GENIUS
&
ANXIETY

HOW JEWS CHANGED
THE WORLD, 1847–1947

NORMAN LEBRECHT

SCRIBNER

New York   London   Toronto   Sydney   New Delhi

Scribner
An Imprint of Simon & Schuster, Inc.
1230 Avenue of the Americas
New York, NY 10020

First Scribner hardcover edition December 2019

SCRIBNER and design are registered trademarks of The Gale Group, Inc.,
used under license by Simon & Schuster, Inc., the publisher of this work.

For information about special discounts for bulk purchases,
please contact Simon & Schuster Special Sales at 1-866-506-1949
or business@simonandschuster.com.

The Simon & Schuster Speakers Bureau can bring authors to your live event.
For more information or to book an event, contact the Simon & Schuster Speakers Bureau
at 1-866-248-3049 or visit our website at www.simonspeakers.com.

Manufactured in the United States of America

3   5   7   9   10   8   6   4   2

Library of Congress Cataloging-in-Publication Data is available.

ISBN 978-1-9821-3422-8
ISBN 978-1-9821-3423-5 (ebook)

CONTENTS

INTRODUCTION

THINKING OUTSIDE

Yom Kippur service for Jewish soldiers in the German Army during
the Franco-Prussian War, outside Metz, October 1870.

Between the middle of the nineteenth and twentieth centuries, a handful of men and women changed the way we see the world. Some of their names are on our lips for all time: Marx, Freud, Proust,

Einstein, Kafka. Others have vanished from our collective memory, but their importance endures in our daily lives. Without Karl Landsteiner, for instance, there would be no blood transfusions or major surgery; without Paul Ehrlich, no chemotherapy; without Siegfried Marcus, no motorcar; without Rosalind Franklin, no model of DNA; without Fritz Haber, not enough food to sustain life on Earth; without Geneviève Halévy, no grand opera; without Emanuel Deutsch, no State of Israel.

What these transformers have in common is being Jewish, some by having Jewish parents, others by practicing the Jewish faith. All appear to think "outside the box," and all of them think fast. Why, at this period, a handful of Jews managed to see what others could not is the subject of this book.

There is a reverse side to the proposition. If Jews remade the world between 1847 and 1947, did the world also change Jews, perhaps beyond recognition? (Short answer: yes.) No historian has, to my knowledge, addressed the story from both aspects. In a multicultural twenty-first century, there may be a wider relevance to these engagements as a template for cultural dialogue and symbiosis.

Folk wisdom has it that five Jews wrote the rules of society:

> Moses said, "The law is everything."
> Jesus said, "Love is everything."
> Marx said, "Money is everything."
> Freud said, "Sex is everything."
> Einstein said, "Everything is relative."

Ha-ha, but more than half true. And Jews have a half truism for most things. A century before Christ, a man demanded to be taught the whole of Torah while standing on one foot. Hillel the Elder said: "Love your neighbour as yourself. The rest is commentary." Two millennia later, Albert Einstein, asked by a journalist to explain the theory of relativity, replies: "Matter tells space how to curve." A Hillelian aphorism. When the hack still looks blank, Einstein tells a Jewish joke. That works (see page 191).

The Jewish mind-set behind the wave of genius has not been successfully explored.[1] How much do Jewish elements in their background inform Mahler, Modigliani, Marcel Proust? How does Freud know that sex is the source of most unhappiness? What makes Marx hate Jews? How much do science and mass migration affect rabbinic thinking, not to mention the physical shape of Jews? When is being Jewish a virtue? Why can't the world see what, to one or two Jews, is blindingly obvious?

The tendency to take a different point of view is illustrated by an anecdote—apocryphal—about the head of a famous Lithuanian yeshiva (rabbinic college) who chides his students for playing football on their lunch break when they could be discussing pearls of Torah. "But football is a beautiful game, *kevod harav* [honored rabbi]," they protest. "Let us show you." At the next weekday league match in Vilna, featuring the nation's best players, the students and their *rav* take seats in the stands. At halftime, the young men ask the *rav* for his response.

"I have solved your problem," he replies.

"How, *kevod harav*?"

"Give one ball to each side, and they will have nothing to fight over."

The *rosh yeshiva*'s way of thinking is counterintuitive to the Western method, which starts with observing the facts on the ground—twenty-two men and a football—before seeking to understand them in a context of social interaction. The *rav*, unaware of the rules, sees the game from a fourth dimension, a world apart from the situation. He offers a solution which, while irrelevant to the game of football, has a certain angelic elegance and ethical rightness.

Aspects of the *rav*'s solution can be sighted in Benjamin Disraeli's deconstructive approach to British politics, in Sarah Bernhardt's exploitation of fame, and, critical for the outcome of the Second World War, in Leo Szilard's cracking of the atom: "he saw a way to the future . . . the shape of things to come." Time and space are flexible for Szilard, as they are for Einstein, Haber, Lise Meitner, and Kafka, because their grasp of time and space is not confined to white lines on green grass. Jews speak of "Jewish time" as a relative measurement; the Talmud establishes a "relative hour," also known as a *halakhic* hour, which varies in length from one day to the next according to the sun's position. Relative time is part of Einstein's genetic heritage long before he announces the discovery of relativity.

Sigmund Freud declares on several occasions that he was brought up in an irreligious home and that he knows nothing about Judaism. It will come as a shock to any researcher with a knowledge of Talmud to find that Freud uses no fewer than six of the thirteen rules of Talmudic exegesis—unconsciously, no doubt—in his analytic approach. It is no less eye-opening to find Marx exposing a profound familiarity with Jewish toilet manners or Trotsky being so sensitive to anti-Semitism that he denounces it in *Pravda* as early as 1923. Proust's madeleine is almost certainly baked with a Jewish recipe. Kafka dreams of waiting on tables in a Tel Aviv café. Their Jewish psyche neither sleeps nor slumbers.

There is another connective factor. In every person of genius who appears in this book, there runs a current of existential angst. Jews in the nineteenth century and the first half of the twentieth are gripped by a dread that their rights to citizenship and free speech will be revoked. After the Dreyfus affair, great minds are driven by a need to justify their existence in a hostile environment and to do it quickly, before the next pogrom. They do not expect acceptance. On the contrary, knowing that their ideas are likely to be rejected leaves them free to think the unthinkable, and forced to do so at speed, before the next crisis. It is no coincidence that Freud, Einstein, Schoenberg, Proust, Herzl, Trotsky, Haber, and Magnus Hirschfeld all rise in the decade after Dreyfus, a turning point whose magnitude is generally unacknowledged outside France. Dreyfus reawakens a primal fear, and his fellow Jews interpret it as a token of their marginality and therefore of their opportunity.

For Kafka, alienation is not a Jewish problem, nor even a personal shortcoming; he extrapolates it as an essential symptom of the universal human condition. George Gershwin, the first American-born songwriter to earn international acclaim, is only happy at parties when he is sitting at a piano in the corner of the room, figuring out the meaning of it all. Arnold Schoenberg, asked if he is the man who makes that horrible atonal music, says: "Well, someone had to, so it might as well be me." A Jew, steeped in concerns for collective survival, is free to go where angels fear to tread, thinking, *Well, what's the worst thing they can do to me?* Angst, a sense of dread or apprehension (from the Latin *anxius*), is regarded by most psychologists as a negative, inhibiting emotion. Freud does not see it that way. Among Jews, anxiety is a primary motivating factor, the engine of fresh thinking.

The word *genius* derives from the Latin *genius*, for inner nature, or *gignere*, to beget. Hebraists trace its origins to *gaon*—greatness, excellence, or arrogance—a noun used first at the Exodus from Egypt

(Ex. 15:7) and forty-one times subsequently in the Bible. It appears in Psalms (47:5) as *geon Yaakov*; the genius of Jacob, an intimation that there might be a kind of genius that is innate to Jews. Samuel Johnson extends the definition of greatness to include two more categories: the ruling power, any person endowed with "superior faculties," and, as an abstract concept, a "disposition of nature by which anyone is qualified for some particular employment." By this he means the untapped aptitude of quite ordinary people to rise to an opportunity or an emergency in a way that others cannot: cometh the hour, cometh the man. This kind of genius, writes the great dictionarist, "is like fire in the flint, only to be produced by collision with a proper subject" (Johnson may be referring to his own utter hopelessness at any other activity). Quite a few of the individuals in our narrative fall into this fleeting category: men and women who rise to a unique moment of emergency or opportunity to display an unlikely, superhuman capacity for action and ingenuity. Some are born to genius; others have it thrust upon them.

I am not about to make a case for Jewish exceptionalism, nor do I believe that Jews are genetically gifted above the average in mathematics, entertainment, and money, as is often claimed, usually with malice. It is impossible to overturn such prejudices by reasoning alone, but a swipe of beauty cream might help. The first woman to become a US dollar millionaire is the cosmetician Helena Rubinstein, a pocket-sized (four-foot-ten) cousin of the philosopher Martin Buber, with a restless urge for self-betterment. Leaving Warsaw in her midtwenties to find a husband in Australia, she discovers that women under the harsh Antipodean sun fear constantly for their skin. Happily, she has brought a cream to protect hers, and she is in the perfect place to manufacture more, having access to limitless supplies of lanolin, a fat secreted by sheep, and to herbs that deodorize it. By the time she leaves Australia in 1908, Helena has outlets in several countries. The following year, a Canadian woman of unmingled Cornish descent goes into business as Elizabeth Arden and battles Rubinstein wrinkle to wrinkle across North America. If Rubinstein opens a showroom in Minneapolis or on Madison Avenue, Arden opens one across the street. They poach each other's executives and hire publicists to do the other down in the press, lording it over the cosmetics sector until Charles Revson and Estée Lauder come along and broaden the competition. There is little to distinguish between the two queens of the beauty business except this: Rubinstein is avowedly Jewish, and Arden is decidedly not. Operating under identical conditions, Arden amasses the same kind of fortune as Rubinstein. She might spend it on racehorses while Rubinstein prefers to collect modern art, but there is no way of telling which of the two is more or less Jewish, whether in mind or in modus operandi. All we can conclude from the comparison is that there is no specific Jewish genius for making money. If there were, someone would have bottled it by now.

If Jews happen to excel in any particular area, it is generally a consequence of culture and experience rather than DNA. Jews learned from adversity to think differently from others, and, maybe, harder. The composer Gustav Mahler was fond of saying: "A Jew is like a man with a short arm. He has to swim harder to reach the shore." Anxiety acts on them like an Egyptian taskmaster in the book of Exodus. It goads them to acts of genius.

What qualifies me, a music historian and novelist, to tell this story? My credentials include an early spell in an eminent Jerusalem yeshiva, followed by a lifelong study of Talmud, fluency in the core Jewish languages of Hebrew, Aramaic, and Yiddish, and an inability to walk past a secondhand bookstore in Tel Aviv, Vienna, Paris, St. Petersburg, or New York without acquiring a dozen esoteric memoirs, many of which now stare at me with reproach from two shelved walls in my office. For unpublished manuscripts, I have resorted to university libraries and the archives of family and friends.

Much of what I touch on has a firsthand origin. At various times in my life I have been fortunate to engage with eyewitnesses and authorities who afforded me untold enlightenment. I used to spend ten minutes each morning with Aharon Lizra, who knew both the Hebrew Bible and the Arabic Qur'an by heart. I could pick up the phone to Raphael Loewy and Michael Weitzman for points of Chaldean and Syriac etymology. Baruch Kurzweil, who left Frankfurt in 1933, guided me into German literature and academic warfare; Leah Goldberg introduced me to Russian greats. Eleanor Rosé, who lived upstairs, grew up among artists in fin de siècle Vienna. Alma Mahler and Lotte Klemperer knew Berlin between the wars. I would phone Berthold Goldschmidt, who had an acute memory for gesture, to ask how Schoenberg or Ferruccio Busoni entered a room. "Come for coffee, and I will show you," he'd say. Their generation, no longer alive, had a ferocious regard for verifiable detail. "I cannot tell you this," Mrs. Rosé would say, "because I am no longer sure if I was actually there or I just heard about it." Today, the Internet provides us with access to more information than we can ever need to know, but it cannot supplant the memories of men and women who were brought up to seek truth, conserve it, and, at all costs, defend it.

This story of genius and anxiety does not begin arbitrarily in 1847, nor does it end exactly a century later. I use these two dates as bookends, marking out an age in which Jews engaged more intensely with the rest of the world than at any other time. The history of the Jews concludes, in a certain sense, with the United Nations' recognition, on November 29, 1947, of the moral justice of founding a Jewish state in the biblical homeland. The fulfillment of a Zionist dream is, however, no more durable a solution to a human problem than Marxism or atonality. The birth of the State of Israel marks a new chapter. It is not the end of history.

Like most post-Holocaust Western Jews, I have long believed that anti-Semitism belongs to the past. The slights and slurs that my father endured as a matter of course throughout his life in England hardly touched me. If I came up against hatred, I assumed either that it was provoked by something I had written or that it was random and irrational. Anti-Semitism persisted in the Soviet bloc, Arab propaganda, and a few fringe groups too powerless to warrant attention, but it did not impinge on my consciousness. Over the past five years, while writing this book, I have been forced to recognize that this assumption is false.

Animosity toward Jews for no reason except that they are Jews has become a tool of our times. Since 2014, we have seen the rise of far-right parties in Germany, France, and Sweden, and especially in Eastern Europe, where the Hungarian-born Jewish financier George Soros has been targeted as a hook-nosed hate figure, the personification of evil. More disturbing still, the political Left in Western Europe has translated a reasoned anti-Zionism into a visceral assault on all Jews, especially those who refuse to denounce the State of Israel for actions which, by any rational measure, are less heinous than acts committed by such Left-favored states as Venezuela, Russia, and China. The British Labour Party, once a homeland for left-leaning Jews, is led by men who believe that the State of Israel has no right to exist. American universities, once havens of free speech, now prevent Jewish students from presenting any point of view on the Middle East conflict that is not anti-Zionist. The abusive term *Zio* is the leftist version of *yid*.

On the news, every hour on the hour, there is fresh cause for concern. An aged Holocaust survivor is brutally murdered in her Paris apartment. A rabbi and three children are shot dead in a school in Toulouse. Polish students give a Hitler salute at the gates of Auschwitz. A Swedish mayor blames anti-Semitism in his city on its Jews. A synagogue in Pittsburgh, Pennsylvania, is attacked during a Sabbath service by a gunman who shouts "All Jews must die," and takes eleven lives, an outrage blamed by one member of the British House of Lords on Israeli policy toward the Palestinians.

In 2017, anti-Semitic attacks rise by 57 percent in the US and by 34 percent in the UK. Jew hatred, long tamped down by Holocaust revulsion and parliamentary legislation, is back among us, on our streets, in our schools, and on the screens of our phones and computers, which, as it happens, are powered in part by the inventions of deplorable Jews. It is cool to be cruel about Jews (though not about other minorities). We have guards at the gates of our synagogues.

Prejudice, fed by ignorance and inflamed by ideology, is growing year after year. Children require school gate protection. No sane person believes anymore that anti-Semitism has been defeated or is under control. Jews feel, to a greater or lesser degree, under attack. French Jews have emigrated en masse; of my mother's extensive family, hardly any remain. The British historian Simon Sebag Montefiore reports that "virtually every Jewish family I know has discussed leaving Britain because of Labour's antisemitism."[2] Many Jews own second homes in Israel "just in case." The only Jewish communities in Europe that flourish are the ones that have returned to the former killing fields of Germany, Hungary, and Poland.

It is a writer's duty to present the truth, and in sufficient detail to give it a fighting chance against the torrent of lies. Kafka calls truth "one of the few really great and precious things in life." In today's post-truth environment, it seems to me imperative to review the impact of Jewish genius on Western civilization and tell it as it truly happened.

NORMAN LEBRECHT, St. John's Wood, August 2019

A SHORT GLOSSARY
OF JEWISH TERMS

Aleph-bet (Hebrew)	first two Hebrew letters of the alphabet
Aliyah (Hebrew)	ascent; in Zionism, migration to the Land of Israel
Amidah (Hebrew)	literally, standing; the central act of Jewish worship
Ashkenazi (Hebrew)	Jews of North European origin
Avot (Hebrew)	fathers; a tractate of the Mishna
Bar mitzvah (Aramaic/Hebrew)	coming of age at thirteen for boys, son of commandment
Bat mitzvah (Aramaic/Hebrew)	coming of age at twelve for girls, daughter of commandment
Batlan (Hebrew)	a bum, pejoratively used for yeshiva students
Beit midrash (Hebrew)	study house
Broiges (Hebrew/ Yiddish)	in a rage; furious with someone, cutting off contact
Callah (Hebrew)	bride
Chabad (Hebrew)	acronym for *Chochmah, Binah, Daat* (wisdom, understanding, knowledge), the mission statement of Lubavitch Hasidim
Challah (Hebrew)	plaited bread loaf for the Sabbath
Chalutz (Hebrew)	Palestine pioneer
Chazan (Hebrew)	synagogue cantor, leader of prayers

Cheder (Hebrew)	elementary Hebrew classes for infants
Chuppah (Hebrew)	Jewish wedding canopy
Chutzpah (Hebrew)	cheek, effrontery, insolence
Daven (Latin/Yiddish)	to pray
Derekh eretz (Hebrew)	literally, the way of the land; the prevailing culture—hence the symbiosis of Torah with Derekh eretz
Ein bereirah (Hebrew)	there's no choice, no alternative
Eretz Yisrael (Hebrew)	Land of Israel
Finjan (Judeo-Arabic/ Persian)	Coffeepot or cup
Freygish (Yiddish)	questioning; in music, the Phrygian mode
Frum (Yiddish/German)	pious Orthodox
Gaon (Hebrew)	genius
Genizah (Hebrew/ Persian)	hiding place
Ghetto (Italian-Jewish)	walled enclosure; possibly from *borghetto*, small borough
Goy (Hebrew)	literally, nation; used to designate a non-Jew
Haham (Hebrew)	wise man; Sephardi leader
Halakha (Hebrew)	code of Jewish law
Hasid (Hebrew)	follower of an ecstatic Jewish group, led by a *rebbe*; plural Hasidim
Hatan (Hebrew)	bridegroom
Hatikvah (Hebrew)	the hope; Israeli national anthem
Herem (Hebrew)	excommunication
Hora	Chalutz dance of Romanian origin
Ilui (Hebrew)	child genius
Kaddish (Hebrew)	memorial prayer accepting God's judgment, recited by mourners
Kevod harav (Hebrew)	honored rabbi

A SHORT GLOSSARY OF JEWISH TERMS

Kibbutz (Hebrew)	Israeli agricultural commune
Kiddush (Hebrew)	Sabbath blessing over wine
Klezmer (Hebrew)	literally, musical instruments, generally used for wedding bands
Kol Nidrei (Aramaic)	literally, all vows; the opening prayer of Yom Kippur
Kosher (Hebrew)	food permitted to Orthodox Jews
Kvetch (Yiddish)	to grumble, gripe, mutter; from medieval German *quetschen* (to squeeze)
Litvak (Yiddish)	Lithuanian
Mashiach (Hebrew)	messiah
Matzah (Hebrew)	flatbread for Passover use
Mazal tov or Mazel tov (Hebrew)	literally, good luck; used as an exclamation of congratulation
Meizid (Hebrew)	deliberate act
Melamed (Hebrew)	elementary teacher
Meshuga (Hebrew/ Yiddish)	mad
Mezuzah (Hebrew)	emblem with Bible texts nailed to Jewish doorposts
Mikveh (Hebrew)	ritual bath
Minyan (Hebrew)	a gathering of ten men, the minimum required for saying Kaddish
Mishna (Hebrew)	first- to second-century six-volume formulation of Jewish law
Misnaged (Hebrew)	opponent of Hasidism, follower of Lithuanian-style scholasticism
Mitzvah (Hebrew)	a duty or commandment derived from Torah
Mohel (Hebrew)	person who performs circumcisions; also Mohler (German-Yiddish)
Musar (Hebrew)	nineteenth-century Lithuanian ethics movement
Neilah (Hebrew)	closure; final service of Yom Kippur

Pletzl (Yiddish)	little place; the heart of Jewish Paris, in the Marais
Pogrom (Russian)	armed attack on Jews
Posek (Hebrew)	a rabbi with authority to determine precedential law
Rachmones (Hebrew)	pity
Rav or rov (Hebrew)	non-Hasidic rabbi
Rebbe (Yiddish)	leader of a Hasidic dynasty
Risches (Heb/Yid)	wickedness, anti-Semitism
Rosh yeshiva (Hebrew)	head of Talmudic college
Schmaltz (Yiddish)	an overload of sentimentality; also goose-fat spread on bread
Schmooze (Yiddish)	to chat, gossip, talk someone around, shoot the breeze; from the Hebrew *shemuos* (things heard)
Schnorrer (Yiddish)	beggar
Seder (Hebrew)	literally, order; the service preceding the Passover meal
Sephardi	Jews of Mediterranean or Middle Eastern roots
Shammes/Shamash (Hebrew)	synagogue beadle or general factotum
Shehecheyanu (Hebrew)	blessing for a new event: "who has given us life and sustained us to this day"
Shema or Shema Yisrael	three passages of Scripture, recited thrice daily, proclaiming, "Hear, O Israel, the Lord our God, the Lord Is One"
Shiduch (Hebrew)	matchmaking; also *shadchan* for matchmaker
Shluchim (Yiddish/Hebrew)	Chabad term for emissary couples
Shochet (Hebrew), shechter (Yiddish)	slaughterer of animals for kosher meat
Shofar (Hebrew)	ram's horn

Shogeg (Hebrew)	unintended act
Shtetl (Yiddish)	village or small town with a large Jewish population
Shtiebl (Yiddish)	small prayer room
Shtum (Yiddish)	silent
Shul (Yiddish)	synagogue
Siddur (Hebrew)	prayer book
Talit (Hebrew)	prayer shawl for men
Talmud (Hebrew)	compendium of rabbinic discussion, fourth to eighth centuries, the foundation of *Halakha*
Tefilin (Aramaic)	leather straps and boxes worn by men for morning prayers, also known as phylacteries
Tikun olam (Hebrew)	repair the world; the idea that man has a duty to complete God's creation
Torah (Hebrew)	teaching, usually meaning the five books of Moses
Tuchslecker (Yiddish)	arse-licker; sycophant
Yallah (Arabic)	let's go; go for it
Yechidus (Yiddish/ Hebrew)	privacy; Chabad word for a consultation with the *rebbe*
Yeshiva (Hebrew)	rabbinic college for Talmud studies
Yid (English)	pejorative for Jew
Yishuv (Hebrew)	collective term for Jewish settlers in Palestine
Yom Kippur (Hebrew)	Day of Atonement
Zakai (Aramaic)	innocent
Zhid (Russian)	pejorative for Jew

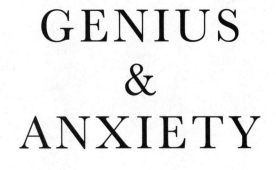

GENIUS
&
ANXIETY

ONE

1847
THE VISITOR

Heinrich Heine goes into exile, 1831.

A week before Christmas 1846. A world-famous composer comes unannounced to his sister's house in Berlin.

She is expecting him. Sister and brother are so close they anticipate each other's thoughts. Fanny Hensel, plump and dark-eyed, rushes to the door and hugs her younger brother, Felix Mendelssohn Bartholdy. Hand in hand, they walk through to the rear of 3 Leipziger Strasse to a garden house which Fanny occupies with her husband, the painter Wilhelm Hensel, and their teenaged son, Sebastian.

Felix looks harassed, in need of a holiday, burdened by his position as Leipzig *kapellmeister*, where he not only conducts the world's premier orchestra but examines every last lazy student in its music academy. Any spare weeks are consumed by concert tours around European capitals. He longs to give up public life and settle in Berlin, in a garden house where he can compose undisturbed. "It has been years since we last spent a birthday together," chides Fanny. She has just turned forty-one and is taking over their late mother's role as family conscience. "Depend upon it," promises Felix, "the next birthday I shall spend with you."

He is never lost for the *mot juste*. Trim and handsome, with curly black hair and eloquent dark eyes, he is described by William Makepeace Thackeray as having "the most beautiful face I ever saw, like what I imagine our Saviour's to have been." Few see the turmoil that rages behind this beatific façade. Few see a man who is living on the last filaments of a fragile confidence.

Felix has a present for Fanny. Christmas and birthday gift combined, it is a proof copy of his new piano trio in C minor, a work of joyous vivacity, possibly a character sketch of his sister's effervescence. Like all his works, it has been snatched up by publishers in Germany, France, Italy, and England. Typically, the score is dotted with last-minute corrections, a mark of Felix's "morbid conscientiousness," his obsessive attention to precision, the mark of a man who is terrified of being caught in error. The finale quotes the Lutheran hymn "Before Thy Throne I Now Appear," also known as "Praise Be to Thee, Jesus Christ." Mendelssohn wears his Christianity loud and proud. The music sparkles with wit and challenge, and is designed for family members to play in the parlor. Fanny is so thrilled with the music that her descendants refuse to part with the score for more than a century.

She, too, has a gift for Felix. It is the first numbered copy of her very first published work: settings of six poems by Heine, Goethe, Eichendorff, and Geibel, issued by the respected Berlin house of Bote und Bock. The work, she knows, treads on family wounds. Felix, she fears, will be shocked.

As a child, Fanny was ordered by her father to stop composing, so as not to steal attention from her genius brother. "Music will perhaps become his profession," declared Abraham Mendelssohn, "while for you it can only be an ornament." Fanny dutifully becomes a wife and mother, but she never loses the urge to compose. Felix, hearing she is talking to publishers, goes prissy with outrage. "This is contrary to my views and my convictions," he tells their mother. "From my knowledge of Fanny I should say she has neither inclination nor vocation for authorship. She is too much all that a woman ought to be for this. She regulates her house, and neither thinks of the public, nor of the musical world, nor even of music at all, until her first duties are fulfilled."[1]

Can this really be his objection? Could the foremost German composer fear that a few piano works by his hausfrau sister might undermine his position? Felix gives no clue to his feelings, but his veto exposes a constant anxiety. Felix is never sure of his success. By the time he consents to Fanny's publication, she has lost two decades. Handing him her songs, she asks mock-innocently, "Why didn't I dedicate these *Lieder* to you?" Fanny is his older sister. She now holds the upper hand.

She opens the door to the music room, and they dash, like children, for the piano. We know what they play, though not in what order. They pound through Fanny's songs, Felix's new trio, and excerpts from his oratorio *Elijah*, an instant hit that year in Birmingham. "No work of mine ever went so admirably at the first time of execution or was received with such enthusiasm," Felix tells his loving family. "How often I thought of you during the time!"

Sharing a piano stool, all elbows and knees, brother and sister blaze away at their music. Wall-length windows cast a wintry light. Parental portraits gaze down from the walls. A tinseled fir tree groans with candles and angels. Nothing in this tableau indicates that these two are grandchildren of Moses Mendelssohn, the great philosopher of Judaism, advocate of a symbiosis between the Jewish faith and German culture. Moses, hero of Lessing's play *Nathan the Wise*, believed his family would live as proud Jews and Prussian citizens. Instead, they go to church, marry Christians, and erase their origins. Fanny loves Christmas. Felix follows up *Elijah* with *Christus*, reassuring the world that he is a New, not Old, Testament composer. His image, external and internal, is founded on his *not* being Jewish. In his voluminous letters and published conversations, he makes only one reference to himself as a Jew, when reviving Bach's *St. Matthew Passion* from a century of disuse: "to think that . . . a Jew gives back to the people the greatest of Christian works." Johann Sebastian Bach is Mendelssohn's spiritual ancestor, not Moses. That past has been silenced.

Parting at the garden gate, brother and sister promise to meet again soon. They never do. Although Felix is in Berlin on business three months later, he has no time to spare. He is needed in England to conduct *Elijah* in Manchester, Birmingham, and London, the last two concerts attended by Queen Victoria. Prince Albert calls him "the noble artist who, though encompassed by Baal-worship of false art, by his genius and study has succeeded, like another Elijah, in faithfully preserving the worship of true art." In the domestic quarters of Buckingham Palace, Felix sits at the royal piano and accompanies Victoria in three of his songs. She asks for a last treat. He plays a lied by Fanny.

On his way home, he is arrested at the Belgian border, mistaken for a Mendelssohn cousin called Arnold, who is on the run for theft and fraud. In Berlin, Fanny premieres her newest score, a piano trio, modeled on her brother's. On May 13, 1847, she writes a song. The next morning, she holds a chorus rehearsal for her brother's *Erste Walpurgisnacht* in the garden house. Raising her arms, Fanny finds that her hands have gone numb. This has happened before, and she knows what to do. She goes to the bathroom and bathes her hands in warm vinegar. Resuming the rehearsal, she collapses to the floor. "A stroke," she gasps, "just like Mother." She falls into a coma. By the time her brother Paul arrives, forty-five minutes later, she is barely breathing. She is laid out in the garden room in a flower-decked coffin. Her widower, Wilhelm, sits there for two days, sketching the scene.

Paul Mendelssohn telegraphs a relative in Frankfurt am Main, asking him to break the news gently to Felix, who is conducting there. Felix gives a cry and faints. Doctors diagnose exhaustion. He cancels the rest of his concerts, taking his family to Black Forest and Swiss resorts, inviting Paul to join them, together with Wilhelm and Sebastian. Ordered to abstain from music, he paints landscapes. At night, he reads a novel by Benjamin Disraeli.

After a visit to Fanny's house in September, he cannot get over the loss. Earaches, a lifelong blight, torment him. He engages in bursts of manic creativity. On October 9, he is composing six morbid lieder, opus seventy-one, when his hands lose sensation. After staggering home, he collapses on a sofa. Doctors apply leeches. Mendelssohn revives, sends a copy of *Elijah* to the king of Prussia, and confirms a November concert in Vienna. He takes morning walks and plays cards with his wife, Cécile, before bed. On October 28, while kissing Cécile, he loses consciousness. Coming round, he is stricken with mortal terror. "His shrieks, which lasted until 10 o'clock, were terrible," writes the Leipzig concertmaster Ferdinand David. "Then he began to hum and to drum as if music were passing through his head and, when he became exhausted by it, he started giving fearful screams and continued to do so throughout the night."

All music is suspended in Leipzig. Two violinists, Joseph Joachim and Niels Gade, sit in vigil in his living room at 3 Königstrasse. His brother, Paul, and sister Rebecka arrive. "Cécile knelt by his bed and burst into tears," writes the pianist Ignaz Moscheles:

> [We] stood around the bed in deathly silence, immersed in prayer. With every breath that was wrested from him I could feel the struggle of his great spirit, wanting to free itself from its earthly shell. I had often heard his breathing while admiring his performing, as if he were riding heavenwards on Pegasus and now these same sounds had to ring out, announcing the terrible end . . . At 24 minutes past nine [on November 4, 1847], with one last deep sigh, he exhaled his soul from his body.

His death, at thirty-eight years old, reminds people of Mozart's at a similar age. Thousands escort his coffin to the railway station and more follow the procession through the streets of Berlin, singing hymns that Mendelssohn composed. Crowned heads send condolences. Queen Victoria is "horrified, astounded and distressed." Musicians are dumbstruck. To Joachim, "it seemed as if the world had ceased." Robert Schumann regards him as "the highest authority" in German music. His death briefly halts Germany's ascent as a musical power. It is a fermata in the history of Western music, an end point.

All the more extraordinary that, within a year, Mendelssohn's reputation falls like a cemetery angel in a winter storm. The new order—Wagner, Schumann, Liszt—rejects his perfectionism, his style, his anguished sincerity, his ethnicity, his transparent vulnerability. Mendelssohn, quips a Wagner ally, is not a serious composer but "a childhood sickness" like measles, to be overcome while young. In England, the Queen's esteem and hundreds of choirboys warbling "Oh, for the wings, for the wings of a dove," maintain his esteem as long as Victoria reigns, only for it to subside in the next century, still performed but not among the greats. How this mighty composer is fallen is an enigma of cultural evolution.

Richard Wagner, in his midthirties, seizes the opportunity. The composer of three operas—*Rienzi, The Flying Dutchman*, and *Tannhäuser*—and conductor in dowdy Dresden, Wagner needs to discredit Mendelssohn to prove his own credentials. A speech by the Russian anarchist Mikhail Bakunin provides him with his leitmotiv. "This whole Jewish world," rants Bakunin, "[is] a single exploiting sect, a blood sucking people, a kind of organic destructive collective parasite, going beyond not only the frontiers of states but of political opinion, this world is now, at least for the most part, at the disposal of Marx on the one hand, and of Rothschild on the other."[2] Wagner makes contact with Bakunin, who teaches him how to make grenades and hurl them from barricades. Wagner rings a bell that sets off the 1848 revolution. When the uprising is crushed, he flees Germany with a price on his head.

In exile, he writes an article for a small magazine, *Neue Zeitschrift für Musik*, under the pseudonym "K. Freigedank" (the freethinker). Titled "Jewishness in Music," it attacks Felix Mendelssohn as a "foreign element" that must be expunged from German music. There is, writes Wagner, "an unconscious feeling which proclaims itself among the people as a rooted dislike of the Jewish nature . . . We always felt instinctively repelled by any actual, operative contact with them . . . involuntary repellence."

The Jew, says Wagner, "speaks the language of the nation in whose midst he dwells from generation to generation but he speaks it always as an alien." Mendelssohn "showed us that a Jew can possess a wealth of specific talents, the most refined and varied culture, the most exalted and gentle sense of honour, without ever being able to arouse in us that profound, heart-and-soul searching effect that we expect from music." If Mendelssohn, the most gifted of Jews, was no more than a pale imitator, it stands to reason—to Wagner's reason—that no Jew can ever create an original work.

With a circulation of fifteen hundred, Wagner's diatribe makes limited inroads on public attention and would have been forgotten had its author failed to deliver works of greater genius. Twenty years later, renowned as the composer of *Tristan und Isolde*, Wagner republishes "Das Judenthum in der Musik" under his own name. *Tristan*, along with *The Ring of the Nibelungen*, addresses the uses and abuses of political power in ways that no art has done before. Beneath them lies Wagner's conviction that German music is for pure-blooded Germans, not addled Jews. His revived essay is a blueprint for the cleansing of German art from alien civilities, restoring the feral values of primal ancestors. If Mendelssohn is Wagner's premier bête noire, the second target of his essay is a poet who has simplified and decluttered the German language, making it accessible and attractive to outsiders. Heinrich Heine, as Wagner begins his ascent, is climbing into his deathbed.

There is no love lost between Heine and Mendelssohn, least of all on Heine's side. Nor, apart from both being Jews, is there much to connect them. The pair differ in character, outlook, morality, and modus vivendi. One is formal, prudent, well dressed, tending to solemnity. The other is rude, roughshod, rebellious, destructive, dandyish, impulsive, unprincipled, and riotously funny. They are the leading German composer and poet of their time; all the more reason to avoid each other as best they can. And Heine certainly does his best. He is good at cutting people dead.

Raised in Düsseldorf, Harry Heine—his birth name—knows two things: that he is a great poet and that he must not try to earn his living by it. "Give me my daily bread," he prays, "that I may not profane Thy name." Poetry, like Torah, is pure. It is not to be used for earthly needs.

His first *Gedichte* (poems) appears as he arrives in Berlin in 1821. Aged twenty-three, he is invited to the best Jewish salons—the Mendelssohns', the Meyerbeers', the Varnhagens'. He enjoys the hospitality but slams his hosts for embracing Christianity. At the Society for Jewish Culture and Science, he debates with the historian Leopold Zunz and the philosopher Eduard Gans, trying to discern what it means to be a Jew in post-Enlightenment Europe. All of a sudden, he gives up. In June 1825, he converts to Lutheranism, taking the names Johann, Heinrich, Christian. When Gans does the same, Heine calls him an apostate. Heine is a law unto himself. His conversion is, he says, a matter of survival. "If the law permitted me to steal spoons, I would not have had to get baptised."[3] Baptism, he quips, is "a ticket of admission to European culture." On ceasing to be a Jew, Heine becomes twice as Jewish.

Poems from his second book, the *Lyric Intermezzo*, are soon on everyone's lips: "In the marvellous month of May," "On the Wings of Song." Franz Schubert takes six Heine poems for his *Winterreise*. Schumann sets forty-three. Mendelssohn composes seven, Grieg eight, Liszt seven, Brahms six, Hugo Wolf eighteen, Richard Strauss six, Alban Berg three. Heine's directness exerts a lasting appeal. "With me," he says, "the old school of German lyrical poetry comes to an end; with me, the modern German lyric begins."

This is no exaggeration. Heine blows away complex sentence structures that end in verbs and morbid romanticism that ends in death. If Goethe is the somber owl of German verse, Heine is the nightingale. He sings day and night, threatening mischief. His fluency is unstoppable. Poems, stage plays, travel journals, and screeds of journalism pour forth. Untroubled by any need for balance or accuracy, he jabs at rich and poor alike, exposes adulterers and names homosexuals. He is bigoted, rumbustious, hypocritical. When editors turn down his submissions, he cadges a stipend from rich Uncle Salomon in Hamburg. In 1831, he moves to Paris, where the censor is less oppressive.

Paris is paradise. He seduces and marries a shopgirl. Mathilde, as he calls her, is illiterate and half his age. "God is all there is, He is in our kisses," he sighs. "Unfortunately," he informs his mother, "her temperament is very unstable and she is irritated more often than is good for me. I am still deeply attached to her. She is my heart's greatest desire— but that, too, will go the way of all human passions." Heine's prophecies often come true. Sex is over within a year. "I used to think love was possession," he tells a friend, "and the last thing I believed in was the theory of abstinence. But there is much to be said in favour of Platonic love. It lets you sleep at night—and it is so inexpensive." He grumbles about sharing a bed with his wife on hot nights and feels no shame in confessing his sexual rejection. Unlike Mendelssohn, Heine lives his life from the outside in. Where Mendelssohn buries his Jewishness, Heine peppers his letters with terms like *rachmones* (pity), *zaar lechayim* (cruelty to living things), *chushem* (senses), *killeh* (community), *Schabbesfrau* (woman who lights the Sabbath stove), and *peiger* (I'm dying).

After an early Jewish novella, *The Rabbi of Bacharach*, he writes an epic poem, *Jehuda Ben Halevy*, 896 lines of empathy with a medieval poet-scholar. In the same volume, he offers a rhapsody on Princess Sabbath, an account of the strict observance of the Jewish day of rest, including two wistful verses on *shalet* (cholent), the slow-cooked midday dish of meat, potatoes, and beans, echoing the meter of Beethoven's melody to Schiller's "Ode to Joy":

> Shalet is the food of Heaven
> Which Lord God himself once taught
> Prophet Moses how to prepare
> On the Sinai mountain.

Yet, with each ode to Jews, Heine finds ways to hurt them. For the opening of a Jewish hospital in Hamburg, endowed by his uncle Salomon, he extols:

> A hospital for sick and needy Jews,
> For poor humans who are triply miserable
> With three great sicknesses
> With poverty, pain and Jewishness . . .
> The worst of these afflictions is the last.
> A thousand-year family disease,
> Dragged from the hollow of the Nile
> The unhealthy beliefs of Ancient Egypt.

Sigmund Freud will borrow this idea in *Moses and Monotheism*, arguing that Judaism is a pagan legacy. Heine calls Judaism "not a religion, a misfortune." Half of Heine hates his other half. This is not the man he wants to be.

To be German is his ideal, his unattainable aspiration. Here, too, he is conflicted. As torchbearer for the Young Germany group of radical writers, he realizes that his Germany is not the same as theirs. Heine's Deutschland is a holy tongue, like Hebrew: a language without a land. The political unification of Germany leaves him cold. Deutschland is his mother tongue, at times his mother. After a family reunion in Hamburg, he writes "Nachtgedanken," one of his most quoted poems:

Denk ich an Deutschland in der Nacht
dann bin ich um dem Schlaf gebracht

When I think of Germany at night
all hope of sleep takes flight

The line between person and nation is blurred. It is unclear if he is writing about motherland or about his mother, Betty:

Years came and years went past,
Since I saw my mother last,
Twelve years lie behind us
While my longing, yearning, rises.
My longing and my yearning rises
The old lady has bewitched me
I think always of the old lady
May God preserve her [*die Gott erhalte*].

This last phrase is the first line of Joseph Haydn's *Kaiserlied*, the imperial Austrian anthem. Who, then, is Heine's "old lady"? And whose God is he praying to? His world is a Sabbath dish of mother, motherland, matrilineality. All this in a poem about Germany. Using elementary nouns and verbs, he revels in dualities. Far ahead of Freud, Heine mines the ambiguities of everyday words. No poet has ever written such simple lines in German or with such subversive intent. He even manages what appears to be a happy ending:

God be praised: through my window, fresh and bright
Breaks a buoyant French daylight;
My wife comes in, lovely as the dawn,
And smiles away my oh-so-German frown.

Can we believe that? Mathilde is no remedy. Heine has gone back to wooing shopgirls. He writes begging letters to Baron Rothschild and inhabits the concert hall after dark. The world's composers are drawn to Paris by high fees. Heine reckons they will pay to have their concerts reviewed by a famous poet. Those who refuse to pay are rewarded with foul reviews. He dislikes composers, as a breed. They use his poems without payment and never bother to send him a published copy. He knows all the big names at the Salle Pleyel: Bellini, Berlioz, Chopin, Liszt, Paganini, Rossini, Wagner, Meyerbeer, and Mendelssohn.

Ah, Mendelssohn. Heine has been biding his time. Mendelssohn is a bubble begging to be pricked, a grudge going back to dull nights in Berlin salons, where he is forced to be polite to bankers about their musical wunderkind. He and Mendelssohn are the first Jewish ambassadors to the court of European culture. They vie for precedence, and Heine does not care to come in second. He disparages Mendelssohn's Christianity by comparing his orotund *St. Paulus* oratorio to a trivial Stabat Mater by the elderly Gioachino Rossini, who is happily gorging himself to death in Paris restaurants.

What makes Rossini a better Christian than Mendelssohn? demands Heine. "Heaven forbid that I should be guilty of reproaching so estimable a master as the composer of *Paulus* and least of all does it occur to the writer of these pages to carp at the Christianity of the oratorio in question because Felix Mendelssohn-Bartholdy happens to be Jewish by birth. But . . ." And here comes the thrust:

> I cannot refrain from observing that in the very year in which M. Mendelssohn began his career as a Christian in Berlin (he was baptised at age thirteen), Rossini had practically fallen away from Christianity and plunged into the worldliness of operatic music. Now that he has himself abandoned the latter and dreamed his way back into youthful memories of Roman Catholicism . . . he has no need to reconstruct the spirit of Christianity in a learned way or much less slavishly to copy Handel or Sebastian Bach . . .

This is an act of emasculation. Heine accuses Mendelssohn of using faith as a smart career move, accusing him of misunderstanding church music and fabricating poor imitations of German masters. No one who reads the review—and everyone does—can fail to admit that Heine has a point. No matter how many prepubescent boys quaver "Wings of a Dove" or how many couples enter holy matrimony to his "Wedding March," Mendelssohn's angelic piety sounds phony beside the smoky incense and muddied incantations of a born Catholic. Mendelssohn might have ceased to be a Jew, but he can never compose like a goy.

Heine is not done with him yet. In *Deutschland: A Winter's Tale*, Heine mocks Moses Mendelssohn, whose grandson has "ventured so far into Christianity/why, he's already a Kapellmeister." Finally, in a letter to the German-Jewish socialist Ferdinand Lassalle, Heine says what he really thinks about Felix Mendelssohn. "I dislike his Christianising," writes Heine:

> I cannot forgive the way this man of independent means puts his great, his prodigious talent at the service of religion. The more impressed I am by his talent, the more angry I am by its vile misuse. If I'd had the good fortune to be the grandson of Moses Mendelssohn, I would never have applied my talents to set to music the urine of the Lamb.

Heine is outraged by Mendelssohn's sanctimony, by his self-denial, and by his failure to be, like Heine, a free soul. He hates Mendelssohn for squandering his God-given gifts on the Church. And, even as he rages, Heine recognizes that he is condemned to be shackled to Mendelssohn for all eternity, as the first composer and first poet of Jewish descent. Mendelssohn hangs around Heine like an unforgiven sin, a constant reproach, an affront to God and man. Mendelssohn is the anti-Heine, and the poet cannot put him out of mind.

When news of Mendelssohn's collapse and death reaches Paris, Heine takes it personally. Toward the end of 1847, he loses the use of his legs. After three months in the hospital, he goes home to Avenue Matignon in May 1848, to spend the rest of his life in a "mattress-grave." The root cause of his illness is uncertain; it might be syphilis, multiple sclerosis, motor neuron disease, or lead poisoning. Whatever the pathology, the condition does not affect his clarity of mind. Over eight years the mattress-grave yields a flood of essays and poems, some of his finest, many of them taken down by a new love, Elise Krinitz, known as Camille Selden, whom Heine calls "La Mouche" (the fly). In letters to La Mouche, Alexandre Dumas, and others, he remains adamant in his ambivalences. "I make no secret of my Judaism," he declares, "to which I have not returned because I never left it." Heinrich Heine draws his last breath just before dawn on February 17, 1856. He is entombed in a catafalque in Montmartre Cemetery. The city of Düsseldorf rejects a statue commissioned for his birth centenary in 1897 (the bust ends up in the Bronx, above the Lorelei Fountain, a short walk from Yankee Stadium). In the summer of 1941, acting on the express orders of Adolf Hitler, German soldiers use industrial hammers to smash Heine's tomb, destroying it totally and irreparably.

When legends meet, facts are blurred. A black-bearded man knocks at Heine's door on or around December 20, 1843. He is a writer, newly exiled, claiming to be a distant cousin. Heine recognizes his name not from the family tree but from a German arrest warrant on which their names appear side by side. He invites the young man in and is impressed by his literary culture. Karl Marx knows Shakespeare by heart, and much of Homer. He is coeditor of a French-German yearbook and wants the great poet to contribute articles. That is Marx's version of the story. Others believe he first met Heine by chance in a newspaper office. Either way, Marx is determined to make a Marxist of Heine.

He never refers again to their common lineage. Marx is descended, through both parents, from generations of rabbis, some eminent. His forefathers minister to the Jews in the ancient town of Trier; his mother's side has rabbis in Krakow, Padua, and Holland. Among disenfranchised Jews, rabbis count as aristocracy. Marx, although his mythmakers fudge the issue, is a blue-blooded Jew.

It is his father who first breaks ranks.

Heinrich (Herschel) Marx does well as a lawyer under Napoleonic rule but is banned, as a Jew, once the Prussians resume control. Herschel duly converts in a Lutheran church and dunks his children, too, but his wife, Henriette, refuses. Karl Marx, their third child (of nine), is an atheist. Relations with his mother are remote, and he avoids the rest of the family, all but for his sister Sophie, best friend of his fiancée, Jenny von Westphalen; and his mother's sister, also Sophie, wife of Lion Philips, head of the Dutch electrical firm. Karl Marx begs for money from Philips of Holland. Letters between the Communist revolutionary and the Dutch capitalist are familial and warm.

Before Marx can formulate an ideology, he must grapple with the leading German thinker, Georg Wilhelm Friedrich Hegel. Like every philosopher, Hegel seeks a purpose for life on Earth. He comes up with a redeeming *geist*—usually rendered in English as "Spirit" or "Mind"—arguing that our capacity for understanding the world is greater than its physical reality. Hegel also propounds a "philosophy of right," which grants Prussia a moral foundation to rule as it pleases. From this aspect, Hegel is an old-school reactionary. Hegel believes in God and the status quo. "What is rational is actual and what is actual is rational," he says, an aphorism that is used to justify every despotism, down to Hitler and Stalin.

But Hegel's logic is powered by a process that he calls "dialectical change." Every force in history, he says, has its opposite. Progress is driven by the collision of two opposites to yield a fusion of the best in both. The Hegel sum reads: thesis versus antithesis equals synthesis. It's a beautiful, revolutionary notion.

Karl Marx joins the Young Hegelians at Berlin University. He takes his doctorate in Jena and becomes editor of a small newspaper in Cologne. He is soon in trouble. An editorial arguing that poor tenants have the right to collect fallen forest branches for firewood gets him a reprimand. An article on miserable housing conditions earns a final warning. In 1843, the paper is shut down after the Russian tsar takes umbrage, and Marx is threatened with arrest.

Married to Jenny and with a child on the way, Marx takes flight, to Paris. Heine visits the couple in their unheated room, steeling themselves for the death of their baby, who is having convulsions. He recommends they give the child a warm bath, and little Jenny recovers (or so her sister relates). Heine is impressed by the suffering Marx is prepared to endure. Marx is dazzled by Heine's fame. He is not yet a Communist, or so he tells Friedrich Engels, a German businessman from Manchester who is researching working conditions in the British garment industry.

Before he can get to grips with Engels's statistics, there are two essays that Marx must fire off. The first is a review of a paper by Bruno Bauer, a student of Hegel who opposes restoring Napoleonic civil rights to Prussian Jews. Bauer, in a paper titled "The Jewish Question," argues: "We ourselves are not free. How are we to free you? You Jews are egoists if you demand a special emancipation for yourselves as Jews."

Marx replies with an essay: "On the Jewish Question." He agrees Jews should not have equal rights, arguing that Jews disenfranchise themselves by being different. Their religious practices—Sabbath observance, kosher food—prevent them from playing a full public role. A Jewish judge or government minister would be unable to attend meetings on Saturdays. Worse, these special needs and separations promote (Marx does not show how) a Jewish tendency to materialism, especially among those who have allowed their religious observances to lapse.

"What is the secular basis of Judaism?" Marx demands. *Practical need, self-interest. What is the worldly religion of the Jew? Huckstering. What is his worldly God? Money.*"

He continues:

Money is the jealous god of Israel, in face of which no other god may exist. Money degrades all the gods of man—and turns them into commodities. Money is the universal self-established *value* of all things. It has, therefore, robbed the whole world—both the world of men and nature—of its specific value. Money is the estranged essence of man's work and man's existence, and this alien essence dominates him, and he worships it. The god of the Jews has become secularized and has become the god of the world. The bill of exchange is the real god of the Jew. His god is only an illusory bill of exchange.

The way to free the Jews is to rid society of Judaism. Marx concludes: "The *social* emancipation of the Jew is the *emancipation of society from Judaism*."⁴ For society to be free, the Jews must be cleansed of their religion, their culture, their history. They must be made to disappear.

This stew of wild generalizations and blind prejudice is textbook anti-Semitism: get rid of the Jews and all will be well with the world. Marx makes anti-Semitism a core doctrine for the revolutionary Left and a rallying cry for his future revolution.

His second essay, "Critique of Hegel's Philosophy of Right," is an attack on all forms of religion, starting with "the God of Israel and his servant Moses" and swiping at a "cringing Shylock, that swears by . . . every pound of flesh cut from the heart of the people." Marxist class theory and the importance of the proletariat emerge first in this essay, whose racialist motivation is never satisfactorily explained. Why would a born Jew, a humanist who identifies with the have-nots, direct his greatest venom at his own people, themselves victims of oppression? Biographers deal with this problem mostly by dodging it. Isaiah Berlin, in his groundbreaking biography of Marx, first published in 1939, ignores the anti-Jewish content. Berlin's antipode, Isaac Deutscher, argues that Marx seeks to redeem Jews and Christians alike from God. A recent Marx apologist, Francis Wheen, proposes—against all literal evidence—that "the essay was actually written as a defence of the Jews."

Why does Marx hate Jews? Berlin circles the question several times in correspondence, finally concluding that for Marx, Judaism is "a personal stigma which he was unable to avoid pointing out to others." In Berlin's view, Marx, ashamed of his origin, is prompted by some inner demon to keep harping on about it by victimizing Jews. It is an obsessive-compulsive disorder, and it is wildly inconsistent. While he calls Lassalle "nigger-like" and moans that a seaside resort is "full of yids and fleas," Marx brings up his daughter Eleanor to introduce herself to working men's groups as a proud Jewess. Marx is deeply conflicted. The roots of his conflict lie, in my reading, in his essay "On the Jewish Question."

For a man whose Jewishness was washed away in the font at six years old, Marx knows a lot more about Jewish practice than, by rights, he ought. He decries Jewish marriage, for instance, in which "the woman is bought and sold" as "an object of trade." The Talmud, in tractate Kiddushin, page one, states that a wife is "acquired" for marriage according to Torah law. But the act of "buying" a wife is outlawed by later rabbis and becomes ceremonial. Marx goes on to state that Judaism is a "polytheism of the many needs, a polytheism which makes even the lavatory an object of divine law." This extraordinary statement betrays a deep personal intimacy with Jewish life. Religious Jews thank God for all mercies great and small, reciting a quiet blessing after each visit to the toilet. These rituals are unknown outside the religious Jewish home. So how is Marx familiar with them?

Undoubtedly through his mother, the headstrong Henriette Marx, who refuses to convert with her husband, clinging to Judaism to impart it to her children. The Jewishness in Marx is naggingly maternal, and he resents it, rejecting the Jewish mother who tells him in a letter that he should try to make some real capital instead of just writing *Das Kapital*. Marx tells Engels he wishes his mother were dead. "On the Jewish Question" is an attempt to kill his mother, perhaps to avenge her insult to his father by refusing baptism. Freud, had he known these letters, would have had an Oedipal field day.

Marx has one other reader in mind. Heine, he knows, is fond of Jewish rituals. If he attacks Jewish habits, Heine must surely respond to the provocation. But Heine says nothing for four months, at which point he writes the most political of all his poems. "The Silesian Weavers" is a hymn of support for a German working-class revolt. The weavers of Peterswaldau are on strike for better wages. Heine takes up their cause and rephrases it in Marxist terms: they are rebelling not so much against wicked mill owners as against a rotten system and an oppressive country.

> Germany, we're weaving in your funeral shroud,
> A triple curse—deep endowed
> We're weaving, we're weaving!

Marx is ecstatic. Unable to publish the poem in the *Yearbook*, which has gone bust, he takes it to *Vorwärts* magazine, funded by the millionaire opera composer Giacomo Meyerbeer. Hundreds of copies are smuggled into Germany. A man is arrested in Berlin for reciting Heine's poem. Engels translates it into English, announcing in his paper, the *New Moral World*: "Henry [*sic*] Heine, the most eminent of all living German poets, has joined our ranks and published a volume of political poetry which contains also some pieces preaching socialism." Marxism claims Heine as its first celebrity convert. A future German Democratic Republic will teach its children that Karl Marx made Heine into a poet of genius.

On balance, one suspects that Heine has more influence on Marx than the other way round. Heine unchains Marx from windy rhetoric and refines his writing to the point where, by 1848, the *Communist Manifesto* becomes almost readable. Suddenly, Marx comes out with succinct slogans. "Communism is the riddle of history solved and it knows itself to be this solution." "Religion is the opiate of the masses."

"Revolutions are the locomotives of history." "The workers have nothing to lose but their chains." While Engels gives Marx hard economic facts, Heine shows him how to write a headline.

Leaving Paris, Marx laments: "The saddest thing for me is parting with the person of Heine; I wish I could pack you up with us and take you along." In London, hearing of Heine's return to God, he smears the poet's wife with poisonous gossip. Heine, on his mattress-grave, denies that he ever flirted with Communism:

> It is only with dread and horror that I think of the time when these gloomy iconoclasts will attain power; when their heavy hands will break without pity all the marble statues of beauty which are so dear to my heart . . . Yet, despite this, I publicly confess that this Communism, which is so inimical to all my interests and inclinations, exerts a magic influence on my soul . . .

In the war of head and heart, Heine ultimately votes with his heart. Like train engines in a shunting yard, Heine and Marx have enjoyed a noisy contact, conjoined by a heritage that neither can escape. Their convoluted friendship leaves a large footprint on the future of human affairs.

London, like patriotism, is the last refuge for all sorts of scoundrels. There are 4,386 fugitives from European revolutions in Britain, half of them in the capital. Many are brigands, roisterers, and street fighters, but there are also Italy's Giuseppe Mazzini, Louis Napoleon (future emperor of France), and Lajos Kossuth, the Hungarian insurrectionist. London is a safe space for political chancers who risk their lives on the prospect of Utopia.

Marx arrives in June 1849, intending to stay for a few weeks. He finds accommodation first in Leicester Square, Chelsea, and finally in Dean Street, Soho; "evil, frightful rooms," where three of his children will die. He is so poor that he pawns his shoes to pay the rent and is unable to attend the British Museum for several days. The Marx family shares a small bedroom with Jenny's German servant Helene Demuth, known as Lenchen. Marx is known as the Moor. One night, when Jenny is away, the Moor impregnates Lenchen. The child, at Jenny's insistence, is given up for adoption.

The author of the *Communist Manifesto* takes a punt on the stock exchange and sends dispatches to the *New York Daily Tribune*. In 1856, a family legacy enables him to move to Grafton Terrace, Kentish Town, where he becomes a bourgeois. The family takes picnics on Hampstead Heath. His daughters have piano lessons. Marx smokes a good cigar. He publishes *Das Kapital* in 1867, to "utter and complete silence." Unlike Mazzini and Kossuth, who are cheered on the streets of London, Marx passes unrecognized. He plots revolution abroad, scarcely bothering with British politics, which is a pity since the two-party system is being shaken up and the most colorful of scoundrels is about to seize power.

Has there ever been a political leader more unpolitical than Benjamin Disraeli? The eldest son of a literary man who quit the Jewish community a year before Benjamin's bar mitzvah, citing an indifference to religion, Benjamin is raised in the Church of England and loves its hymns. His identity, however, remains defiantly Jewish, and he never hesitates to assert it in a political cause; here, for instance, in a biography of his mentor, Lord George Bentinck: "The Jews represent the Semitic principle; all that is spiritual in our nature. They are the trustees of tradition and the conservators of the religious element. They are a living and the most striking evidence of the falsity of that pernicious doctrine of modern times, the natural equality of man." His Jewish pride is so infectious that even the self-denying Karl Marx, in a letter to his Philips uncle, refers to Disraeli as our "Stammegenosse"—a fellow Jew who shares our roots. While Marx hates Jews as a populist tactic, Disraeli wonders how people can ever be so dumb as to hate the Jews who brought them so many benefits: "The toiling multitude rest every seventh day by virtue of a Jewish law; they are perpetually reading . . . the records of Jewish history and singing the odes and elegies of Jewish poets." In May 1835, he delivers one of his great put-downs when the Irish MP Daniel O'Connell calls him "a lineal descendant of the blasphemous robber, who ended his career beside the Founder of the Christian Faith."

"Yes," declares Disraeli, "I am a Jew. And when the ancestors of the Right Honourable gentleman were brutal savages in an unknown island, mine were priests in the temple of Solomon."

Just over thirty years of age when this quip is uttered, he is already the sharpest tongue in British politics, a diamond wit with a quiver full of killer lines. No one skewers an opponent with such precision. His prim opponent, William Ewart Gladstone, is "a sophistical rhetorician, inebriated with the exuberance of his own verbosity," a vicious jibe at Gladstone's abstinence from alcohol. Of his own party leader, the northern industrialist Robert Peel, Disraeli snipes: "He traces the steam train always back to the kettle" and his smile "is like the silver fittings of a coffin." Feared on both sides of the House of Commons, Disraeli is impossible to pin down on any issue, changing policy as the wind blows.

A prolific novelist, he packs his plots with public figures in thin disguise, obliging powerful men and women to read them in case they are mentioned. His sales are small compared to Dickens and Thackeray, three thousand copies at most, but he revels in the literary hustings and makes enemies wherever he goes. Thackeray, under the pseudonym D. Shrewsberry, Esq., publishes a parody of a Disraeli novel, titled *Codlingsby*. Dickens caricatures Disraeli as the foppish James Harthouse in *Hard Times*. Both these novels are soaked in racial prejudice.

Disraeli takes a trip to Egypt and the Holy Land. On his return, he is elected to Parliament in 1837, amassing debts equivalent to half a million pounds in today's terms. He spends the next years hounded by creditors. Sporting coats of many colors where other men are decked in black, he tosses his curly hair at conformity. To the horror of Tory grandees, he sleeps with political wives, and sometimes with their husbands. Eventually, he marries a rich MP's widow, twelve years his senior. Mary Ann knows her Dizzy is a rogue. There is no deception on either side, and the union proves unexpectedly devoted.

Like Marx among workingmen, Disraeli is an odd fish in his party. The Tories are a mix of hereditary landowners, urban manufacturers, city bankers, and fiscal speculators. Run by blue bloods, the party is self-interested and backward-looking. Peel, an austere man of sensible and humane instincts, introduces a police force (called "Bobbies"), income tax (at 3 percent), and a Factory Act limiting the working hours of women and children. For generally humane and sensible reasons, he refuses to have a Cabinet with Disraeli in it.

The outsider dashes off three novels—*Coningsby* (1844), *Sybil* (1845), and *Tancred* (1847)—capturing the disaffection of young Tories. Peel is caricatured in *Sybil* as the "gentleman in Downing Street" who instructs his secretary to tell visitors only what they want to hear. The novel, subtitled "The Two Nations," is Disraeli's manifesto for a One Nation party.

Unable to topple Peel with a page-turner, Disraeli awaits the next reading of the Corn Law. In the thick of the Irish Potato Famine, Peel proposes to scrap import taxes on corn in order to feed the hungry masses. The landowners object. Disraeli, who has no opinion one way or the other, leads his young Tories into the lobby against the prime minister, bringing down the government. Peel, overwhelmed by a sense of betrayal, crosses the floor of the House with his protégé, Gladstone, to join the Whigs, who form the next government. The Tory Party enters opposition with Disraeli, at forty-two, as its coleader in the Commons. He has overturned political loyalties and rewritten the boundary lines of British politics.

What does he do next? He stakes his future on a Jewish issue. The banker Lionel de Rothschild is elected to Parliament for the City of London constituency. The Rothschilds have risen from money-changers in Frankfurt to a major economic force across Europe. Lionel's father, Nathan, supplied finance for British armies in the Napoleonic wars. Cousin Salomon in Vienna is funding railway networks. In Paris, cousin Jacob is a patron of the arts. To have a Rothschild in Parliament would be good for the British economy.

There is just one drawback. Lionel, who owns a chunk of Buckinghamshire and rides with the local hunt, clings devoutly to his Jewish faith. To enter Parliament, a member must swear allegiance "on the true faith of a Christian." Lionel, as a Jew, refuses to do so.

A bill is put forward to amend the oath and permit Jews to affirm in their own faith. The bill splits the house. Peel speaks in favor. The Tories are against. The Church of England is lobbying every MP it can lunch. All eyes are on Disraeli. If he backs the so-called Jew Bill, he will defy his party and lose his leadership. He has every reason to keep *shtum*. Being Disraeli, he speaks out.

"What you owe to this people," he hectors the House, is "your Christianity." He goes on: "Yes, it is as a Christian that I will not take upon me the awful responsibility of excluding from the Legislature those who are of the religion of which the Lord our Saviour was born." Jesus, he reminds them, could not be a British MP. The Jew Bill is passed by 257 votes to 186. Disraeli and his coleader, Bentinck, are the only Tories in favor. The House of Lords, obedient to the Church, vetoes the bill. Rothschild stands again for election and is once more returned. Disraeli speaks fervently for the bill. Charles Dickens, from the gallery, grudges him a rare compliment. "It delights me that D'Israeli [sic] has done such justice to his conscience-less self, in regard of the Jews," writes Dickens. The Lords junk it again.

Back and forth the bill shuttles, between Commons and Lords, until, after ten weary years, on July 26, 1858, Lionel de Rothschild enters Parliament. Rothschild, having taken his seat, never makes a speech or takes any part in political life. Nor is he grateful to Disraeli. "You know what a humbug he is," he tells his wife.

That leaves us to wonder why Disraeli would risk political suicide standing up for Jews when he ceased to be a Jew before his bar mitzvah. To read his mind-turns, we have to place him in the same frame as the other breakthrough Jews: with Mendelssohn, who quashes his inner Jew; with Marx, who hates the Jew within him; and with Heine, who is torn between love and distaste. Disraeli is the first to proclaim his origin as a political asset, the flair that sets him apart from the gray Tory pack. He refuses to accept the disability of being Jewish. Instead, he flaunts it as a token of historical superiority and a splash of color and diversity in dull political life. The Jew Bill, as he sees it, is a platform for his special set of talents.

The Jews represent, for Disraeli, everything he wants England to be: entrepreneurial, restless, quizzical, cultured, philanthropic, productive, contentious, and colorful. He backs the Jew Bill because it is good for England, a breach with past persecutions and a gateway to a new era in which genius need have no regard for its ancestry. He speaks up also out of friendship. Mr. and Mrs. Rothschild and Mr. and Mrs. Disraeli dine together every Sunday night. Disraeli remains close to Anglo-Jewry. Lionel's uncle, Sir Moses Montefiore, is president of the Board of Deputies of British Jews and head of the Spanish and Portuguese synagogue from which Disraeli's father absconded. Late in life, Disraeli takes a house next door to Sir Moses on Park Lane, opposite Hyde Park, reconciling his father's rupture.

By the time Rothschild enters the Commons, Disraeli is chancellor of the exchequer in the Earl of Derby's Tory government. His budget speech is favorably scrutinized by no less an economist than Karl Marx:

> Mr. Disraeli's speech on the Budget . . . is pleasant to read . . . As to lucidity of analysis, simplicity of composition, skilful arrangement and easy handling of details, it stands in happy contrast with the cumbersome and circumlocutory lucubrations of his Palmersto-nian predecessor. Neither does it contain or pretend to any striking novelty. Mr. Disraeli found himself in the happy position of a Minister of Finance who had to deal with a deficit not of his own making, but bequeathed by a rival. His part was that of the doctor, not of the patient . . . Mr. Disraeli roundly told the House that, if they wanted a policy of invasion and aggression, they must pay for it and that their loud cry for economy was a mere mockery, blended, as it was, with an unscrupulous readiness for expenditure.

Marx seems to understand Disraeli better than most of his own party. His review of the Disraeli budget is one of his chattiest and most reader-friendly articles, before his commissions dry up and he is once more reduced to want. His last years are pain-stricken and unproductive. His death on March 14, 1883, at the age of sixty-four, is mourned in Highgate Cemetery by a handful of cultists. Engels eulogizes him as "the greatest living thinker." Marx cannot have foretold that his doctrines would one day rule half the human race, that his Highgate tomb would be a major tourist attraction, or that his birthplace would erect a 4.4-meter-high statue, paid for by the Chinese government.

I have just given a lecture at the Gewandhaus when the *kapellmeister*, Kurt Masur, insists that I accompany him to a derelict building. It's my second wreck of the day. There is no shortage of them in the post-Communist Leipzig of 1992. That morning I found the site on Lessing-strasse where my brother-in-law grew up before fleeing the Nazis. Leo has given me a sketch of the interior—his father's surgery, the waiting room, living quarters, kitchen, balcony, maid's bedroom. The site is now a car park. Weeds grow where lives were saved and Sabbath hymns were sung.

Masur takes me to the house where Felix Mendelssohn lived and died. It is scheduled for demolition. First the Nazis banned his music, then the Communists turned his home into a factory. Masur aims to save the house and, by doing so, to reclaim Mendelssohn for the German *geist*. I wonder where he will find the money. East Germany is broke. But Masur is about to become music director of the New York Philharmonic, and he is nothing if not resourceful.

Four years later, I enter the restored Mendelssohn home. Here is the dining table where he ate, the desk where he composed, the sofa on which he collapsed. Down a stark corridor, I glimpse something of the spartan life of this overconscientious musician. I ask Masur if he understands Mendelssohn's personality. He shakes his head. I ask if he hears Jewish elements in his music. "Mendelssohn was a great German composer," says Kurt Masur, "a symbol of our tragedy."

There is more to Mendelssohn than this, I am sure. His name "son of Mendel" has an emotive context. Mendel is a Yiddish diminutive of the Hebrew Menahem, meaning "comforter"—a reference to God's promise to comfort the mourners of Zion. Felix is familiar with Jewish history. His letters are littered with clues. Although the ones selected for publication are bowdlerized of Jewish terms, some of the unedited family letters are notably unbuttoned. In an unpublished letter from London dated July 23, 1833, Mendelssohn uses a Hebrew word in German transliteration.[5] The word is *rohsche*.[6] It means a wicked person, and it is family code for an anti-Semite.

In the letter, Mendelssohn reports that he went to the House of Commons to hear the debate on an emancipation bill to remove "all civil disabilities at present existing affecting His Majesty's subjects of the Jewish religion." The bill is opposed by a group of MPs led by the independent member for the University of Oxford, Sir Robert Inglis. Mendelssohn writes: "Early today the Jews were emancipated. That makes me proud. *The Times* . . . suggests that it is better for *us* in England. There were some Jew haters: Mr Finn, Mr Bruce and the *Rohsche* Inglis . . . The bill was carried by 187 ayes to 52 noes." Mendelssohn glows at this victory for Jewish rights. He counts himself as one of *us*. He dreads the Jew-haters. In this suppressed letter, unseen until the twenty-first century, Mendelssohn proclaims himself a Jew. It is not his only such admission.

On the score of a new composition,[7] he writes four small letters: *L.e.g.G*, a German acrostic for "please, God, let it go well." This inscription is in the top right-hand corner of the page, on the spot where Jews write the Hebrew acronym *be'h* or the Aramaic *bs'd*, meaning "with God's help." Mendelssohn's superstitions are Jewish. His best friends—Moscheles, Ferdinand David, Joachim, Ferdinand Hiller, Julius Benedict—are Jews. His family language is Jewish, as is his frenetic energy.

My first encounter with a Jewish theme in Mendelssohn's music comes at a concert of the *Reformation Symphony* at the Schleswig-Holstein Festival in 1994. Members of an Israeli orchestra are asking the conductor, Noam Sheriff, what to play for an encore. "'Hevenu Shalom Aleichem,'" he beams. The tune, a Romanian Hasidic ditty played on El Al planes as they land at Ben Gurion Airport, opens the third movement of Mendelssohn's ultra-Christian symphony. Does Mendelssohn know "Hevenu Shalom Aleichem"? The melody is a common Jewish trope, not unlike the wedding song "Choson, Kallah, Mazel Tov." Mendelssohn sets it in the *Reformation Symphony* just ahead of the Lutheran hymn "A Mighty Fortress Is Our God." What is he trying to tell us?

Two themes from Mendelssohn's *Elijah*—the baritone aria "Send Us from Heaven" and the chorus "He That Shall Endure to the End"— are sung in synagogues every Sabbath to this day. The first is chanted to *"va-anachnu"* as the Torah is returned to the ark. The second is a Friday-night tune, *"eidoteicha ne'emnu me'od."* We have no idea whether Mendelssohn took these tunes from Jewish liturgy or whether synagogue cantors raided *Elijah*. What is plain, however, is that Mendelssohn's music fits Hebrew prayers to the letter. The composer's unconscious is tuned to a Hebrew rhythm. How did that happen? Jews hate silence. They hum and drum while waiting in line, walking in the street, or cooking supper. The infant Felix must have heard synagogue melodies at his mother's knee.

Other clues abound. The glorious incidental music for *A Midsummer Night's Dream* is stopped stone-dead by a klezmer clarinet wail in the eighth episode, titled "Funeral March." The music anticipates the child's funeral in Gustav Mahler's first symphony (the affinity is clearest in a recording by the Hungarian-Jewish conductor Iván Fischer). Mahler goes on to steal one of Mendelssohn's *Songs Without Words* (volume five, number three) to begin his fifth symphony. Mendelssohn's *Three Psalms*, opus seventy-eight, resembles rabbinic recitation.[8] The Capriccio movement in *Four Pieces for String Quartet* (1843) uses a Hebrew rhythm and a ground bass that fits the Friday-night hymn "Lecha Dodi." None of these examples is conclusive. Mendelssohn is a Christian. If he expresses a Jewish theme, he may do so unawares. Many regard the violin concerto in E minor as his most Jewish work. It contains no trace of a Jewish tune. How, then, does it feel so Jewish?

A hint lies in its troubled incubation. Mendelssohn, to whom writing music has always come easily, composes the concerto for Ferdinand David in July 1838 and then abandons it, blocked. Four years on, he pesters David with technical queries. He writes out a cadenza in full, allowing the soloist no license for improvisation. Six years and two months after he began, he makes a last-minute decision to strike the orchestral introduction and put the soloist in charge from the outset. There is no classical precedent for such an opening. Mendelssohn, for the first time in his prudent life, has broken a mold. It leaves him anxious. He writes again and again to David. He rehearses the concerto at the piano until his fingers are numb. He makes multiple changes on the printed score.

And then, on the evening of the premiere, March 13, 1845, he sends a message that he is ill. Something—a headache, migraine, anxiety attack—has rendered him incapable of conducting. The premiere of what proves to be the most popular violin concerto of all time is directed by the baton of Niels Gade. Felix never writes another concerto. That is how much the work has taken out of him.

The concerto's performance history is defined by Jews: Joachim, Kreisler, Heifetz, Huberman, Elman, Szeryng, Milstein, Oistrakh, Menuhin, Kogan, Spivakov, Stern, Perlman, Zukerman, Vengerov, Znaider. The music speaks with a directness that avoids the verbosity of Mendelssohn's oratorios and the starchiness of his five symphonies. In the violin concerto, Felix casts off his paralyzing inhibitions and glimpses a freedom that he dare not, at the last minute, grasp. Freedom does not come naturally to Mendelssohn and his kind.

Being Jewish is not what makes Mendelssohn a genius. Nor Heine, Marx, or Disraeli, for that matter. Their gifts are unique and particular;

their problems self-generated as much as genetic. No other human fits in their shoes. There is nothing collective in their triumphs and failures. Each is sui generis.

On the other hand, biographers who play down the heritage factor risk losing a vital perspective. All four confront the same prejudice. Each is acutely aware of what one might call *the indignity of their difference*: the need to apologize for not being the same as others, for being part of a long-scorned, barely tolerated faith and racial minority. Each develops a method for dealing with the indignity. Mendelssohn cultivates a faultless urbanity that conceals his fretful self. When insults start to fly, Heine and Marx get their retaliation in first. Disraeli disarms animosity with wit. Being Jewish takes up strategic space in their brains. They have to think hard how to handle it.

Their phenomenal productivity—Mendelssohn writes a symphony in days; Disraeli a novel in weeks—arises from being the first to burst out of the ghetto, brimming with the bottled energies of two millennia. They know that nothing will come easily. "A Jew is like a swimmer with a short arm. He has to swim twice as hard to reach the shore," says the composer Gustav Mahler. Being different, they do not expect easy acceptance. However, knowing that their difference cannot be erased gives them the freedom to express an idea without being inhibited by the fear of criticism or the need to please those in power. They can trash the room with impunity, recognizing no authority above their own.

Heine, Marx, and Disraeli are iconoclasts, as reckless in their mold-breaking as they are confident in its necessity. Heine unpicks the corsets of the German language, exposing fragile beauties. Disraeli turns England's stupid party into One Nation conservatives. Marx calls for class war and the confiscation of wealth. Mendelssohn infiltrates a Hebrew tune into, for heaven's sake, his *Reformation Symphony*. The turning points in their lives in 1847 set the tone for a century of Jewish invention, liberating their successors from the craving for approval. On their foundations Freud can name the unspeakable—sex—as our darkest drive and Einstein can imagine a world equipped for self-annihilation. Schoenberg can inflict painful atonality on cultivated ears and Trotsky can propound the nightmare of perpetual revolution. Sarah Bernhardt will invent celebrity and Sam Goldwyn its means of dissemination. Jonas Salk prevents polio and Gregory Pincus pregnancy. Larry Page and Sergey Brin will make all mortal knowledge available at the click of a key; Mark Zuckerberg will get all human faces to connect on a screen. The desire to change the world is their unifying purpose. Some may recognize it as the Jewish religious impulse known as *tikun olam*.

Much as the radicals abandon Judaism, they are imbued with its values and attitudes, especially in relation to authority. Jews have an "I/You" dialogue with God that casts the Creator as a remote, if ultimately benevolent, member of the tribe. Heine, on his deathbed, is asked how he stands with God. Heine has no doubts on the matter. *"Dieu me pardonnera,"* he announces. *"C'est son métier"* (God will forgive me, it's his job). This may be more profound than he knows. Heine is drawing a line between Christian forgiveness, which can be dispensed by human agency (church or state) before it reaches God, and the Jewish concept in which only God can forgive: "For with You there is forgiveness, that you may be feared."[9] But the expectation is that God *must* forgive. If He does not, He will be left without people. Heine, like many Jews, knows better than God what He ought to be doing. God may have created the world, but the Jews knew Him when He was young.

Their perception of God is shifting among the Jews. Ever since Moses Mendelssohn broke bread with Christians, Reformers have pushed hard to "modernize" Judaism, while traditionalists have held even harder to arcane practices. Reform seats men and women together at services, excises prayers for the restoration of temple sacrifices, and whittles away at prohibitions on Sabbath work and nonkosher foods. Traditionalists refuse to modify a word in the liturgy. Reformers argue that since most Jews no longer observe the strict letter of the law, the letter must be modified. "Frum" Jews—a Yiddish term from the German *fromm* (pious)—resist. In France and Germany, Reform leaders seize control of community assets and represent the Jews to the state. Orthodox groups lose the right to speak for their communities and receive state subsidies. As Jews make their first impact on Western civilization, a violent storm is breaking over their ancient faith.

TWO

1851
THE WARS OF THE JEWS

The unfathomable enigma
that was Alkan.

Frrom his study window, the rabbi sees rolling hills and green for-
ests, a lake twinkling in sunlight. He is at the very center of central
Europe, a town called Nikolsburg in Moravia, and he looks out on an

earthly paradise. The rabbi thinks of writing a book on how the changing seasons affect the philosophy of Judaism, but this is no time for bucolic reveries. He has won an important battle during the 1848 revolution, persuading the Austrian emperor and Parliament, who took refuge in Moravia, to remove anti-Jewish laws such as punitive taxes on Sabbath candles and kosher foods and, most onerous, the right of only one Jewish male in a family to register a marriage, making all other children bastards.[1] Samson Raphael Hirsch serves ex officio in Parliament as the Moravian chief rabbi, shepherd of fifty thousand souls. He could remain here more or less contentedly for the rest of his life, writing learned books while the seasons change beyond his window. He knows, however, that this would be an unpardonable sin.

On his desk sits a letter. Eleven men in Frankfurt am Main invite him to be their rabbi. The job they offer has no state salary or public status. The men, who have resigned from Reform-run institutions, meet to pray in private houses. The rabbi would be sacrificing his career, putting his children's future at risk. Hirsch, after consulting his wife, Johanna, accepts the offer. He informs the Moravian government that the Frankfurt secession is "the most promising development that has occurred in Jewry for decades."

Samson is aptly named. A fighter by nature, the war he joins looks like a lost cause. Almost all Jewish communities in Germany are in Reform hands. A Reform conference of 1842 has rejected the Talmud as the source of Jewish law, discrediting the foundation of Jewish religious practice. The Reform temple is a place of contemplation and decorum, far removed from chaotic *shtiebls* with their babble of Hebrew prayer and Yiddish conversation. Reform offers dignity and grace in worship, together with a permission to discard practices that no longer appear meaningful: the morning ritual of phylacteries, for instance, or the waving of palm branches in the Tabernacles festival. It recites some prayers in German, to the accompaniment of an organ. A mixed choir sings from the high place, the *bimah*. Reform abolishes circumcision, two-day festivals, thrice-daily prayers, and all reference to Zion and Jerusalem. Samuel Holdheim, a Berlin rabbi, even proposes to shift the Sabbath to Sunday, to conform with Christian neighbors.

At this point, Reform is a German movement with a French offshoot and a tenuous foothold in America. Elsewhere, Jews in Italy, the Balkans, and the Arab crescent show no appetite for change. In Eastern Europe and Russia, where Orthodoxy prevails, Jews are split between Hasidic mysticism and Lithuanian scholasticism. Modernity is off the menu. In Pressburg, Moses Sofer, the supreme authority on Jewish law, proclaims: *"Chadash asur min haTorah"* (Anything new is forbidden by the Torah). Orthodoxy sees Reform as a one-step gateway to apostasy. Statistics support that contention. Some 22,500 German Jews convert to Christianity during the nineteenth century, a rate of six a day.[2] This is the crisis that Samson Raphael Hirsch confronts throughout his life.

Hirsch, at ten years old, sees the world's first Reform temple open in Hamburg, his hometown. In his bar mitzvah year, 1821, Hamburg installs Isaac Bernays as chief rabbi. Bernays, the first German rabbi to obtain a PhD, is acutely aware of the parlous state of faith. His brother, Adolphus, professor of German at King's College London, has become a Christian. His son Michael demands to convert at the age of fourteen. Bernays, to stop the drift, draws on the synthetic philosophy of the twelfth-century rabbi Maimonides, whose Judaism is infused with Greek and Islamic ideas. Bernays, taking the Sephardi title "Haham" (wise man) to distinguish himself from Reform "rabbis," teaches German history in the Orthodox cheder, sends teenagers to university, and promotes women's literacy, to the chagrin of ignorant fathers and husbands. He argues that Judaism has been revitalized down the ages by contact with other cultures. Heinrich Heine says of his inaugural sermon: "He is an ingenious man . . . [but] none of the Jews understand him."[3] Bernays declares war on the Reform temple through the medieval act of blowing the black shofar, signaling an act of excommunication which places Reform Jews outside the religious fold. Taken to a harsh conclusion, the *herem* prohibits Jews from having any communication with members who have been banned, excludes them from marriage and burial, and denies them the right to enter a synagogue and commemorate bar mitzvahs and anniversaries. It literally cuts them dead. Bernays pronounces a second *herem* on the Reform prayer book, an unnecessary provocation. He wants the split to be irrevocable. Samson Raphael Hirsch is his bedazzled disciple. Another is Nathan Marcus Adler, future first chief rabbi of the British Empire.

At university, Hirsch forms a society for Jewish studies with Abraham Geiger, who shares his passion for making Judaism relevant to a post-ghetto world. Hirsch graduates and becomes rabbi in Oldenburg. Geiger stays on to write a doctoral thesis titled "What did Moham-med take from Judaism?" Terminally indecisive, he dithers seven years before marrying his fiancée, Emilie Oppenheim, and, when he finally accepts a rabbinic call to Wiesbaden, it is to serve the Reform com-munity. Hirsch, wounded by Geiger's defection, responds with an unexpected bestseller. *The Nineteen Letters of Ben Uziel* is a Socratic dialogue between a young Orthodox rabbi and his disillusioned best friend, who is straying from the path. Named Naphtali and Benjamin, they are recognizable as Hirsch and Geiger.

In the book, Hirsch characterizes Reform as morally weak and intellectually unjustifiable. "Judaism seeks to lift us up to its height," he writes, "how dare [they] attempt to drag it down to our level?" Faith is essential and immutable:

> If you consider yourself born only to possess and enjoy; if the quan-tity and extent of your possession and enjoyments are for you the measure of your importance; if you look upon these things not as a means but as ends in themselves . . . if you believe that your strength and the power of your hand can carry the edifice of your prosperity to its limit; not God but you alone and that all other considerations must yield to this one ambition, well—then, indeed . . .

The Nineteen Letters, published in 1836, galvanizes German Jews on both sides of the rising barricade. Geiger writes no fewer than four reviews of the book, one of them fifty-four pages long, extolling "the moral loftiness of [Hirsch's] presentation of Judaism." But he finds a weak spot in Hirsch's hotheaded denigration of Maimonides's synthesis and in one of his harsher reviews castigates Orthodoxy for its absolut-ism and compares it to infallible Roman Catholicism: "rule of the old without necessity, naked assumption without foundation."[4]

Hirsch never speaks to him again. Geiger moves to Breslau, becom-ing "the first real theologian of Reform Judaism."[5] Hirsch, aged twenty-eight, is the engine of a modern form of Orthodoxy. Young men flock to Oldenburg to sit at his feet. The most excitable is Heinrich (Hirsch) Graetz, a youth of nineteen who, having lost his faith at a pre–Yom

Kippur ceremony in which live chickens are waved above men's heads, regains it on reading *Nineteen Letters*: "Avidly I devoured every word. Disloyal though I had been to the Talmud, this book reconciled me." Graetz moves in with Hirsch as his house pupil for three years, while completing a PhD and starting work on an eleven-volume *History of the Jews*.

With a swaggering self-assurance and considerable speculation, Graetz's history challenges the presumed dates of biblical works, dismisses Kabbalah as a fraud, and ignores social and economic causes in a trimillennial tale of heroes and villains. He surmises that Jesus of Nazareth is a member of a mystic Essenes cult, he denigrates Polish Jews, and he lambasts Reform, calling the Berlin rabbi Holdheim "the greatest enemy of Judaism since Paul of Tarsus." Geiger counterattacks, calling Graetz "a first-class swindler and charlatan." Hirsch maintains his support of Graetz until the fourth volume, on temple ritual, which he calls "a piece of fantasy derived from superficial combinatory mannerisms." Graetz concedes some errors in citations but refuses to revise. Banned by Hirsch, he joins a moderate seminary in Breslau founded by Zacharias Frankel, whom Hirsch calls "a complete heretic." Geiger, unsettled by Graetz's arrival in Breslau, moves to Frankfurt, where Hirsch refuses to see him. These three willful men would reshape the outlook and practice of Judaism as we know it today.

Hirsch is the hardest to fathom. "His demeanour was serious and introverted. He was not talkative," writes a student.[6] There are few archival clues to his personality. Three extant photographs—from youth, adulthood, and old age—show a dark pair of eyes, no hint of a smile, and a well-trimmed beard covering a clenched jaw. His marriage is said to be contented. Aloof by choice, Hirsch recognizes no way but his own. Yet he is far from being inflexible or fundamentalist. In his commentary to the Torah section that contains "an eye for an eye, a tooth for a tooth," Hirsch likens the text of the Torah (and the relation of written to oral law) to a student's notes on a scientist's lecture: "For those who did not attend the instructor's lecture, these notes would be of no use whatsoever. If they were to attempt to reconstruct the entire lecture solely from these notes, they would of necessity make many errors." Hirsch's statement that Torah cannot be grasped without the oral law of Mishnah and Talmud is the standard Orthodox position.

But his analogy of Torah text to a student's notes is startlingly original, accepting by inference that the "notes" might be erroneous or misleading and that only by means of evolving analysis down the generations can Torah be understood as a living body of thought. The rabbi's role is to interpret; he is the Moses of his time.

In Frankfurt, Hirsch finds a total absence of Jewish amenities: no *mikveh* (ritual bath), no kosher butcher. His first act is to rebuild a *mikveh* that the Reformers have bricked up. Next, he sets up a school for the study of Torah and secular subjects. Only then does he agree to build a synagogue, paid for by Baron Wilhelm Carl "Willi" von Rothschild, the last banker in the dynasty to observe Orthodoxy (his London and Paris cousins fear "that his religious devotion will be followed by fanaticism"[7]). Willi attends daily services and shuts his bank on the Sabbath. Hirsch declines Rothschild's offer to cover the full costs of the building, insisting that other members raise a third. At the inauguration ceremony, Catholic and Protestant bishops occupy the seats of honor. Reform rabbis are excluded.

Hirsch's Orthodox shul differs from all others in the beauty and dignity of its worship. It has a male voice choir with a professional conductor. Hirsch demands punctuality and decorum, glaring at whisperers and latecomers. He wears a floor-length canonical cloak, spotless and imposing. His sermons cite Hegel and Goethe as much as the biblical elucidators Rashi and Radak. German and Jewish cultures have much to learn from each other, he proclaims.

His school syllabus includes Hebrew grammar and syntax, eliminating the arid casuistry known as *pilpul*. He teaches boys and girls without discrimination. Unlike many Christian prelates, he discusses Darwin's theory of evolution with an open mind and recommends modern science when it contradicts Talmudic folk remedies. The Talmud is a guide to Jewish life, not a remedy for pain relief, he quips. "*Torah im derekh eretz*" is his motto: "God's law in the real world."

Before long, his community has six hundred families, and Frankfurt is the hub of modern Orthodoxy. He founds a monthly magazine, *Jeschurun*, and publishes lucid translations of the Pentateuch, the Psalms, and the book of Isaiah. He successfully lobbies the Reichstag in Berlin to win Orthodox Jews the right of state recognition, separate from Reform, a triumph not universally endorsed by his congregation.

Only a third of his members break ties with Reform institutions, and Baron Willi carries on funding charities on both sides of the divide. Hirsch, as he ages, becomes isolated from his own followers.

He dies, aged eighty, on the last day of 1888. Sixteen boys carrying his published works walk behind the coffin, followed by 520 boys of the senior school and three hundred of the junior. A Hirsch synagogue opens in New York, another in London. "Rabbi Samson Raphael Hirsch . . . was in favor of reform," writes Bernard Revel, first president of Yeshiva University, "but with him it was the reform of the Jews, not of Judaism."[8] Hirsch, not unlike Johann Sebastian Bach, has synthesized a worn tradition and made it transmissible to an empirical age.

Early in 1851, the foremost French pianist disappears. Charles-Valentin Alkan is not dead; he writes to colleagues, assuring them that he is perfectly all right. Any who knock at his door are told: "M. Alkan is not at home." Asked when he might be available, the concierge says, "Never." Alkan is lost to the world, not seen for twenty years, a reaction as extreme as it is inexplicable. But Alkan has his reasons, and he has done this sort of thing before.

Alkan is a phenomenon, a pianist without rival and a composer of wild invention. Liszt and Chopin live in awe of his abilities. Frédéric Chopin, at his death in May 1849, leaves Alkan a manuscript to complete. The loss of Chopin is one cause for his seclusion, but not the main one.

Alkan is an Alsatian Jew, born in Paris on November 30, 1813. Aged six, he enters the Conservatoire as a piano student. At fourteen, he is praised by Rossini. At nineteen, he performs his own concerto. After swamping his Paris publisher with too many works, he goes to London to find another outlet. No other pianist can play his thick cascades of notes. Even he struggles with the *Grande Sonate*, describing a man's life at twenty, thirty, forty, and fifty years of age. Liszt writes of Alkan's piano suite *Le Vent* that it "marvellously conveys the sound of those prolonged winds that moan monotonously for whole days." Schumann calls it "a crabbed waste overgrown with brushwood and weeds, the best of it borrowed from Berlioz." Alkan, at twenty-four, is dividing serious opinion.

Then, after a duo recital with Chopin, he drops out. For five years, between 1839 and 1844, Alkan retires from the concert hall. He teaches private pupils and visits salons, but he is no longer seen onstage. The clue to his withdrawal is the birth, on February 7, 1839, of a baby named Élie-Miriam Delaborde. Neither parent is named on the birth certificate. Delaborde is the maiden name of George Sand's mother (make of that what you will). Alkan brings up the child as his own. On his fifth birthday, he begins to teach Delaborde to play the piano.

In April 1844, Alkan completes a symphony, adorned with the Hebrew verse "And the Lord said let there be light and there was light."[9] He destroys the score unheard but resumes his famous recitals. His piano études sell like fresh croissants. The *Grande Sonate*, dedicated to his father, appears when "all the Parisian pianists are in London" during the 1848 revolution. Contention arises when his Conservatoire teacher, Joseph Zimmermann, retires as head of the piano department. Four candidates are named: Alkan, Émile Prudent, Louis Lacombe, and Antoine François Marmontel, who is Alkan's pupil and a protégé of the Conservatoire director, Daniel Auber. Alkan, naming Chopin and Liszt as his references, asks George Sand to lobby on his behalf. "If you collect the votes of all the leading musicians in Europe," declares Alkan in his application, "I will be elected."

In September 1848, as sure as keys are made of ivory, Marmontel gets the coveted position. "In spite of my positive rights, in spite of your all-powerful support, Madam, I have failed," Alkan tells George Sand. "The Republic, for which I have a most ardent love, allows strange blunders to be made . . . I felt disposed to educate a whole generation in musical matters and I have to give way, not to a worthy or even unworthy rival but to one of the most total nonentities."[10]

Devastated, he retires again, moving from the artists' quarter around the Square d'Orléans and returning only for the first nights of George Sand's plays. Upon his father's death in 1855, he moves to the rue Daru in the eighth arrondissement. Richard Wagner lures him out one last time with a pair of concert tickets. Alkan says afterward: "Wagner is not music; it's a sickness." He wants nothing of such vanities.

Locked inside his own four walls, his music acquires a baffling complexity: an *allegro barbaro*, forty-eight *esquisses*, and three *grands études*, one for each hand and a third to be played together. His style spans classical Bach and Romantic Mendelssohn and has some futuristic atonalities that anticipate Arnold Schoenberg. As well as writing music, every day he translates two verses of Scripture, the Old Testament from Hebrew and the New from Syriac. He keeps a set of the Talmud on his top shelf. He hires and fires fifty-one housemaids and is ultimately forced to make his own bed. "My situation makes me horribly sad and wretched," he writes to the Jewish composer Ferdinand Hiller.

In 1871, during the siege of Paris, a bullet pierces his piano. Suddenly, unprompted, he rents the Salle Érard for six late-night *petits concerts*. "Delaborde must not be told," he warns. After dark, on the night of February 15, 1873, at nine p.m., Alkan takes the stage for the first time in a generation. He plays Bach and Handel, Chopin and Alkan. The audience, mostly professional pianists, is dumbstruck. Alkan is the last of the golden age of keyboard artists, only quicker and more fearsome than Chopin or Liszt. He seeks neither applause nor approval. For the next eight years, he turns up every day at Érard's practice rooms. "I am Charles-Valentin Alkan," he introduces himself to the composer Vincent d'Indy, "and I'm just preparing for my annual series of six Petits Concerts, at which I play only the finest pieces. Listen well. I am going to play for you, for you alone, Beethoven's Opus 110." D'Indy, a pronounced anti-Semite, finds his playing "more humanly moving" than Liszt.

Unwary concertgoers are daunted by his appearance. A pencil sketch at the Canadian National Library shows the wild-bearded Alkan in a broad-brimmed black hat, looking like a Hasidic *rebbe* from Hungary or Bessarabia.

His death, on March 29, 1888, is the most celebrated fact of his life. "He was found crushed beneath his upturned bookcase from which he had been extracting a Hebrew religious book" is the legend circulated by his probable son Delaborde (who will reenter our story before long), but the police report mentions no such mishap. It says Alkan expired in the kitchen while preparing his evening meal. He is buried on Easter Sunday in Montmartre Cemetery in the presence of family members and four musicians. "He had to die," writes a Paris obituarist, "in order to prove his existence."

The music almost dies with him, since hardly anyone can play it. So full of notes, so unyielding to the ear, it takes huge hands and single-minded determination to scale this musical Matterhorn. His music is written, like a page of Talmud, as a conceptual problem to be unraveled by argument. It propels the piano out of the Romantic drawing room and into a space-age future, unlocking sonorities that would remain unheard until the age of John Cage and Pierre Boulez. The first to attempt it in Berlin is Ferruccio Busoni, the half-Jewish Italian-German composer, who is greeted with cries of "preposterous French rubbish." Busoni, unfazed, plays Alkan's cadenza in the middle of Beethoven's third piano concerto, causing audience consternation. No more Alkan is heard in a major hall for forty years until the Dutchman Egon Petri plays it on the BBC in January 1938, a lone star in a night sky of oblivion. In 1953, the New York pianist Raymond Lewenthal, recovering in Paris after having both arms and hands broken in a brutal Central Park mugging, finds some Alkan scores in a junk shop. Remembering that his piano teacher was a pupil of Delaborde, he persuades RCA to let him record the *Symphonie* for solo piano. Harold Schonberg, in the *New York Times*, calls it "prophetic." *Life* magazine proclaims an "Alkan revival." Lewenthal goes home to Manhattan and enjoys a brief celebrity. As his fame fades, he holes up in a studio apartment, where, like Alkan, he is found dead one morning by the neighbors.

In England, the BBC asks Ronald Smith, a Busoni expert with huge hands, to have a go at Alkan. Smith, totally bald and almost blind, makes the composer his life's mission. Alkan, for Smith, is the harbinger of modernism. His "Funeral March for a Dead Parrot" matches the title of Gustav Mahler's first work. The bleak foreboding of Mahler's sixth symphony and the emotional ambiguities of Schoenberg's *Verklärte Nacht* are anticipated by Alkan. Smith writes a two-volume biography, founds the Alkan Society, and fills the Royal Festival Hall with Alkan lecture-recitals. I approach him for a tutorial, and he talks me through the Jewish elements in Alkan, mostly to do with minor-key themes. There is a distinctive Star of David design in his *esquisses*, as well as a cantorial trope and numerical *gematriya*-style games.[11] Alkan is proud to be Jewish. What neither Smith nor anyone else can fathom is why he writes such intractable music and why he locks himself away in a one-man ghetto. Smith sees it as an overreaction to anti-Jewish prejudice at the Conservatoire, but this is unsupported by the facts. Alkan's brother Napoléon is made professor of *solfège* (ear training) at the Conservatoire. Delaborde becomes professor in 1873. There is no ban on Jews.

Clinical depression can also be discounted. Alkan functions capably in seclusion, and his letters betray none of the usual symptoms: low energy, concentration difficulties, and helplessness. He seems in control of his situation and content with his actions. What pushes this unusual, improbably gifted man into becoming a hermit?

A Jewish analyst might recognize his behavior as a *broiges*, a huff or strop that falls midway between a childish tantrum and an adult vendetta. From the Hebrew *be-rogez*, meaning "in rage," a person in *broiges* declares to the world: *Look what you are making me do to myself. Broiges*, a retreat from confrontation, is twice as aggressive as a fight. It says: *You can't touch me because I am hurting myself more than you possibly can. You cannot release me from the pain you have caused me; only I can end it.*

The *broiges* is a default position for many Jewish thinkers. Karl Marx rejects much-needed apostles, Sigmund Freud excommunicates disciples, Samson Raphael Hirsch turns Graetz from ally to apostate. No one, though, does *broiges* as totally as Alkan. Furious at the French Republic, this Jew makes his own ghetto.

Rages are what rabbis do. A Rhineland Reformer, Samuel Adler, is renowned for violent rhetoric. He attacks "shocking lies" in the traditional prayers, the "fustian" shackles of Talmud, Hirsch's "twisted, hyper-Orthodox brochures," and Geiger's moderation.[12] An 1848 revolutionary who is lucky to escape jail, Adler receives a summons from Temple Emanu-El in midtown Manhattan. This, he declares, is a sign of "the rule of God in the world."

Arriving in New York in 1857, Adler, a distant cousin of the British chief rabbi, sets about creating an authentic American place of worship. He takes down partitions between the men's and women's seating areas. Men pray bareheaded, the skullcap gone. The rabbi's sermon, delivered in German, replaces the reading of the Torah at the heart of the service. Adler preaches citizenship and social responsibility. To be a good Jew is to be a good American. He is first to preach the morning after President Lincoln's assassination. "As God said to Abraham the patriarch that he was to be the father of many peoples, so did God select Abraham Lincoln to be the protector and father of a great people," orates Samuel Adler, before (as the *New York Times* reports) he breaks down in tears.

Samuel Adler makes Temple Emanu-El the cathedral of New York's upper crust, the mark of God's blessing on those who just a few years before and a few blocks away were selling rags. Most New York Jews start out poor, with sacks on their backs, heading down south where the richest pickings are to be found. The Lehman brothers save enough money to open their first store in Alabama, where the Seligmans have four. In Philadelphia, the son of peddler Marcus Goldman marries Joseph Sachs's daughter and starts a bank. The Kuhns, the Loebs, the Guggenheims, the Lazard brothers, all from Germany and France, start up in much the same way.

In the California gold rush, the Seligmans sell a $5 blanket for $40. When their store burns down, they open a money-transfer service, shipping half a billion dollars back east in six years and themselves returning in glory. By 1857, Joseph Seligman has a fine mansion in Murray Hill, New York's prime residential area, and a family pew in Temple Emanu-El for Sabbath worship.

Levi Strauss, a Bavarian clothier, treks through fever-ridden Panama to San Francisco, where he finds that panhandlers keep wearing out the seats of their pants. With Levi's investment, a Russian Jew, Jacob Davis, fixes the problem. He makes tough jeans of denim cotton, fastened with rivets to prevent splitting. The jeans are known as Levi's. Levi Strauss builds a western Temple Emanu-El on Sutter Street, the first synagogue to employ a female cantor.

When General Ulysses S. Grant threatens to expel Jews from territory under his control, he gets a reminder from Jesse Seligman that his family used to extend him credit when he was a penniless lieutenant and that they are now selling $200 million in US bonds to Europe to support the Union cause. Grant rescinds his expulsion order.

The most flamboyant New York Jew is August Belmont, national chairman of the Democratic Party and the Rothschilds' man in America. The *New York Evening Post* reports that he is an illegitimate son of the Rothschilds. Belmont marries the daughter of a US naval hero in an Episcopalian ceremony; it is said that he remains Jewish during business hours and is Christian on Sundays. During the 1864 election, he is attacked by the *Chicago Tribune*, a Republican newspaper: "Will we have a dishonorable peace in order to enrich Belmont, the Rothschilds, and the whole tribe of Jews, who have been buying up Confederate bonds, or an honorable peace won by Grant and Sherman at the cannon's mouth?"[13] Allan Pinkerton, of the detective agency, spreads a rumor that Belmont is plotting to assassinate the president. Belmont's Democrats are routed 212 votes to 21 in the electoral college, but the Rothschild banker emerges more powerful than ever.

He is New York's first master of the universe, a man of limitless wealth who can put any politician in his pocket while maintaining a pretense of public good. The Democrats' kingmaker for two decades of defeat, he is nonetheless regarded as the savior of the two-party system. Belmont collects Old Masters, fine wines, and racehorses. An outsider wherever he goes, he stays in touch with the Temple Emanu-El crowd—the Lehmans, the Goldman-Sachses, the Seligmans, the Kuhns, and the Loebs—who now have shields on Wall Street and whose sons and daughters marry one another, keeping the dynasties within temple walls. Temple Emanu-El moves up in the world. In 1868, it reopens on Fifth Avenue and Seventy-Sixth Street with stained-glass windows and a Moorish interior with Persian carpets and Turkish tiles, a larger model of the Liberal synagogue on Berlin's Oranienburger Strasse. Untold wealth and the liberation from Talmudic rules inspire midcentury, midtown Jews to reimagine a Mediterranean golden age.

Samuel Adler's son, Felix, shocks the community from its complacency with a debut sermon on "The Judaism of the Future," in which God is abolished. The bankers find him a teaching post at Cornell University, but Felix has bigger ideas. He founds a Society for Ethical Culture for New York Jews who have outgrown religion, along with a school and kindergarten that remain popular with Liberal parents in the twenty-first century.

Jews have lived in the French provinces of Alsace and Lorraine since Roman times. After Napoleon grants them full citizenship, they remain faithful to tradition when the rest of France turns to Reform. Their Grand Rabbin, Salomon Wolf Klein, is a brilliant orator who urges his "*chers frères, chers soeurs*" to embrace the totality of French culture alongside their Jewish practice. Klein, a warrior against Reform, is supported by 95 percent of the Jews in Alsace.[14]

Raised in a village on the outskirts of Strasbourg, he is made chief rabbi at the age of thirty-six. He publishes works of Hebrew grammar and Torah commentary and raises a family of fifteen children, whom he burdens with orotund French names: Théophile, Virginie, Cléomène, Théophraste, Eugénie, Angélique, and Palmyre. His sons are sent to university to become doctors or lawyers; some also take ordination as rabbis, at ease in both worlds. In his own province, the Grand Rabbin is shepherd to a flock of sixteen thousand Jews.

Paris is another matter, a den of Reform. Summoned to a national conference of rabbis, Salomon Wolf Klein agrees to attend on condition there is no vote on ritual matters. The opening banquet, strictly kosher, is thrown by Baron Edmond de Rothschild, president of the Consistoire. The baron offers his carriage to drive Grand Rabbin Klein back to his hotel. Klein declines. The baron is puzzled: no one turns down a Rothschild. Klein says: "Thank you, Baron, for your kindness, but I cannot accept, for it is written in the Bible (Isaiah 55:8), '*lo darkeichem derachai*' [your ways are not mine]."

Next morning, the conference votes "to introduce an organ into the synagogue, provided that on Sabbaths and festivals it is played by a non-Jew." Klein adds a codicil: it can only be played with the permission of the Grand Rabbin. He outsmarts inferior minds. Reformers ask the minister for religion to suspend Klein for forming a separatist association of Orthodox rabbis. Klein makes an ally of Adolphe Crémieux, a future minister of justice. Crémieux, a Liberal Jew, assures Klein that he observes the Ten Commandments. Klein offers him a riddle: "Let's say you find your safe broken and you call a Jewish locksmith on the Sabbath. He does the job but steals all the money in the safe. What do you do?"

"I'd have him arrested for theft," declares Crémieux.

"But not," demands Klein, "for breaking the Sabbath, an earlier Commandment?"

In 1866 the post of chief rabbi of France falls vacant. Klein seems likely to win election until Reformers join forces with a feeble Orthodox minister, Lazare Isidor. In Colmar, Klein starts a school and a rabbinical college with the aim of filling France with rabbis in his own symbiotic mode. The school proves his nemesis. Education in France is centrally regulated. Reformers inform the Ministry for Education that the rabbi is running a school "which does not even have legal standing."[15] The minister shuts it down. Salomon Wolf Klein, dismayed at the treachery of his fellow Jews, is felled by a heart attack and dies in November 1867, aged fifty-three. Samson Raphael Hirsch roars in a Frankfurt eulogy that "this unique event [the closure of his school] broke the heart of this man." The wars of the Jews are not bloodless. Good men lose their lives in defense of faith. Salomon Wolf Klein is my direct ancestor, the grandfather of two of my grandparents.

THREE

1863

BROUGHT TO BOOK

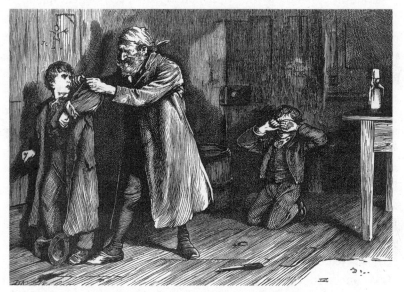

How Charles Dickens toned down the worst of Fagin.

The city is a nineteenth-century organism. In 1800, London has a million inhabitants; by 1900, 6.7 million. Vienna goes from 200,000 in 1800 to half a million in 1851 and 1.77 million in 1900, of whom 9 percent are Jews. New York, home to 60,000 in 1800, has 3.8 million by the end of the century. Its Jewish population swells from 16,000 in 1850 to 598,000—17.4 percent of the total population[1]—and to 1.6 million by 1920. Never have so many Jews gathered in a single place at the same time.

At first, they huddle in low-rent "Jewish quarters": the East End of London, Berlin's Alexanderplatz, Vienna's Leopoldstadt, the Marais in Paris, New York's Lower East Side. Opportunity beckons. The city invents leisure. No longer obliged to draw water, wash clothes, or hew wood for daily needs, the middle classes have time to waste and money to spend. Department stores turn shopping into fun. Theaters fill empty evenings. Jews enter the entertainment industry. The city grows and grows.

London expands to the west and north. Paris is redesigned by Baron Haussmann in a web of concentric boulevards. Vienna tears down its walls in 1857 to make way for a *Ringstrasse* that opens space for cultural interaction. The first building on the ring is the majestic opera house, followed by two museums, the Burgtheater, Musikverein concert hall, the university, city hall, various ministries, and the Parliament. The patches of land in between are snapped up by newly made millionaires. There are five Palais Rothschilds on the ring, housing some of Europe's most treasured works of Renaissance art. The Ephrussis, grain merchants from Odessa, own the world's largest collection of Japanese *netsuke*. The Palais Wittgenstein, built by a railroad baron and the birthplace of an important philosopher, is filled with musicians. Johann Strauss, himself part Jewish, likes to dine at the Palais Todesco, where the two Todesco daughters sponsor next-generation poets and novelists led by Hugo von Hofmannsthal and Stefan Zweig. *Jugendstil* art is conceived in the salons of Jewish hostesses who sit (in the nude, it is rumored) for Gustav Klimt. With his friends Koloman Moser, Josef Hoffman, and Otto Wagner, Klimt founds a Secession gallery, funded by Jewish patrons. The Secession proclaims a shocking eroticism alongside a devotion to functional beauty in small household objects. Secession architects remove encrusted ornaments from ring façades. Vienna is reshaped lastingly by the influence of its ringside Jews.

The spreading city needs new means of transportation. A self-taught engineer, Siegfried Liepmann Marcus, constructs an internal combustion engine in 1864 and sets it on a four-wheeled cart. It takes six years until the car, running on benzene, manages five hundred meters, but Marcus has seen the future and keeps working at it. He upgrades his engine from one cylinder to two, then to four, registering more than seventy patents for his inventions, which include an electric table lamp and the first carburetor. In 1888, his Mark 2 rolls down the Mariahilferstrasse. Marcus's original automobile, which can be seen in Vienna's Technical Museum, has no clutch and not much speed. Still, it predates Daimler and Benz by a decade and Henry Ford by a quarter of a century. Until the Nazis erase Marcus's Jewish name from the record, he is known across central Europe as the inventor of the automobile. A stone statue on the Karlsplatz commemorates him.

The Jewish influence is slower to reshape New York. As the city surges up Manhattan Island, developers hit a barrier at Fifth Avenue and Fifty-Ninth Street. The 843 acres beyond, running up to 110th Street, are reserved for a Central Park. A pair of landscapers, Frederick Law Olmsted and Calvert Vaux, win the design contract in 1857. Sixteen hundred squatters, mostly escaped Southern slaves and Irish pig farmers, are evicted. Bedrock is blasted with gunpowder. Four million trees and shrubs are planted. The state of New York appoints a Republican commission to protect the park from Tammany Hall Democrats. The first section of Central Park opens in 1858.

Jewish neighbors set up an outcry. North of Sixtieth Street is where Wall Street comes home to sleep. August Belmont wangles himself a seat on the park commission, with a view to keeping "fast-trotting men and other rowdies" out of the area.[2] He wants a private zoo in the park, strictly for subscribers. When that scheme is shot down, Belmont changes tack and invests in New York's first subway line, running from the Battery up to the park, bringing the huddled masses to their Sunday breath of fresh air. Belmont, one of the makers of New York, can flip like a pancake.

He figures in two major works of literature. In Anthony Trollope's masterpiece *The Way We Live Now* (1875), Augustus Melmotte is a "horrid, big, rich scoundrel," a "gigantic swindler." The novelist hardly bothers to disguise Belmont's name or alter his appearance:

> Melmotte himself was a large man, with bushy whiskers and rough thick hair, with heavy eyebrows, and a wonderful look of power about his mouth and chin. This was so strong as to redeem his face from vulgarity; but the countenance and appearance of the man

were on the whole unpleasant, and, I may say, untrustworthy. He looked as though he were purse-proud and a bully.

Trollope makes Melmotte loathsome and other Jews worse. The crooked Member of Parliament for Staines, Samuel Cohenlupe, is "a gentleman of the Jewish persuasion." The "fat, greasy" Ezekiel Brehgert is "fat all over, rather than corpulent—and had that look of command in his face which has become common to master-butchers, probably by long inter-course with sheep and oxen." An outrageous libel. Trollope's defenders exempt him from anti-Semitism by arguing that the rest of his charac-ters are equally repulsive: social climbers, aristocratic wastrels, young women desperate to make a rich match. Trollope's dislike of Jews—"an accursed race"—reflects his repugnance for Benjamin Disraeli, whose rise he both resents and secretly admires (his next novel, *The Prime Min-ister*, has a Jewish banker attempt to bring down an upright British gov-ernment). *The Way We Live Now*, claims his biographer, is "a great shout in the long conversation that Anthony Trollope sustained, and sustains, with his readers about the betrayal of all that is honest and true."[3] Yet, far from being demeaned by deprecation, Melmotte (Belmont) emerges so powerful, so far above the petty manipulations of lesser men, that he is almost venerable. His moral dignity is preserved by a face-saving suicide when his finances collapse. Here, for the first time in an English novel, the Jew is respected and feared. No longer a creature of contempt, Melmotte is a man who can make or break Britain.[4]

Belmont's second appearance is as Julius Beaufort in Edith Whar-ton's *The Age of Innocence*. Set in 1870s New York, the novel is a peep-hole into the drawing rooms and ballrooms that look over Central Park. Beaufort is a grasping, women-groping banker: "His habits were dissi-pated, his tongue was bitter, and his antecedents were mysterious." His wife "grew younger and blonder and more beautiful each year." Such people, scorns Wharton, "were not exactly common; some people said they were even worse." Wharton, who traces her descent to early Dutch settlers, drips contempt onto the swaggering class of arriviste Jewish bankers. Like Trollope, however, she is obliged to concede that Belmont and his type have changed the world she inhabits, for better or worse.

• • •

The city connects and disconnects. People can be neighbors for thirty years without knowing each other's names. Charles Dickens, chronicler of London life, glitter to gutter, does not meet a Jew until near the end of his life.

In 1859, Dickens puts his house on the market after separating from his wife. Tavistock House is the birthplace of *Bleak House*, *Hard Times*, and *A Tale of Two Cities*. He wants it to go to a sympathetic buyer. There are two records of the sale. The deeds are transferred to William Spencer Johnson and William Bush,[5] but letters by Dickens announce a sale to a West End solicitor, James Phineas Davis. The disparity, perhaps a legal device, need not detain us. "The purchaser of Tavistock House will be a Jew Money Lender," writes Dickens. He makes other disobliging remarks: "I shall never believe in him until he has paid the money." He warns a local acquaintance: "I hope you will find the Children of Israel good neighbours." James Phineas Davis is a solicitor with a practice in New Bond Street. Like many lawyers, then and now, he handles monetary transactions for clients. Dickens's description of him as a moneylender is willfully disparaging.

Davis offers two thousand guineas for the house. Dickens then asks if Mrs. Davis might like to keep the furnishings. Eliza Davis chooses a Turkish carpet and the drawing room cornices, adding £20 to the price.[6] The transaction is completed in September 1860, to Dickens's satisfaction. Eliza Davis, he writes, "appears to be a very kind and agreeable woman. And I have never had any money transaction with any one more promptly, fairly and considerately conducted than the sale of Tavistock House has been."

This is a delicate moment in Dickens's life. He is burning piles of letters at his Kent estate, to protect his reputation. He does not want readers to know of his failed marriage, let alone his infatuation with a young actress, Nelly Ternan. He grows a beard, both for privacy and to frighten audiences when he recounts the horrible deaths of Nancy and Bill Sikes in *Oliver Twist*. He is on tour much of the time, with Nelly as his companion.

Mrs. Eliza Davis is four years younger than Dickens, a mother of ten. Raised in Jamaica, the daughter of a synagogue cantor, she is averagely educated and a clumsy writer. Plump and pale, with a stubborn set to her lips, she is not the sort of person a celebrity writer would normally befriend. Yet the most famous living English writer finds himself engaged with Eliza Davis in "one of the most sustained exchanges of letters we have between Dickens and someone outside his immediate circle."[7]

Eliza opens the conversation on June 22, 1863. "Dear Sir," she writes, "Emboldened by your courtesy throughout my correspondence with you, I venture to address you on a Subject in which I am greatly interested." She wants to solicit his help in raising funds for a Jewish convalescent home named after Judith, Lady Montefiore, "who conjointly with her husband exerted herself at great personal sacrifice to relieve her oppressed people in distant lands." This is a routine charity appeal, one of many that Dickens must receive every week, but hers has a sting in the tail.

Out of the blue, without a prefatory word, Eliza Davis attacks Dickens for offenses against the Jews. "In this country," she writes:

> . . . in which where the liberty of the subject is fully recognised, where the law knows no distinction of Creed, the pen of the novelist, the gibe of the pamphleteer is still whetted against the "Sons of Israel." It has been said that Charles Dickens, the large-hearted, whose works plead so eloquently and so nobly for the oppressed of his country and who may now justly claim credit for the fruits of his labour, the many changes for the amelioration of the poor now at work, has has encouraged a vile prejudice against the despised Hebrew.

One can read the erasures as a mark of anxiety, but Eliza is not to be deflected from her self-appointed task.

"Fagin I fear"—(she goes on)—"admits only of one reading interpretation; but while Charles Dickens lives, the author can justify himself or atone for a great wrong." In plain English, she wants Dickens to rewrite his most popular work and make good the offense he has given to Jews by means of a handsome donation to her charity. There is a Hebrew word for what she is doing, a term that will enter English use: *chutzpah*.

Eliza Davis does not let up: "The amount of the donation is unimportant but we Wanderers from the far East desire to shew that we have found friends in the land in which we have pitched our tents." (Is this Jewish irony? Dickens knows she lives in Tavistock House, not in a Bedouin tent.) "I must again apologise for intruding so long on your very valuable time and awaiting a favourable reply. I remain, dear Sir, faithfully and sincerely yours, Eliza Davis."

The substance of her criticism is not new. Fagin, in the first thirty-eight chapters of *Oliver Twist*, is referred to 257 times as "the Jew" and forty-two times as "Fagin" or "the old man." There is no mistaking the author's prejudice. Fagin is introduced as "a very old shrivelled Jew, whose villainous-looking and repulsive face was obscured by a quantity of matted red hair." His business is snatching small boys and turning them into thieves, a variation on the blood libel by which Jews are accused of stealing Christian boys for their blood at Easter time. Dickens has defended himself to the *Jewish Chronicle* by arguing that *Oliver Twist* is a work of fiction and that he knew no Jews at the time of writing. Now he takes his time—eighteen days—before replying to Eliza Davis.

Friday Tenth July, 1863.

Dear Madam.

I hope you will excuse this tardy reply to your letter. It is often impossible for me by any means to keep pace with my correspondents.

I must take leave to say that if there be any general feeling on the part of the intelligent Jewish people, that I have done them what you describe as "a great wrong," they are a far less sensible, a far less just and a far less good tempered, people than I have always supposed them to be. Fagin in Oliver Twist is a Jew, because it unfortunately was true of the time to which that story refers, that that class of criminal almost invariably *was* a Jew. But surely no sensible man or woman of your persuasion can fail to observe—firstly, that all the rest of the wicked dramatis personae are Christians; and secondly, that he is called "The Jew," not because of his religion but because of his race. If I were to write a story, in which I pursued a Frenchman or Spaniard as "The Roman Catholic," I should do a very indecent and unjustifiable thing but I make mention of Fagin as the Jew, because he is one of the Jewish people and because it conveys that kind of idea of him, which I should give my readers of a Chinaman by calling him a Chinese.

The enclosed is quite a nominal subscription towards the good object in which you are interested but I hope it may serve to shew you that I have no feeling towards the Jewish people but a friendly one. I always speak well of them, whether in public or in private and bear my testimony (as I ought to do) to their perfect good faith in such transactions as I ever had with them. And in my "Child's History of England" I have lost no opportunity of setting forth their cruel persecution in old times.

Dear Madam.

Faithfully Yours,

Charles Dickens

It's a good letter, a conversation closer. Any other charity lady would have cashed the check and saved the autograph. But Eliza Davis is not easily put off. She sniffs vulnerability and opportunity. Dickens is on the back foot. He need not have bothered to respond in more than polite generalities. The fact that he has taken the trouble to address her concerns in such detail is, to her mind, a mark of a guilty conscience. So Eliza, unliterary Eliza, proceeds to blow a hole in his story.

In her next letter, three days later, she demands of him: "Does anyone designate Mr Disraeli as 'the Jew'?" True, she adds:

> I cannot dispute the fact that at the time to which *Oliver Twist* refers there were some Jews, receivers of stolen goods and although in my own mind it is a distinction without a difference I do not think it could at all be proved that there was one so base as to train young thieves as in the manner described in that work . . . If, as you remark "all must observe that the other Criminals were Christians" they are at least contrasted with favourable characters of good Christians, this poor wretched Fagin stands alone "The Jew."

If Fagin is "the Jew," then all Jews are, by imputation, child abductors. Eliza is onto something and she won't let go. Knowing how sensitive authors can be to comparison with their peers, she points out that other writers—she names Sir Walter Scott and the Irish novelist Mrs. S. C. Hall—depict Jews in the round. She might also have mentioned that Dickens's very good friend Wilkie Collins, author of *The Woman in White*, has a number of sympathetic Jewish characters.[8] Dickens, implies Eliza, is one-eyed and off-key. To assist his reeducation, she encloses a pamphlet on the customs and practices of British Jews "to represent them as they really are." She concludes with a promise "not to trouble you any more."

A year passes without further contact. Does Dickens put Eliza Davis out of mind? Not in the least. He allows her to invade his creative process while writing what proves to be his last completed novel, *Our Mutual Friend*. In a large cast of characters, one of the last to be added is Mr. Riah, an elderly, Jewish employee of an odious Christian loan shark. Mr. Riah does his boss's bidding, fearing all the while that his activities reflect badly on his fellow Jews. "In bending my neck to the yoke I was willing to wear," he frets, "I bent the unwilling necks of the whole Jewish people." A pious Jew, he risks his life to rescue two impoverished Christian girls, Lizzie Hexam and Jenny Wren, who might otherwise have fallen into bad ways. "I think there cannot be kinder people in the world," cries one of the girls. Near the end of *Our Mutual Friend*, Riah addresses the charge that Eliza Davis has hurled at Dickens, that one bad Jew can blight an entire people. Riah says:

Men say, "This is a bad Greek, but there are good Greeks. This is a bad Turk, but there are good Turks." Not so with the Jews. Men find the bad among us easily enough—among what peoples are the bad not easily found?—but they take the worst of us as samples of the best; they take the lowest of us as presentations of the highest; and they say "All Jews are alike."

G. K. Chesterton, an avowed Jew-hater, finds Riah "a needless and unconvincing character."

Riah is Dickens's atonement for Fagin, his amends to Eliza Davis. When *Our Mutual Friend* starts to appear in weekly installments, she writes to Dickens in November 1864, apologizing for breaking her promise not to bother him again. "Your introduction of the Jew, Riah, in the 7th No. of 'Our Mutual Friend' impels me to thank you most earnestly for what I am so presumptuous as to think a great compliment paid to myself and to my people," she writes, taking credit for this desired outcome. But Eliza Davis is not yet satisfied. She finds fault with the book and will not hold back from letting the author know that he lives in unforgivable ignorance of the Jews and their beliefs. "Riah is made to say 'they curse me in Jehovah's name,' " she thunders. "You are not then aware that no Jew ever utters this appellation of the 'Creator,' even in our prayers," and she goes on at some length to give chapter and verse as to precisely how Jews address God. Dickens is humbled and dumbfounded. He takes her words to heart. In 1866, he writes an article in a literary weekly, describing the Jews as:

> sober and self-denying, prudent and careful . . . Their ceremonial law teaches what we polite Christians call etiquette to the commonest man of the tribe. They are a people who wash their hands and anoint their heads, and pay respect to times and seasons and observances. The character of Jews has too long been wronged by Christain [*sic*] communities.

Eliza Davis sends him the gift of a beautiful Hebrew-English Bible:

> *Presented to CHARLES DICKENS ESQ in grateful and admiring recognition of his having exercised the noblest quality man can possess; that of atoning for an injury as soon as conscious of having inflicted it,*
> *by a Jewess.*

Dickens replies:

> The terms in which you send me that mark of your remembrance are more gratifying to me than I can possibly express to you; for they assure me that there is nothing but good will between me and a people for whom I have a real regard and to whom I would not wilfully have given an offence or done an injustice for any worldly consideration.

And there the letters end, ignored by most Dickens biographers not just as a reversal of Dickens's attitude to Jews now that he has finally met one, but as a mark of his humanity, his humility, and his open-mindedness, attributes uncommon in world-famous authors. Dickens is, and wants to be seen as, a good man, with malice toward none. The final proof of Eliza Davis's influence can be found in the galleys of a version of *Oliver Twist* made for a collected edition of his works. Dickens goes through the proofs from chapter 39 on, striking out the word "Jew" and substituting "Fagin" or "the old man." The title of chapter 52 is altered from "The Jew's Last Night Alive" to "Fagin's . . ." Dickens dies in June 1870. Two months later, Eliza Davis advises his daughter that Tavistock House "will again be changing owners or occupants." With Dickens gone, she no longer wants to live in his house. Eliza outlives Dickens by thirty-three years and is buried in Willesden, in United Synagogue Cemetery.

She has no idea that her intervention has altered forever the image of the Jew in English literature, far beyond the amendments Dickens has made to please her. After Eliza, there are still Jewish villains in best-selling novels by Anthony Trollope, G. K. Chesterton, John Buchan, Agatha Christie, and more, but none is so villainous as Fagin in Dickens's original; that stereotype has been laid to rest. And when Fagin is portrayed on film, it is with a third dimension that exposes viewers to mitigating depths in his character. Alec Guinness's depiction in *Oliver Twist* (1948) is initially banned in America until wiser opinions prevail, and Ron Moody's quasi-cuddly character in the musical *Oliver!* is based heavily on Guinness's multilayered, empathetic creation. The Jewish monster is no more.

In a back room of the British Museum, an anemic assistant pores over a manuscript written in a script that might be Amharic, early Arabic, or a variant of Hebrew. Emanuel Oscar Menahem Deutsch is the only man in England who can decipher the fragment. It is, he writes:

> my privilege to dwell in the very midst of that Pantheon called the British Museum, the treasures whereof, be they Egyptian, Homeric,

Palimpsest, or Babylonian cuneiforms, the mutilated glories of the Parthenon, or the Etruscan mysterious grotesqueness, *were all at my beck and call, all days, all hours*—Alexandria, Rome, Carthage, Jerusalem, Sidon, Tyre, Athens.

A Talmudist from Silesia, recommended to the museum by a Berlin bookseller, Deutsch is fluent in all Indo-European and Middle Eastern languages. He is a walking encyclopedia, a workaholic bachelor who shares his £300-a-year salary (around $40,000 in 2019 values) with his parents back home and earns extra money writing for reference works: 190 entries in *Chambers's Encyclopaedia*, others in Smith's *Dictionary of the Bible*.

Short, stocky, and indifferent to dress and social niceties, he mingles with fellow outcasts. At a soirée in 1866, he meets "a woman with next to no feminine beauty,"[9] "magnificently ugly, deliciously hideous."[10] Her name is Mary Anne Evans; she is better known as George Eliot. She is the author, up to this time, of *Adam Bede*, *The Mill on the Floss*, and *Silas Marner*, earning a popular readership and (unlike Dickens) literary accolades. Deutsch is drawn to Eliot, moth to flame. Eliot, for her part, is intrigued by "this bright little man."

He sends her an advance copy of a sixty-page essay he has written for the *Quarterly Review*, the first guide for English readers to the history, content, and philosophy of the Talmud. He aims, he says, to trace "so much that is really fine in Christianity" to its Jewish sources, "to shame shrieking fanaticism and ignorance out of its existence by a few simple facts and adages."[11] George Eliot is engrossed. As the translator of two works of theology, she has an interest in the roots of religion and counts Jews among her circle, which is, of necessity, marginal. George Eliot lives in sin with a married journalist, George Henry Lewes, whose undivorced wife, Agnes, cohabits with the editor of the *Daily Telegraph*. Placed beyond the pale of polite society, George Eliot fills her Regent's Park home with fringe people.

She engages Deutsch, "a very dear, delightful creature,"[12] to teach her Hebrew once a week. Hebraism is in the air. In 1864, Robert Browning composes the epic poem *Rabbi Ben Ezra*, an echo of Heine's *Jehuda ben Halevi*, and Matthew Arnold stokes a Heine revival. Someone describes Deutsch as "a living embodiment of Matthew Arnold's ideal union of

Hebraism and Hellenism." Deutsch, when his Talmud essay appears, is the talk of the town. The government asks him to accompany a military expedition to Abyssinia as resident scholar, Disraeli invites him to dinner, and the Khedive of Egypt requests his attendance at the opening of the Suez Canal. Heady with celebrity, Deutsch takes ten weeks' leave and sails for the Middle East in March 1869. He visits Cyprus, Egypt, and the Holy Land, "all my wild yearnings fulfilled at last." Entering Jerusalem and pressing his head against the cold stones of the Wailing Wall, "he was himself astonished at the emotion that choked him."[13] He has a dream that Jews will return to live in the Bible lands as foretold by prophets of old.

He returns home with a stomachache. A surgeon undertakes an exploratory operation. The rest of Deutsch's short life is pain. On weekdays, he works at the museum, and on the weekends, on his essays. In January 1871, when his strength gives way, the vicar of St. James's Church in Marylebone, Reverend Reginald Haweis, and his wife, the author Mary Eliza Haweis, take him in as a houseguest. "I used to . . . think him plebeian and ugly and a bore," writes Mary Eliza Haweis. "And now I am very fond of him and respect him very much."[14] Deutsch teaches her Arabic poetry.

George Eliot visits him across Regent's Park while writing *Middlemarch*, her masterpiece. "Dear Rabbi," she writes, finding him depressed. "Remember, it has happened to many to be glad they did not commit suicide, though they once ran for the final leap, or as Mary Wollstonecraft did, wetted their garments well in the rain hoping to sink the better when they plunged."[15] Deutsch hungers for sun and for national revival. He sails for the Holy Land, stopping in Italy and Egypt. In Alexandria, he is taken to the Prussian Hospital, where he dies on May 12, 1873. A postmortem reveals stomach cancer. Emanuel Oscar Menahem Deutsch, aged forty-three, is buried in the city's Jewish cemetery beneath an epitaph composed by Hermann Adler, son of the British chief rabbi.

George Eliot learns of his death as she goes on holiday to France. She immediately declares the title of her next novel, *Daniel Deronda*. Half of it is finished before the year is out. The other half is almost a misfit. (A Cambridge don, F. R. Leavis, proposes to retitle the better half *Gwendolen Harleth*, throwing away the "bad" Deronda bits.) Gwendolen is an English rose, frustrated by expectations that a woman of her class must marry well. At a German spa, she meets Deronda, apparently a well-bred Englishman. Gwendolen, despite liking Deronda, marries a rich brute and is primly unhappy. Deronda, out rowing on the Thames, saves a young woman from committing suicide. Mirah Lapidoth has been looking for her long-lost brother. Deronda scours London's Jewish districts for clues. Passing Ezra Cohen's pawnshop as the owner is shuttering down for the Sabbath, he is invited to stay for the Friday-night meal. At the table he sits beside a consumptive tenant, Mordecai, who calls for a revival of Jewish nationhood in the Holy Land. Mordecai suspects the English gentleman might be Jewish, which Deronda denies. But he is drawn to Mordecai and becomes his disciple.

The plot turns on two twists. Deronda learns that Mordecai's first name is Ezra; he is Mirah's brother. He then finds out that his own mother is Jewish, an opera singer who fled marriage for a stage career. He tracks down the diva to her deathbed in Genoa. "I relieved you from the bondage of having been born a Jew," she cries. Deronda, far from relieved, is delighted by his exotic identity. He decides to marry dark-eyed Mirah, telling Gwendolen (whose husband has conveniently died), "I am going to the East to become better acquainted with the condition of my race . . . The idea that I am possessed with is that of *restoring a political existence to my people, making them a nation again* . . . I may awaken a movement in other minds, such as has been awakened in my own." Gwendolen's heart is broken. Deronda and Mirah take Mordecai to the Holy Land; he dies in their arms. Curtain.

While writing *Daniel Deronda*, George Eliot badgers Lady Strangford, Deutsch's literary executor, for his essays (Lady Strangford is—small literary world—the sister-in-law of the hero of Disraeli's *Coningsby*). Mordecai is plainly Emanuel Deutsch. Other characters in the novel are likewise drawn from life. A musician, Julius Klesmer, is based on the Russian-Jewish composer Anton Rubinstein. Deronda's mother has traces of Jenny Lind, the Swedish Nightingale. Gwendolen Harleth presents, in Leavis's analysis,[16] an idealized image of George Eliot herself, classically beautiful where the author is not and secretly in love with an unattainable Jew. Deronda remains forever an enigma.

Determined to get the details right, George Eliot attends synagogue, watches Orthodox rituals, and amasses a huge reading list in English and German, including Graetz's histories and the writings of Leopold Zunz, father of an emergent Wissenschaft des Judentums, a science of Judaism. Rabbis applaud her accuracy. Hermann Adler expresses his "warm appreciation of the fidelity [to] . . . some of the best traits of the Jewish character." So intense is her Jewish immersion that George Eliot fears the novel may deter Christian readers. In a letter to the *Uncle Tom's Cabin* author, Harriet Beecher Stowe, George Eliot confesses:

> As to the Jewish element in *Deronda*, I expected from first to last, in writing it, that it would create much stronger resistance and even repulsion, than it has actually met with. But precisely because I felt that the usual attitude of Christians towards Jews is—I hardly know whether to say more impious or more stupid when viewed in the light of their professed principles, I therefore felt urged to treat Jews with such sympathy and understanding as my nature and knowledge could attain to. Moreover, not only towards the Jews, but towards all Oriental peoples with whom we English come in contact, a spirit of arrogance and contemptuous dictatorialness is observable which has become a national disgrace to us. There is nothing I should care more to do, if it were possible, than to rouse the imagination of men and women to a vision of human claims in those races of their fellow-men who most differ from them in customs and beliefs. But towards the Hebrews we Western people who have been reared in Christianity have a peculiar debt, and whether we acknowledge it or not, a peculiar thoroughness of fellowship in religious and moral sentiment.

George Eliot, who has done more than any writer to raise the English novel from entertainment to intellectual engagement, has an agenda in *Daniel Deronda*. She seeks respect for the Jews and justice for their national cause. Hers is the first non-Jewish voice in two millennia to call for a return to Zion. Published in 1876, it is her final work.

The novel appears quickly in German, French, Italian, Dutch, Russian, and Yiddish. The Hebrew translation, by David Frishman, cuts out the Gwendolen section to accentuate the Deronda bits.[17] A rabbi's son notes that *Daniel Deronda* "turned our hearts to Eretz Israel." David Ben-Gurion cites the novel as a prime cause of a future Jewish state. Theodor Herzl reads it on the eve of the first Zionist Congress. His aide Nahum Sokolow writes that "*Daniel Deronda* paved the way for Zionism."

The word *Zionism* does not exist in George Eliot's lifetime, nor for decades after her death. It is coined by a Galician, Nathan Birnbaum, and acquires political force at Herzl's first Congress in 1897. Twenty years later, in the Balfour Declaration, the British government endorses Zionist aims. None of this is presaged in *Daniel Deronda*, although some hold George Eliot accountable. In a 1979 essay, "Zionism from the Standpoint of its Victims," Columbia literary professor Edward Said writes: "Eliot's account of Zionism in *Daniel Deronda* was intended as a sort of assenting Gentile response to prevalent Jewish-Zionist currents; the novel therefore serves as an indication of how much in Zionism was legitimated and indeed valorized by Gentile European thought."[18]

Streets are named after George Eliot in Israeli cities. The boulevard that runs from the Tel Aviv town hall down to the sea is named Frishman, after *Daniel Deronda*'s translator. Nothing is named after Emanuel Deutsch, the scholarly spark that lit the Zionist flame.

FOUR

1875

CARMEN, *QUAND-MÊME*

Sarah Bernhardt, inventor of
celebrity, c. 1875.

In the pit of a theater where her name once appeared in lights, an
actress in a nurse's uniform is scurrying from pallet to pallet, tending
to the wounded. The plush seats have been removed from the Odéon,
replaced by straw mattresses. Whiffs of greasepaint and gaslight min-

gle with the acidic odors of urine and antiseptic. The fall of France has come so fast that most are paralyzed by shock. On August 1, 1870, the Germans invade Alsace. On September 2, at Sedan, they take Emperor Napoleon III prisoner and accept the surrender of a hundred thousand men. In Paris, a Republic is declared. The Germans close in. On September 19, Paris is encircled. Krupp guns lob shells into the streets. When Paris refuses to surrender, the Germans dig in for the winter. Food and fuel supplies are soon exhausted. Restaurants serve *gigots* of rat. The population is fearful, confused, and divided. It is in these fragile circumstances that Sarah Bernhardt becomes a national heroine.

Born Jewish to a high-class prostitute and baptized by order of her mother's lover, she enters the theater but gets blacklisted for bad-mouthing a Comédie-Française star. She moves to Brussels, becomes pregnant by a prince, and gives birth to a much-loved son, Maurice. Back in Paris, she joins the Odéon in 1866, catching the eye as a ten-year-old boy in Racine's *Athalie*. She is Cordelia in *King Lear*. In 1869, she makes a hit of François Coppée's first play, *Le Passant*.

An actor's life is always precarious, especially with a child to support. She poses nude for the society photographer Nadar. Like her mother, she takes lovers, aristocrats and artists, and discards them, usually remaining on good terms. When fire destroys her apartment, leaving her destitute, the big draw at her benefit concert is the opera diva Adelina Patti, whose husband is Sarah's ex-lover.

When war breaks out, she puts her family on a train to Holland and requisitions the Odéon as an infirmary. She applies to the *préfet du police* for essential supplies. He, an ex-lover, provides her with "ten barrels of red wine, two of brandy, thirty thousand eggs . . . a hundred sacks of coffee, twenty canisters of tea, forty cases of Albert biscuits, a thousand canisters of preserves and a quantity of other things." As she leaves, she grabs his fur-trimmed greatcoat. "I need it for my convalescents," declares Sarah. "You permit me to keep my scarf?" pleads the *préfet*. The story is pure Bernhardt: she can get any man to do what she wants.

Commandeering two ambulances, she trawls the streets for wounded. Her theater is packed to the rafters, with patients rather than patrons. For weeks, Sarah does not leave the Odéon, sleeping in an office. In her memoirs, she records every shade of bravery and coward-ice. Soldiers beg for her autograph. One of the ones she favors is Fer-dinand Foch, future supreme commander of Allied forces in the First World War.

Outside, the city crumbles. In January 1871, the Germans open a full bombardment lasting several days. Sarah shelters twenty injured men in her own apartment. A lover asks her to go up with him in a bal-loon to drop bombs on the Germans. She throws him out, deploring the use of a beautiful invention to destroy human life. At the armistice—emaciated, exhausted, oddly exhilarated—she talks her way through the German lines to meet her mother, her sister, and her child. That night there is a fire in their hotel; she flees in a nightgown through the snow. Everything in her life is drama.

Paris, "effervescent and grumbling," declares a Commune, with the poet Paul Verlaine as chief press officer and Gustave Courbet as head of the artists' union. Auguste Renoir, sketching beside the Seine, is almost shot as a spy. Sarah Bernhardt, aware that fame is no protection, with-draws to an outer suburb, Saint-Germain-en-Laye, with a pair of lov-ers, a Jewish banker and a free-shooting brigand. In May, the national government attempts to regain control of Paris, slaughtering twenty thousand citizens in a week. Karl Marx writes: "Working men's Paris, with its Commune, will be forever celebrated as the glorious harbinger of a new society."

As the dust settles Sarah Bernhardt, not yet thirty, rejoins the Comédie-Française. She does not have long to wait for a role. Victor Hugo, returning from exile, rehearses a revival of his early romance *Ruy Blas*. Sarah, as the Spanish queen who falls in love with a slave, enjoys an epic triumph on February 19, 1872. Never has Hugo's text sounded so lyrical as it does in her *voix d'or*. Fighting her way through adoring crowds to her dressing room, she finds the seventy-year-old lion of French literature stuttering out his congratulations. "She said to me: 'Kiss me. *Bise de boca*' [on the mouth],'" writes Hugo in his diary. They become lovers.

Sarah can now do as she pleases. She plays Cherubin in Beaumar-chais's *The Marriage of Figaro*, Desdemona in Shakespeare's *Othello*, and Doña Sol in Hugo's *Hernani*. Each play she chooses is a calcu-lated strike for the primacy of spoken French theater over the work's equivalent Italian opera. Her crowning role is Marguerite in *La Dame aux Camélias* by Alexandre Dumas, a play hijacked by Giuseppe Verdi for *La Traviata*. The heroine is a retired courtesan, incurably ill. Sarah Bernhardt acts it her way. Where Patti sings Violetta as an almost respectable society lady, long past much interest in sex, Sarah presents Marguerite in full sensuality, wearing a red carnation to signal unavailability during menstruation and otherwise rampant among men. She breathes life into Dumas's French play and stands up for the rights of women like her, who reject the corsets and conventions of marriage—a feminist ahead of her time. Over three decades, she gives three thousand performances as Marguerite, leaving no audience member untouched and making herself the city's number one tourist attraction. Sigmund Freud, a medical intern, tells his fiancée:

I have never seen a funnier figure than Sarah Bernhardt in Scene II, when she appears in a simple dress, I am really not exaggerating. And yet one was compelled to stop laughing, for every inch of this little figure was alive and bewitching. As for her caressing and pleading and embracing, the postures she assumes, the way she wraps herself round a man, the way she acts with every limb, every joint—it's incredible.[1]

"For years," Freud will confess in *Interpretation of Dreams*, "I dreamed only of Paris."[2]

D. H. Lawrence, who sees Sarah Bernhardt in 1908, writes to his girlfriend, Jessie:

I feel frightened. I realize that I, too, might become enslaved to a woman . . . She is not pretty—her voice is not sweet—but there is, the incarnation of wild emotion which we share with all live things but which is gathered in us in all complexity and inscrutable fury. She represents the primeval passions of woman and she is fascinating to an extraordinary degree. I could love such a woman myself, love her to madness; all for the pure, wild passion of it. Intellect is shed as flowers shed their petals. Take care about going to see Bernhardt. Unless you are very sound, do not go. When I think of her now I can still feel the weight hanging in my chest as it hung there for days after I saw her. Her winsome, sweet, playful ways; her sad, plaintive little murmurs; her terrible panther cries; and then the awful, inarticulate sounds, the little sobs that fairly sear one and the despair and death; it is too much in one evening.[3]

Sarah Bernhardt evokes a kaleidoscope of emotions, from desire to terror, without yielding her selfhood, her original brand, her incomparability.

She is by far the most famous woman in France, and this is just the beginning. What she seeks is not so much fame as an idea that is larger than fame, a framework in which she can harness name recognition to a concrete purpose. At this early stage, she applies her fame to raise the morale of a downcast nation, a relief from the thuds of German boots and the scratching of political machinations. She knows what to do to hold the front pages. Her carousel of new lovers and exotic acts is endlessly distracting. She keeps a menagerie of wild animals in her mansion and sleeps at night in a coffin. When undertakers come to take away her half-sister Régine, dead at nineteen, they find two coffins, side by side. "I was at that moment with my mother . . . ," writes Sarah, "and I just got back in time to prevent the black-clothed men taking away my coffin. . . . The papers got hold of this incident. I was blamed, criticised, &c. It really was not my fault."[4]

It really is, of course. She manipulates the media with Machiavellian cunning, knowing that nothing sells papers like Sarah. Her friends call out two journalists for duels over scandals they have fomented, probably at her instigation. A scurrilous pamphlet, "The Love Affairs of Sarah Bernhardt," appears in America. In 1880, she plays a London season, in French. Monoglot Englishmen storm the box office for a glimpse of her notoriety. On her first crossing to America, she saves a lady on deck from being swept away by a wave. "Her husband, President Lincoln, had been assassinated by an actor and it was an actress who prevented her from joining him," boasts Sarah. The *New York Times* is smitten by her beauty: "a faultless nose of the best Hebrew type reveals in its delicate chiselling the aesthetic artist and her race." On her debut in New York, she receives twenty-seven curtain calls. Thomas Edison records her reciting a speech from *Phèdre*. She crosses America and Canada by private train, giving 157 shows in fifty-one cities, all in pure French. With profits of 194,000 gold coins, she declares:

"I planted the French verb in the heart of a foreign literature, and it is that of which I am most proud."[5] On July 14, in Paris, she declaims "La Marseillaise" for the president of the Republic. Overwhelmed, he asks her to recite it twice more.

Victorien Sardou writes her two plays, *Fedora* and *Tosca*, and Oscar Wilde writes *Salomé*; all three become operas. Wilde, in an English jail for homosexual offenses, takes heart from knowing that Bernhardt "and other great artists are sympathising with me." Sarah puts her fame behind victims of prejudice. During the Dreyfus affair, she rallies theater people to support the Jewish officer, falling out terminally over the issue with Coppée, her first playwright, and temporarily with her own son, Maurice. In January 1898, reading Émile Zola's explosive article "J'accuse!" she writes to its author: "Allow me to speak of the intense emotion I felt when I read your cry for justice. As a woman I have no influence but I am anguished, haunted by the situation, and the beautiful words you wrote yesterday brought tremendous relief to my great suffering."[6] As a woman I have no influence? She has overturned that rule. The right-wing press goes berserk on hearing that she is writing to Dreyfus in his cell: "The great actress is with the Jew against the army."[7] She will champion Dreyfus's cause until he is released.

The price of fame entails a loss of privacy. Jules and Edmond Goncourt, purveyors of café gossip, report that Alexandre Dumas:

> . . . talked amusingly about Sarah Bernhardt who fell into his arms yesterday at the Variétés. He expatiated on the masculine build of her body, which has no breasts but a plump stomach and on the amazing stamina of the woman, who is never tired, never weary and who spits blood with no more effect on her constitution than if she were spitting gobs.[8]

Some of the writing about Sarah verges on verbal rape.

She paints, she sculpts, she writes novels, she founds a theater, she commissions new work. The premiere of Alfred Jarry's *King Ubu* in December 1896 is as much a turning point in theater as Stravinsky's *The Rite of Spring* will be in orchestral music, provoking a riot with its opening word, "*Merde!*" Everything Sarah Bernhardt does is reported, debated, exaggerated. An unknown Czech artist, "Alphonse Mucha," designs her distinctive advertisements, making her the icon of the age, the never-aging face of France. In her sixties, she takes a lover half her age. At seventy, she signs a Hollywood deal with Adolph Zukor.

She hurts her leg in Rio de Janeiro and undergoes an amputation. Unstoppable, she tours the First World War trenches, carried around in a white sedan chair, declaiming classic roles for Marshal Foch's troops at Verdun. Sailing to America in U-boat-infested waters, she refuses the captain's offer to station two seamen at her side, saying, "Their young lives are more important than my old one."

As her kidneys fail, she erects a film studio in her home so that she can work to her final breath. At eight p.m. on March 26, 1923, a doctor throws open a window and declares to a waiting crowd: "Madame Sarah Bernhardt is dead." At the Théâtre Sarah Bernhardt, the audience troops silently home at the end of the first act of *L'Aiglon*. Half a million Parisians turn out for her funeral. The tombstone inscription reads: "Sarah Bernhardt." No need to say more.

"What was her secret?" wonders the playwright Pierre Wolff:

> I believe above all that Mme Bernhardt knew primarily she must be a woman and an artist . . . with all her body and all her sex. Moreover, she was a musician through her voice—that voice of gold which was a song, a lullaby, a melody—a voice without power, however, which rose high without crying out but which could be modulated to an infinite sweetness, obeying secret laws which seemed always impromptu, always changing, always new. Above all she was an artist. She loved the truth but more than truth she loved beauty.

She chose theater as her occupation to achieve fame, but her fame is of a different order from all that came before. There is nothing frivolous about her fame. It has a purpose, a strategy, a lasting significance. Its first engine is patriotism: she becomes famous for the sake of suffering France, for the restoration of its élan and the salvation of its culture. She personifies French resistance to German occupation; she elevates French theater above Italian opera. In London and New York, she acts in French. She is the face of Art Nouveau, the first French star on film. In 1945, after another national humiliation, she will be immortalized on a postage stamp of the République Française as Marianne, goddess of French liberty. Not since Joan of Arc has a woman so personified France to itself and to the world.

Her love of France, genuine as it is, requires deconstruction. Sarah Bernhardt's patriotism is protested so loudly and so often that one has to wonder why she needs to prove how much she loves the land of her unwanted birth. Is it because she casts herself as an outsider: as a harlot and a Jew? She uses her fame to demand respect for outsiders. At the height of the Dreyfus witch hunt, when Jews are beaten up at random on the streets of Paris, she tells *Le Figaro*: "I am a daughter of the great Jewish race."[9] Mark those words: the adjectives *great* and *Jewish* are nowhere else juxtaposed in the Dreyfus era. Having restored French pride after military defeat, she now affirms the dignity of her own embattled people. When men tell her she does not look Jewish, Sarah flashes back, "What does a Jew look like?" She has a point: Sarah changes the physical prototype of Jewish women in the culture of her times.

There is a swagger to Sarah, a hauteur which proclaims that nothing anyone can write or anything she does can harm her because she is at all times totally exposed. Her catchphrase response to a setback is *quand-même*. "So what? Whatever." It is the grandest of grand shrugs. It says, *You can't touch me; I am untouchable.* Her calculated, iconic self-exposure will be adapted in a distant future by Princess Diana and the pop star Madonna.

Sarah Bernhardt is the first to grasp that fame is more powerful than wealth. It is an asset, an intangible commodity, that can influence millions, change the cultural climate, and rewrite the world to one's own script. It is also a promise of immortality. Millions who never saw Sarah alive will recognize her face and her name. In the mid-twentieth century, when I am growing up, children are told, "Don't be such a Sarah Bernhardt."[10] We have no idea who she was or what she did, but she annoys and unsettles our controlling adults, and Sarah Bernhardt is someone we immediately want to be.

She is the prime inventor of the twenty-first-century cult of celebrity, the first person to grasp the meaning of soft power and its manipulation. There is no sign that she understands the forces she has released or that she knows where they might lead. Like Albert Einstein, she discovers the formula without foreseeing the consequences. In her own account, she is simply being herself, *quand-même*. From a historical perspective, she is the Einstein of fame.

The world premiere of *Carmen* is staged at the Opéra-Comique on the night of March 3, 1875. The cream of Paris ought to be there, but many have been warned off. The premiere has been postponed several times while people try to persuade the composer, Georges Bizet, to modify the score, which the orchestra finds unplayable. Women in the chorus refuse to appear onstage smoking and flirting like tarts. Subscribers are advised they may find some scenes offensive. Among many opening-night absentees is the composer's wife, Geneviève.

The first night does not go well. Critics look pointedly at their watches at midnight, with one act still to go. Afterward, only three or four friends go backstage to congratulate Bizet. The rest are too embarrassed. "These bourgeois did not understand a word of the work I wrote for them," wails the composer. He spends the rest of the night walking the streets of Paris, arm in arm with his assistant, Ernest Guiraud.

The reviews are tetchy and inconsistent. One critic calls *Carmen* Wagnerian, another undramatic, and a third denounces the sight of prostitutes onstage. The playwright Jean-Henri Dupin tells a member of the production team:

> Your *Carmen* is a flop, a disaster! It will never play more than twenty times. The music goes on and on. It never stops. There's not even time to applaud. That's not music! And your play—that's not a play! A man meets a woman. He finds her pretty. That's the first act. He loves her, she loves him. That's the second act. She doesn't love him anymore. That's the third act. He kills her. That's the fourth! And you call that a play? It's a crime, do you hear me? A crime!

As the theater has no backup, *Carmen* continues its run. Slowly, night by night, the house fills as word gets around about the gypsy girl who raises her skirts to any man who takes her fancy. The Comique, with an unexpected hit on its hands, offers Bizet another commission, but he is in no fit state to accept. Distraught at the critical "insults," he takes to bed with a sore throat. Feeling a bit better, he goes for a walk in the country beside the river Seine with his wife, Geneviève, and her close friend Delaborde, disreputable son of the hermit composer Alkan. The day is warm, and Bizet, a keen swimmer, accepts Delaborde's challenge to jump in. Next morning, he has a fever. Three days later, three months to the day since *Carmen*'s premiere, he dies. The cream of Paris, which missed the premiere, attend his funeral. Bizet is proclaimed a genius, his death at thirty-six years old a disaster.

Carmen now takes off worldwide. In Vienna, Johannes Brahms sees it twenty times. The American mezzo-soprano Minnie Hauk takes on the role in New York and sings it five hundred times. By 1882, when it returns to the Comique, *Carmen* is a global sensation, acclaimed by the philosopher Friedrich Nietzsche as the most perfect opera ever written. It is also the most popular. In the twenty-first century it is, year after year, one of the three most performed operas, its profits paying year after year to keep open opera houses that might otherwise have to close. *Carmen*, in many companies, is the first work to go on the season's schedule.

How could it be that all the great composers there on opening night—Gounod, Saint-Saëns, Massenet, Offenbach, Delibes, Ambroise Thomas, and more—fail to spot its brilliance, let alone its staying power? The music is, at first listen, tuneful, well written, and original, and the plot is gripping, fast-moving, and not too alarming. What stops the great composers from throwing their hats in the air and acclaiming a masterpiece? If it is not the music that confounds them, it must be something else. The first cause, in Paris, would be *cherchez la femme*. Carmen, shucking off lovers like soiled shirts, telling men they are all the same, is a palpable threat to male egos, a stopcock to their swagger. Carmen is in their faces. Die though she must, she leaves the elite of French musicians guessing. Who the heck is Carmen? She seems familiar. Do we know her? Hang on, I think we do.

The composers have known Bizet since he was a child at the Conservatoire in the class of Jacques Fromental Halévy, composer of *La Juive*, the first grand opera with a Jewish heroine (she is killed in a cauldron of boiling water). *La Juive* is a one-off. Halévy goes the rest of his life without another hit, cutting class to bang on theater doors with his unwanted wares. When he does show up, he is kind to Bizet, inviting him to Friday-night soirées at Jacques Offenbach's, the German-Jewish can-can composer whose comic operettas are the nectar of Napoleon III's Second Empire. Offenbach employs Halévy's nephew, Ludovic, as his librettist; small world.

After Halévy's death in March 1862, Bizet wastes a year tinkering with his teacher's works, less from altruism than because he has fallen for the composer's thirteen-year-old daughter. Geneviève Halévy is a dark-eyed, febrile child, in a family with a history of mental instability. Halévy's widow, Léonie, member of a Sephardic banking clan, is a hysteric who spends long periods in expensive sanatoria. The elder daughter, Esther, engaged to the librettist Ludovic, dies of an unspecified cause at the age of twenty-one. Geneviève, known as Bébé, employs a froth of gaiety to mask her highly strung nature. "Bébé," notes the composer Émile Paladilhe, "is more and more unbalanced."

Bizet, smitten by her beauty and her family, fails to notice anything untoward. His experience with women is limited; he has fathered a child with a housemaid and fools around with actresses. Geneviève is the first "good" girl he has met. She believes, he writes, "neither in the God of the Jews nor in the God of the Christians but in honour, duty; in short, in morality." Her Jewishness seems to him a guarantee of purity. When Geneviève's uncles object to her marrying a goy, cousin Ludovic swears that Bizet has "spirit and talent. He should succeed."[11] The uncles' bank fails and is taken over by the Rothschilds. In June 1869, Bizet marries Geneviève in a civil ceremony. Her mother is in a sanatorium, "incapable of giving permission."

Their honeymoon year is sweet. Geneviève can live with a husband who, like her father, thinks first of his music. Bizet showers her with gifts. Then the Germans invade. Bizet joins the National Guard, Geneviève suffers a nervous breakdown. Bizet takes her to Bordeaux, where Léonie drives her to distraction. "Take me, take me away quickly," pleads Geneviève, "quickly or I shall die the way Esther did."[12] Madness is near at hand. Liberated by Bizet, Geneviève returns to Paris and gives birth to a son. They name him Jacques, after Halévy. Bizet composes a *jeux d'enfants* and a one-act opera, *Djamileh*, which flops.

Asked by the Comique for another score, he comes up with *Carmen*, a salacious 1845 novel by the louche Prosper Mérimée, author of the aphorism: "There are two kinds of women; those who are worth the sacrifice of your life, and those who are worth between five and forty francs." Bizet's choice does not go down well with the owners of the Opéra-Comique, who protest that it is a family theater, a place where courting couples come to get engaged. Librettist Ludovic tries to deflect him, but Bizet is dead set on this opera and no other. It is the one he was born to write. "Please try not to have her die," beg the theater owners. "Death on the stage of the Opéra-Comique! Such a thing has never been seen—never!"

For the title role, Bizet chooses Célestine Galli-Marié, lover of the composer Paladilhe (and, it is said, of various others), a mezzo of high volatility. She is Bizet's ally against the world: his librettists, the owners, the orchestra, his wife. Jules Massenet reports Bizet to be plunged in a "habitual" melancholy. What no one knows is that Bizet and Geneviève are living apart, their marriage in trouble. Geneviève, out of town, consorts with the pianist Delaborde, a notorious womanizer. Bizet, in his wife's absence, becomes Galli-Marié's lover.

Geneviève returns to Paris for the premiere. That morning, as Bizet receives a thrilling letter telling him he will receive the Légion d'Honneur, she announces she has an abscess in her eye and will miss the first night. Bizet cannot go home that night, unable to face Geneviève after the failure of *Carmen*, terrified of her rages. In the brief life they have left together, Bizet is sick and Geneviève blooming. Does it occur to her that sunny afternoon beside the Seine that swimming in a river is not a good idea for a man with a sore throat? Probably not. Like Carmen, Geneviève wastes no time on what men might think.

Bizet, with his dying breath, begs Delaborde to look after Geneviève. At the funeral, Gounod reads a tribute from Geneviève: "There is not an hour, not a minute of the six years of happiness which my married life brought me that I would not gladly live over again." The biographer Minna Curtis, who acquires the Halévy family papers, calls the eulogy a blatant fabrication.[13] Bizet is dead and Geneviève is rewriting the record.

A year on, she becomes engaged to Delaborde. Within weeks, she sends cousin Ludovic to call it off. Two years on, they are reengaged; Delaborde signs a marriage contract, only for Geneviève to annul it.[14] Is she feeling torn about the lover whose rash challenge brought on her husband's death? Like Carmen, Geneviève gives no clues.

She chides her son, Jacques, for "unbelievable cowardice" when he refuses to learn how to swim.[15] Does it not occur to her that the boy might associate swimming with his father's death? Eventually, she marries a wealthy lawyer, Émile Straus, in a ceremony conducted by the chief rabbi of Paris, Zadoc Kahn. Asked why she married boring Émile when she has so many livelier suitors, Geneviève replies, "What else could I do? It was the only way I knew to get rid of him." She acquires a reputation for dry wit.

On October 7, 1886, Geneviève starts a new life as Madame Émile Straus, society hostess. In a showy mansion at 134 Boulevard Haussmann, she invites musicians and artists to a Sunday-afternoon salon to mingle with government ministers and rich patrons in search of cultural validation and sexual liaisons. Madame Straus presides over her salon in a large winged chair, stroking her black poodle, Vivette.

Fusty paintings by the Romantics Fragonard and La Tour adorn her walls, mingled with the new impressionists. She employs Edgar Degas as her art buyer and hat designer. She has the photographer Nadar take her portrait in a triangular hat with a black bow at its center, her dark curls peeking out in front. Léon Blum, a rising socialist, gives his first oration in her chamber. On a typical Sunday afternoon, Henri Meilhac, colibrettist of *Carmen*, reads an act of his new play, Guy de Maupassant recites a short story, Gabriel Fauré plays an étude on the grand piano, Camille Saint-Saëns turns pages. Asked if she is fond of music, Geneviève says, "They played a great deal of it in my first family."[16] Geneviève never speaks of her past. Few imagine, and none dare suggest, that she might be the life model for rapacious, ruthless, man-taunting Carmen. The respectable Madame Straus? *C'est pas vrai.*

Is she? Carmen has elements of all the women in Bizet's life: his lover, Célestine; his half-mad mother-in-law; and a dash of Sarah Bernhardt. But none fits the role as closely as Geneviève, a woman whom men fear even as they succumb, an exotic creature who trusts no man and cannot be trusted in love. The clue that Bizet's Carmen might be Jewish is found in a Mérimée passage that Bizet keeps quoting at his librettists. In the original novella, when the narrator meets Carmen, he asks about her origins and she equivocates. "So you are, perhaps, Moorish," he suggests. Then, "I stopped myself, not daring to say: *Jewish.*"

Could Carmen be Jewish? There are strong indications. Mérimée winks at us that Carmen is Jewish, since no gypsy girl has ever captured the public imagination in a French novel. A Jewess is the subject of Halévy's opera that is Bizet's blueprint. Sarah Bernhardt is the biggest draw in town. Bizet lives with a Jewess who is at once desirable and unknowable, declaring her love for him and sharing it with another. He tells his mad mother-in-law that he does not know what it will take to make Geneviève happy. He is mystified by his Jewish wife and obsessed with her. As he writes the opera, he allows no one to curtail her character.

His music is worlds apart from the gypsy tunes of Dvořák and Brahms or the operettas of Johann Strauss. Nor is it vividly Spanish but vaguely Mediterranean, hinting at the Moorish monodies of Geneviève's Sephardic ancestors. *Carmen* does not live in a caravan on the outskirts of society. She is, rather, a forerunner of the Technicolor musicals of Rodgers and Hammerstein, whose heroines are capricious and unattainable, possibly Jewish.

From the very beginning, argues the Wagner scholar John Deathridge, many in the Paris audience recognize *Carmen* as "an attempt to present a threatening Jewess on stage, who was both sensual and a threat. And also, incidentally, intellectual because Carmen has mastery of all these languages."[17] That helps explain the first-night failure. Carmen conforms to a Gentile archetype of the Jewish woman as sexually alluring, too clever by half, and seducible only on her own emasculating terms. She is anyone from the biblical Salome to Barbra Streisand, a woman impervious to male expectations. If Carmen is Jewish, then she can only be Geneviève. Madame Straus devotes the second half of her life to burying this supposition beneath the magnificent persiflage of a flowery hat designed by Degas and an intellectual pretension to nurture the next French genius of world significance.

One Sunday afternoon in 1888, Jacques Bizet brings a friend to his mother's salon, his coeditor of a school journal. The newcomer, pasty-faced and seventeen years old, sports a white camellia in his buttonhole. Soft-spoken and painfully middle-class, he holds his own in a discussion of new poetry and music against serious writers and composers. The boy has an opinion about everything: M. Eiffel's steadily rising tower, the latest exhibitions, the talk of the day. Before he leaves, the boy invites Madame Straus and her son to share his box at the Odéon for the first night of Edmond de Goncourt's play, *Germinie Lacerteux*. His precocity makes adult guests squirm with embarrassment.

The boy becomes a regular at the salon, sitting literally at Madame Straus's feet, flattering her, declaring one of her art purchases to be "lovelier than the *Mona Lisa.*" He is a fountain of aphorisms—"the artist does not invent; he discovers"—and very well mannered. Geneviève lets him hold forth, but he needs no encouragement. This is where he wants to be: in a room where fine ideas are traded for lubricious gossip, each accorded equal merit and analysis. He makes himself at home chez Madame Straus, a precise half class above his parents' professional milieu. He courts his friend's mother not so much for her beauty, though she is still desirable, but for her circle, a privileged realm that he means to plunder for a monumental work of art.

The boy is Marcel Proust. The son of a professor of hygiene at the Faculty of Medicine at the University of Paris, Marcel shares two points of alienation with his friend Jacques Bizet. Both feel displaced in a society that values status above talent, and both struggle to cope with the unsought blessing of having a domineering Jewish mother of privileged background. Proust's *maman*, Jeanne Weil, a cousin of the justice minister Adolphe Crémieux, is fifteen years younger than her eminent husband. His Catholic family refuses to attend his wedding to a Jewess, and he does not ask her to convert. After the birth of two sons, Adrien Proust installs an attractive mistress in a rented apartment and visits her every day, *comme il faut*. Madame Proust immerses her sons in classical texts, quoting liberally from Voltaire, Racine, and Molière. Marcel suffers terrible asthma attacks; his younger brother, Robert, robust as their father, becomes a surgeon (he proves so adept at removing enlarged prostate glands from middle-aged men that the operation is known in Paris as a "Proustatectomy").

Adrien Proust is professionally offended by Marcel's frailty. He publishes a study of asthma and another of neurasthenia. Jeanne attends to Marcel with stifling devotion. As a grown man, he is obliged to report every day to his mother on all his activities, down to the color and consistency of his bowel movements. "Got up at . . . Went to bed at . . . Hours outdoors . . . Hours of rest . . . &c.," she specifies. When he omits a detail, she persists: "*je demande et je redemande.*" Jeanne instills in Marcel a respect for the significance of small things. She fosters his chronic hypochondria. He is unable to step outdoors unless he is swaddled in sweaters and three overcoats. She frets and fusses over his diet, making him feel all the while that it is his fault she must nag. Marcel blames himself. "In worrying her through my health, I made her very unhappy." Their interdependence, mutually fulfilling, horribly unhealthy, is the trigger of his art, the starting point of *À la recherche du temps perdu*, a work that changes world literature forever.

The narrative opens with a boy lying awake in bed in anticipation of—and an adult later remembering—the ceremony of receiving his mother's good-night kiss. The lives of man and boy are interleaved. The narrator begs his mother not to leave his room, to stay until he sleeps. No sooner has he done so than he is filled with regret:

> I ought to have been happy: I was not. It seemed to me that my mother had just made me a first concession which must have been painful to her, that this was a first abdication on her part before the ideal she had conceived for me, and that for the first time she, who was so courageous, had to confess herself beaten.

The world's first stream-of-consciousness novel is actually a voyage into the interior of the yet-to-be-defined Freudian unconscious.

Marcel manipulates Maman, who appears to fulfill his wishes while dangling him like a fish on a rod. He cannot escape her, nor does he want to. There is a famous falling-out in the 1890s when Marcel slams the door so hard in his parents' apartment that a glass panel breaks, and the family is shocked by his lack of etiquette. Maman writes to Marcel that evening, sending him a good-night kiss and warning him not to enter the living room without his shoes because there may still be glass fragments in the carpet. Whatever remorse he feels for the violence of his reaction is now redoubled by her manifest anxiety for the soles of his feet. He is hooked on the certainty of her concern.

What is the cause of the row? We cannot be entirely sure, but it seems to be a delicate moment in the parents' coming to terms with Marcel's homosexuality. Dr. Proust offers a traditional response. He sends Marcel, aged eighteen, to a brothel to procure sexual intercourse with a female prostitute at the prix fixe of ten francs. Marcel, unable to perform, breaks a chamber pot. He is made to pay three francs for the damage. Well-bred boy that he is, he writes to his Jewish *grandpère* asking him for thirteen francs so that he can revisit the brothel because, he reasons, ". . . it can't happen twice in your life that you're too distraught to fuck."[18] In fact it does; he never tries again. In his twenties, Marcel declares his love for men. He finds a kindred spirit in the light *chanson* composer Reynaldo Hahn, a Venezuelan-born Jew with a mother as intrusive as Proust's, and they become lovers and friends for life.

Maman accepts Marcel's homosexuality as God's will and a blessing. It means no other woman will ever take him away from her. In her letter about the broken door, she connects the glass fragments on the carpet to the climax of the Jewish wedding ceremony, when a glass is smashed by the groom beneath the chuppah (canopy), to commemorate the fall of Jerusalem. "It shall be, as in the temple, the symbol of an indissoluble union," she informs Marcel, implying that, by smashing the glass (as his father never did), he is now married to her by Jewish law. The incident of the door panel is repeated, complete with the wedding quote, in his early novel *Jean Santeuil*, a work that Proust decides not to publish in his lifetime for fear it might discommode his *chère petite maman*.

As if one Jewish mother is not enough for Marcel Proust, he finds another in Geneviève Straus. The precise nature of their friendship is hard to establish with certainty since letters have been incinerated on both sides. There is, however, no doubting its centrality. Marcel meets effete aristocrats in Geneviève's salon and converts them into characters. Having feared that he might seduce her ill-adjusted son (Jacques Bizet is prone to drink and drug addictions), Geneviève comes to terms with Marcel's homosexuality. What she wants from him is a work of genius that will place her in the literary pantheon and eclipse her painfully compromised role in the making of *Carmen*. In the end, she gets her wish. Proust casts her as the ennui-ridden Duchesse de Guermantes, a hostess full of bon mots, some of which Geneviève recognizes, thrillingly, as her own. The duchess's snobbery, hypocrisy, and white-gloved heartlessness are unforgettable. Proust, in a passage cut from the first edition for reasons we can only conjecture, modifies Madame Straus's negativity with a slash of authorial pity, a trace of sympathy for her inability to comprehend the futility of her condition.

"That is why life is so horrible, since nobody can understand anybody else," Mme de Guermantes concluded with a self-consciously pessimistic air, but also with the animation induced by the pleasure of shining before the Princesse de Parme. And when I saw this woman who was so difficult to please, who had claimed to be bored to death with an extremely impressive minister-academician, going to so much trouble for this uninspiring princess, I understood . . .[19]

This and other original omissions, advises Proust editor Terence Kilmartin, should "on no account be overlooked." They need to be read both for depth of character and for clues to the real people on whom they are based. Geneviève once asks Proust if she can consider herself his muse. Marcel evades the question, reassuring her only that his narrator is "mad about the Duchesse de Guermantes."[20] Marcel is too keenly aware of Geneviève's flaws to fall in love with her, although there is a kind of love between them in which each is unsparing about the other's flaws. Marcel writes to Geneviève in an early letter:

The truth about Madame Straus: At first, you see, I thought you loved only beautiful things and that you understood them very well—but then I saw that you care nothing for them—later I thought you loved people, but I see that you care nothing for them. I believe that you love only a certain mode of life which brings out not so much your intelligence as your wit, not so much your wit as your tact, not so much your tact as your dress. A person who more than anything else loves this mode of life—and who, nevertheless, casts a spell.[21]

He keeps Geneviève dangling to the end of an overlong sentence for the gift of a compliment, maintaining the upper hand and never succumbing to the helpless dependency that he so enjoys with Maman.

Jeanne Proust dies in September 1905, outliving her husband by two years. She faces kidney failure with the stoicism of a doctor's wife, refusing the intervention of the top nephrologists in Paris. "She has died at fifty-six, looking no more than thirty," laments Marcel. "She takes away my life with her, as Papa had taken hers." Arranging for Jeanne to be buried beside Adrien, Marcel takes care to ensure that she receives a proper Jewish funeral, attended by all her Jewish relatives from Alsace, alongside her two sons, who are nominally Catholic. Does Marcel recite the Kaddish at Maman's grave? We shall never know. He takes to his bed for a whole month after the funeral, horrified at the realization that he will finally, at thirty-four years old, have to leave the parental home and not report daily on his poo.

Still in mourning, he asks Geneviève Straus to book a room for him in a clinic for nervous disorders, specifying that he will stay for three months to treat his insomnia and his asthma.[22] At the clinic a physician, Paul Sollier, talks to him about "emotional memory." Proust leaves after six weeks, better informed about the ways the human mind can process the dimension of time. On February 1, 1907, he writes a front-page article in *Le Figaro* about a man who murders his mother because he cannot bear to watch the effects of age and illness on her beauty and her personality. Proust, whether he knows it or not, is exhibiting a form of the Oedipus complex, as recently defined by Sigmund Freud. He loves his mother almost to death.

Having begun *À la recherche du temps perdu* (*Remembrance of Things Past*) in 1895, around the time of the smashed glass door, Proust gives up before very long, unready for concentrated effort. He resumes in 1908, writing in bed all day and much of the night. It is an unusual way to work. The German philosopher Walter Benjamin envisages him as Michelangelo, "lying prone, head thrown back, painting the world's creation on the Sistine chapel ceiling." Such is the scope of Proust's world that the comparison does not seem altogether excessive.

No matter how big the canvas, Proust does not miss a detail. His plot evolves slowly, imperceptibly, drawing the reader into an acceptance that this story can be told only in this way, no other. He revises each page ten times. Proust knows his readers well. When he observes that "one cannot read a novel without ascribing to the heroine the traits of the one we love," he does so in full confidence that readers will heave a sigh of self-recognition. Readers respond to Proust as dogs to Pavlov.

In 1912, he publishes extracts from his work in progress in *Le Figaro*, hoping for a publisher to take the bait. Three big houses turn him down, the most hurtful refusal coming from his gay friend André Gide, an editor at Gallimard. Salving his wounds, Proust decides to pay for publication through a boutique imprint, Editions Grasset. *À côté de chez swann* (*Swann's Way*) appears on November 14, 1913. It is

523 pages long, and described as "volume one." Jean Cocteau calls it "a giant miniature, made up of mirages." Another critic "began this book with enthusiasm but ended up casting it aside with a feeling of dread."[23] Some of the reviews are written by Proust himself under assumed names. Accused of dishonesty, he makes a distinction between the narrator "who says 'I' and is not always myself."[24]

A sequel is promised, but during the First World War Proust can hardly bring himself to get out of bed, except occasionally for dinner at the Ritz and other social obligations. Exempted from the draft, he escapes into an alternative reality, where time is stopped at a point before the world went mad. He summons a string quartet to his bedroom to give him ideas for the fictional *Vinteuil Sonata*. He watches a German air raid from a balcony, describing it to Geneviève as "a wonderful apocalypse, in which aeroplanes going up and down made and unmade different constellations."[25] Immune to physical fear, he is gripped by sudden panic that he has lost his exemption certificate and might get sent to the front. A speech difficulty sends him scuttling to a surgeon, claiming he has suffered a stroke and requires brain surgery. A doctor calls at his apartment every Friday. Celeste, his housekeeper, burns thirty-two black notebooks to cover his tracks.

Gide comes round, all contrite, begging him to publish with Gallimard. The next volume, *À l'ombre des jeunes filles en fleurs* (*In the Shadow of Young Girls in Flower*), is published in June 1919 and wins the Prix Goncourt for "the best and most imaginative prose work of the year." International attention ensues. Proust, people say, has changed the novel forever. One night he shares a taxi home from the Ritz with then unknown James Joyce. Proust asks if Joyce knows a certain duchess; Joyce asks if Proust has read his work. They both say no and have nothing more to say to each other.

Gide agonizes over *Sodome et Gomhorre*, fearing prosecution for homosexuality, but Proust is now protected by fame and artistic merit. He has defied the tenor of the times, inventing a world in which all is calm and mannered on the surface, just above the seeds of its destruction.

In October 1922, he contracts bronchitis, which turns into pneumonia. Jacques Bizet, his oldest friend, shoots himself in the head at the end of a masochistic love affair. Marcel is distraught. Robert Proust says he needs to be in the hospital, but Marcel orders an iced beer from the Ritz to help him work through the last night of his life. Robert is there to hear his last word: *"Maman."* At five thirty in the afternoon of November 18, 1922, at the age of fifty-one, Marcel Proust draws his final breath. His great work, running to twelve French volumes, will fill three thousand printed pages. Geneviève Straus, her world preserved, dies on December 22, 1926, aged seventy-seven. Both glimpse immortality.

The most famous opening sentence in modern literature—*Longtemps, je me suis couché de bonne heure*—resists translation. In English, its meaning is "I used to go to bed early for quite a while," which misses the dark, baritonal resonance, the drawn-out languor of the original. The adverb *longtemps* suggests both sweep and scale; not just a long time but an eternally long time, a time beyond time, a word that prepares us for the unknown. *Longtemps* gives balance to the rest of the sentence in a way that "for a long time" cannot. It hints at a time long past while the rest of the sentence is in the present continuous. Proust is a brute to translators. His mot juste taps into melody. He hears, like Sarah Bernhardt, a secret temple music in the French language. No one speaks French like Sarah; no one writes it like Marcel. As Jews in a hostile environment, they listen like cats, alert to whispers and quavers that elude Gentile ears. French is Proust's mother tongue yet, in his phrasing, it is inimitably his own language, maintaining a cordon sanitaire from the rest of French letters. Proust is both the greatest French writer of his time and the least French. The paradox is rooted in his Jewish identity, an insider-outsider status that he shares with fellow Jews.

Proust's affinities with Freud are striking. Proust remembers minute childhood sensations and analyzes them as the source of character. He builds personality by aggregating infant incidents and observations. He attributes adult motives to the mother-son relationship, the trope of Jewish jokes and the focus of Freud's attention. An Oxford scholar, Malcolm Bowie, finds no fewer than ten of Freud's theories in Proust's work, yet, so far as we know, Proust never read Freud or referred to him.[26] Their similarity of approach arises from a classic Jewish way of observing and understanding small things that others take for granted. Both know that great laws can be deduced from tiny details without being aware that this is one of the key principles of Talmudic exegesis. Proust, baptized and godless, is bonded to Judaism by the crunch of broken glass.

The Jewish connection extends further. Proust's concept of "lost time" is not light-years apart from Albert Einstein's insights into the relativity of time. An hour, to Einstein, is a unit of time whose length varies in space. Proust writes: "An hour is not merely an hour; it is a vase full of scents and sounds and projects and climates." By no stretch of the imagination is Proust a scientist, nor is he much concerned with the workings of the universe. Nevertheless, Proust perceives time as a metaphor and a continuum; a zone in which past, present, and future commingle, where history is not a finite action—In the beginning God created the heavens and the earth—but a spectrum of continuous development. Time, for Proust as for Einstein, is a key to God's cabinet of secrets, assuming a god exists. Where do Proust and Einstein receive this idea of time? From the Hebrew Bible which, read literally, is written in the present continuous tense and in a chronology that is not fixed but relative. The six days of creation are not twenty-four-hour days. According to rabbinic interpretation, they could be a million years, or variable lengths. A Talmudic ruling states: "There is no before or after in Torah."[27]

The Talmud, which forms the basis of Jewish law, is a dialogue between rabbis who live across four centuries in different parts of the world, yet engage with one another on the same page as if they are contemporaries, in much the same way that characters from past and present populate Proust's search for lost time. Proust may take ten pages to describe something that happens in half a minute, or ten words to outline a whole life. Time varies according to one's position in space.

Einstein looms large in Proust's last year. The French-Jewish philosopher Henri-Louis Bergson, who is married to Proust's cousin (Marcel is best man at his wedding to Louise Neuberger), issues a challenge to Einstein's theory of relativity. Bergson's book *Duration and Simultaneity* argues that space can be measured but time cannot. On April 6, 1922, Bergson and Einstein meet for a debate on the nature of time at the Société française de philosophie in Paris. It is never a meeting of minds. Einstein's French is shaky and Bergson's argument shakier still. Claiming to be "more Einsteinian than Einstein," he waffles that "to act on the future one must start by changing the past." Einstein, indicating that he has no idea what the philosopher is getting at, delivers a rude riposte: "There is no time in philosophy."

Einstein defines time as the fourth dimension of the universe, adding, "There remains only a psychological time that differs from the physicist's." The poet Paul Valéry calls their debate the "*grande affaire du siècle*" (of the century). Einstein wins the Nobel Prize in Physics that year. Bergson wins the Nobel Prize in Literature. He then suffers a precipitate reputational collapse, descending from a man everyone quotes to one whose name no one remembers, as if all his substance has been nothing but hot air. Proust, who attends Bergson's lectures at the Sorbonne and names him as an influence on his concept of "*temps perdu*," caricatures him as Bergotte in the novel. He does not respond to the debate of the century, but many literary analysts and physicists share the view that Proustian time has uncanny affinities with Einstein's.[28]

Proust is credited with many things by his admirers, with innumerable insights and mystic powers. A self-help manual advises *How Proust Can Change Your Life*. Another is titled *Proust Was a Neuroscientist*. A third recommends one should read nothing but Proust for a year in order to be whole and healthy. Of which other author could such things be said? Might Proust contain the elixir of life? I am tempted to think he might.

In my thirties, I would take Proust with me on holiday to Collioure, a French fishing village. In the early morning, my wife and daughters still asleep, I slip out and walk down to the harbor to sit with Proust and black coffee on a bench beside the sea. My exhilarating sensation of freedom is qualified by two forms of guilt: that I have fled from my loved ones and that I should have needed to do so. Guilt, however, does not occlude the joy of reading Proust. On the contrary, the pleasure is enhanced by my exquisite self-bifurcation. I read for an hour. At seven thirty, I bend the corner of a page, shut my book, buy fresh-baked croissants at a boulangerie across the road, and walk back up the hill to rejoin my beloved family, who are just waking up as the sun pierces the shutters. With each step I take, I know that I will not forget this sensation for as long as I live. I know, too, that I owe the indelibility of this moment to Marcel Proust, who is the alchemist of memory. The more that my other memories are blurred with the passing of years, the more I give thanks to Proust for saving me this perfect recollection. Proust, whatever else he does, teaches us to live in the moment. And then he rewards us with a madeleine of past happiness that is forever present.

FIVE

1881
THE TSAR'S HAMBURGER

Gateways to heaven and hell: Ellis Island.

O n the first day of March 1881, a Sunday, Tsar Alexander II—
Emperor of Russia, King of Poland, Grand Duke of Finland—is
urged to cancel his attendance at military roll call. There is intelligence

of a murder plot by Nihilists. A man under arrest has told police that nothing can save the tsar.

Alexander listens with grave attention before donning his uniform to review his troops on the grounds of the Mikhailovsky Manège. There have been three attempts on his life in two years. In April 1879, a Nihilist fired five shots and missed. In November, a radical group, the People's Will, opened fire on the tsar's train. In February 1880, they placed a bomb under the Winter Palace dining room, killing eleven people and injuring fifty-six, but missing the tsar. Alexander, normally the most punctual of monarchs, was delayed by the late arrival of his nephew, the prince of Bulgaria.

A workaholic who cooks his own breakfast and chops firewood for exercise, Alexander spends much of his day signing appointments across his empire. No magistrate can take the bench, no midwife is licensed to practice, without his signature. Known as the Benevolent Tsar, Alexander II has freed millions of serfs, built railways, and founded state schools. Russia enjoys a culture boom. Dostoevsky writes *Crime and Punishment*, Tolstoy publishes *War and Peace*, Tchaikovsky composes four symphonies, and Russian ballet leaps to world attention. The system is founded, however, on state terror, practiced by the Okhrana secret police. The pressure has begun to tell on the tsar. In his last photograph, Alexander, sixty-two years old, stares into the camera from behind a bushy mustache, his pale eyes haggard with overwork. His only relief is a lively sexual dalliance with Catherine Dolgorukov, whom he marries in June 1879, weeks after the first tsarina's death.

On March 1, 1881 (March 13 by the Western calendar), Catherine begs him to skip the parade. At twelve forty-five, Alexander sets out. What follows is reported by an exiled anarchist, Prince Peter Kropotkin:

> It is known how it happened. A bomb was thrown under his ironclad carriage, to stop it. Several Circassians of the escort were wounded. [Nikolai] Rysakóff, who flung the bomb, was arrested on the spot. Then, although the coachman of the Tsar earnestly advised him not to get out, saying that he could drive him still in the slightly damaged carriage, he insisted. He felt that his military dignity required him to see the wounded Circassians, to condole with them as he had done with the wounded during the Turkish

war, when a mad storming of Plevna, doomed to end in a terrible disaster, was made on the day of his fête. He approached Rysakóff and asked him something; and as he passed close by another young man, [Ignatz] Grinevétsky, the latter threw a bomb between himself and Alexander II, so that both of them should be killed. They both lived but a few hours.

There Alexander II lay upon the snow, profusely bleeding, abandoned by every one of his followers! All had disappeared. It was cadets, returning from the parade, who lifted the suffering Tsar from the snow and put him in a sledge, covering his shivering body with a cadet mantle and his bare head with a cadet cap. And it was one of the terrorists, Emeliánoff, with a bomb wrapped in a paper under his arm, who, at the risk of being arrested on the spot and hanged, rushed with the cadets to the help of the wounded man. Human nature is full of these contrasts.

Taken to the Winter Palace, his guts spilling from a gash in his abdomen, the tsar dies that night. His son, Alexander III, unleashes the Okhrana. St. Petersburg is sealed off. Fifty Nihilists are arrested and, under torture, confess. Five People's Will members are tried and, on April 3, hanged. A sixth, Nikolai Sablin, shoots himself as police burst through the door; his lover, Gesia Gelfman, is arrested. A member of the People's Will executive committee, she is condemned to death, but, as the judge pronounces sentence, Gesia declares that she is pregnant. Under Russian law, she cannot be hanged until the baby is forty days old. Gesia gives birth in prison. Her child dies, followed by Gesia herself, of medical neglect. She is twenty-six years old.

Gesia Gelfman's arrest has world-changing consequences. The Okhrana traces her to a Jewish family in Belarus and puts out the word. In Zhmerinka, a small town in Podolia, a mob starts shouting: "The Jews killed the tsar!"

Two days after the tsar's assassination, the Earl of Beaconsfield struggles to his feet in the House of Lords to offer a vote of condolence to Queen Victoria on the death of her cousin. Beaconsfield, the former Benjamin Disraeli, affirms the British people's undying loyalty to the Crown.

His own devotion needs no declaration. Never has a British monarch enjoyed such intimacy with a prime minister. "His affectionate sympathy, his wise counsel—*all* were so invaluable even out of office," sighs the Queen. Nothing about Disraeli is solemn or safe. A bisexual peacock dressed in "green velvet trousers and a canary-coloured waistcoat," he flaunts his difference whenever possible. Victoria loves him for his chutzpah. He has named her Empress of India and bought her a stake in the Suez Canal by means of a £4 million private loan from his friend Lionel de Rothschild. "When do you need it?" asks Rothschild. "Tomorrow," says Disraeli's envoy. Rothschild, legend has it, pauses to remove the skin of a muscat grape from between his teeth.

"What is your security?" he inquires.

"The British government."

"Then you shall have it," said Rothschild.

Disraeli eulogizes Alexander II as "the most beneficent prince that ever filled the throne of Russia," which everyone knows is a lie. Disraeli hates Russia, its feudal absolutism, its anti-Jewish laws. He backs Turkey against Russia, to the fury of the Liberal leader William Gladstone, who accuses him of "holding British foreign policy hostage to his Jewish sympathies." At the 1878 Congress of Berlin, Disraeli recognizes Romania, Serbia, and Montenegro as independent states, diminishing Russian influence in the Balkans. The German chancellor Otto von Bismarck is impressed. *"Der alte Jude,"* says Bismarck, surveying a roomful of European leaders, *"dass ist der Mann"* (The old Jew, he's the man). Dizzy promptly shares the compliment with his delighted Queen.

Time, though, is catching up with the old Jew. Within days of his lament for the tsar, he sickens with bronchitis. The Queen receives daily bulletins. Gladstone leaves a sanctimonious prayer at his door: "May the Almighty be near his pillow." Dying, Dizzy proofreads the official Hansard report of his final speech, saying: "I will not go down to posterity talking bad grammar." Coughing painfully, he quips: "I have suffered much. Had I been a Nihilist, I would have confessed all." His last political words are a Jewish joke.

Benjamin Disraeli dies, aged seventy-six, in the early hours of April 19, 1881. The Queen writes:

I can scarcely see for my fast-falling tears . . . Never had I *so* kind and devoted a Minister and very few such devoted friends . . . I have lost *so* many dear friends but none whose loss will be more keenly felt. To England (or rather Gt. Britain) and to the *World* his loss is *immense* and at such a moment. God's will be done! I have learnt to say this, but the bitterness and the suffering are not the less severe. As yet I cannot realize it.[1]

Winston Churchill offers a timeless epitaph:

Disraeli, the Jew Prime Minister of England and Leader of the Conservative Party, who was always true to his race and proud of his origin, said on a well-known occasion: "The Lord deals with the nations as the nations deal with the Jews." Certainly when we look at the miserable state of Russia, where of all countries in the world the Jews were the most cruelly treated and contrast it with the fortunes of our own country, which seems to have been so providentially preserved amid the awful perils of these times, we must admit that nothing that has since happened in the history of the world has falsified the truth of Disraeli's confident assertion.[2]

The Russians need no reminder of his significance. With Disraeli gone, Russia sets about punishing the Jews for the murder of their tsar.

The *Novorossisskij Telegraf*, published in Odessa, reports "rumours of impending anti-Jewish rioting." These are not rumors. The report, planted by the Okhrana, is a summons to pogrom. The noun *pogrom*, from the verb "to destroy," has one meaning: attack Jews. Odessa is Russia's fourth-largest city; one-third of its inhabitants are Jews.

Some 250 kilometers to the north, in the town of Elizavetgrad (population sixty thousand), three glasses are smashed in Shulem Grichevsky's bar. Shulem demands payment. The drunks refuse. Yelling, "The yids are beating up our people," they run into the street and throw stones at shopwindows. That night, a mob lays siege to the main synagogue. Troops arrive, and the crowds disperse. Next morning, three corpses are found; one Jew, two drunks. Disturbances continue for two days. An old Jew named Pelikov, trying to save his daughter from being raped by soldiers, is thrown off a roof to his death. A hundred shops and five hundred Jewish homes are sacked.

As pogroms go, Elizavetgrad is no more than a skirmish, one that would have faded from history but for its primacy. Eleven days later, there is a three-day riot in Kiev. Four Jews die; twenty-five are raped. "The police actually witnessed the gross outrages without making the least attempt to arrest the ruffians," notes an eyewitness.[3] Before Kiev settles down, two more pogroms flare elsewhere.

Over the next twelve months, Jews are attacked in 175 towns and villages. Eleven Jews are murdered at Nezhin in July. The tsar signs a public order act, and there is a summer lull, only for violence to blaze again at Christmas in Warsaw, where Jews are bizarrely blamed for a church stampede that left twenty-eight worshippers dead. The worst outrages come at Easter 1882 in Balta, where forty Jews are reported murdered (later assessments indicate around twelve) and there are multiple incidents of rape and pillage. Twelve hundred Jewish homes and shops are destroyed. In Yekaterinoslav, a Russian woman runs screaming out of a Jewish shop after a sales assistant slaps her child for stealing. Two hundred men attack the store, beat the assistant to death, and rampage along the street. Three thousand railway workers put down their tools and join in. Rapes continue even after troops open fire.[4] The *Jewish Chronicle*, headlining a "Reign of Terror," warns that "life is no longer tolerable in the districts where religious hatred and commercial jealousy have aroused the evil passions of the populace."[5]

The interior minister, Count Nikolay Pavlovich Ignatyev, blames the Jews. "The conduct of [Jews]," he explains, "called forth protests on the part of the people, as manifested in acts of violence and robbery." The tsar enacts a series of May Laws, punishing the Jews by forcing them back into the Pale of Settlement and forbidding them to take property mortgages.

"We expect a pogrom at any minute," writes a man from Vilna, Lithuania, in February 1882:

> What kind of life is this? If I had the courage, I would kill all those close to me and then myself and the farce would be over. If I do not,

some drunken riffraff will come along, ravish my wife and daughter and throw my infant Sonia from the third-floor window. Would it not be better for me to kill everyone? What a miserable creature is the Jew! Even when the advantage is clear to him he cannot summon the courage to do a good thing. Death awaits us in any case, so why should we wait?[6]

Across the western border with Austria, the town of Brody, population eighteen thousand, takes in twelve thousand refugees. A young refugee describes the accommodation.

> From a distance, it looks as if the walls are covered with ants moving one on top of another. Upon closer observation one is chilled at the sight. Here a Jew clad in rags and perspiring, who seems to have been here many hours, has managed . . . to get midway through the crowd. He tries to figure out a way to get to one of the windows as quickly as possible. He does a somersault hoping to hurdle over the heads of several people and thus advance his position. This causes chaos. He is beaten, his clothes are rent and finally, still alive, he nears the window, only to be pushed back by a strong, armed man who has tried to clear a space. He falls and drags others with him. Immediately the space is occupied by others . . .[7]

The Brody episode is widely reported. The Lord Mayor of London makes a charity appeal, raising £108,759. Sir Moses Montefiore, ninety-seven years old, offers to travel to Moscow and intercede with the tsar. Two French barons, Rothschild and de Hirsch, sponsor farm schools for refugees in Palestine and Argentina. A relief conference is held in Vienna. Several thousand Brody refugees are accepted in Western Europe, a smaller number reaches America, and eight thousand are sent back to Russia, resentful, rejected, and fearful for their lives.[8]

Brody opens a gulf between Western Jews, who live in relative comfort, and those who tremble in shtetls (small towns and villages) within the Pale. Shtetl Jews live in "naked misery and frightful poverty,"[9] observing rabbinic Orthodoxy, studying Talmud, praying for messianic redemption. During the pogroms, rabbis write learned responsa about the legal status of raped women. For secular Russian Jews, the pogroms mark the end of integration. "I [once] saw myself as a faithful son of Russia, which was to me my raison d'être and the very air that I breathed," writes Haim Hissin, a student from Mir. "Each new discovery by a Russian scientist, every classical literary work, every victory of the Russian Empire would fill my heart with pride. I wanted to devote my whole strength to the good of my homeland . . . Suddenly, those I considered my countrymen tell me I should leave."[10]

The violence unleashed by the tsar's assassination sputters on for a generation, climaxing in two horrendous rampages through Kishinev, the Moldovan capital, in 1903 and 1905. An Irish nationalist MP, Michael Davitt, is appalled by what he sees:

> From their hiding places in cellars and garrets the Jews were dragged forth and tortured to death . . . in not a few cases nails were driven into the skull and eyes gouged out. Babies were thrown from the higher stories to the street pavement. . . . The local bishop drove in a carriage and passed through the crowd, giving them his blessing.[11]

Davitt calls Russian Jew hatred a "barbarous malignancy."

Russia remains in denial. "There is no feeling against the Jew in Russia because of religion," says Count Arthur Cassini, the Russian ambassador in Washington. "It is as I have said—the Jew ruins the peasants, with the result that conflicts occur when the latter have lost all their worldly possessions and have nothing to live upon."[12] After nearly one hundred deaths in Kishinev, only two youths are brought to trial. They are given short sentences.

Halfway across the hemisphere, another head of state is assassinated. On July 2, 1881, President James A. Garfield leaves the White House with his two sons to spend a vacation on the New Jersey seashore, where his wife is recuperating from malaria. As the president enters the Sixth Street station waiting room, arm in arm with his secretary of state, a man steps forward and shoots him in the stomach and the arm. "My God, what is this?" cries Garfield.

The killer pockets his pistol and leaves the station, only to run into a passing policeman. The shooter is named as Charles Guiteau, a malcontent who thinks Garfield owes him a job. Guiteau is tried for attempted murder and hanged. The president lingers for eighty days, attended by sixteen physicians who ignore antiseptic measures. When he dies, the country is prepared. No minority is blamed. Wall Street is unmoved.

Markets, in fact, begin to stir. Bumping along the bottom since an 1873 Union Pacific Railroad scam crashed three hundred banks, Wall Street awakes in 1881 to a clatter of new shingles on its stone fronts. The firms have German or French names and Jewish owners: Kuhn, Loeb & Co.; Lehman Brothers; Goldman Sachs; Warburg; Bache & Co.; Lazard Frères; and Seligman. Described as "investment banks," the start-ups are ex-peddlers from the Deep South and the California gold rush. Clannish and convivial, they cluster around Temple Emanu-El and marry their daughters to one another's sons, within the clan.

Solomon Loeb's son-in-law, Jacob Schiff, is Kuhn, Loeb & Co's head of policy. Descended from the rabbinic exegete Maharam Schiff, and educated at Samson Raphael Hirsch's Frankfurt school, Schiff ascribes his analytical skills to Jewish learning. Blue-eyed, high-principled, first at his desk every morning, Schiff is a game changer who invents the role of investment banker in an expanding economy. Where old merchant banks lend money that they hold on deposit, investment bankers go out in search of new money to invest in new industry. Schiff raises money on the Frankfurt market to refinance railroad owners, shock-starting a stalled development sector. Before long, he is going head-to-head with the establishment banker John Pierpont Morgan. One weekend, the pair come close to crashing the US economy in an injudicious hyping of railroad stock.

Morgan, who dislikes Jews, says, "We and Barings are the only white banks in New York."[13] Schiff dines at home on Friday nights and spends every Saturday morning in his Temple Emanu-El pew. Morgan is tall, powerfully built, facially disfigured, and astonishingly rude. Schiff is short, smartly dressed, and athletic, striding sixty blocks from home to work in all weather, listening to people who stop him with tips and market gossip. He greets customers with extravagant affection, judging good manners to be good business, but wastes no time on small talk or wit. Humor is alien to his character. Schiff's presence changes the mood on Wall Street from hucksterism to hushed calculation. In 1882, Charles Dow and Edward Jones start tracking stocks.

Morgan builds the Metropolitan Club, from which Jews are excluded. He founds the Metropolitan Opera, where Jews are barred from owning boxes, and the Metropolitan Museum, where their gifts are refused. *Metropolitan*, in Manhattan, means "Jew-free." Joseph Seligman, taking his family on vacation to Saratoga Springs' Grand Union Hotel, is told on arrival: "Mr. Hilton has given instructions that no Israelites shall be permitted in future to stop at this hotel." The *New York Times*, Jewish-owned, reports the incident on its front page.[14] Judge Henry Hilton responds, calling Seligman "disreputable." Seligman, shocked by a hatred he thought he had left far behind, dies soon after. An obituary calls him "America's leading Jew."

Schiff transcends animosity with style. He sets aside 10 percent of his earnings for charity and then gives more for what he calls "philanthropy." Thanked for a donation, he replies, "That wasn't my money." What he gives as charity is God's money. The rest is philanthropy. Schiff endows the Hebrew Union College to train Reform clergy and the Jewish Theological Seminary to educate rabbis of a "reasonable Orthodoxy." He establishes the American Jewish Committee, known as "the Joint," as an international relief agency. In December 1881, he gives $10,000 to set up the Schiff Refuge on Wards Island, at the bottom of 110th Street, to receive fugitives from the Russian pogroms. He hates the tsar. "A system of government . . . capable of such cruelties and outrages at home . . . ," he declares, "must be overhauled from the foundations up in the interests of . . . the world at large."[15]

Schiff's outrage has lasting political ramifications. In 1904, he buys Japanese war bonds, floating $200 million in loans to help defeat the Russians. During the First World War, he refuses to support a British loan unless he gets assurances that Russia, Britain's ally, will not benefit from it. In 1917, he rejoices at the fall of the tsar and announces loans for the new Russia.[16] He is accused of backing the Bolsheviks, which he denies, and of pro-German sentiments. "My sympathies for the land of my birth are as warm as anyone's," Schiff declares, "but I have been an American for fifty years and mean to remain so first and for the remainder of my life." At his death in 1920, Schiff leaves

$50 million, equivalent to half a billion in twenty-first-century values. His son succeeds him as bank president. His daughter marries a War-burg. His granddaughter, Dorothy Schiff, owns the *New York Post*. But the lights are going out for German Jews in America. The Schiffs and the Warburgs are soon to be outshone by Russian masses who trans-form American society and popular culture.

A noun is born.

It appears first in an essay in January 1881 in the Viennese daily *Neue Freie Presse*, a Jewish-owned newspaper of Liberal outlook. Soon after, it is the title of a book, *Zwanglose Antisemitische Hefte* (informal anti-Semitic pamphlets). The author is Wilhelm Marr, a Prussian jour-nalist who gives Jew hatred its modern name and secular identity, dis-tinct from Christ-killing. Marr is "the father of antisemitism."[17] Seldom has a popular ideology had feebler parentage.

A member of the 1848 Frankfurt Parliament, where he calls for equal rights for Jews and women, Marr sails to South America to make his fortune, and returns penniless. A man of weak features—the only known portrait shows a goatee beard and a thin, jutting nose—Marr marries a Jewish woman with a monthly allowance from her father. Elected to the Hamburg Parliament, he witnesses a fight for state rec-ognition between the Orthodox and Reform Jewish communities and is disgusted by the display of doctrinal strife. He writes a book, *Der Judenspiegel* (*The Jewish Mirror*), attacking Judaism as irrational and its communities as "a state within a state." It attracts scant attention. In 1869, he is jailed for ten weeks for defaming the Hamburg govern-ment. He divorces his wife and marries another Jewish woman, who is "not rich, not young, and not pretty."[18] She dies after bearing a still-born child. Marr marries a third Jewess; they have a son and divorce. In 1878, he takes a Christian wife. He is done with Jews.

"There is no stopping them," writes Marr in *The Victory of Judaism over Germanism*, the book that makes his name in 1879:

Jewry's control of society and politics is increasing . . . In England, the Semite Disraeli, a German hater, holds in his huge pocket the key to war and peace in the Orient . . . Dear reader, while the German is skinned alive, I bow my head in admiration and awe before this Semitic people which has put us beneath its heel.[19]

As Asiatic "Semites," Jews cease to be German citizens and can be extirpated without constraints of legality and compassion.

Preaching the expulsion of Jews from Germany, Marr founds a League of Antisemites and launches a newspaper, *The German Guard*, which soon folds. His claim that Germany is eroded by Semites is contradicted by the reality that Germany has never been stronger. Bismarck has defeated Denmark, Austria, and France, financing his army through Gerson von Bleichröder, the first Jew to receive a Prussian "von." Richard Wagner vilifies Bleichröder as an evil Jew who sponsors "the degenerated German taste for war."[20] Marr visits Bayreuth but is sent packing by Cosima Wagner, who finds his ideas "too close" to her husband's. The League of Antisemites disintegrates without ever holding a meeting, but its sentiments take root.

In April 1881, the Berlin Reichstag receives and rejects a petition with more than a quarter of a million signatures, and supported by the kaiser's personal chaplain, Adolf Stoecker, calling for the removal of Jews from public life. In Austria, an anti-Jewish leader, Georg Ritter von Schönerer, styles himself "Führer." In September 1882, on Yom Kippur, an International Anti-Jewish Congress convenes in Dresden. Led by Stoecker, a Bavarian state treasurer, and three Hungarian Parliament members, it appeals to "the Governments and Peoples of Christian Nations Threatened by Judaism" to expel "the Semitic race of Jews" from Europe. Marr is pointedly omitted from the delegates list, having retired to Hamburg to write his memoirs. "After thirty years of war against the Jews I have come to despise this cheating business of anti-semitism," he wails.[21] Failure though he is, Wilhelm Marr effects a step change in political discourse. His terminology shifts Jew hatred from theology to public policy. Anti-Semitism, he argues, is essential for German survival. Removing the Jews defines the German nation. Nebulous, imprecise, pseudo-intellectual, Wilhelm Marr's new word makes Jew hatred politically palatable.

In a small town in Bavaria, a musician invents a new religion. The world should have ended for Richard Wagner with the immolation scene of his four-night *The Ring of the Nibelungen*. But that is five years ago, in 1876, and the world has moved on. *The Ring* has failed to set the world alight. The composer is not, after all, God Almighty, so Wagner writes *Parsifal* to design his own divinity.

The plot is static. Amfortas, knight of the Holy Grail, is stabbed by the witch Kundry, who works for the sorcerer Klingsor. Kundry steals Amfortas's manhood, his holy spear. Along comes Parsifal. He penetrates Klingsor's castle, resists Kundry's sex appeal, retrieves the spear, and returns it to Amfortas. A surge of Good Friday music delivers redemption. In an essay on art and religion, Wagner proclaims: "When religion becomes artificial, art has a duty to rescue it."

The essay betrays his obsession with Jews. "That the God of our Saviour should have been identified with the tribal god of Israel, is one of the most terrible confusions in all world-history," he declares. In February 1881, he adds: "The Jew . . . is the most astounding instance of racial congruence ever offered by world-history. . . . [He] has no religion at all—merely the belief in certain promises of his god which in nowise extend to a life beyond . . . but simply to this present life on Earth, whereon his race is certainly ensured dominion over all that lives and lives not." Wagner warns his patron King Ludwig that *Parsifal* will need protection "from a world which fades in cowardice in the face of the Jews." The king tells him that it will be premiered by his court conductor, Hermann Levi. Wagner goes berserk. "It would be an overwhelming hardship for me if *Parsifal*, this all-Christian work, was to be conducted by a Jew," he expostulates. The king ignores him. "People are basically brothers," he replies.[22]

Levi is not just a Jew. He is the son of a chief rabbi, Benedikt Levi of Hesse. As a boy, Hermann played the organ at his father's Sabbath services. He remains close to his father, corresponding with him throughout his Bayreuth duties. "I am addicted to [Wagner] body and soul," he writes.[23]

Wagner recognizes that Levi is an outstanding conductor, preferable to Hans Richter, who led the first *Ring*. He commends Levi for keeping his Jewish surname, rather than blurring it to Löwy. But he is damned if he is going to let a Jew conduct his "most Christian of all artworks." Before Levi can conduct *Parsifal*, he says, "we shall go through a ceremonial act with you"—baptism.[24] The conductor declines. Wagner persists: if only "a formula could be found for baptising such a poor creature as Levi."[25] The conductor shows signs of depression. "Marry my wife," suggests Wagner, "then you'll be cheerful."[26] What is going on? Does Wagner think Levi will be redeemed by having sex with Cosima? "As a Jew," Wagner tells his wife, Levi "merely has to learn to die."[27]

On June 28, 1881, Levi arrives a few minutes late to lunch. Wagner berates him in front of the whole family for the un-German sin of unpunctuality and orders him to go to his room, where a letter awaits him. The anonymous letter is an appeal to Wagner "to keep his work pure and not let a Jew conduct it." It goes on to suggest that Levi is having an affair with Cosima.

Levi returns to the dining room, sits silent to the end of the meal, and then leaves for the train station. He sends Wagner a resignation letter from the first stop, at Bamberg. Wagner, fearing King Ludwig will withdraw his court orchestra, replies, accusing Levi of being too sensitive, too Jewish: "With all respect to your feelings, you don't make things easy for yourself or for us."

He abandons the demand for baptism. "For God's sake," writes Wagner, "come back at once and get to know us properly. *Lose none of your faith* but be bold. Perhaps this will be a great turning point in your life. At any event, you are my *Parsifal* conductor." This does the trick. On July 2, 1881, Levi returns to Bayreuth, arriving in time for lunch. "Very relaxed, even very cheerful mood," notes Cosima. "Richard calls for *Hebrew* wine!"

There are no further stumbling blocks on the path to *Parsifal*. Levi conducts the premiere on July 26, 1882, with the rain hammering on the theater roof. He finishes in a rapid four hours and eighteen minutes (Arturo Toscanini takes five hours) and gives sixteen performances in all. At the last, on August 29, Richard Wagner slips into the pit in the third-act finale, takes Levi's baton, and conducts to the end. It is a reassumption of power, his victory over the Jew.

The Wagners leave for Venice, where Hermann Levi visits them in November and again in February 1883. "On Monday midday I left Venice," he writes. "The *Meister* accompanied me to the stairs, kissed me several times." Twenty-four hours later, Wagner is dead. Levi, devastated, writes to his father: "In my dreadful, indescribable grief, you are in my loving thoughts. Generations to come will realize what he was to the world and what the world has lost in him . . ." His father wonders why Hermann is so besotted with a sworn enemy of their people.

Their correspondence, which comes to light in a 1959 Bayreuth program book, offers acute insights into the cultural schizophrenia of German Jews, torn between their heritage and their devotion to German *kunst* (art). Rabbi Levi's fear that his son has been seduced by a Jew-hater is met by Hermann's insistence that Wagner's *kampf* (struggle) against the Jews stems from "the noblest of motives" and must not be mistaken for "*kleinliches risches*" (petty malice). *Risches*, a Hebrew-Yiddish word, denotes wickedness. The rabbi sees evil in Wagner. His son writes: "Wagner is the best and noblest of men . . . I thank God daily for the privilege to be close to such a man. It is the most beautiful experience of my life."

The rabbi wants to know if Hermann is being paid. "Don't worry about my wages," comes the reply. "Our orchestra members get 250 marks a month, plus travel and accommodation. I shall ask for 500 marks, which is all I need. I don't want to make a profit out of Bayreuth." There is a note of rebuke in this riposte: Hermann hints that the rabbi is thinking like a money-grubbing Jew. He continues:

> The Wagners are so good to me that I am quite touched. I arrived here on June 12th and from that day until July 1st I have lunched and dined every day at Wahnfried. Frequently I called at 12 noon and left only at midnight. . . . In the evenings, the Meister reads to us and we have the most absorbing discussions. Never have I lived through a happier time.

After *Parsifal*, the rabbi asks if his son will receive an award. The conductor replies wearily: "I refuse to consider whether I deserve an order or any other kind of recognition for *Parsifal*. As for my 'prestige,' I have plenty of it already and am, anyway, far too well rewarded."

What are we to make of Hermann Levi's *kulturkampf* (culture wars)? The Freudian scholar Peter Gay reads it as a case study in Jewish self-hatred, arguing that Levi abases himself before Wagner to the point where he accepts that a "Semite could never produce anything immortal."[28] To read these words in Levi's hand is to feel shame at his surrender and concern for his sanity. He absorbs Wagner's prejudice and recycles it uncritically. He also accepts a kind of martyrdom, knowing that after *Parsifal* he will go down in history only as Wagner's baton, never for any other achievement. Trapped between loyalty to his father and his reverence for German culture, Levi is a tragic figure, a totem of the choice German Jews will have to make under Hitler: to stay or to go, to be German first or Jew.

Levi is chosen by Cosima as one of Wagner's pallbearers. He shares conducting duties at Bayreuth for a dozen years with Felix Mottl and Richard Strauss, retiring at fifty-six to marry a rich widow and live in a villa in Garmisch, where he dies in 1900 and is buried in the garden. Nazis desecrate his tomb in 1935, and the site is never repaired. The local authority orders its removal. In September 2018, preparations are made for the remains of Hermann Levi to be transferred to the Jewish cemetery in Munich. Six months later, in the face of an international media outcry, the tourist-dependent town reverses its decision and pays to restore Levi's grave.

A Protestant musician in Berlin befriends a Jewish cantor, who teaches him the tune for "Kol Nidrei," the opening incantation of the Day of Atonement. The musician Max Bruch makes it into a concert piece for cello and orchestra, assuring his publisher in December 1881 that it is not, God forbid, a celebration of Jewish worship but a cold-headed commercial proposition. "The success of *Kol Nidrei* is assured," writes Bruch, "because all the Jews in the world are for it." Jews form a sizeable chunk of the Berlin concert audience. The new anti-Semitism is eager to exploit the Jews.

At a café on Boulevard Montmartre, a thin young man spreads his documents on an outdoor table and studies travel plans. Eliezer Perlman wants to get his girlfriend out of Russia and meet her in Vienna. He has no money, no prospects, no qualifications, nothing other than a vision he glimpsed in this same café two years earlier, when he minted the first word of a new language.

A medical student at the Sorbonne, Perlman carries two dangerous germs: a tuberculosis bacillus that nearly kills him, and a streak of Jewish nationalism. On his first visit to the café—biographers can't agree if it was the Lapin Fou or the Chat Noir[29]—Perlman talks for two hours with a man he thinks is called Zundelman but it might be Adelman.[30] The pair attempt a conversation in biblical Hebrew and fail. "That showed me straight away how hard it was to talk Hebrew, how far Hebrew still was from being an adequate expression for the needs of daily life."[31] That afternoon, Perlman coins the first word in modern Hebrew. He needs to say *dictionary*. He calls it *milon*.

Hebrew is a dead language, as defunct as Latin, confined to daily prayers and dusty yeshivas. Yet, unlike Latin, Hebrew has continued to evolve posthumously. In medieval Spain, Solomon Ibn Gabirol, Moses Ibn Ezra, and Yehuda Halevi compose Hebrew love poems. In Egypt, Moses Maimonides writes lucid Hebrew. Moses Mendelssohn in eighteenth-century Berlin inspires a slew of Hebrew novels. The great Yiddish storyteller Sholem Aleichem, forefather of *Fiddler on the Roof*, tries his hand first in Hebrew. The holy tongue is taught to every child in cheder. But its antiquity disables it for modern use. How can one order a drink in a language that uses only the present continuous tense and has a constipated emotional vocabulary? The verb *ohev* can mean anything from a liking for vodka to an overwhelming passion for a sexual partner. Hebrew has no word for lover. Or bathroom. Or underwear. Or coffee. Or kids' toys. Nor is there any agreement on how words are pronounced. Ashkenazi Jews in Europe cannot understand the prayers of Sephardim in North Africa.

Eliezer Perlman has his work cut out for him. Confined to the Rothschild hospital with tuberculosis, he chats with the man in the next bed, a fellow Lithuanian, A. M. Lunc, who tells him he has heard Jews in a Jerusalem market trading in simplified Hebrew in the Sephardi pronunciation. Perlman practically leaps out of bed. He quits medicine for linguistics. "One day I decided, 'This gap I will fill,' and the thought of writing the Dictionary was born."[32] The Hebraic Dr. Johnson starts work at a café table in Montmartre.

Perlman leaves Paris in September 1881, meets Devora Jonas in Vienna, and marries her in Cairo. They head to Jerusalem, a walled ghetto sweating beneath a fierce sun and Ottoman misrule. Jews, Muslims, Christians, and Armenians are allocated separate quarters in the Old City; Russians, Greeks, and Abyssinians have settlements outside the walls. A nonpartisan source estimates the 1882 population at twenty-one thousand, of which nine thousand are Jews, seven thousand Muslims, and five thousand Christian.[33] The city is small, inward-looking, and crammed with fanatics of every kind.

Perlman makes Devora wear a wig to eavesdrop on the Hebrew usage of ultra-Orthodox women. He names their firstborn Ben-Zion (son of Zion) and speaks to the baby in Hebrew, flying into a rage when his wife sings a Russian lullaby. Intemperate, obdurate, unfeeling, he will do whatever it takes to resurrect the language. Devora dies in 1891 of tuberculosis. The ultra-Orthodox, dismissing her husband as a heretic, refuse to bury her. Perlman takes a new surname, Ben-Yehuda (son of Judea). The ultras tell the Turks he is planning an armed uprising. He is arrested, convicted of sedition, sentenced to a year in jail, and excommunicated by a rabbinic court. On release, he marries Devora's sister, Hemda.

Making a language involves decisions, deliberations, and compromise. It is 1912 before Ben-Yehuda gets his Va'ad Halashon (language committee) to accept Sephardi pronunciation as standard. A lack of syntax and a deficiency of grammar make it difficult to construct a sentence. Should subject precede object? Might noun follow verb? The Pentateuch and Prophets, rich in sacrificial ritual, are useless for shopping, cooking, flirting, and debating, the essentials of modern existence.

Ben-Yehuda composes new words. He takes *hashmal* (electricity) from a psychedelic vision of the Prophet Ezekiel, a word that denotes immediacy and speed. *Machine* (*mechona*) re-vowels a Latin noun. *Motorcar* is *mechonit*. Foodstuffs come mostly from the French— *ananas* for pineapple and *tapuah adama*, apple of the earth, from *pomme de terre*. A Jaffa orange is *apple of gold*, *tapuz* for short. Domestic interiors—*prozdor* or *mizderon* for corridor, *traklin* for lobby—are Aramaic. *Lavatory* uses a rabbinic euphemism—*beit shimush*, utility house. The word for *newspaper* (*iton*) comes from the German *zeitung*, to do with *zeit* or time. *Gelida*, for ice cream, is taken from the Italian *gelato*, followed by the verb *to freeze*, *higlid*.

More than any other source, Ben-Yehuda raids indigenous Arabic. Terms used by neighbors and tradesmen—*nadir* for rare, *adiv* for polite, *mercaz* for center, *bul* for postage stamp, *letifah* for caress—are absorbed unaltered into Hebrew, along with slang words—*kef* (fun), *finjan* (kettle), *yallah* (let's go), *sababa* (feeling good).

He reads forty thousand books and copies half a million citations. Day by day, Hebrew revives. Newspapers appear, followed by novels and recipe books. Tinned foods carry Hebrew labels. Math is taught in Isaiah's tongue. When General Edmund Allenby liberates Jerusalem from the Turks in December 1917, his inaugural proclamation is printed in Hebrew, followed by Arabic, Russian, and Greek.

Mother tongue to the next generation, Hebrew is policed by the pedantic Va'ad Halashon (as a 1970s broadcaster on Israel Radio, I receive regular rebukes from these guardians of lexical correctness). Ben-Yehuda's son, the first Hebrew-speaking child in two thousand years, renames himself Itamar Ben-Avi (son of my father) and writes in English as correspondent for the London *Times* in Jerusalem. Ben-Yehuda dies in 1921. A century later, close to ten million people speak Hebrew as their first language and perhaps ten million more as their second. The scale of Ben-Yehuda's achievement may be measured against other language revivals. Finnish has five million speakers, Welsh three million.

There is opposition to the revival. In Warsaw, the optician Eliezer Ludwig Zamenhof tries to get Jews to speak Esperanto, his "universal language," designed to promote world peace and understanding. His *Lingwe uniwersala* appears in 1878, followed by grammar in 1887. An Esperanto Congress is held in 1905 at Boulogne-sur-Mer, France. In the twenty-first century, two thousand people speak Esperanto from infancy and two million claim adult fluency.[34] Ben-Yehuda beats Zamenhof by ten to one (both have roads named after them in Tel Aviv).

Ultra-Orthodox Jews reject modern Hebrew as an abomination (thought they speak it in Israel), and academics mistrust its improvisations. Raphael Loewe, a noted Near Eastern linguist, calls modern Hebrew "the worst thing Zionism ever did to the Jews."[35] And Yiddishists fight a civil war against Hebrew over glasses of lemon tea in Warsaw cafés until Hitler annihilates the Yiddish heartland.

In 1978, Isaac Bashevis Singer, a Polish-Yiddish novelist living in New York, is awarded the Nobel Prize in Literature as an epitaph for his mother tongue. In his acceptance speech, Singer strikes a hopeful note from the Hebrew revival: "For 2,000 years Hebrew was considered a dead language. Suddenly it became strangely alive. What happened to Hebrew may also happen to Yiddish one day." On a visit to his son, who lives in Israel, Singer is told that the prime minister, Menachem Begin, wants to meet him. Two Warsaw Jews, Singer and Begin, take tea in a Tel Aviv hotel overlooking the sea. "Tell me," says Singer, "why did you have to reinvent Hebrew when we have such a beautiful Jewish mother tongue in Yiddish?"

Begin explains that Yiddish is unfit for government. It has no administrative terms, and its elaborate courtesies are unsuited to military situations. To order *shoot!* in Yiddish, an officer would have to speak a full sentence to indicate the possibility of a shot being fired. Why, cries Begin, Yiddish has no words for weapons, no word even for *army*.

Singer surveys the Israeli prime minister with sad, gray eyes. He raises a forefinger in the air and utters a single Yiddish syllable. "Oh!" says Singer. Meaning: *just imagine a world without such things.*

The two men never speak again.[36]

On the site of the tsar's assassination, they build the Church of the Savior on Spilled Blood. The earth burns beneath the feet of Russian Jews. The tsar's chief adviser, Konstantin Pobedonostsev, holds uncompromising views: "The characteristics of the Jewish race are parasitic; for their sustenance they require the presence of another race as 'host' . . . Take them from the living organism, put them on a rock, and they die."[37] Pobedonostsev's remedy for Russia's Jews is "one-third to convert, one-third to migrate, the rest can starve to death." The *Jewish Chronicle* reports in June 1882: "The emigration of the Jews is now the all-absorbing topic of the hour."[38]

Exact numbers are hard to pin down. Between 1881 and 1897, when the first Russian census is taken, it is estimated that something over 1,000,000 Jews take flight. In the 1897 census, there are 5,215,805 Jews left in Russia, mostly within the Pale (in Lithuania-Belarus, they make up 52 percent of the populace). Of these, one-quarter—1,288,000—leave between 1897 and 1914. The total outflow is around 2,500,000 Jews. At this time, there are 10.6 million Jews in the world.

They go wherever they can get in. France is a popular destination. The Jewish population of Paris, thirty thousand in 1881, trebles by 1914. Four streets in the Marais, the "armpit" fourth district of Paris, become *le pletzl*, a yiddishism for *la place*. Others name it Vilna on the Seine for the Lithuanian origin of many immigrants, the intensity of their intellectual discourse, and their future influence on the course of French philosophy, notably through the teachings of the "Litvak," Emmanuel Levinas.

England, with forty-six thousand Jews in 1882, gains a quarter of a million by the First World War. By 1900, there are fifteen kosher butchers on Wentworth Street in London. Bagels replace the breakfast roll on bakery counters. Yiddishisms enter everyday English usage: *shmatter, schmooze, spiel, chutzpah*. The vicar of St. Jude's, Whitechapel, writes to the London *Times*, complaining that his church is "as little used as ever" by immigrants, resistant to the temptations of Anglicanism. A sanitary inspector finds chickens sharing a room with a family of four, "twelve fowls feeding under the bed."[39] Rents soar; wages fall. Men and women work in sweatshops, fourteen hours a day. Life is no easier than it was in *der heym* (home and hearth; both a landscape and an intimate place). But Jews in London have recourse to their own hospital and to a free school that saves children from future indigence. Communities spring up in Hull, Sunderland, Leeds, Liverpool, Derby, Cardiff, Glasgow, and Dublin, where the young James Joyce mingles fruitfully with Jews.

In the German and Austrian capitals, the influx of "Ostjuden" is concentrated in two districts; the Alexanderplatz in Berlin and the Leopoldstadt section of Vienna are recognized Jewish habitats. There is safety in numbers within them; danger beyond. Anti-Semitic attacks are frequent, instigated by student fraternities and tavern drinkers. "I gaze into the gloomiest future," warns the German-Jewish folklorist Berthold Auerbach.[40] More than a quarter of Berlin's Jews come from Russia and Poland. By 1890, Jews amount to 12 percent of Vienna's population, and they do not feel safe.

An alternative destination beckons. In January 1882, a student in Kharkov calls a meeting at his apartment. Israel Belkind has been reading a pamphlet titled *Rome and Jerusalem* by Moses Hess, a sometime ally of Karl Marx, who now calls for a Jewish uprising in the Land of Israel, modeled on the Italian Risorgimento. Hess is one inspiration for Belkind, *Daniel Deronda* another. A third, published on January 1, 1882, is *Auto-Emancipation* by an Odessa physician, Leon Pinsker, a pamphlet in German subtitled *A Warning to His Brethren by a Russian Jew.*

Pinsker analyzes the situation of Jews in Russia and finds it hopeless. He applies a quasi-scientific logic:

> Judeophobia, together with other symbols, superstitions and idiosyncrasies, has acquired legitimacy among all the peoples of the earth with whom the Jews had intercourse. Judeophobia is a variety of demonopathy with the distinction that it is not peculiar to particular races but is common to the whole of mankind, and that this ghost is not disembodied like other ghosts but partakes of flesh and blood, must endure pain inflicted by the fearful mob that imagines itself endangered.
>
> Judeophobia is a psychic aberration. As a psychic aberration it is hereditary, and as a disease transmitted for two thousand years it is incurable.
>
> It is this fear of ghosts, the mother of Judeophobia that has evoked this abstract—I might say Platonic hatred—thanks to which the whole Jewish nation is wont to be held responsible for the real or supposed misdeeds of its individual members, and to be libeled in so many ways, to be buffeted about so shamefully.
>
> Friend and foe alike have tried to explain or to justify this hatred of the Jews by bringing all sorts of charges against them.

Having read Hess, Eliot, and Pinsker, Belkind decides that the moment has come. On January 21, 1882, he forms a group named Bilu, an acronym of Beit Iakov Lechu Venelkha (Isaiah 2:5), a verse they take to mean: "House of Jacob, let's go." Within weeks, Bilu has five hundred members. In summer, they set forth. The first to reach Jaffa, on July 7, 1882, is Isaac Shertok of Pinsk, father of a future prime minister, Moshe Sharett. Belkind follows with his sister, along with Haim Hissin of Mir and Vladimir Dubnow, brother of the celebrated historian Simon Dubnow. In all, fifty-three Bilu members reach the Holy Land that year.

They go to work first at Baron Edmond de Rothschild's farming school in Mikveh Yisrael, until Belkind falls out with the baron's managers and decamps to Gedera. Conditions are brutal. The heat is fierce, disease rife, provisions scarce. "If the Arab storekeepers were not absolutely convinced that we are [secretly] incredibly rich, we would certainly be dead of starvation," writes Hissin.[41] One by one, the Bilu'im drop out. By mid-1883, just twenty-eight remain. Dubnow informs his brother: "The ultimate aim, the *pia desiderata*, is in time to take over the Land of Israel. The Jews will yet arise and, arms in hand (if need be), declare that they are masters of their ancient homeland."[42] Eliezer Ben-Yehuda invites the eight remaining Bilu'im to his Passover meal. He tells them: "The goal is to revive our nation on its land. There are now only five hundred thousand Arabs, who are not very strong and from whom we shall easily take away the country if we do it by stratagem and without incurring their hostility."[43]

As Bilu fizzles out, a bookkeeper from Kremenchug, Salman David Levontin, pays £1,837 to a pair of Arab brothers for 3,340 dunams of sand dune.[44] Levontin, with ten Hovevei Zion (lovers of Zion), calls his hamlet Rishon LeZion (first unto Zion). Baron Rothschild shows them how to plant vines, buys their failed crops, and founds the Carmel winery. "These hands of mine, used only to holding a pen and calculating profits and losses, will they be capable of handling a plough to produce bread for me, my wife and my children?" wonders Levontin.[45] At night, there are armed raids by Arabs. By day, malaria lurks. For recreation, they sing Russian folk songs with Hebrew words and dance a Romanian circle jig, the hora, around the campfire. Together, Bilu and Hovevei Zion form the First Aliyah (Hebrew: ascent). They are the forerunners of the future State of Israel.

For most Jews, America is an unattainable dream. The cost of a third-class ship passage is $125 (£25), plus travel from home to the point of embarkation and a few dollars to maintain them on arrival. Every step of the way is fraught with hazard. "It was two o'clock in the morning when my guide, whose business it was to smuggle out travelers without passports to Germany, called for me," notes Benjamin L. Gordon, of Neustadt, Lithuania. "After walking silently in the dark for about an hour we reached a forest near the frontier . . . From behind trees we could see the guards marching to and fro . . . we heard the shots of revolvers."[46]

Fearing the next pogrom, Russian Jews start to move. In 1881, the number of Jews reaching the US from Russia, Austria-Hungary, and Romania is 5,692. By 1886, arrivals from Russia alone are 14,029. In 1891, they reach 43,457. The total peaks in 1906, post-Kishinev, at 125,234.[47] By 1908, some 62 percent of Jewish arrivals have their passage paid by family already in America; 94 percent give the name of a relative they intend to join.[48] Four out of five Jews who leave Russia sail to America. It is the most significant ethnic influx to the United States since the Irish Potato Famine of the 1840s.

The main departure point for Jewish migrants is Hamburg. The city regulates conditions, specifying minimum bunk space and food per passenger, mostly rusks and salted pork. The US government intervenes, imposing a $100 fine on carriers for each invalid arrival. Shipowners set up screening camps outside Hamburg where passengers wait for a clean bill of health and an available space; ships do not sail until they are absolutely full.

In 1881, things speed up. The North German Lloyd company introduces the Schnelldampfer, a modern liner that cuts journey time across the Atlantic from twenty-two days to fourteen, then to nine. Fares start to fall and crowds to swell. In 1881, exit levels reach a record 123,000. At this moment, a teenaged entrepreneur spots an opportunity.

Albert Ballin is the thirteenth child of a Hamburg travel agent whose business is going bust. Albert, seventeen years old and a school dropout, takes over Morris & Co. on his father's death. No point selling tickets on behalf of other operators, he decides. Better to run one's own line. Ballin persuades a British shipowner, Edward Carr, to convert two cargo ships into people carriers. By dispensing with first-class cabins, they cram in 640 passengers and cut ticket prices by one-third, to 82 marks. Within a year, Ballin has 17 percent of the emigration trade. At twenty-nine, he is recruited at a salary of one hundred thousand marks to run the North America business of Hapag, Hamburg's biggest shipping line. Soon, he is president of Hapag, head of the German shipping industry, and a trusted friend of the emperor, Wilhelm II.

In Hamburg, they look down on him as a Jew. Ballin marries a Christian woman and pays synagogue dues. His best friend is the banker Max Warburg:

Every afternoon, Ballin—often accompanied by his friend Max
Warburg, their top hats tilted toward one another—walked to the
stock exchange. . . . [In] the realm of society Hanseatic custom
sometimes prescribed a rigid segregation of the races. Thus Jews
and Gentiles, who had negotiated with each other at the exchange,
took separate tables at the Alster Pavilion during the coffee hour at
the close of the day's trading.[49]

Short, unhandsome, and irascible, Ballin puts in sixteen-hour days at
the office and is ruthless in crushing worker unrest, but he treats his
penniless passengers well. He bans salted pork and provides kosher
food. He tears down Hapag's rough camps and builds respectable, even
imposing, halls of residence, where travelers find refreshment and
clean beds. "At the HAPAG depot, those who were able paid a mark a
day for room, board, baths, disinfection, and any medication required.
The indigent paid nothing."[50] A model of Ballin's emigrant town is
shown at the 1900 World Exhibition in Paris. It is a harbinger of future
airports, full of air and light and things to buy.

After an 1892 cholera epidemic kills 8,600 Hamburg citizens, Ballin tightens sanitary procedures, in scenes uncomfortably prescient of
Holocaust imagery:

On arrival at the *Auswandererhallen*, the emigrants were relieved
of their clothing and the contents of their baggage, all of which
was then hung on revolving racks and passed through an elaborate steam disinfection process. . . . Maintaining high standards
of cleanliness in the emigration center was rendered very difficult because of the resistance of many emigrants, whose hygienic
obscurantism made them suspicious of the rite of purification.[51]

Hamburg's Social Democratic Party raises a ruckus: "Lord protect you
from Ballin and his hygienic control stations."[52]

Ballin makes Hapag the world's biggest shipping company, with 175
liners and twenty-nine thousand employees. He travels from Africa to
China, promoting global trade. He builds a country house, Little Pots-
dam, a miniature kaiser's palace. Wilhelm II visits for advice on foreign

affairs. Pierpont Morgan offers Ballin $1 million to form a transatlantic shipping monopoly. Ballin has a better idea: he gets a consortium of German shipowners to sign a treaty with Morgan that cuts British lines out of transatlantic passenger traffic. Cunard appeals to the British government for emergency aid. Ballin the failed travel agent is now a power on the high seas.

Scrutinizing Hapag's expenses, he knows to the last crumb exactly what food is served in his halls and on his ships and in what quantities. He tests the menus himself. They need to be nutritious, inoffensive, and cheap. They will now offer Albert Ballin's greatest claim to immortality.

Nobody knows for certain who first thought of roasting a patty of minced beef and serving it inside a fresh-baked bun. The hamburger is a meal in the hand, eaten by workers on their lunch breaks, or on days out by families who cannot afford fancy restaurants. It is the great comestible leveler, suitable alike for country-house barbecues and the front steps of tenement houses. It is a staple food of American democracy, yielding cheeseburgers, bacon burgers, franchise brands, and drive-in outlets with total annual sales of five billion units. Its precise origin, however, remains opaque.

The earliest use of the name is for an eleven-cent dish, the "Hamburger steak," served at a New York restaurant, Delmonico's, in 1873. There is no mention of buns or relish. The first recipe for the Hamburg steak, in *Mrs. Lincoln's Boston Cook Book*, of 1884, is also bun-free. A hamburger joint in Seymour, Wisconsin, claims to have served a hamburger at an 1885 fair in Hamburg, New York. A further claim is made for Louis Lassen, of New Haven, Connecticut, who in 1900 slapped two slices of bread around hot fried beef. The *Chicago Daily News* in 1896 reports "a hamburger sandwich" being sold from a cart. None of these accounts has independent corroboration.

Such evidence as there is points to the German city from which the item takes its name. Food historians suggest the hamburger was created by Hamburg shipping lines to feed passengers fast and cheap; others contend it was devised in America by ex-Hamburg passengers.[53]

The former supposition is the likelier of the two. Hamburg ship-owners need a quick, cheap way to feed the masses. The early Hanseatic moguls dispense salted pork. Albert Ballin feeds kosher food to Jewish migrants: beef, properly slaughtered and salted. Minced and packed, it is frozen as individual portions and quickly flamed into food. Hapag, under Ballin, sets the Atlantic standard for onboard refreshment. In the absence of conclusive evidence to the contrary, I venture to suggest that Albert Ballin of Hamburg is the inventor of the American hamburger. Ballin, a shy man who forbids the Hapag press department to publish anything about him, takes no credit for his culinary and sanitary reforms. He has bigger geopolitical ambitions. His motto is "The world is my field."

> Give me your tired, your poor,
> Your huddled masses yearning to breathe free,
> The wretched refuse of your teeming shore.
> Send these, the homeless, tempest-tost to me,
> I lift my lamp beside the golden door!

The writer of these famous lines is dead long before they are etched into a bronze plaque and affixed to the Statue of Liberty, harbinger of a new life in a new land. The writer, Emma Lazarus, is fifth-generation New York. Her ancestors built the first Sephardi synagogues in Manhattan. Her family is among New York's "upper ten thousand," wealthy and patrician. A cousin is an associate justice of the United States Supreme Court. Emma's parents worship at Temple Emanu-El.

Aged eighteen, Emma Lazarus meets Ralph Waldo Emerson and is blessed by the seer of American letters. She dedicates a collection of poems to Emerson and forms an epistolary friendship with Henry James. Wealthy enough not to worry about work or marriage, she breezes through the 1870s on a dilettante cloud of essays, poetry, and translations. She is more society poet than popular muse, her archaic usages ("tempest-tost") and clumsy meters written for a class that affects culture and receives her efforts with fond warmth. She knows everyone in media, from Joseph Pulitzer down.

At thirty, Emma Lazarus undergoes an identity crisis. She reads *Daniel Deronda* with immediate empathy. A family member, Mrs. Alfred Tobias, is turned away by Judge Hilton from his hotel. Another hotelier, Austin Corbin, declares: "We do not like Jews as a class . . . I am satisfied we should be better off without them."[54]

Lazarus responds to American anti-Semitism with a four-hundred-line poem, "Raschi in Prague," a fantasy about the medieval French-Jewish exegete in a hostile European city. She writes a play that imitates Halévy's opera *La Juive* and sets about producing an American edition of poems by Heinrich Heine, in whom she finds "ineradicable sympathy with things Jewish and . . . inveterate antagonism to the principles and results of Christianity."[55] When boatloads of Russian Jews begin docking in New York, Emma is among the first volunteers at Wards Island, teaching English and American skills to the huddled masses. Speaking no Yiddish, she employs sign language. "When I arrived," recalls Abraham Cahan, founding editor of the *Yiddish Forverts* newspaper, "the immigration committee included one wealthy young Jewish lady who belonged to the cream of the monied aristocracy. She was Emma Lazarus. She often visited the immigrants' camp on Wards Island in the East River, but this never undermined her status as an aristocrat."[56]

In September 1882, she publishes *Songs of a Semite*, followed by *Epistle to the Hebrews*. "Wake, Israel, wake!" she cries. "Recall today the glorious Maccabean rage . . . Oh for the Jerusalem trumpet now!" Her assertion of Jewish nationalism draws the wrath of Temple Emanu-El Jews who fear the light she shines on their ethnicity will impede their advancement to full integration. Among her antagonists is a member of the Sulzberger dynasty, owners of the *New York Times*.

Mingling with pogrom victims is the making of Emma Lazarus. She speaks out for human dignity and resists Jewish plans to disperse refugees out of New York. A committee of bankers furnishes new migrants with long-distance, one-way train tickets. "Go [they say]. Our land is big and fruitful, go ahead and live on it by begging."[57] Schnorrers besiege far-flung communities. Destitute widows and daughters resort to prostitution. A Reform rabbi in Fort Worth gets "Jew whores" arrested to protect his synagogue's reputation. "I went to the jail and took with me a man who could speak Yiddish. The stories we heard were tragic. They were in the sordid business because it was the only way they had of earning bread and butter. Some were supporting their children . . . their parents . . . Our women's committee wouldn't even speak to them."[58] "We don't want any kikes in our congregation," says one synagogue leader, turning an anti-Jewish pejorative on his own folk. "If you're a Polack, don't come back," thunders a Chicago rabbi.[59] In Louisiana, an agricultural settlement for thirty-four families from the Elizavetgrad pogrom is wiped out when the Mississippi River floods. Settlements in Oregon and the Dakotas founder in similar fashion.[60]

Against the current of American Jewish self-interest, Emma Lazarus expounds a pride in Jewish identity and a faith in the American dream. She writes her signature poem, "The New Colossus," to be recited on December 3, 1883, at a fund-raiser for the future Statue of Liberty. Joseph Pulitzer publishes it in the *New York World* and Adolph Ochs in the *New York Times*. Emma Lazarus composes a sequel, "1492," linking Columbus's discovery of America to the expulsion of her Jewish ancestors from Spain.

She then sails to Europe to reflect on her life. Marriage is out of the question; none of her sisters has bothered to get hitched, why should she? Emma takes a keen interest in what are known as "Boston marriages"—two women living together as a couple. While there is no evidence of any love affair with another woman, a sonnet hints at unfulfilled desires:

> Last night I slept, & when I woke her kiss
> Still floated on my lips. For we had strayed . . .

She sails a second time to Europe in 1885, returning critically ill with Hodgkin's disease. At the dedication of the Statue of Liberty by President Grover Cleveland, her poem is not recited. Emma Lazarus dies in New York on November 19, 1887, at the age of thirty-eight. Her devoted sisters take care to remove "anything Jewish" from her collected poems.

In May 1903, a bronze plaque is mounted on the Statue of Liberty, bearing the words of "The New Colossus" and its author's dates. The poem becomes a foundation text of the American dream, taught in schools and quoted by successive presidents. Emma Lazarus has given the United States of America its human face. Her country as "a mighty woman with a torch," the Mother of Exiles. She defines an America that millions hold dear and millions more will, in harsh times, seek to deny.

SIX

1890
TWO BEARDS ON A TRAIN

Two beards in search of a story: Theodor Herzl, Solomon Schechter.

For the first time in history, Jews are found on five continents. Six thousand Jews register in an 1895 census in Argentina, most of them in Entre Rios province, where Baron Hirsch trains Jewish gauchos in flying fringes to ride across his ranches. There are sixteen thousand Jews in Australia, sixteen hundred in New Zealand. Dishonest sea captains dump Lithuanian Jews in South Africa, assuring them that they have reached America. By the 1890s, their number exceeds fifty thousand.

Two thousand Jews live in China, many in Shanghai, operating family trading networks that run through Singapore, Bombay, and Calcutta and back home to Baghdad and Aleppo. Shanghai's waterfront, known as the Bund, is built up by the Kadoories, the Hardoons, the Ezras and Nissims, Abrahams and Gubbays; most of all by the Sassoons, who create the iconic Cathay Hotel, a landmark of 1920s decadence that the Communists rename the Peace Hotel. Jews learn to eat Chinese kosher. Preachers see a harbinger of messianic times, quoting Isaiah (11:12) that the Lord will gather in the dispersed of Judah from all four corners of the Earth.

Dispersion disrupts the old order. In the Old World, Jews consult a rabbi on moral, ritual, and legal issues. In the pampas and the paddy fields, there may be no rabbi, or none a troubled Jew can trust. Disoriented, the Jew turns to bookstores. The most popular ethical tract is by Israel Meir Kagan of Radin, known as the Chofetz Chaim (Hebrew: the life seeker). Vilifying loose talk and advocating personal asceticism, Kagan sells his books door-to-door. "The journey is never too hard if you know you are going home," he assures believers. "You cannot attack darkness with weapons" is another of his aphorisms. "Light a candle [of Torah] and the darkness will disperse of itself." Responding to inquiries from all four corners, he is the first super-rabbi of a connected universe. The Chofetz Chaim dies in 1933, aged ninety-five, revered for his poverty, his humility, and for never holding an official post.

Of comparable stature is the troubled figure of Israel (Lipkin) Salanter. Founder of a Musar stream (ethical movement) that advocates intensive self-examination, Salanter suffers from midlife depression and moves to Prussia to recover in the home of wealthy supporters. "To succeed in business you need talent," he tells his hosts, "but if you have such a talent, why waste it on business?" His writings ripple with paradoxes. The first Lithuanian rabbi to set up in the godless West and the first to attempt a translation of the Talmud into German, Salanter writes about morality and motivation, about conscious and unconscious impulses, in a manner that anticipates Sigmund Freud. Some see him as a pioneer of mindfulness, others as a forerunner of self-improvement books. He drifts to Paris, combating Reform with mild wit. "Reform," he would say, "came to reform Judaism. I come to reform Jews." His mailbox bulges with far-flung requests. Hasidim designate him the rebbe of the intellectuals.

In Shanghai, the perplexed send their questions to Baghdad. If Shanghai Jews need to know whether an exotic bird is kosher, a divorcée marriageable, a contract legal, or a partnership dissoluble, they write to Haham Yosef Hayim, the supreme *posek* (interpreter) of Jewish law in the Sephardi world. The Haham holds no official position. His status is established at fourteen years old, when he intercepts a query to his father from Jerusalem rabbis and replies within hours, with an immaculate resolution. By his midtwenties, his spiritual authority holds sway from Tunisian Djerbah to British Calcutta. His responses fill four thick volumes, among twenty-four books that appear under his chosen name, Ben Ish Hai (Hebrew: son of a living man). The Ben Ish Hai fulfills no public duties, other than giving four sermons a year in the great synagogue, but each Sabbath afternoon he sits at a low table and teaches for three hours. His lectures open with an item from the day's Torah reading, expanding to its ramifications in Talmud, its mystic connotations in the Zohar, and, finally, its application to everyday life. The Ben Ish Hai regards all branches of Jewish law and lore as equal and indivisible. He is the first sage to teach Talmud and Kabbalah as parallel streams of Judaism.

His writings are a repository of social history. A handbook for women, written in Baghdad Arabic, shows more concern than the Ashkenazi *poskim* for women's rights in marriage. He orders women not to perform any "humiliating" act demanded by the husband, and he requires men who divorce a wife "without reason" to compensate her for reputational damage. Other responses shed light on relations between Jews and Arabs in Baghdad, to all appearances convivial. A Jew asks if, on his way home from synagogue on a Sabbath, he may drop into his regular coffeehouse and drink a shot of Turkish coffee. Although commerce and cooking are prohibited on the Sabbath, the Haham decides that if the man is used to settling his café bill at the end of the month and if the *finjan* is already on the hob and not put there specially for him, there is no reason to deny him a Saturday *qahwa* with Muslim and Christian friends.

These are the decisions of a sage who, while personally frugal, encourages the simple pleasures of life. In a further departure from Western Orthodoxy, he allows members of the community to send their children to secular Alliance Israelite schools.[1] The Jews of Iraq in the time of the Ben Ish Hai engage with the world at large.

Between the Ben Ish Hai and Western scholars lies a gulf of mysticism. In the Haham's view, every human act has a critical bearing on the balance of the universe. The routine of getting dressed in the morning must be conducted in a stipulated order to avoid impurity and refrain from awakening dark forces that might blight the offender's life. He advises followers to rise at midnight; sleeping later in the night does not refresh the soul. He advises frequent hand washing, three times each hand, and deplores the Western invention of toilet paper as inefficient and impure. Cleanliness is the route to godliness.

Visiting the Holy Land, he receives a revelation. At the tombs of patriarchs and prophets near the town of Safed, he discovers that he is the physical reincarnation of Benayahu, son of Yehoyada, one of King David's warriors. He affixes a stone from the tomb into the wall of Baghdad's great synagogue and kisses it each time he passes. "In the time of Haham Josef Hayim," writes a community historian, "a great longing for visiting and dwelling in the Holy Land took hold of the pious among Baghdadi Jews."[2]

At his death, in September 1909, Baghdadi Jews shut their shops for a week. He is the greatest Sephardi legalist in three centuries, revered from the Mediterranean to the Pacific; his many publications are consulted to this day. Through the Ben Ish Hai, the thirteenth-century school of mysticism known as Kabbalah invades the heart of Jewish learning. Lubricating arid legalism with phantasmagorical tales of angels and demons, miracles and revelations, the Ben Ish Hai regards Kabbalah as integral to Torah, inseparable from Talmud and its commentators. What has hitherto been a logical, lexical approach to textual analysis of Talmud is now conjoined to Eastern mysticism.

In the second-class carriage of a train to Cambridge, in October 1890, a full-bearded man is immersed in his papers, oblivious to the student din around him. The man looks like a junior lecturer or a country vicar. The gingery beard hints at iconoclasm. Untrimmed, it exudes repressed energies. Something about the man does not fit. His coat is creased, his accent untraceable. He is an alien and proud of it, a man of no fixed abode. In Cambridge, Solomon Schechter's beard will acquire a life of its own, bursting into rooms, bristling at opponents. Schechter, in the next decade, will overturn the received history of the Jewish people; after that, he will alter the state of American Jewry for all time.

None of this can be foretold from his curriculum vitae to this point. At the age of forty-two, Schechter has never held a job. He has lived for learning alone until late fatherhood requires him to earn an income. The death of Solomon Schiller-Szenessy, Cambridge University's first reader in rabbinics and Talmud, presents an opportunity. The post consists of helping Anglican divines with details of Jewish law and teaching Aramaic to theology students. Friends assure Schechter that he will have plenty of time to examine rare manuscripts in the university library. Archives are Schechter's greatest joy in life; he pesters the librarian, Francis Jenkinson, at all hours of the day, night, and weekend, "until the last candle burns out." It is not clear to Jenkinson, on first acquaintance, what Schechter is after.

The son of a *shochet* (slaughterer) in Foscani, a Romanian town, Schechter is named Shneur Zalman after the founder of the Lubavitch dynasty. Lubavitch, using the acronym *Chabad* (Hebrew: wisdom, understanding, knowledge), is a hybrid of Hasidic and scholastic Judaism, moderating ecstatic worship with immersive study of its rebbes' texts. The founding rebbe, Shneur Zalman of Liadi (1745–1813), leaves a Torah commentary, the *Tanya*, which is amplified by the third rebbe, Menachem Mendel Schneersohn (1789–1866). The Lubavitch movement is little known beyond Russia. Like all Hasidim, Lubavitch trust their rebbe in all matters, spiritual and personal; none would ever marry without his blessing.

Shneur Zalman Schechter studies Torah with his father at three years old and supposedly knows it by heart at five. A restless child, he is forever having to be rescued from treetops. Designated an Ilui, or "prodigy," he is married at eighteen, at the rebbe's suggestion, to a girl from a wealthy family. It is a horrific mistake. Within months, Schechter leaves his wife and never speaks of her again. His faith severely tested, he turns to secular books. In the first study of Hasidim ever to be published in English, Schechter writes:

119

I confess there was a time when I loved the Hasidim and a time when I hated them. And even now I am not able to suppress these feelings. I have rather tried to guide my feelings in such a way as to love in Hasidism what is ideal and noble and to hate in it what turned out bad and pernicious for Judaism.

He soon adds:

As an active force for good, Hasidism was short-lived.[3]

At twenty-four, Schechter renames himself Solomon and goes to Vienna, where he attends a year of university, searching for a sustainable faith. He moves on to Abraham Geiger's reformist "Academy for Jewish Science" in Berlin while privately observing Orthodox rites. No longer a fundamentalist, he needs the comforts of prayer, the warmth of Hasidic song. Torn between head and heart, Schechter formulates his own definition of Halakha, the code of Jewish law, as the conscience of the Jewish people, evolving as it moves through time. He blames Reform for "disloyalty to the law"[4] and embracing the critical hypothesis of the Protestant Julius Wellhausen, who claims the Torah is the work of four male authors and that rabbinic Judaism stems from a minor Babylonian sect. Schechter calls Wellhausen's Higher Criticism "the Higher Antisemitism."

He is rescued from Berlin by a wealthy English student, Claude Goldsmid Montefiore, who brings him to London in 1882 on the promise of access to British Museum manuscripts. From his first day in Britain, Schechter is as happy as a boy in a toy shop, intoxicated by the must of urtexts and enchanted by the lack of fanaticism among English Jews. He meets the acting chief rabbi, Hermann Adler; the Reform rabbi of West London Synagogue, Albert Löwy; and the Haham of the Spanish and Portuguese community, Moses Gaster. All warm their hands on his expertise, knowing that he has no designs on their pulpits. All Schechter wants is to develop a "science of Jewish learning." With a subsidy from Montefiore, he publishes the eighth-century *Avot de Rabbi Nathan*, a collection of rabbinic sayings, possibly an offshoot of the Mishna tractate *Avot*. Reviewers, both Christians and Jews, get so excited by his insights that the intemperate Schiller-Szenessy accuses

Schechter of copying from his blotting pad at the British Museum. With the writer Israel Zangwill, Schechter founds a debating society in Kilburn, North London. They call it "The Wanderers," because they drift from one member's home to another's. Members include the *Law Journal* editor Herbert Bentwich, the artist Solomon J. Solomon, and the *Jewish Chronicle* editor Asher Myers. "I can see him," says Bentwich, "rising from his chair, pacing up and down the room like a wounded lion and roaring retorts."[5] Schechter is almost forty, his promise inchoate, his destiny unclear.

One day in the British Museum he finds himself sitting next to Mathilde Roth, a young woman from Breslau who is studying English literature and boarding with the principal of Jews' College. Over tea at the Vienna Café on Oxford Street, Schechter falls in love, but he cannot bring himself to tell Mathilde, inhibited as he is by the trauma of his early marriage. Haham Gaster, taking matters in hand, buys four tickets to a concert of Joseph Haydn's oratorio *The Creation* at St. James's Hall, Piccadilly, and, on the way home, gets Schechter to ask Mathilde to marry him.

An impediment arises. It appears Schechter has never divorced his first wife. Letters fly between London and Foscani. On June 22, 1887, in Charles Dickens's former home at Tavistock House, now the residence of Jews' College, a marriage is solemnized between Solomon and Mathilde. Three rabbis—Adler, Gaster, and Löwy—officiate beneath the chuppah, each representing a rival splinter of Jewish faith. The guest of honor is Heinrich Graetz, the notoriously revisionist historian. In this rare moment of Jewish harmony, a vision forms in Schechter's brain. He names it Catholic Israel, and it becomes his lifelong ideal.

Cambridge provides a framework for his life. Settling with Mathilde in a rented cottage near the railway station, he is known as "that wild man of stupendous genius" for his vibrant interventions at High Table, where he refuses food and wine until Christ's College provides kosher refreshment.[6] The Arabist William Robertson Smith, editor of the *Encyclopaedia Britannica*, becomes an admirer. Another is the master of St. John's College, Charles Taylor, a mathematician and Hebraist who has made his own edition of the Mishna tractate *Avot*. Known as "Jumbo" for his vast girth, Taylor is a Cambridge bachelor of substantial wealth who attends Schechter's Tuesday-afternoon class to keep up his Hebrew fluency and court his friendship. Despite such useful contacts, Schechter feels like a fish out of water. There are hardly any Jewish students in the university, and degrees are not granted to women. "Slightly unwelcome" is how one modern scholar describes his situation.[7] "I have no influence among the Christians here," grumbles Schechter. "Is the mission of theology, like that of the leader-writer in *The Times*, . . . to register public opinion and throw it in some shape of Oxford English with a touch of sham philosophy so that the Philistines are almost astonished at the depth of their own wisdom?"[8]

His Gladstonian rhetoric is founded on new English novels, supplied by his librarian Jenkinson. On a Sunday, the former Lubavitch Hasid might be found walking arm in arm beside the Cam with a Jesuit from Trinity, or with the reclusive James George Frazer, author of *The Golden Bough*. His cottage by the station provides an easy getaway for spending the Jewish Sabbath in London.

He has been in Cambridge for five years when, in the spring of 1896, two Scottish Presbyterian sisters, Mrs. Lewis and Mrs. Gibson, return from Egypt with a stash of manuscripts. The sisters, who are twins, have stayed in Cambridge after being widowed to pursue researches in Semitic studies, their passion since girlhood. Intrepid travelers, they climbed Mount Sinai in 1893 to retrieve the earliest extant copy of the Gospels in the original Syriac—Agnes Lewis's specialist language—and returned to Egypt in pursuit of further treasures. Margaret Gibson, a fluent Arabic speaker, does much of the sifting, checking, bargaining, and photography. On their 1896 adventure, they recover objects from the *genizah* (hiding place) of the ancient Ben Ezra Synagogue at Fustat, outside Cairo. In Cambridge, they seek Schechter's help in clarifying and classifying their finds.

Schechter is none too excited at first. He knows about the *genizah* at Fustat: Jewish law forbids the misuse or destruction of any document that bears God's name. Old Torah scrolls, disintegrating books, marriage and divorce certificates, and the like are either stored in a *genizah* or buried in a cemetery. In the Ben Ezra Synagogue, built in 1040, there is a room of scraps dating back to before the time of Maimonides. Its existence has long been known. An uncle of Heinrich Heine's, Simon Van Geldern, visited in 1752 and took away some fragments. Local treasure hunters are deterred by rumors of a fearsome serpent. A Russian called Firkovitch plunders papers for the tsar's library. A Jerusalem rabbi, Solomon Wertheimer, employs a Yemenite Jew to filch morsels for sale to British libraries. The British chief rabbi's brother, Elkan Adler, risks his neck on a rickety ladder, the only access to the attic, in September 1888. "The steps were rotten and as I stood on the topmost rung I swayed and felt like Mahomet, 'twixt heaven and earth."[9] Adler, who comes away with nothing much, informs Schechter of his failure.

Now, on May 13, 1896, Schechter doffs his hat to Agnes Lewis on Kings Parade. Mrs. Lewis tells him about two Hebrew documents she and her sister just brought back. Schechter, himself a twin, feels a kinship with the Presbyterian widows, who are scoffed at by stuffy dons at High Table. He identifies one manuscript without ado as "a part of the Jerusalem Talmud, of which few copies exist." A welcome discovery but not earth-shattering. The other item he takes away for close scrutiny in his cottage. It does not take him long to reach a momentous conclusion. That night, Schechter dashes off an exhilarated response.

Dear Mrs Lewis,

I think we have reason to congratulate ourselves. For the fragment I took with me represents a piece of the Original Hebrew of Ecclesiasticus. It is the first time that such a thing was discovered. Please do not speak yet about the matter until tomorrow. I will come to you tomorrow about 11 p.m. and talk over the matter with you how to make the matter known.

In haste and great excitement,
Yours sincerely,

S. Schechter[10]

Such is his agitation that he writes *p.m.* for *a.m.* and has to ask Mathilde to send another letter to correct his mistake. Before they go to bed that night, he impresses on his wife the significance of this day: "As long as the Bible lives, my name shall not die. Now telegraph Mrs. Lewis and Mrs. Gibson to come immediately."[11]

The book of Ecclesiasticus is the work of a Jewish scribe, Ben Sira, written in Jerusalem two centuries before Christ. Omitted from the Hebrew Bible, it is referenced in the Babylonian Talmud and included in the Greek version of the Christian Bible. The Hebrew text has been lost for so long that its very existence is denied by Christians. Schechter has a section in his hands: Might the whole book be buried in the same Fustat attic? The possibility is almost too thrilling to contemplate. Ben Sira is a major player at a formative time. He would have been an observer at meetings that resolved the final edition of the books of the Bible. His teachings are both authentically Jewish and influential on the Christian Apostles. Be humble, he says, because man's future is worms. A man who holds back his employee's wages is shedding his blood. Sin begins with woman; because of her, we die.

Ben Sira's book discusses death, friendship, finance, sex, and sin. Its homilies are drawn from Torah and filtered through generations of prophets and rabbis, as described in *Avot*: "Moses received Torah at Sinai and gave it to Joshua and Joshua [passed it] to the Elders and the Elders to the Prophets and the Prophets to the Men of the Great Assembly." Ben Sira died in the same year as the last of the Men of the Great Assembly. He is a vital missing link between Torah and Mishna, proof positive, *pace* Wellhausen, of Jewish integrity and continuity. The fragment, for Schechter, is an object of unparalleled importance.

To ward off their common enemy, the dusty Anglican academics, he asks the sisters to announce their find in *The Athenaeum* while he decides what to do next. Elkan Adler, just back from a second trip, confides that the *genizah* is now a bit easier to reach after building work at the Ben Ezra. Schechter hears a warning shot from Oxford; Adolf Neubauer, reader in rabbinics, has found Ben Sira scraps in the Bodleian and is threatening an expedition to Egypt. Schechter tells his Cambridge friends there is no time to lose. A philosopher, Henry Sidgwick, offers to finance Schechter's research trip to Cairo, only to be trumped by Charles Taylor, who, as Schechter's friend and student, insists on defraying all costs without telling or involving anyone else at the college.

In December 1896, Schechter takes a train to Marseilles and a ship to Cairo, sweltering on deck in his English tweeds. He carries a letter of introduction from chief rabbi Adler to the rabbi of Cairo, Raphael Aharon Ben Shimon, and another from the vice-chancellor of Cambridge University to the British representative, Lord Cromer. But he is nervous. He has no idea whether the Jews will grant him access to the *genizah*, and he has no clear plan for how he might export the bulk of its contents. He will have to rely on charm, cigarettes, and some of the pound notes that Taylor has stuffed in his jacket pockets as ready bribes.

The chief rabbi of Cairo turns out to be a handsome, scholarly man, fluent in five languages and happy to introduce Schechter to leading families, who will make the ultimate decision about the *genizah*. Days and weeks are wasted "smoking endless cigarettes, drinking endless cups of tea." He does not know from one week to the next if he will be granted access. Schechter takes the rabbi to visit the pyramids, which he has seen only from afar. Feasts and fasts occasion further delays, as do preparations for the Sabbath, which start in the middle of the week. Schechter finds Cairo "a glorious place, enjoying an Italian opera, French dancing masters, English administration and Mohammetan houris."[12] But still no *genizah*. Agnes Lewis turns up to see how he is getting along. A Dutch journalist, Anna de Wit, wants to interview him for an article. Finally, Rabbi Ben Shimon takes Schechter to the *genizah*.

"The entrance is on the west side," he reports, "through a big, shapeless hole reached by a ladder. After showing me over the place and the neighbouring buildings, or rather ruins, the Rabbi introduced me to the beadles of the synagogue, who are at the same time the keepers of the Genizah, and authorised me to take from it what, and as much as, I liked."

> Now, as a matter of fact, I liked all. Still, some discretion was necessary. I have already indicated the mixed nature of the Genizah. But one can hardly realize the confusion in a real old Genizah until one has seen it. It is a battlefield of books, a battle in which the literary production of many centuries had their share, and their *disjecta membra* are now strewn over its area. Some of the belligerents have perished outright, and are literally ground to dust in the terrible struggle for space, whilst others, as if overtaken by a general crush, are squeezed into big unshapely lumps, which even with the aid of chemical appliances can no longer be separated without serious damage to their constituents.[13]

This account of his activities is published in the London *Times*. At the dawn of classical archaeology and exploration, the excavations of a Cambridge scholar in a Cairo attic are cause for public excitement.

125

Schechter's *Times* articles are syndicated to American media. His work is world news.

He spends a month in the attic, surrounded by boxes, examining scrap after scrap for removal or rejection. By January 12, he has thirteen sacks of "many glorious things."[14] What next? Concerned for the integrity of the *genizah* and his own rights to it, he writes that night to the librarian Francis Jenkinson, alternately his ally and adversary, in a letter far less laid-back than his published articles:

Hotel Metropole
Cairo 12 Jan 97
(c/o Cook's Agency)

<u>Private</u>

Dear Mr. Jenkinson,

I am now here since three weeks. After making the ~~acqai~~ acquaintance of the Chief Rabbi here and the president of the Jewish community I set to work on the "Genizas" where I ~~spent~~ spend the most of my time in the dust of centuries. The beadel & other infernal scoundrels are helping me to clear away the rubbish and the printed matter. I have constantly to bakeshish them but still they are stealing many good things and sell them to the dealers in ~~an~~ antiquities. I cannot possibly prevent it, but I found out the said dealers and bought from them the fragments which have interest for me. In the <u>Genizah</u> itself which is dark dusty and full of all possible ~~in~~ insects there is no opportunity of examining the content of MSS. My policy is to take as much as I can (for which I have the full permission of the authorities). I have till now thirteen large ~~sacks~~ bags of fragments, ~~of~~ which though not examined, I am ~~su~~ sure, contain many most important things.

Now I have a great request on you. I do not consider it desirable to the MSS here and am anxious to send the first lot ~~hone~~ home to England. Will you ~~receive them~~ give them a place in the University Library till I return. The MSS will probably belong soon to your Library. I want only to hear first whether you and the Syndics will agree to certain conditions which I have to make. Money plays no important part in these conditions and I am sure you will find them <u>very</u> fair and <u>just</u>. <u>But till then I want the MSS to be considered as my private property; so that the boxes must not be opened before I have returned. For I am very anxious to [be] the first to examine them properly.</u> ~~Can~~ If you cannot agree to these conditions will you do me the ~~favou~~ favour to send at once—when the boxes ~~to~~ arrive for Mrs Schechter (2 Rock Road) and hand her over the boxes, who will bring them into some place of ~~saf~~ safety till I return p.g.

I repeat again that I do not mean to make a bargain with the University. I have not the least doubt that you will find the terms just and fair. What I am chiefly anxious is that no body would ~~th~~ see the MSS before I have examined them. Therefore I want you to consider them as my private property till then.

I feel fairly well and am rather thankful that it is cold. Otherwise it would be unbearable to live in this dus[t] & underground. How are you? PG I intend to stay here another three weeks as the Jews have here so many feasts and fasts in which I cannot work.

With best regards,
yours very truly

S. Schechter[15]

A Fustat photograph shows Schechter, sitting at a trestle table at the far end of the attic, his huge head resting on his right hand while his left riffles through a millennium of detritus. By the end of the month he is done. He believes he has set aside 140,000 items for shipment; in fact, there are 190,000. Working every day, except Saturday and much of Friday, Schechter has chosen 6,000 pieces a day, making snap decisions, lacking time to set things to one side for a second guess. Scholars a hundred years hence will marvel at his eye, "an eye that spotted, seemingly at first glance, the important, the significant and the extraordinary from the great mass of texts that confronted him."[16] His confidence is all the more astounding when we learn that, for all his expertise in Hebrew and Aramaic, he cannot read Judeo-Arabic, the vernacular of much of the collection, and has only just begun to learn Arabic. His is not, by any criterion, a scientific search. It resembles more a journalistic raid on a conquered city, scooping up whatever comes to hand with a fast-scanning eye for a story and an awareness of predatory competitors and a looming deadline.

Not content with ransacking the loft, Schechter digs up graves in the cemetery with Mrs. Gibson and Mrs. Lewis. Sweating in a black frock coat, his activity is frenzied, his health impaired. Savaged by mosquitoes, his lungs congested with the dust of ages, Schechter cries himself to sleep at night, missing Mathilde and their three children, longing to be back in Francis Jenkinson's nice clean library in Cambridge, where order and silence prevail and the milk in his tea has not gone sour. Like Dr. Livingstone on the Zambezi, he suffers every single inch of the way and longs to rejoin civilization. In one of his last letters home, he promises Mathilde that he will never travel again without her.

But he does not go straight home. Leaving Egypt, he sails to the Holy Land to see his twin brother for the first time in twenty years in his new village, Zikhron Ya'akov. Schechter falls in love with the ancient land and endorses the Zionist cause. He is almost tempted to stay, but there is work to be done, and he parts in tears from his twin.

It takes all of three months for his cargo to be shipped from Cairo, unloaded in London, and delivered to Cambridge. On the morning of May 11, 1897, Francis Jenkinson opens the first box. At two p.m., he calls in Taylor, Schechter, Mrs. Lewis, and Mrs. Gibson, who are awed by the magnitude of the task ahead. "Looking over this enormous mass of fragments about me, in the sifting and examination of which I am now occupied," sighs Schechter, "I cannot overcome a sad feeling that I shall hardly be worthy to see the results which the Genizah would add to our knowledge of Jews and Judaism."

This is no understatement. Schechter's find will open vast fields of study: into the eighth-century editors of the Talmud, the working life of Maimonides, the isolated Jews of Yemen, and the traders of Bombay, adding an entire hemisphere to the known history of the Jews. There are varied early editions of the Jewish prayer book, poems by Yehuda Halevi in Spain, and an account of how the kingdom of the Khazars, in southern Russia, converted to Judaism in the eighth century. I have seen an Amidah prayer, unknown in Europe, calling down curses on the heads of early Christian defectors. There is a draft in Maimonides's hand of his *Guide to the Perplexed*, possibly the most contentious Jewish theology of all time. The oldest *genizah* document dates to the fifth century CE.

The sheer range of material refutes Christianity's view of Judaism as defunct by demonstrating its vivid evolution through engagement with other cultures. For Cambridge scholars, the greatest thrill lies in a discarded parchment containing Greek Bible commentaries, over-written with Hebrew devotional verses. One wispy academic actually crashes his bicycle on seeing the script of an early Gospel writer in its basket. From Schechter's point of view, the Ben Sira find is of the highest importance. Last seen by Saadiyah Gaon in tenth-century Baghdad, it connects the central works of Jewish thought and history: Torah, Mishna, Talmud, Midrash. Schechter has found the key to Jewish connectivity, and he is impatient to do more.

Jenkinson, a lonely widower who lives for his work, is our most trustworthy witness of Schechter's temperament, charting his moods as closely as he does the day's temperature, the wind direction, and the weather, which he logs at the top of each page. On Saturday, May 15, four days after the first crate is opened, Jenkinson writes:

> When I got to the Library I found Schechter had been making a row & declaring someone had cut one of his fragments—(it had been folded & then snipped so as to leave diamond-shaped holes). Luckily I had noticed it before, & had in fact myself put it on his table; so I was able to give him a good setting down for his impertinence and violence.

These are strong words, tantamount to a denial of service. Schechter apologizes. Relations between librarian and explorer remain tense:

> Saturday August 21
> Schechter called but I did not go with him. At the Library, I had too much of him. He had found 2 more leaves (doubled to make four) of the Aquila Psalms (?) He wanted to take out a novel he could not have. The puff preliminary of the Aquila in The Atheneum does not mention his name (which ought to have been done). And being Saturday he had nothing to do. C. Taylor came in and Robinson identified Wednesday's palimpsest . . .

Jenkinson is the first to record that Schechter is calling at his place of work on the Jewish Sabbath. There can only be three reasons for this. Either he is losing his faith, he has fallen out with Mathilde, or he is looking for the exit. One day, Schechter blows up at Mrs. Lewis, who refuses to touch another fragment unless asked to do so by Jenkinson.[17] Schechter's focus has gone.

On a visit to Philadelphia and Baltimore, a year before the *genizah* excavation, he finds himself for the first time since childhood in towns that are heavily Jewish. In Cambridge, he is an oddity, a bearded wonder, an object of mild amusement. He fears for his children's education. In America, he could be a man of consequence. A letter arrives from the Jewish Theological Seminary, announcing the death of its founder, Sabato Morais. The JTS trains what its financier Jacob Schiff calls "reasonable" rabbis. Schechter sees it as the potential incubator of "Catholic Israel." In the spring of 1902, after firing off four acrid essays on Anglo-Jewry at the *Jewish Chronicle*, Solomon Schechter takes his family to New York for the crowning epoch of his life.

As president of the Jewish Theological Seminary, Schechter is the preeminent rabbi in America, a dazzling teacher, provocative thinker, counter-Reformation leader. He revives the Jewish Publication Society, coedits the *Jewish Encyclopedia*, and is the first Jew to receive an honorary doctorate at Harvard, sharing the platform with Henry James. He preaches, publicizes, punches friend and foe alike. In the First World War, he affronts Schiff by condemning German aggression and urging America to enter the war on the British side.

He gathers middle-ground communities into a United Synagogue of America, modeled on the British prototype. His timing is pinpoint. Jews arriving from Russia find no warmth in Reform temples and no sympathy from Orthodox rabbis for their need to work on Saturdays. Schechter's organization offers all the old tunes from back home without angry sermons. His rabbinic students are taught tolerance above all other values. On November 19, 1915, Schechter suffers a heart attack at home and, calling for Mathilde to bring him a book because he cannot lie idle until the doctor arrives, expires at the age of sixty-seven. He leaves behind the largest, most powerful synagogue body in the world and a network of Solomon Schechter Schools across America.

As for the *genizah*, Cambridge has no idea how to handle it after

Schechter leaves. Some, over the next half century, call for it to be removed or destroyed. A German-Jewish ethnographer, Shlomo Dov Goitein, recognizes it in the 1950s as an unparalleled resource for studying a millennium of social and economic life around the Mediterranean. It is now a treasured part of the library of Cambridge University, accessible by appointment. The chief takeaway for the non-specialist visitor like me is the dynamism it reveals within Judaism, a faith that adapts to all weathers without compromising its core. This is the grail that Schechter has sought, the proof of his people's resilience.

On a wintry Sabbath morning, in a Conservative synagogue in the middle of North America, the rabbi pulls up in his car, followed by the cantor. They enter the building, switching on the lights. The rabbi dons a prayer shawl without uttering a blessing, clips a microphone to his lapel, and goes, "Testing, testing." The cantor plugs in an electronic keyboard. Solomon Schechter would have been horrified at these clerical violations of Halakha.

The community I am visiting is Conservative chiefly in the sense that it does not employ a female or gay rabbi. Families who have prayed here for five generations have resisted rapid-onset diversity. They want things to stay the way they were. Like most static bodies, this shul is in precipitate decline. The main synagogue is too expensive to heat, so we commune in a side chapel. Most of the worshippers are past retirement age. The rabbi throws in a few Yiddish words for the most senior attendees. The least mobile members are watching the service online.

This is Schechter's Catholic Israel a century after his death. The middle ground of American Jewry has caved in to waves of assimilation, alternative belief systems, emigration to Israel, and rampant neo-Orthodoxy. All the United Synagogue has left to offer is warmed-up sentiment. The Coen brothers' much-praised movie *A Serious Man* exposes the helplessness of a suburban Jew in a Conservative synagogue that offers no answers to life's crises. In the synagogue that I visit, the rabbi's sermon has words of praise for the Maharishi Mahesh Yogi, an Indian guru who lured away 1970s Jewish seekers of mystic experience. The cantor chants a prayer for the State of Israel, which absorbs the most idealistic American Jews. And the return of strict Orthodoxy spells doom for Schechter's dream. Chabad-Lubavitch has a thriving prayer house in this town.

This is the same Chabad that Solomon Schechter fled in his youth. The movement, reenergized by its seventh rebbe, Menachem Mendel Schneersohn, has become evangelist and inclusivist, welcoming Jews of all degrees of practice with abundant food and drink and a simple, one-size theology: be a better Jew. Schechter's thoughtful, "reasonable" Judaism has no defense against Chabad's dynamism formula. His Catholic Israel, so apt for his time, is overthrown by the ancestral heritage that he never fully escaped.

Another train, another beard. October 1891. The beard is rectangular, jet-black, a portent of authority. Its owner, Theodor Herzl, is traveling from Vienna to Paris, as the new correspondent of the *Neue Freie Presse*. Herzl, who is thirty-one and of no fixed ambition, tells his parents that this job will be the making of him. It will earn him equal rank to an ambassador, such is the prestige of the *NFP*, a newspaper which manages to reflect both the reactionary views of a decaying Habsburg court and the liberal currents of enlightened urban opinion. By inflating the newspaper's importance, Herzl is busy cultivating his own myth. More fantasist than journalist, his track record in print up to now is a series of travel pieces from Italy, France, and Spain. Herzl tells everyone he doesn't want to be a journalist. He has seen one of his plays, *Der Flüchtling* (*The Fugitive*), put on at the Burgtheater, and he is busy writing more.

No one can figure out how Herzl has become a foreign correspondent, but the job could not have come at a better time. His best friend, Heinrich Kana, has just shot himself in Berlin, unable to make ends meet as a writer. His other pal, Oswald Boxer, is in Brazil helping Russian pogrom refugees. Herzl's marriage to a rich young blonde, Julie Naschauer, is a disaster that begins on the honeymoon night and grows steadily worse. Julie's family are crass traders, socially far below the cultured Herzls. Julie shows signs of mental instability. Theodor himself is prone to depression. Julie attempts suicide. The birth of a son, Hans, brings them no closer. "I shall bring up my son as lovingly and wisely as I can," Herzl informs Julie. "You can be sure of that. I will also teach him to love and honour his mother." Beyond stiff courtesies, he threatens her with physical violence:

> Despite the fact that you have never understood me, I shall try one more time to explain myself. It will be the last time. I don't need to tell you that our marriage has been a most unhappy one . . . For two full years my house has been a hell to me and when I came home it was in fear. It was not you, my dear, that I feared but myself. I was afraid that I would completely lose my self-control and would react to your torments with a blow that would make you into a cripple or maim you. I thank God that so far I have managed to hold myself back.[18]

So far.

Herzl is prey to other dangerous urges. Before his marriage, he writes troubling love letters to a thirteen-year-old girl. Unlike his university acquaintance Arthur Schnitzler, he does not relieve his sexual needs with shopgirls and seamstresses, nor, once in Paris, does he sample its erotic banquet. Herzl is serious, solitary, repressed. That so emotionally inert a man could trigger a national redemption movement is a mystery as deep as the forces that he unleashes.

He is, by any reckoning, not much of a Jew. Raised in a German-speaking family in Budapest, he rejects religion after his bar mitzvah. The death of his sister, Pauline, from typhus, sends the family to attempt a new beginning in Vienna, where Herzl enters university to study law. He joins a dueling fraternity, Albia, only to resign over anti-Semitism; or so he claims. Albia is notoriously Germanic. Why does he join it in the first place unless he is trying to pass as an Aryan? Walking out on Albia is his only Jewish act for a decade. He refuses to have his son circumcised. Part of the lure of Paris is that it will give him a second chance, as a foreigner, to pose as a Gentile.

France is in the grip of anti-Jewish fervor. Edouard Drumont's newspaper *La Libre Parole* vilifies the Jews for the collapse of the Panama Canal Company, which wipes out many people's savings. "If only it were a simple question of right and wrong," sighs Herzl. From August 1892, he writes one article after another on French anti-Semitism. It is a phenomenon of immediate interest in Vienna, where a charismatic, handsome demagogue, Karl Lueger, is running for mayor, promising to ban Jews from public life. Herzl regards Lueger and Drumont as a common threat. He proposes a radical solution. In a meeting with the *NFP*'s Jewish proprietors, he suggests that all Jews become Christians. In Paris, he has a dream that he, Theodor Herzl, in his big, black beard, leads the Jewish people in procession to the Stephansdom on a Sunday afternoon to accept mass conversion. This is his first fantasy of national redemption. In every scenario that runs through his head, Herzl is always the national hero.

He has just finished a play, *The New Ghetto*, a polemic on Jewish segregation, when late in 1894 a Jewish officer in the French Army, Captain Alfred Dreyfus, is charged with spying for the Germans. Herzl hares off to cover the trial. Dreyfus, a stern defendant, has no chance against a battery of state evidence. The trial splits France into hostile camps. Brothers sever relations and never speak again. Artists hiss and snarl at each other. Pissarro and Monet are vehemently pro-Dreyfus; Renoir and Cézanne furiously anti. Madame Straus fires Edgar Degas for anti-Semitic outbursts. Jews are spat on in the streets of Paris.

In December 1894, Dreyfus is found guilty of treason and sentenced to deportation for life to Devil's Island, a penal colony off French Guiana. As the verdict is read, Herzl hears the crowd outside cry, "Death to the Jews." At the degradation ceremony on January 5, 1895, when the captain's sword is snapped in two and the epaulettes are ripped from his uniform, Herzl hears Dreyfus shout, "I declare and solemnly swear that you are degrading an innocent man. *Vive la France!*" Herzl reports:

> The crowd surged towards the gates to watch the condemned man being led away. There were passionate shouts. "Bring him out here and we'll tear him to pieces!" But the crowd waited in vain. There was a curious excitement among those who had been able to witness the ceremony of degradation. The strange, firm bearing of the prisoner had made a profound impression.[19]

On no more than the evidence of his eyes, Herzl proclaims Dreyfus's innocence in several polemics. He makes no effort to investigate the case. He is not much of a journalist. Later, Herzl will maintain that Dreyfus has changed his life, but his diaries do not suggest a Damascene conversion. Nor does he hang around much longer in Paris to see how the Dreyfus saga plays out.

The Dreyfus conspiracy takes years to be exposed. Georges Picquart, head of military intelligence, discovers that prosecution witnesses have forged documents. He is exiled to Tunisia and told to keep quiet. The novelist Émile Zola, on January 13, 1898, splashes "*J'Accuse*" across the front page of the newspaper *L'Aurore*. He is tried for criminal libel and flees to England. One of the anti-Dreyfus plotters is found hanged in a hotel room. Another confesses. In 1899, Dreyfus is brought back for a retrial. He is once more found guilty but walks free due to "extenuating circumstances." In 1906, Dreyfus is acquitted. He serves on the front line through the First World War, dying in 1935. Another sixty years pass before the French Army formally confirms his innocence. In 2006, the president of France, Jacques Chirac, offers a public apology.

The Dreyfus case rips the blindfold from the eyes of French justice. For Herzl, the story has only one lesson. If France, home of liberty, fraternity, and equality, can convict a Jew for being a Jew, then there is no state on Earth where a Jew can feel safe. Jews must make plans for a separate future. He visits a synagogue, noting "the family resemblance of their faces—bold, misshapen noses, shy and cunning eyes."[20] He fills his diary with fantasies and bombards his editors with Jewish issues. Called back to Vienna in 1895, he witnesses Karl Lueger's election victory. Herzl becomes feuilleton editor, in charge of the bottom half of the front page of the *NFP*, the bit "under the fold" that café society reads over a *kleine braune* and *kipferl* (small brown coffee and cookie) before going to work. The feuilleton is his platform to mold public opinion. The *NFP*'s owners order him not to use the space for his Jewish preoccupations.

Happy to be home, Herzl contacts his university acquaintance Schnitzler, whose debut play, *Anatol*, is an international hit, showing young men categorizing women into ones they sleep with and those they marry. Herzl wants to be Schnitzler's friend. Schnitzler tells his diary: "I don't take to Herzl very well. His pompous manner of speaking . . ." Herzl keeps chasing Schnitzler:

I have a great need of a good friendship. I am on the point of publishing an advertisement: "Man in prime of life seeks a friend in whom he can confide without fear all his frailties and absurdities"... I don't know: am I too distrustful or too diffident or are my eyes too clearsighted? I find none such among my acquaintances. One is too stupid, another too treacherous, the third irritates me at my most sensitive point when he takes advantage of a burgeoning familiarity ... Tell me, do you, too, feel like this with a new friend?[21]

Socially maladroit, emotionally unfulfilled, he will go to any lengths to win Schnitzler's approval. Herzl does not take *no* for an answer.

Before leaving Paris, he calls on Baron Maurice de Hirsch, a plutocrat who is resettling Russian Jews, not altogether fruitfully, in South America. Herzl tells Hirsch: "What you have undertaken until now has been as magnanimous as it has been misapplied, as costly as it is pointless. I will show you the way to become something more."[22] Accusing Hirsch of breeding schnorrers, he demands financial support for his own scheme. Hirsch is sufficiently taken with his chutzpah to demand a prospectus. Herzl returns to his hotel and, at high speed, writes a sixty-page proposal that becomes the nucleus of his manifesto *Der Judenstaat*, commonly translated as *The Jewish State* but better rendered as *A State for the Jews*. His plan is for the Jews to reoccupy Palestine. The costs of mass migration and resettlement will be underwritten by a Jewish National Fund, supported by contributions great and small from members of the tribe, each according to his or her means. A blue collecting box for the fund will be put on every Jewish mantelpiece. Young people will be trained to drain the malarial swamps and turn the desert green. The Jews, with a land of their own, will never bother Europe again. "No one ever thought of looking for the Promised Land where it actually is—and yet it lies so near," cries Herzl. "This is where it is: within ourselves."

He sends a copy of his draft to the Rothschilds, who do not reply. He writes to Bismarck and the kaiser. A fellow journalist, Max Nordau, suggests he try his luck in London. Nordau, author of a mass-selling tract called *Degeneration*—on the moral impact of modern life—is, like Schnitzler, a man Herzl dearly wants to emulate. Nordau, for his part, sees that a Jewish agrarian state would reverse all the ills he has outlined in *Degeneration*.

Herzl reaches London with a letter from Nordau to Israel Zangwill, author of a popular novel, *Children of the Ghetto*, about the lives of poor Jews in the East End (the *Jewish Chronicle* decries its "unsavoury details"). Zangwill is putting the finishing touches to his American edition when Herzl turns up on his Kilburn doorstep. Herzl, in his hapless way, takes issue with Zangwill for mocking "lovers of Zion" in his novel and differs with him over whether the Jews are, as Zangwill sees it, a race or, as Herzl insists, "a historical unit." Herzl describes Zangwill as a "long-nosed Negroid type, with very woolly deep-black hair parted in the middle."[23] Zangwill speaks no German, and Herzl no English, so they converse in clunky French. Zangwill warms to the force of Herzl's fervor and invites him to address the Maccabaeans, a club of intellectuals founded by Schechter and Zangwill. Here, Herzl is inspired. Speaking German and French, with simultaneous translation by the Anglo-Jewish *siddur* editor Simeon Singer, he delivers an oration that recruits powerful men to his cause. Herbert Bentwich becomes his international lawyer, Asher Myers puts the *Jewish Chronicle* at his service, and Solomon Schechter bestows blessings. Haham Gaster hosts Herzl at his home in Maida Vale. He proceeds to Wales to meet Colonel Albert Goldsmid, a British officer who has converted to Judaism with his wife. The colonel, strictly Orthodox, declares: "I am Daniel Deronda!" They sit in the parlor, listening to the Viennese pianist Moriz Rosenthal play Schumann and Brahms. Goldsmid, a man of action, appoints himself head of the British Zionist movement. Herzl now has an organization.

He returns to Vienna by way of Paris, where Nordau, a medical doctor, expresses concern at his bronchial condition. In his Paris hotel, on the rue Cambon, Herzl writes the final draft of *Der Judenstaat*. "Let sovereignty be granted us over a portion of the globe adequate to meet our rightful national requirements; we will attend to the rest," he declares. Three thousand copies are printed in February 1896. One finds its way to the chaplain to the British ambassador in Vienna, the Reverend William Hechler, who proclaims Herzl to be the harbinger of the Messiah. Hechler, who has witnessed pogroms in Russia, tells Herzl that redemption is nigh. Hechler has "calculated in accordance with a prophecy dating from Omar's reign (637-638) that after 42 prophetical months, that is, 1,260 years, Palestine would be restored to the Jews. This would make it 1897-1898."[24] Herzl is informed that Hechler has been tutor to Kaiser Wilhelm II's cousins. Might he effect an introduction?

Hechler escorts Herzl to Karlsruhe, where the kaiser is visiting. Wilhelm says: "Hechler, I hear you want to become a minister of the Jewish State." Herzl does not make it onto the reception line.

He is suddenly in a panic. The bronchial condition is rediagnosed as congenital heart disease, a death sentence with an unfixed execution date. In June, he is in Constantinople, asking the grand vizier to sell him land in Palestine, offering money he has not yet raised. Officials tell him Turkey will never agree to a Jewish state in Palestine. How about Cyprus? Herzl is not averse to the idea. He hangs around awhile but does not meet the sultan. His interview with the grand vizier appears in the *NFP*, whose owners are losing patience. Under pressure, he nurtures young writers—Hermann Bahr, Hugo von Hofmannsthal, Richard Beer-Hofmann, Stefan Zweig—raising the tone of the newspaper's front page and proving himself to be a good judge of literary quality.

Baron Edmond de Rothschild snubs his request for a £2 million loan to the sultan in exchange for a slice of Holy Land. Stymied, he starts a Jewish newspaper, *Die Welt*. The *NFP* owners are irritated. His heart bangs away in his chest. Herzl needs to make headway. He decides to call a Zionist Congress. "It should be a magnificent demonstration which will show the world what Zionism is and what it wants," he tells Bentwich, more in hope than in confidence.

The Swiss town of Basel has a casino that is empty in the last week of August 1897. Its concert hall is deceptively spacious—big enough for Gustav Mahler to stage a performance of his *Resurrection Symphony*—and far enough away from Vienna to blindside his employers. This, says Herzl, will be the first parliament of the Jewish people, to be conducted with British decorum and no trace of rowdiness. Delegates must wear white tie and tails for the opening; Nordau, who turns up in a frock coat, is sent home to dress. The banner will be a blue Star of David on a white background between two blue stripes, designed by a Cologne businessman, David Wolffsohn. "Hatikvah"—verses by Naphtali Herz Imber, the music a mash-up of a sixteenth-century Mantuan ditty and a tune from Smetana's *Moldova*—is the movement's anthem.

Until the opening hour, Herzl has no idea who will turn up. When heads are counted, there are 196 members (some say 208) from sixteen countries. They include black-hatted rabbis from Russia, bareheaded atheists from Lithuania, traveling salesmen from the Balkans, a serving member of the Swiss National Council, pioneers from Palestine, four Americans, ten Christians (including Hechler), a professor from Bulgaria, and the Reverend Dr. Shepsel Shalter from Baltimore. The list is never finalized; disputes persist as to who is or is not an official delegate. Women are registered as observers, without voting rights. Absent are any delegates from the Sephardi crescent, which extends from Casablanca to Calcutta. Herzl, myopic or plain ignorant, has not thought to invite Eastern Jews.

On the first day of the penitential month of Elul, a Sunday morning, the oldest delegate takes the stage to pronounce the blessing "Shehecheyanu," thanking God for keeping Jews alive to witness the new dawn. Herzl, the unbeliever, has acknowledged the power of religion. The opening speaker, a Romanian physician called Karpel Lippe, ignores Herzl's exhortations to keep it short and puts the hall to sleep. Herzl, up next, combines flowery rhetoric and practical politics to deliver a vision of a modern Jewish state. "We are laying the foundation stone of a house that will one day accommodate the Jewish people," he cries. When he sits down, the hall erupts. Tables and chairs are overturned. "Hatikvah" is sung. There are shouts of "Long live the king!" A man from Czernowitz swears he has seen the Messiah. Zangwill reports: "On the rivers of Babylon we sat and wept when we remembered Zion. On the river of Basel we now sit and resolve: We will weep no more." Max Nordau announces: "We do not believe in failure." A policy statement is adopted: "Zionism seeks to secure for the Jewish people a publicly recognised, legally secured homeland in Palestine." Rubbing their eyes, these two German-speaking foreign correspondents, Herzl and Nordau, discover that they have invented a nation. Herzl records in his diary: "Were I to sum up the Basel Congress in a word—which I shall guard against pronouncing publicly, it would be this: At Basel I founded the Jewish state."

It is his finest hour, and it is quickly over. A year later, addressing the second Congress in the same hall, Herzl has no progress to report. The middle classes in Western Europe and America oppose his idea, fearing that, if Zionism succeeds, they will be turfed out of their suburban homes and packed off to a desert. Reform and Orthodox rabbis denounce his nationalism. Moses Gaster is ordered by communal elders to desist from preaching his cause. Edmond de Roth-schild refuses to underwrite a national bank. Herzl's only gain is the 913 Zionist groups now affiliated with his movement.

Back in Vienna, on the edge of despair, he receives a summons to visit the Grand Duke of Baden in Karlsruhe. The grand duke, a sympa-thizer, is beside himself with excitement. Someone has told the kaiser that Zionism could help rid Germany of Jewish "usurers." The kaiser is on his way to Constantinople to see the sultan, says the grand duke. He is available for a meeting.

Herzl catches the Orient Express and checks in at the Hotel de Lon-dres. On October 18, 1898, he is called to the kaiser. Wilhelm greets him warmly, confiding that "there are elements among your people whom it would be good to settle in Palestine" and volunteering that German intelligence never had contact with Alfred Dreyfus: the whole affair was a French anti-Semitic hoax.

"Tell me in a word what I should ask of the Sultan," demands the kaiser.

"A Chartered Company—under German protection," replies Herzl. The kaiser dismisses him with a handshake and declares that their next meeting will be at the walls of Jerusalem. Herzl books passage to Palestine together with David Wolffsohn; Moses Schnirer, a doctor; a Cologne lawyer, Max Bodenheimer; and an engineer, Josef Seidener, who plans to introduce electricity to the Holy Land. Wolffsohn is offi-cial photographer. He snaps Herzl on a Russian ship bound for Alex-andria, sitting cross-legged on deck with five Arabs in kaffiyehs in the background. Herzl barely notices them. His tour diary refers just once to "Arab beggars, women, children and horsemen."[25] He refuses to rec-ognize that the land is partly occupied by other peoples.

On seeing the Jaffa shoreline, he embraces Wolffsohn and cries, "Our country, our mother Zion!" They visit agricultural settlements. Herzl suffers sunstroke and takes to his bed. On reaching Jerusalem, he is annoyed by beggars at the Wailing Wall and wades through excre-ment in the streets. "If Jerusalem is ever ours, and if I were still able to do anything about it," he records:

> I would begin by cleaning it up. I would clear out everything that is
> not sacred, set up workers' homes beyond the city, empty and tear

down the filthy rat holes, burn all the non-sacred ruins, and put the bazaars elsewhere. Then, retaining as much of the old architectural style as possible, I would build an airy, comfortable, properly sewered, brand new city around the Holy Places.[26]

The meeting with the kaiser is perfunctory; the mood at court has changed, and the foreign minister Bernhard von Bülow lets slip a calculated anti-Semitic barb. Worse, Wolffsohn misses the propaganda shot of the kaiser on his horse extending a hand to the top-hatted Herzl. "When we went to the photographer in Jaffa and had the negatives developed, it turned out that the first picture showed only a shadow of the kaiser and my left foot; the second was completely spoiled."[27] The publicity shot is forged from a montage of four separate images.

Schnirer is concerned about Herzl's irregular heartbeat. Catching a ship at Jaffa proves harder than anticipated. They are rowed from one freighter to another in the harbor before a captain agrees to take them. Herzl, not yet forty, remakes his will, cutting out his wife, Julie, and all her family. Back in Vienna, he writes a play about an adulterous wife and a polemical novel, *Altneuland*. Its hero is a Viennese journalist who goes on a cruise with a millionaire friend, disembarking in Jaffa and touring Palestine, which they find primitive and revolting. Twenty years on, they return to find the country transformed under the enlightened rule of David Littwak, a doppelgänger for the Litvak David Wolffsohn. Jerusalem is spotless. The temple has been rebuilt. A Muslim intellectual thanks the Jews for the new prosperity. *Altneuland* is a potboiler, a work of wishful thinking that makes Herzl more foes than friends. The novel is scorned by reviewers, most pungently by "Ahad Ha'am," the Kiev essayist Asher Ginsburg, who picks holes in Herzl's totally superficial grasp of Jewish culture and civilization. If ever a novel should not have been written, it is this one.

Yet, despite its paucity of ideas, *Altneuland* has two vital resonances. Its flyleaf motto—"*Wenn du willst ist es kein Märchen*" (If you wish, this is no fairy tale)—becomes the driving slogan of Palestine pioneers. Herzl, like Freud, understands that dreams reflect a collective unconscious. The second strike belongs to Herzl's Hebrew translator, Nahum Sokolow, who replaces Herzl's original title with two words from Ezekiel 3:15—*Tel Aviv*, meaning "springtime hill." The name catches on among the pioneers and is pinned to the first modern Jewish city, a scattering of white-fronted buildings running north up the sand dunes from Arab Jaffa. Founded in 1909, Tel Aviv is a magnet for new Jews. One of its first residents is the Kiev skeptic and Herzl critic Ahad Ha'am.

Herzl reconfigures his Jewish National Fund (JNF) from a general development fund to a resource aimed specifically at buying land from Arab and Turkish owners, many of them absentee landlords. It does not cross Herzl's mind that subsistence Arab farmers on the land may be evicted after the sale. He sees the fund as a parachute for refugees from the latest pogroms.

The first JNF donors, giving £10 sterling each, are intriguingly international. The first is Professor Dr. Hermann Schapira, a noted Heidelberg mathematician. He is followed by Dr. Theodor Herzl of Vienna; Jacob Moser, a textile philanthropist and town councillor of Bradford, Yorkshire; Sir Francis Montefiore of London; David Wolffsohn of Cologne; and a "Mr. Vecht" of New Zealand.

Aron Vecht is a glorious adventurer, unknown to Zionist historians. A Dutch Jew of impeccable Orthodoxy and an urge to see the world, "throughout all his ceaseless globe-trotting, although constantly exposed to hardship and privation, he never once transgressed the dietary laws."[28] Starting in London, where he marries a member of the wealthy Van den Bergh clan, Vecht launches the *Jewish Standard* newspaper, with Zangwill as star columnist, to combat the *Jewish Chronicle*. Unable to settle anywhere for long, he takes his family to Argentina, where he founds a frozen kosher meat export business, approved by European rabbis. Vecht moves on to South Africa, then to Australia. His children are born on four different continents. In New Zealand, which he explores from top to tip, he finds the populace afflicted by trichinosis, a parasitic disease caused by eating raw or undercooked pig meat. Without much fuss, Vecht applies his expertise in freezing kosher beef to set up New Zealand's first bacon-curing plant, charging one shilling for each carcass he treats.[29]

Reading Herzl's manifesto, Vecht turns up in Basel for a Congress and sets about forming Zionist societies below the equator. Concern for his children's education prompts Vecht to head north to Antwerp, where he undergoes gallbladder surgery. Delegates to the eighth Zionist Congress send fond greetings to his sickbed, but Vecht dies of postoperative complications. In all his wanderings, he never sees the promised land. One of his sons takes his body for burial on the outskirts of Tel Aviv.

The pressure on Herzl is now unremitting. He fears losing his job and his followers if he does not produce results. As the screws tighten, he makes unprompted errors, or rather, errors that are prompted by his need to demonstrate momentum. The British, alert to his talks with the Germans and the Turks, suggest Cyprus as an alternative Jewish homeland. Herzl is tempted, as is Zangwill, but many religious supporters tear up their membership cards. The British colonial secretary, Joseph Chamberlain, follows up in 1903 with an offer for a long lease on land in East Africa. Herzl unwisely commends the proposal as "an emergency measure" to the sixth Zionist Congress. The Uganda Project splits the movement. The Odessa delegation, led by Menachem Ussishkin and Ahad Ha'am, calls Herzl a traitor. A fanatic tries to kill Nordau. Zangwill is ousted for having a non-Jewish wife. Herzl retreats in disarray. His resilience is running out. In May 1904, he is sent for six weeks to a spa. Chaplain Hechler, first of the true believers, pays him a visit. "Tell them I have given my heart's blood for my people," he begs Hechler, whose account is error-strewn.[30] "How I wish to rest," he tells a doctor, in his last recorded words on the afternoon of July 3, 1904. Herzl dies at forty-four years old.

What follows is a scene from one of his dreams. Vienna, deserted in summer heat, turns black in broad daylight, as Eastern Jews in their thousands converge for the redeemer's funeral. "From all the provinces and all the little towns they hurried excitedly, the shock of the news still written on their faces," records Stefan Zweig:

> Never was it more clearly manifest what strife and talk had hitherto concealed—it was a great movement whose leader had now fallen. The procession was endless. Vienna, startled, became aware that it was not just a writer or a mediocre poet who had passed away, but one of those creators of Ideas who disclose themselves triumphantly in a single country, to a single people at vast intervals . . . All regulation was upset through a sort of elementary and ecstatic mourning such as I had never seen before nor since at a funeral.[31]

The *Jewish Chronicle* gives its entire front page to the funeral: "Cheek by jowl with the correctly attired Western Jew one noticed the caftaned, heavy-bearded Jew from Galicia and side by side with the dark-eyed Rumanian was the fair-skinned North German. But on every face was the mark of a huge and lasting sorrow." As the coffin is laid to earth, David Wolffsohn calls on the multitude to recite the Psalmic verse: "If I forget thee, o Jerusalem, may my right hand lose its function." Herzl has earned the immortality he craved.

The coda is unbearably sad. Julie outlives him by just three years. Unwilling to be buried among Jews, she is cremated, but her ashes are subsequently mislaid. Herzl's son, Hans, undergoes an adult circumcision and wins a scholarship to Cambridge, only to suffer a nervous breakdown. He becomes a Roman Catholic in 1924. When his sister Pauline dies of morphine addiction, Hans shoots himself in a hotel room. Herzl's third child, Trude, spends her life in mental asylums and dies in the Nazi concentration camp of Theresienstadt. Her only child, Stefan Theodor Neumann, jumps off a bridge in Washington, DC, in 1946, ending the family line. Herzl's body is removed from Vienna in 1949 and reburied in Jerusalem on a bare hilltop that is hastily named Mount Herzl.

The State of Israel would never have come into being without Theodor Herzl's vision, charisma, and relentless pursuit of imperial powers. He is at once the Garibaldi of Zionism and its Verdi, the caller of an uprising and its composer. His bold good looks, shining eyes, and signature beard are indispensable to the acceptance of his core idea that the only solution to European rejection is a Jewish state on another continent. Without his activity in the 1890s, nothing would have changed. None of his successors—Nordau, Chaim Weizmann, David Ben-Gurion—can claim his unifying appeal.

Yet, in contrast to Garibaldi, he is a revolutionary leader detached from his people, ignorant of its religion, deaf to its dynamics, a leader who prefers the prelate Hechler to any rabbi ("these simple Christian hearts are much better than our Jewish clerics who think of their wedding fees from rich Jews"). Herzl, longing to the last to be an acclaimed playwright, is unsuited in almost every aspect to his self-appointed task. He is the least Jewish of Jews and the least sensitive of leaders.

His success rests on zeitgeist and chutzpah. Herzl has the luck to be alive at a time of an awakening to ancient history. The Greek excavations of Hermann Schliemann and the *genizah* retrievals of Solomon Schechter help prepare public opinion for the restoration of the Jews to Jerusalem. Herzl's indomitable self-belief accounts for the rest. From the moment he designs a state for the Jews, no shadow of doubt crosses his mind. A good journalist would have called on his training to consider the other sides of the argument and reflect upon the realities of Palestine's other residents. Herzl looks neither right nor left, up nor down. He is convinced, like Karl Marx, of his historic inevitability. Nobody, be it Rothschild or the kaiser, will deflect him. He is Herzl, hope of the Jews. Over time, his will prevails. Even the elderly Sigmund Freud admits that "Zionism awakened my strongest sympathies, which are still faithfully attached to it today."[32]

Rabbis relent their initial enthusiasm. One after another, they put a fence between their faith and this Messiah. Starting with Hermann Adler in London and the Parisian Zadok Kahn, Herzl loses pulpit support. Solomon Schechter, while broadly sympathetic, rejects "extreme Herzlism" and warns that "the Messiah cannot be brought by proxy." Schechter, however, joins the Zionist movement in the aftermath of Herzl's death and joins the search for a successor. "It must be a great man," he specifies, "and even a better Jew."[33]

SEVEN

1897

SEX IN THE CITY

Nazis ransack Hirschfeld's Institute of Sexual Science.

O n May 15, 1897, a Berlin physician signs off on what will become
his life's work. Magnus Hirschfeld is twenty-nine years old, newly
established in a family practice in the prosperous suburb of Charlot-
tenburg. Originating from Kolberg on the Baltic, where his father is
chairman of the Jewish community, Hirschfeld renounces his faith at
university and deviates from medical orthodoxy by offering naturo-

pathic treatments. Angry colleagues drive him out of his first surgery in Magdeburg, accusing him of causing a patient's death by withholding "invigorating alcohol."[1] In Berlin, Hirschfeld has more freedom to develop his healing instincts.

On this particular Saturday, with three close friends, he forms the Scientific-Humanitarian Committee, a group created for the purpose of revoking paragraph 175 of the German penal code. Law 175, dated 1871, makes sex between two men a criminal offense, punishable by long prison terms. Hirschfeld, himself discreetly gay, has been stirred to action by the suicide of a patient, an army officer, who shoots himself the night before his wedding, saying he cannot marry a woman when his natural urges are to be with men. His doctor duly writes an educational monograph: *Sappho and Socrates, or What Explains the Love of Men and Women for Persons of Their Own Sex*. It draws little attention. His committee, on the other hand, makes waves. It consists of a Leipzig publisher, Max Spohr; a railroad official, Eduard Oberg; and an aristocrat, Franz Joseph von Bülow. Two of the four are respectably married. In eighteen months, they collect two thousand signatures on a petition to decriminalize homosexuality. Among the supporters are the playwright Frank Wedekind, the poet Rainer Maria Rilke, and the novelists Heinrich and Thomas Mann (who quickly asks to be removed). Hirschfeld then presents the petition to the Reichstag.

Consider, for a moment, the date. The year is 1897. In England, Oscar Wilde is released from jail, having served two years with hard labor for homosexual acts. In Russia, musicians mourn the composer Pyotr Ilyich Tchaikovsky, hounded to death over his homosexuality; Tchaikovsky's death, ascribed to cholera, is never satisfactorily explained. In France, one of the rumors used to incriminate Captain Dreyfus is an imputation of homosexuality. In New York, police raid bathhouses to catch gay men in the act. For an inexperienced young doctor in Berlin to confront the illiberal German Parliament with a demand to legalize homosexuality is an act of social and professional folly, if not suicide. Hirschfeld does not flinch. When his petition is rejected, he presents it at the Reichstag year after year, until its acceptance is finally tabled in 1929.

Morally impelled, inflexibly principled, Hirschfeld is a stocky man with a luxuriant mustache and, at this point, a discreet private life.

Rising each morning at five, he writes for three hours before seeing patients. Passionate about music, he hosts string quartets in his house. Hirschfeld has all the attributes of suburban respectability, except regarding his sexuality. He is powered by an instinct that this might be a historic moment of sexual enlightenment. Something is in the air. As Hirschfeld presents his petition, Albert Moll, author of a clinical book on hypnotism, publishes a pathbreaking book on child sexuality, arguing that homosexuality (which he calls sexual inversion) is a symptom of retarded emotional development:

> Consider, for instance, the case of a homosexual man. He remembers that, as a small boy, he was very fond of sitting on his uncle's knees, and he believes that the pleasure he formerly experienced was tinged by sexual feeling. In reality this was by no means the case. His uncle took the boy on his knee in order to tell him a story. Possibly, also, the riding movements which the uncle imitated by jogging his knees up and down gave the child pleasure, which, however, was entirely devoid of any admixture of sexual feeling. But in the consciousness of the full-grown man, in whom homosexual feeling has later undergone full development, all this becomes distorted. The non-sexual motives are forgotten; he believes that even in early childhood he had homosexual inclinations, and that for *this* reason it gave him pleasure to ride on his uncle's knees.[2]

Moll, a Jewish-born Lutheran, claims to be the founder of the field of medical psychology and is called as an expert witness in criminal cases involving homosexuality. He also dabbles in the occult. Hirschfeld abominates Albert Moll. Two Jewish doctors, lifelong bachelors, are mortal enemies.

Hirschfeld founds his research into homosexuality by gathering masses of data. Applying newfangled American sociological methods that he picks up on a visit to cousins in Chicago, he asks three thousand Berlin students to answer a questionnaire about their sexual urges. Next, he questions five thousand metalworkers. He tours bars and bathhouses for contacts and evidence. Finally, he draws the conclusion that, between male and female, there exists a third sex that is attracted chiefly to itself. He launches a *Yearbook of Intermediate Sex-*

ual Types and publishes a book, *Berlin's Third Sex*. It proves remarkably timely. In November 1902, Berlin is shocked by the suicide of the arms magnate Friedrich Alfred Krupp, after he is exposed in the press as a predator of boys on the Italian island of Capri. At Krupp's funeral, Kaiser Wilhelm II accuses left-wing politicians of spreading lies about Krupp. A magazine editor, Maximilian Harden, responds by threatening one of the kaiser's close friends, Philipp, Prince of Eulenburg, with exposure as the lover of General Kuno Augustus von Moltke, military commander of Berlin and adjutant to the kaiser.

As political scandals go, this is highly explosive. Eulenburg, a Wagnerian anti-Semite, is Germany's ambassador in Vienna. Moltke belongs to one of Prussia's most glorious military dynasties. Harden is a socialist and a Jew. One morning a man wearing women's clothing is found dead on the grounds of one of the kaiser's residences. The kaiser fires Moltke from the army. Moltke sues Harden for defamation. Harden calls Dr. Magnus Hirschfeld as his expert witness, to the fury of Dr. Albert Moll.

The trial is one of the most lurid in German jurisprudence. Moltke's ex-wife, Lily, comes forward to testify that the general only made love to her twice in three years and that she tried beating him with a frying pan in an effort to arouse his desire. Lily swears under oath that Moltke is gay and that Eulenburg is the love of his life. Moltke's lawyers protest that a woman who declares in public that she wants sex must be deranged. The court consults Hirschfeld, who says that in his view, Lily is perfectly normal. Hirschfeld is asked if he can tell whether Eulenburg, who is sitting in court, is homosexual or not. Hirschfeld says that, from his observation, the ambassador is rather effeminate, as is common with many homosexuals.

Barely are these words out of his mouth when Hirschfeld knows he is in trouble. The opinion he has given is both subjective and unscientific, as flimsy as any of Moll's fantasies. He wants the court to believe that Eulenburg is gay in order to normalize homosexuality in German society, but he has laid his scientific flank open to attack. Moll bursts into print, calling Hirschfeld an apologist for depravity. Nationalists declare him a race enemy for shaming their heroes Moltke and Eulenburg. Posters are pasted on the walls of his building, warning patients against "Dr. Hirschfeld, a public danger." He takes a trip to Turkey and Italy, ostensibly for research, until things cool down. In London, he addresses the International Congress of Physicians, in a meeting organized by the British Medical Association at the Royal Albert Hall, showing more than a hundred photographic slides to support his theories on homosexuality. He meets fellow campaigners Henry Havelock Ellis and Edward Carpenter. His Reichstag petition now has five thousand signatories, among them Albert Einstein, Hermann Hesse, Stefan Zweig, and Martin Buber. Hirschfeld knows he is not alone.

Having read reports of Sigmund Freud's new talking cure, he forms the Berlin Association for Psychoanalysis, together with "Freud's best pupil" Karl Abraham,[3] and the ambitious Iwan Bloch, founder of Sexualwissenschaft, the science of sexuality. Bloch is determined to overturn Richard von Krafft-Ebing's contentious statement that Jews have "abnormally intensified sensuality and sexual excitement that leads to sexual errors that are of etiological significance." One such "sexual error" is homosexuality. Bloch declares that that "unnatural vice is of conspicuously rare occurrence" among Jews.[4] Albert Moll retorts that there is certainly the same proportion of gay men among Jews as there is among Christians. Bloch declares he has never met a Jewish homosexual. Most of the early sexologists are quarrelsome Jews, and there is much interest in their argument.

Hirschfeld is the most thoughtful contributor to the debate. His book on Berlin associates sexual ignorance with city life. In the countryside, sex is no mystery. Every child sees what goes on in the fields. It is the growth of cities that has suppressed discussion and driven sex underground. Hirschfeld looks at Berlin and sees not a military garrison but one of the world's gay capitals. "*Ich bin ein Berliner*" becomes a coded statement of sexual curiosity and diversity.

He quickly breaks with Freud, who has tried to use him to discredit a former ally, Wilhelm Fliess.[5] When Freud, in 1911, refers to homosexuality as an "inversion," adopting Moll's term, Hirschfeld quits the Association for Psychoanalysis. Freud tells Carl Jung: "Magnus Hirschfeld has left our ranks in Berlin. No great loss, he is a flabby, unappetizing fellow, absolutely incapable of learning anything. Of course he takes your remark at the Congress as a pretext; homosexual touchiness. Not worth a tear."[6]

Despite the breach, each concedes the other a measure of respect.

Both are working to dispel sexual ignorance and reduce human misery. Both have a rabbinic bent to their mission. They teach personal redemption through self-examination and self-awareness. They engage in ferocious disputation and denigration. Both believe they have a monopoly on understanding the human soul. At the outbreak of the First World War, both are gripped by nationalistic fervor, believing in a German victory and a better society. Hirschfeld sends gifts of food and books to gay soldiers at the front. He writes two pamphlets, *On the Psychology of War* and *Why Do Nations Hate Us?* Freud, with three sons in uniform, tries to work out why some battle troops suffer shell shock while others don't. Moll persuades insurance companies to extend their health cover to include fees for psychiatric consultation. Freud emerges famous from the world war. Hirschfeld, revitalized, is ready for liftoff.

A landmark year as it is for sex in Berlin, 1897 is no less seminal for Vienna. Momentous changes are afoot. The anti-Semite Karl Lueger is sworn in as mayor, the Jewish conductor Gustav Mahler becomes director of the opera, and forty artists quit the old society of artists, the Künstlerhaus, to follow Gustav Klimt into the Art Nouveau Secession. Lueger electrifies the transport system, takes control of utilities, and carves his name in large letters on the outside of every new public building, fostering a personality cult that will redound through the next century. Mahler galvanizes the opera, introducing a coherent production style and consistency of performing standards. As Vienna engages for the first time with modernity, Freud and Schnitzler think mostly of sex. Schnitzler suffers two bereavements and writes a play so shocking it cannot be staged for decades. Freud makes a catastrophic error that will, in time, undermine the science he aims to establish. Both are dancing barefoot on broken glass.

Schnitzler is keen on sex and success, in that order. His first play, *Anatol*, about a middle-class woman-chaser, premiered four years earlier and is staged everywhere from Scotland to South America. The royalties make him rich and anxious: Can he do it again? He gives up his job as a hospital doctor but continues to see private patients, many coming from the theater. Freud, overwhelmed by the first act of *Anatol*, calls Schnitzler "a researcher of psychological depths" and wonders how he obtains such penetrating insights into the human condition, especially the feminine side.

He does not know that Anatol is Arthur Schnitzler himself. The playwright, since he was sixteen years old, has been a seducer of women, flitting between "sweet young things," often virgins from the serving classes, and married bourgeois ladies. The pursuit of sex consumes his existence. He fills a thick diary and a secret autobiography with accounts of his sexual exploits, logging every orgasm. He prefers sex outdoors in the Vienna Woods, where he can howl like a wolf at climax, as if in great pain. He falls in love at the flash of an ankle and out of it twice as quickly. With one young lover, a seamstress, he achieves orgasm 326 times in eleven months, on top of many times more with casual conquests. He is compulsively concupiscent, unable to walk past a young woman without thinking, *Why not?*

There are setbacks—pregnancies, suicide threats, infections, and bouts of conscience—but nothing stops the young Lothario until his father breaks into his private drawer and reads his diaries. Johann Schnitzler, a laryngologist, orders his son to read every page and scrutinize every illustration in the standard three-volume medical work on venereal disease, "so that I might learn . . . the possible consequences of a sinful life." Arthur appears chastened. He becomes editor of his father's journal of laryngology and works at the same hospital. But at lunch breaks and after hours, he propositions women for sex. He blames his father for his bad feelings. "I couldn't forget for a long time the treacherous method he had used," he complains, "and if we were never able to establish a completely open relationship, the memory of this betrayal of trust surely played its part."[7] If there is one thing Schnitzler learns from his father, it is that no man can be trusted in matters of sex. His father's admonition saps his confidence. Arthur Schnitzler cannot see a patient without feeling inadequate or write a play without fearing it will flop. Vienna's premier dramatist looks into the mirror and sees a man who has been failed by his father. Instead of reflecting on the psychological causes of his fragility, he ups the frantic pace of his promiscuity. "Faithfulness," he writes, "was something I saw, at best, as . . . unlikely."[8]

After his father's death, he visits his mother daily to play new symphonic scores by Strauss, Goldmark, and Mahler four-handed at the piano. He seeks reassurance from his contemporaries: from the distracted Herzl, from the admiring Hofmannsthal, and most of all from a hotelier's wife in Merano whom he befriends while on holiday. Olga Waissinix is his own age, not Jewish, trapped in a loveless marriage. They begin a "metaphysical" epistolary friendship. Olga refuses to meet Schnitzler, to protect her marriage, hollow as it may be. "I have thrown away five years of my life, the most beautiful, the best and I do not know for what," she tells Schnitzler. The more she refuses to see him, the more dependent Schnitzler becomes. He tells her of his love affairs, sends his manuscripts for criticism. Olga moves closer to Vienna, to ninety kilometers south of the city, but will not see him. In November 1897, missing her letters, Schnitzler learns that she has died, at thirty-five, of a cancer she never mentioned. He is devastated, blaming himself for failing to rescue Olga from a sexless jail in which he has tortured her with confessions of his own sexual freedom.

His grief is deepened by a second loss, no less covert. Schnitzler's main mistress, the actress Maria Reinhard, becomes pregnant and, in September 1897, gives birth. The baby dies within days. Schnitzler is racked with guilt. He loves Maria, whom he calls Mizzi, and has furnished a home for her and the baby. He keeps a second girlfriend, also called Mizzi, or Mizzi-2. And he continues to go to the woods for casual sex. He is thirty-five years old, acting like a schoolboy in an unattended candy store. His conduct is inexcusable. He is walking proof of Krafft-Ebing's "abnormally intensified sensuality" among Jews, and he is profoundly confused. Freud's biographer, Peter Gay, argues that by copying the promiscuity of gay men Schnitzler reveals a suppressed homosexuality. Take this theory or leave it, Schnitzler is either an incurable sex addict or an indefatigable social scientist.

Schnitzler, in 1897, writes a taut play called *Reigen*, later to be filmed as *La Ronde* (1950) and *Eyes Wide Shut* (1999). Styled as a social comedy, *Reigen* gives a graphic account of the destructive outcomes of sex without love. In ten scenes, a prostitute has sex with a soldier, who then sleeps with a parlor maid. The maid is seduced by a young gentleman, who goes home to his wife, who has a lover of her own . . . and round it goes until, at the end, a member of the nobility is reduced to copulating with the whore from the opening scene. In Max Ophüls's 1950 film, the plot is a case history of the spread of venereal disease. In Stanley Kubrick's 1999 script, it explores sex and fantasy within marriage, the permissible and the prohibited. Almost twenty other films are based on *Reigen*. It is a play of limitless possibilities. Above all else, it is a morality tale.

Schnitzler's text, printed in a limited edition, serves both as a biopsy of Viennese sexual hypocrisy and as a summary of all that one man has learned during twenty years of sexual addiction. The sex in his diary has not been undertaken purely for pleasure but, in part, at least, as research into what happens when humans have sex outside marriage, a subject so off-limits that Schnitzler is not the least surprised when his play is banned by the imperial censor. He is not a typical philanderer. Unlike the notorious London womanizer Frank Harris, he shows interest in his women and evokes sympathy for them in his works; Mizzi-1 appears in his 1908 novel, *Der Weg ins Freie* (*The Road into the Open*). Schnitzler is, at once, an avid participant in sex, an observer, and a social reformer: too many roles for one man to play and stay sane. On the verge of a breakdown, he is relieved to know that no less an authority than Sigmund Freud considers him a pioneering sexologist.

Although they live in the same district, Freud and Schnitzler avoid each other for years. Like math wizards in a Monte Carlo casino, they look the other way and cross the room. It is Schnitzler who breaks the ice in May 1906, on Freud's fiftieth birthday. "My dear Professor," he writes, "Even if you have almost forgotten who I am, allow me to add my congratulations to the many that you will receive today. I am indebted to your writings for a host of strong and profound ideas . . ." Freud's reply is effusive. "For many years," writes Freud:

> I have been conscious of the far-reaching conformity existing between your opinions and mine on many psychological and erotic problems. . . . I have often asked myself in astonishment how you came by this or that piece of secret knowledge which I had acquired by a painstaking investigation of the subject, and I finally came to the point of envying the author whom hitherto I had admired.
>
> Now you may imagine how pleased and elated I felt on reading that you too have derived inspiration from my writings.[9]

There are intimations here that Freud fears being outshone, even unmanned, by Schnitzler. The sentence "I finally came to the point of envying the author whom hitherto I had admired" is a Freudian slip of the first order. *Envy* is a key word in the Freud lexicon, primarily associated with the penis. Freud appears to defer to Schnitzler's superior knowledge of the sexual act, a unique concession by a man who never yields to any other in his field. He also hints at a secret jealousy of Schnitzler's prowess, so exotic compared to Freud's dull and conventional matrimonial situation.

They exchange letters twice more over sixteen years, still avoiding a formal meeting. Freud writes to Schnitzler on his sixtieth birthday in May 1922: "Whenever I get deeply absorbed in your beautiful creations I invariably seem to find beneath their poetic surface the very presuppositions, interests, and conclusions which I know to be my own."[10] He is Schnitzler's most devoted reader.

Schnitzler visits Freud on June 16:

> He was very welcoming. Enjoyable about [our] hospital and military times, the bosses we shared, etc.—Lieutenant Gustl, etc.— then he shows me his library—his own works, translations, his students' works;—all kinds of small antique bronzes etc.;—he no longer ordains [analysts], trains only pupils who let themselves be analyzed by him. Gives me a nice new edition of his lectures.— Accompanies me at a late hour from Berggasse to my apartment.— The conversation becomes warmer and more personal;—About aging and dying.[11]

Each mirrors the other's concerns. The monologue of Schnitzler's suicidal *Lieutenant Gustl* (1900) bears close resemblance to a patient's narrative on the psychoanalytic couch. Gustl blames his unhappiness on the army's archaic code of honor and on the wretched Jews. The first of Schnitzler's works to address Austrian anti-Semitism, it gets him sacked from the military reserves and attacked as an enemy of the state. His novel *Der Weg ins Freie* shows Vienna exercising oh-so-courteous prejudice against a Jewish composer, possibly Gustav Mahler. In *Professor Bernhardi* (1912), a Jewish hospital physician, who could be Schnitzler's father, is persecuted by church and state for his alleged neglect of a dying girl, whose dreams he interprets in quasi-Freudian fashion. In 1913, one of Freud's favorite disciples, Theodor Reik, publishes

Arthur Schnitzler as Psychologist, a monograph undoubtedly written with Freud's approval.

Reigen, above all, speaks to Freud's agenda. It shows how in a sexually repressed society, sex subverts the social order. If a serving girl in coitus can humiliate a middle-class doctor, how do they behave with their clothes on? Schnitzler sees that sex weakens social superstructures and endangers social order. He anticipates Freud in declaring sex to be the source of all neurosis and, like Hirschfeld, ascribes its confusions to the artificiality of city life. The difference is that Vienna, unlike Berlin, where Hirschfeld uncovers a bold sex club land, buries its urges deep in the rustling woods. It needs Freud to bring them out. The refrain in Schnitzler's works is *this will not end well*.

His own miseries are suddenly beyond relief. The deaths of Olga and the baby capsize his charmed life. Two years later, in 1899, Mizzi becomes pregnant again. During the week of her twenty-sixth birthday, she suffers an appendicitis attack. She is rushed in excruciating pain to the hospital, where she dies on the operating table, or soon after. The attending physicians are Schnitzler's brother Julius and his cousin Ludwig. There is no postmortem. This could be a cover-up for medical negligence. Schnitzler, bereft, pays for a funeral in the central cemetery. "I loved her best of all people on earth, my beloved, friend and bride," he tells a colleague, suspending his diary and his woodland hunts for several weeks.[12] For the rest of his life, he wears mourning on March 18, the anniversary of Mizzi's death (in 2014, to mark her connection with Schnitzler, the city of Vienna declares her grave a historical monument).

Four months later, his eye falls on an actress, Olga Gussman, "not pretty but sharp for 18." Olga is middle-class, Jewish, and a virgin. She bears the name of his first true love, Olga (what might Freud make of that?). She visits Schnitzler at his consulting rooms. He, turning forty, seduces her. She becomes pregnant. Schnitzler, undecided, frets over "the two spectres that stand over our bed—my [sexual] past and her future." Olga gives birth to a son, Heinrich, on August 9, 1902. Schnitzler writes in his diary: "At 4 o'clock the baby came into the world. At 5 I began a novel." They marry a year later, under pressure from both families, in the Schopenhauergasse synagogue on the outskirts of the city, close to the Vienna Woods. Their daughter, Lili, is born in 1909. The Schnitzlers pose for a smug, plump, famous photograph. It appears on the cover of several Jewish anthologies as a portrait of the perfect Viennese bourgeois family, secure in its social status.

Behind the façade, the marriage, like Herzl's, is doomed. Olga resents Schnitzler for disrupting her stage career. He blames her for the decline in his output. "You know, it isn't the political situation but our relationship that makes me incapable of working," he tells her.[13] Olga matches him blow for blow. In 1921, she confesses to having an affair with her voice teacher, the composer Wilhelm Gross. Schnitzler agrees to a rabbinic divorce and a judicial separation. Olga leaves Vienna and reassumes her maiden name. Lili, who stays with her father, has tantrums at school and is sent for assessment to Anna Freud the child psychologist. Sitting in the waiting room while the assessment is being conducted, Schnitzler finally meets Sigmund Freud. They exchange courtesies, nothing more. They meet again in 1926, when Freud consults Schnitzler on his heart condition. In all matters of the heart, Freud recognizes Schnitzler as the superior authority.

In 1921, the year Schnitzler's marriage ends, *Reigen* reaches the stage. In Vienna, it is shut down after anti-Semitic outbursts. In Berlin, there are thirty-four arrests, a trial, and thirty-four acquittals. On tour in Czechoslovakia, Schnitzler faces swastika flags and threats of violence. A bachelor once more, he becomes involved with three young women, playing each off against the others. Passion has gone from his life. He receives a letter from the sister of his second Mizzi, informing him that Mizzi has ended her life with poison.

On holiday in Venice, his daughter, Lili, seventeen years old, falls in love with a uniformed fascist, Arnoldo Cappellini, twenty years her senior. Schnitzler consents to the marriage. The next summer, about to go for an evening walk with her husband, Lili slips into the bathroom and shoots herself with Arnoldo's revolver. The breast wound is not thought to be life-threatening. Cappellini telegraphs to Schnitzler that Lili is in the hospital, recovering. Anna Mahler, the composer's daughter, follows with a second telegram, informing him that Lili is gravely ill. Schnitzler heads to the airport, where he finds Olga ahead of him in the queue. In Venice, she heads straight to the hospital. Schnitzler refuses to go. This former hospital doctor and chronicler of human foibles cannot bring himself to set eyes on his beloved daughter—alive or, hours later, dead. His terrible inertia is recounted to me, years later, by a shocked Anna Mahler.

He spends weeks reading his daughter's private diary, repeating his own father's transgression. His son, Heinrich, directs a play at the Volkstheater. His latest mistress, Clara Katharina Pollaczek, takes an overdose of sleeping pills when he refuses to marry her. Schnitzler, by now, has no explanation for the things women do from love. Clara survives. On October 21, 1931, aged sixty-nine, Schnitzler suffers a brain hemorrhage and dies, his head in Clara's hands.

The Nazis suppress his works. By the time his plays are staged again, society and sexuality have moved on. Class is no longer a factor in sexual relations. Penicillin has reduced venereal disease. Anti-Semitism is muted by Holocaust awareness. Schnitzler's themes become redundant. All that remains is the strong supposition that, without Schnitzler, there could have been no Freud.

At the start of 1897, Sigmund Freud is forty years old, a nonentity, barely able to afford the rent for the two connecting apartments he inhabits at 19 Berggasse, in the genteel ninth district of Vienna. Freud requires twelve rooms on the second floor of a new building to accommodate his family of six children, his household staff, and a struggling medical practice. So far, every discovery he has announced has been shot down in derision. His seduction theory—the idea that neurosis stems from repressed memories of childhood sexual acts—is scorned by Krafft-Ebing as "a scientific fairy-tale." Freud is more puzzled than pained. He believes he has revealed "the solution to a more than thousand-year-old problem—'a source of the Nile!'"[14]

Confident as he tries to sound, his situation is parlous. Freud's grand ideas are derived from his patients, who are mostly middle-class Viennese Jewish women with time and money to lavish on their neuroses. His pet hypothesis, the seduction theory, postulates that many women show the delayed effects of forgotten sexual assaults in their infancy. Freud believes pedophilia is rife in Vienna, particularly in Jewish families. He cannot get anyone to concur.

His father dies at the age of eighty-one. Freud, not the most devoted of sons, is distraught. He describes his bereavement as "the most significant event, the most decisive loss, of a man's life." He spends the first half of 1897 mourning his father and examining his own soul. To break through to the infantile sexual roots of adult emotional disturbance, he must empty his mind of all unnecessary clutter. In the course of this clear-out, Freud makes a single, terrible error in judgment, a slip so serious that it will ultimately topple his reputation.

In September 1897, Freud returns from his summer break—"refreshed, cheerful, impoverished, at present without work," he tells his friend Wilhelm Fliess, a Berlin ear, nose, and throat specialist with whom he has spent seven years developing the seduction theory. In the next sentence, he informs Fliess that he "no longer believes" in the theory. His reasons are, first, that he has failed to "bring any analysis to a real conclusion," and, second, that if adult hysteria is caused by childhood sexuality, every father, "not excluding my own," would have to be suspected of "being perverse" with his children. Since Freud refuses to believe that his father abused him as a child, the theory must be wrong. Instead, he now thinks that hysteria is caused by repressed *fantasies* of sexual activity in the infant mind. He has no evidence for this idea beyond his present line of logic. In practice, if a patient now tells him she remembers an adult playing with her sexually as a girl, Freud will consider this to be the child's imagination, acting as a cause of her adult sexual problem. Freud orders Fliess not to discuss his change of mind. He is happy with the outcome, adding with Jewish equivocation, "I have more the feeling of a victory than defeat (which is surely not right)."[15]

Two weeks later, delving into his own infancy, Freud tells Fliess that self-analysis has raised no sexual memories of his father, only of his mother. This is the start of his Oedipus theory. When, later that year, a patient recounts that she was bloodily raped at two years old by her own father, Freud interprets her memory as fantasy. From now on, he refuses to take his patients' stories literally. The seduction theory is dead. "This renunciation," concludes a Freudian apologist, "opened a new chapter in the history of psychoanalysis."[16] This is, in fact, the moment when Freud becomes fraud. What history fails to perceive is that he crosses the bridge from failure to fame by means of deceit.

More books have been written about Freud than any other person of his time. Most, even those by enemies, acknowledge him as a historic personality. Freud, in his dreams, cherishes "the expectation of eternal renown."[17] For half a century after his death, he is recognized as one of the makers of modern civilization. He is quoted by world rulers and studied by philosophers. His ideas infiltrate every niche of society, arts, and scholarship. The letter in which he abandons the seduction theory goes unnoticed until the 1980s, when Jeffrey Moussaieff Masson, project director of the Freud Archives, brings to light Freud's exchanges with Fliess and publishes them, with Anna Freud's permission. Masson argues at first that rejecting the seduction theory is the key to Freud's goal:

> The question whether psychoanalysis could have emerged had Freud retained his earlier belief that the memories of his patients were real, not fantasies, is hardly peripheral to the practice of psychoanalysis (and perhaps to the practice of psychotherapy in general since most therapies are based, openly or implicitly, on Freudian theory). Psychoanalysts, beginning with Freud himself, agree that the abandonment of the seduction theory was the central stimulus to Freud's later discoveries.[18]

However, Masson's charge that Freud suffered "a failure of courage"[19] outrages the Freudian establishment, which bans him from the archives and shuts down his research. Most of Freud's papers are lodged at the Library of Congress in Washington, DC, under an arrangement that withholds documents from public view until, successively, 2020, 2038, 2053, 2057, and, in one instance, 2113. There are many things that Anna Freud and her clique do not wish us to know about Freud, starting with the bad move he made in 1897.

Suppression, Freud believes, breeds neurosis. The Masson incident opens the gates to a new breed of demolitionists, who attack Freud as a liar and sociopath. The most hostile is the literary scholar Frederick Crews, who depicts Freud as an egotist, drug addict, bully, and megalomaniac. "Freud, who cared only about the cause to which his name was attached," writes Crews, "found it imperative to inflate his results, to make promissory claims, to meet objections through sophistry, scorn, and ad hoc tinkering, and to pile further theory atop postulates that had never been validated."[20]

By the time Crews wields his pickaxe in 2017, even orthodox Freud-ians call themselves post-Freudian, and Freud's stature as a scientist is ruined. At best, he is seen as a philosopher of human conduct; at worst, as a speculator. Between these reputational extremes, the personality of Sigmund Freud recedes into a spiritual limbo, awaiting a judgment that will be conclusive only when the last of the documents is released by the Library of Congress in 2113. What we know of Freud consists of what he wants us to know, what he vehemently denies, and what has seeped out through neutral sources. Freud, at once enticing and forbid-ding, will always divide opinion. Among the most intriguing untapped mysteries are his deep—and strongly denied—roots in Jewish faith and thought.

On his thirty-fifth birthday, May 6, 1891, Sigmund Freud receives a gift from his father. Opening it, he finds the family Bible, rebound in fresh leather and embellished with a flyleaf message in classical Hebrew addressed to *"ben yakir li Shlomo"* (the son who is dear to me, Shlomo). Jacob Freud expects Sigmund, whom he calls by his Jewish name, can read and understand cursive Hebrew script and will recog-nize five microquotations that he takes from verses in Judges, Num-bers, and Psalms. Jacob's message is one of moral encouragement: "You have looked upon God's face, you heard and rose and you flew upon the wings of the Spirit." Jacob expresses happiness at Sigmund's ascent. He signs off, "from your father who loves you with everlasting love, Jacob, son of Rabbi Shlomo Freud."[21] Earlier messages on the flyleaf record the death of Jacob's father and, days after, Sigmund's birth.

Jacob's motives are, like his handwriting, not entirely deciphera-ble. He is a proud father who, aware that his son has forsaken God, is nonetheless entrusting him with a religious heirloom as a reminder of his everlasting love (*"mazkeret vezikaron ahava"*) and a gentle exhorta-tion to return to the faith. Jacob is an elderly man, passing on a baton that he himself has neglected, but he does so with a certainty that his son shares the same foundations. We learn from Jacob's inscription that Sigmund Freud, at thirty-five, is literate in the Hebrew language and familiar with Scripture. Sigmund may dismiss God as an illusion and religious observance as "a compulsive obsessive neurosis," but Freud does not, then or ever, disavow his Jewish identity. "My parents were Jews, and I have remained a Jew myself," he writes in a 1925 memoir. He repeats this statement in a seventieth birthday letter, written to the B'nai B'rith social club, recalling that he joined their lodge "in the years after 1895," a time when he felt most alone in Vienna. "That you were Jews could only be agreeable to me; for I was myself a Jew, and it had always seemed to me not only unworthy but positively senseless to deny the fact." Freud goes on to ascribe two traits in himself that he recognizes as Jewish: "Because I was a Jew I found myself free from many prejudices which inhibited others in the use of their intellect; and, as a Jew, I was prepared to join the Opposition and to do without agreement."[22] These are significant declarations of faith or something close to it.

Freud being Freud, however, he promptly contradicts himself. "I have always been an unbeliever and was brought up without any religion," he tells B'nai B'rith. This, we know, cannot be true if he can read his father's inscription, and if one follows the facts of his life. Born in Freiburg (Pribor) at the eastern edge of the Austrian empire, Sigmund Freud is circumcised at eight days old and raised in a Jewish community of one hundred souls. Freiburg is not an East European shtetl, rather a melting pot of Austrian and Russian Jews where Yiddish, German, and Czech intermingle in the marketplace. Its surrounding lakes and wooded hills are spectacularly beautiful; Freud will always long for this paradise lost.

Both parents come from Hasidic families. Jacob Freud, a traveling salesman (*wanderjude*) in wool, salt, suet, hides, and other products, is a dreamer who never brings home much money. Amalia is his third wife, twenty years his junior; they married in a Reform ceremony.[23] In 1859, Jacob's business fails, and his brother goes to jail for currency fraud. The family, fleeing Freiburg, descends on relatives in Leipzig, then moves on to Vienna, where Amalia's father has a wool business.

Vienna in 1860 has 6,200 Jewish residents; by 1870, there are 40,000; by the turn of the century 150,000. The city offers Jews the option of assimilation without ostracism. Jews and ex-Jews remain friends. The Freuds settle in Leopoldstadt, the Jewish district. Amalia speaks Yiddish to her children, never learning German. In common with most Jewish boys, Sigmund's thirteenth birthday is marked by some form of bar mitzvah. Freud mentions receiving "in his fourteenth year" an edition of Ludwig Börne's works, a typical bar mitzvah present of the time.

At school, he is taught religious studies by an observant Jew, Samuel Hammerschlag, a man whom Freud cherishes as a "fatherly caring friend." In a glowing obituary in November 1904, Freud writes that "religious instruction served [Hammerschlag] as a way of educating towards humanism." Freud cannot admit that Hammerschlag taught religion simply because he believed in it.

Freud has a pen pal, Eduard Silberstein, in the Romanian town of Iasi. In letters to Silberstein, Freud jokes about the quirks and rules of Jewish festivals, habits he can only have observed in his parents' home. He cites passages in the Passover Seder and mentions the chicken ceremony that precedes Yom Kippur.[24] Freud is not a man who knows nothing of Judaism. In an introduction to the 1939 Hebrew edition of *Totem and Taboo*, he claims to be "an author who is ignorant of the language of holy writ, who is completely estranged from the religion of his fathers—as well as from every other religion—and who cannot take a share in nationalist ideals, but who has yet never repudiated his people, who feels that he is in essential nature a Jew and who has no desire to alter that nature." Replying to a Yiddishist who sends him a book on Hasidism with a Hebrew inscription, Freud regrets that "today I am not even able to read your dedication which is evidently in Hebrew characters."[25] *Evidently?* Freud is able to read his father's message inside the family Bible. Why he now denies recognizing Hebrew script is puzzling. It looks like a classic Freudian case of willful suppression, and its effects are not insignificant in his work.

At medical school in Vienna, he hates the sight of blood and decides to study diseases of the mind. That takes him to Paris for twenty weeks to observe the neurologist Jean-Martin Charcot, who treats hysteria as an illness rather than a feminine affectation. Charcot, a man of personal warmth and paternal solicitude, becomes a role model to Freud, who names one of his sons Jean-Martin. Freud, writes his reverent biographer Ernest Jones, is "curiously dependent for reassurance" on mentors.[26]

He translates Charcot's lectures into German and copies his use of hypnosis—unsuccessfully—on Viennese patients with neurosis. Then he reads Charcot's claim that "nervous illnesses of all types are innumerably more frequent among Jews" and his adulation fades.[27]

164

Charcot's star pupil, the Parisian Pierre Janet, invents the useful term *subconscious*, a term which Freud adapts to *the unconscious*. Janet connects childhood incidents with adult trauma and fosters a kind of transference between patient and analyst. Accusing Freud of plagiarism, Janet sneers that his fellow pupil's form of psychoanalysis is applicable only to a specific Viennese, meaning Jewish, type of sexual angst. One of Janet's pupils is the Swiss physician Carl Jung.

Freud is almost thirty before he is licensed to practice. His next priority is to get married. His feelings for Martha Bernays during their four-year celibate engagement overflow in nine hundred–odd letters, which Ernest Jones extols as one of the world's great love stories. The letters that have been released so far show Freud to be a controlling lover, restricting Martha's freedoms to meet whom she likes and telling her what kind of wife she should be. He is rude to her mother and orders Martha to terminate relations with her brother, Eli, who is about to wed Freud's sister Anna. (Eli migrates to New York; his son, Edward, a public relations guru, saves Freud from poverty in 1920 by publishing a US edition of *Introductory Lectures on Psychoanalysis*.) Freud, an Eastern Jew, feels cultural inferiority to his in-laws.

Martha is the granddaughter of Haham Bernays, pioneer of modern German orthodoxy. Their wedding, in the Haham's Hamburg synagogue on September 14, 1886, is Freud's last concession to Judaism. From that day on, he orders Martha to abjure religion. She confides in a cousin that "not being allowed to light the Sabbath lights on the first Friday night after her marriage was one of [her] more upsetting experiences."[28] Freud promises Martha that, even without religion, their home will contain "something of the core, of the essence, of this meaningful and life-affirming Judaism,"[29] an assurance he has no intention of fulfilling.

Martha has six children in eight years, and then no more. She employs a cook, a housekeeper, a nanny, a governess, and a cleaner, far more than Freud can afford. He is a paterfamilias who presides, daily at one o'clock, over a family meal from which no child can be absent. Martha is excluded from Freud's work, or decides to exclude herself. Theodor Reik, on a walk with Frau Doktor Freud in the hills outside Vienna, "got the decided impression that she not only had no idea of the significance and importance of psychoanalysis, but had intensive emotional resistances against the character of analytic work. On such a walk she once said, 'Women have always had such troubles, but they needed no psychoanalysis to conquer them. After the menopause they become quieter and resigned.'"[30] Martha Freud is talking about sexual troubles. Her role in the marriage is to attend to Freud's needs, putting out his clothes in the morning and squeezing paste on his toothbrush. "In the fifty-three years of our marriage, there was not a single angry word between us," she says after his death, "and . . . I always tried as much as possible to remove the *misère* of everyday life from his path."

Instead of discussing work with his wife, Freud confides in her sister, Minna, who joins the household in June 1896. Minna helps Martha with the children, chats to patients in Freud's waiting room, writes some of his correspondence, and reads his proofs for publication. Minna is bright, witty, unafraid of speaking her mind. According to Carl Jung, she is Freud's mistress: "Freud has no idea that I knew about the triangle and his intimate relationship with his sister-in-law." Jung asks Freud to explain Minna's role. Freud replies stiffly: "I could tell you more, but I cannot risk my authority," an extraordinarily revealing confession, if true.[31]

Many years later, a researcher finds a hotel logbook showing that Freud and Minna booked a double bed while hiking together in the Swiss Alps in 1898. This is either evidence of a sexual tryst or proof of Freud's pinchpenny ways: Why pay for two rooms when one will do? Either way, if they have an affair it is short-term. At 19 Berggasse, Minna's bedroom is next to Freud and Martha's; she has to cross their room to reach hers. She is close to her sister, often sharing private jokes that no one else finds funny. She works with Freud every day and keeps up Jewish customs in defiance of his ban. As for sexual attraction, there are indications that, at the time of their Alpine trip, Freud feels no sexual desire, having told Fliess that "the libido is now a thing of the past." Shocking as it may seem, the man who places sex at the center of modern consciousness is himself sexually inactive.

By shutting Martha out of his work, Freud deprives himself of a shrewd and fearless critic who might have saved him from a run of disasters. In a hurry to make his name with a bold new cure, Freud experiments with cocaine, testing the drug on himself and Martha and publishing a paper which attracts much attention. Two Viennese ophthalmologists use the drug to numb the cornea during eye surgery. One of them, Carl Koller, has the procedure named after him. Freud, fuming, congratulates Koller on his discovery, which proves to be the drug's only respectable medical application. Freud, undeterred, continues to take cocaine in small quantities for about ten years.[32]

His next flutter is to order a small generator, to administer electric shocks to women with urinary leaks and men with erectile dysfunction. He inserts the wire in the urethra and throws a switch. Patients pay a premium rate for the treatment, which is completely useless. Freud, nonetheless, persists with shock therapy until the early 1890s, unable to admit that he is wrong.[33]

Josef Breuer, fourteen years his senior, becomes his Vienna mentor. Dr. Breuer lives in Hammerschlag's apartment block, and his wife, Mathilde, is a calming presence. Freud writes of Breuer: "He became my friend and helper in my difficult circumstances. We grew accustomed to share all our scientific interests with each other. In this relationship, the gain was naturally mine."[34] Breuer shows Freud the case notes of a young woman he is treating. "Anna O develops disturbances after the death of her father." Twenty-one years old and highly verbal, she complains of headaches, memory loss, paralysis, stomach cramps and hallucinations about snakes and skulls. Breuer, visiting her daily, is alarmed at her deterioration. One evening, he asks her to tell him a story in order to distract her from pain. As she talks, her symptoms ease. Breuer asks for childhood memories. One by one, her faculties return. The origins of her distress are "talked away [*wegerzählt*]." After two years, Anna O writes an account of what she calls Breuer's "talking cure." Freud acknowledges it as the start of psychoanalysis.

Breuer withholds parts of Anna O's story; "the plunging into sexuality in theory and practice is not to my taste."[35] Freud suspects the young woman fantasizes that Breuer has made her pregnant. Anna O, whose real name is Bertha Pappenheim, goes on to set up homes for battered wives, campaigning against rabbinic oppression of women; she is a figure of substance in early feminism. Breuer and Freud publish her case in 1895 in *Studies in Hysteria*. The book is widely read. One newspaper comments on Freud's narrative skills. Freud boasts that Breuer "has become fully converted to my theory of sexuality." Later: "At the College of Physicians Breuer gave a big speech in my honour and introduced himself as a converted adherent to the sexual aetiology. When I thanked him for this in private, he spoiled my pleasure by saying, 'But all the same, I don't believe it.' "[36] Freud, writes Breuer in 1907, "is a man given to absolute and exclusive formulations: this is a psychical need which, in my opinion, leads to excessive generalisation." Freud recasts his mentor as a mortal enemy. "Our intimate friendship gave way to total estrangement . . . I fell into the habit . . . of also avoiding the neighbourhood and the house."[37] When Josef Breuer, old and frail, sees Freud on the street, he throws opens his arms in greeting. Sigmund Freud just walks by.

He owes to Breuer his connection to Fliess, a fashionable Berlin quack who thinks that men have sexual cycles, like women, only twenty-three days instead of twenty-eight. Freud believes him. Fliess believes all men are a bit bisexual and, dangerously, that the roots of sexual neurosis are located in the nose. Freud sends Fliess a patient, Emma Eckstein, to have her nose operated on for the relief of premenstrual tension and (in Freud's view) excessive masturbation. Fliess leaves a piece of gauze inside her nasal cavity and Emma almost dies of postoperative infection. She emerges permanently disfigured, with a caved-in face. Incredibly, she stays friendly with both doctors and soon takes patients herself for psychoanalysis. In 1904, she writes a book on sexual education of children for which Freud offers an approving citation, perhaps by way of apology for her appalling mistreatment.

The letters that fly between Freud and Fliess are extravagantly affectionate and extraordinarily revealing. Freud is in love with Fliess, dazzled by his crackpot self-confidence. He addresses him as "dearest friend," "dearest Wilhelm," "cherished Wilhelm" and hangs his picture on his wall. He has dreams about Fliess, and would have named his last child Wilhelm had she not been a girl. He admits to a homosexual element in his infatuation and seems a little proud of it, as if he has personally confirmed Fliess's theory of bisexuality. He shares his own "original" suppositions with Fliess, among them the idea that there are two types of female orgasm, vaginal and clitoral, that coitus interruptus can damage male virility, and that witches use broomsticks as a penis substitute. In an 1893 memorandum, he advocates "free sexual intercourse" between young men and women as a remedy for masturbation. Freud inadvertently becomes the first medical champion of free love.

In October 1897, Freud informs Fliess that he remembers a thrill of sexual excitement as an infant at seeing his mother naked. "I have not yet grasped anything at all of the scenes themselves which lie at the bottom of the story. If they come and I succeed in resolving my own hysteria, then I shall be grateful to the old woman who provided me at such an early age with the means for living and going on living."[38] This fragment is the final piece in his Oedipus theory.

From this point on, Freud no longer needs Fliess, whom he casts, like Breuer, into outer darkness. Freud goes on to publish *The Interpretation of Dreams*, a year later *The Psychopathology of Everyday Life*, and in 1905 *Three Essays on Sexuality*. He has invented psychoanalysis and ordains strict rules for the session. The patient must lie on a couch, the therapist "behind him, out of sight." The patient "must be left to do the talking and must be free to choose at what point he should begin." Each session lasts fifty minutes and must be paid for on the spot. Freud, during the session, smokes cigars, strokes his dog, Jofi, and leaves the room to relieve himself. In one instance, he pays a patient, known as the Wolf Man, to continue attending so that Freud can complete his analysis. The Wolf Man is not cured. In the 1970s, the Wolf Man (real name Dr. Sergei Pankejeff) is found by a Viennese journalist, living in a care home. Karin Obholzer spends a year interviewing him. "If Freud was so great," Pankejeff says to her, "why do I still feel so rotten?"[39]

Freud's failures are frequent. One of the earliest and by far the worst is the case of Pauline Silberstein, wife of his teenaged pen pal, who suffers from depression. On May 14, 1891, Pauline, aged nineteen, jumps to her death from an upper story of Freud's building. It is not known if she jumps before or after seeing Freud. He never mentions her again to Silberstein, and both Jones and Gay omit Pauline from their authorized biographies. Better known is the case of "Dora" (Ida Bauer), a seventeen-year-old who walks out on Freud in October 1900 after eleven weeks of being treated for "hysteria," manifested in a troublesome cough. Dora tells Freud that her father's friend has made sexual advances toward her. Freud, writing up the case as an erotic fantasy, a fantasy that is largely his own, suggests that his failure is really hers: "I do not know what kind of help she wanted from me, but I promised to forgive her for having deprived me of the satisfaction of affording her a far more radical cure for her troubles."[40] Dora, who lives opposite Freud on Berggasse, dies in

New York in 1945 (her son, Kurt Herbert Adler, is a gifted conductor who becomes director of the San Francisco Opera).

There are more lapses. When an American analyst, Horace W. Frink, whom Freud is training, suffers a psychotic breakdown, Freud misinterprets the symptoms and persists with his plan to appoint Frink head of the New York Psychoanalytic Society. He urges a wealthy patient of Frink's to dump her husband and marry her analyst. Frink dies in 1936, in the throes of a manic episode.

Darker still, Freud welcomes the friendship of Stefan Zweig, an immoderately wealthy author of historical biographies. Zweig has a sexual problem. He is a compulsive flasher, who bursts out of bushes to expose his penis to passing girls. He carries about his person a note from Freud, explaining that he is receiving treatment for mental illness. There is only one source, a homosexual friend of Zweig's, for this lubricious information, but Freud, if he were aware of Zweig's habits, would have had an ethical duty to treat his condition and a civic duty to stop him being a public menace.[41] He continues to cultivate Zweig as a friend.

Freud makes up his rules as he goes along. A male patient, ending a long course of analysis, is invited to join the Freud family for dinner. His youngest child is named after another patient, Anna Lichtheim, daughter of Samuel Hammerschlag. His lack of boundaries knows no bounds, and his love of celebrities is legion. He boasts of treating Princess Marie Bonaparte—"a Napoleon on my couch!"—and goes on to train her as a psychoanalyst. He breaks a family holiday in Holland to see Gustav Mahler when the composer requests an emergency intervention during a marital crisis.

Patients flock to 19 Berggasse because it is the only place in Vienna where they can speak openly about their sexual problems. Freud is a safety valve on a seething cauldron of secrets. His apostles meet on Wednesday nights at his apartment. The Vienna Psychoanalytic Society includes Wilhelm Stekel, Alfred Adler, Karl Abraham, Otto Rank, and, a little later, Viktor Tausk, Hanns Sachs, and Sándor Ferenczi; all are Jews. Not all are medically trained. One, Max Graf, is a journalist, a music critic who sends his son "little Hans" to Freud for analysis. Starting with Adler, Freud falls out one by one with his followers as they become successful. Like Karl Marx, he turns a humanitarian impulse into a totalitarian charismatic movement. Unlike Marx, he needs non-Jewish validation.

In 1907, he recruits the Swiss psychologist Carl Gustav Jung. On their first encounter, Freud and Jung talk nonstop for thirteen hours. Before long Freud talks of Jung as "the ablest of my helpers." Jung asks for their friendship to be one of father and son. Freud replies, "If I am Moses, you are Joshua." Jung is professor at the Burghölzli, a psychiatric hospital of world renown. Freud considers moving to Zurich, exhilarated at having a follower of Jung's stature and un-Jewishness. Freud asks Karl Abraham, who mistrusts Jung, to:

> . . . please be tolerant and do not forget that it is really easier for you than it is for Jung to follow my ideas, for in the first place you are completely independent, and then you are closer to my intellectual constitution because of racial kinship, while he, as a Christian and a pastor's son, finds his way to me only against great inner resistances.[42]

That phrase "finds his way to me" belongs more to a cult leader than a scientist. Jung, he tells Abraham, "has saved psychoanalysis from becoming a Jewish national concern."[43]

Freud assimilates Jung's ideas on word association, the unconscious, and dementia. Their union lasts six years and ends badly. Jung renounces Freud's faith in the sexual origin of absolutely everything. He maintains the unconscious is not necessarily repressed but an active part of everyday life. He shows interest in paranormal phenomena—ghosts and poltergeists—and adopts a holistic approach to the entire life span, rather than just childhood and the sexually active years. In November 1912, Jung refers in a Munich lecture to "differences of opinion." Freud, who is in the audience, faints. Jung rushes over, lifts him up, and carries him to a couch, as if for analysis or burial. Freud pooh-poohs his faint as "a bit of neurosis that I ought to look into," telling Ernest Jones, his second non-Jewish associate, that there is "some piece of unruly homosexual feeling at the root of the matter."[44] Did Freud pass out for love of Jung? If so, the feeling is reciprocated. Jung admits to "an undeniable erotic undertone" in his relations with Freud, but he denounces these "abominable feelings." Jung hates homosexuals. He is also wary of Jews. He writes of "a difference between Jewish and Christian psychology."[45]

Their breach takes the form of a blunt ultimatum from Jung to Freud: "If ever you should rid yourself entirely of your complexes and stop playing the father to your sons and instead of aiming continually at their weak spots took a good look at your own for a change, then I will mend my ways and at one stroke stop being in two minds about you." Freud's response to this gauntlet is to propose "that we abandon our personal relations entirely."[46] Freud puts out word that Jung is anti-Semitic. Jung retorts that many of his best pupils are Jews. In the 1930s, linked to Nazi psychotherapists, he decides that "the Aryan unconscious has a greater potential than the Jewish unconscious."

Acrimonious as the parting is, Freud recognizes the rigor that Jung has brought. Jung, for his part, calls Freud's work "epoch-making," with a range of ideas that "touched nearly every sphere of contemporary intellectual life." Freud, without Jung, goes on to develop the idea of ego, id, and superego. Jung, without Freud, develops the "collective unconscious." In retrospect, it is amazing that they get along for as long as they do, given Jung's resistance to contradiction and Freud's propensity to obliterate anyone and anything that threatens his theories.

He banishes, in reverse order, Jung, Adler, Fliess, and Breuer. The Bernays family is demonized. Judaism is outlawed. God is declared dead. Time after time, Freud covers his traces to remove clues to his true self. His hostility to Judaism is so persistent that the last coherent work of his life, *Moses and Monotheism*, attacks the source of revelation by hypothesizing that the Giver of the Law is, in fact, an Egyptian. Freudians argue that he detests religion because it is irrational. Neutrals, using Freudian analysis, wonder whether Freud's hatred of God is not, at root, an Oedipal fixation. Freud has to kill the father to liberate the Jews from the tyranny of faith.

But so much of Freud's methodology derives from Judaism that his denial takes on the force of affirmation. Is Freud trying to conceal his debt to Jewish sources? Here are six Freudian themes that arise from the Talmud and the Old Testament.

1. Free association

A patient rambling through random thoughts and memories resembles the way the Talmud presents an argument, using voices from different schools, centuries apart, circling an issue without resolving it. "Talmudic scholars anticipated the modern 'stream of consciousness' technique," writes Victor Schermer, a Philadelphia psychotherapist. "It was as if they were seeking to decipher the flow of thought of higher and lower powers hidden within a human-authored text."[47]

2. The unconscious

Rabbinic literature discusses the conscious mind and its opposite, the unconscious. A leading analyst of the unconscious—defined as the force that drives one to sin—is the Musar thinker Israel Salanter. In Hasidism, the unconscious is a state of transcendence, removed from the material world. Schermer concludes: "If one substitutes 'Unconscious' for 'G-d,' the detective work involved in psychoanalytic interpretation is almost identical with Talmudic exegesis."[48]

Put another way, in a Talmudic court of law, the verdict is not guilty or innocent but guilty (*mezid*) or unintended (*shogeg*). An involuntary act is the unconscious at work. (The post-Freudian Viktor Frankl envisages a third state, above conscious and unconscious, which he calls the superconscious. That state equates both to the Jewish view of God's overview of the universe and to Freud's über-ich, the superego.)

3. The interpretation of dreams

In the famous biblical story, Joseph hears two prisoners recount their dreams and interprets their fate according to their unconscious motives. Joseph finds the butler to be blameless when a fly drops in the wine but suggests the baker may have unconsciously intended harm by leaving a stone in his dough. Freud contradicts Joseph in *The Interpretation of Dreams*, but he protests too much.

The Talmud is full of dreams. There is even a discussion in Berachot (56b) on how to separate true dreams from false. Karl Abraham informs Freud that psychoanalysis is based on Talmudic reasoning: "After all, our Talmudic way of thinking cannot disappear just like that."[49] Freud's denial is looking thin. Ken Frieden of Syracuse University: "I am less concerned with Freud's borrowings from ancient sources than with his persistent efforts to avoid such influence—or *to avoid the appearance of such influence.*"[50]

4. *Transference*

On the Day of Atonement, the sins of Israel are transferred to a goat, which is pushed over a cliff. Its death cleanses the people of guilt but, the rabbis specify, only for unconscious or unintended sin. Just like Freudian transference.

5. *Word association*

In August 1910, Gustav Mahler consults Freud about his wife's infidelity. The two men, both middle-aged Moravian Jews, walk for four and a half hours beside a Dutch canal. The conversation is mutually fulfilling. Freud reckons that no one has ever understood psychoanalysis as swiftly and comprehensively as Mahler; unsurprising, perhaps, given their shared Jewish background in bucolic small Czech towns.

Freud asks Mahler for his wife's full name. "Alma Maria," he replies. And his mother's? "Maria." Freud then offers an instantaneous deduction: Mahler has fallen in love with Maria, mistaking her for his mother. Placing her on a pedestal, he "withheld his libido from her" for fear of incest. Mahler has "a Holy Mother complex," says Freud. He should ignore Alma's infidelities, given that he himself is unable to satisfy her. Does Freud suspect that Mahler, like himself, has an underactive libido?

He goes on to propose that Alma, an artist's orphan daughter, loves Mahler both because he is much older and because his name sounds like *maler*, the German word for "painter." Freud's wordplay is based on a Talmudic exegetical device known as *gezera shava*, where the occurrence of a word in one text can clarify its appearance in another. One Maria explains the other. All Mahler has to do is revise his attitude to his wife and they will live happily ever after.

The composer responds with childhood flashbacks. He remembers hearing an organ grinder play a tune as his parents fight in their bedroom. This, he now understands, explains why his symphonies veer without warning from deadly serious to trivial and mundane. Mahler has grasped how the unconscious works.

He cables Alma that Freud's "magic word" has solved their problem; Freud tells Marie Bonaparte that he cured Mahler's impotence. Be that as it may, the "two Marias" trick is fake. Mahler's wife is called Alma. No one uses her middle name, Maria, nor could this frisky, cosmopolitan, bohemian Catholic woman be mistaken for Mahler's devout, disabled, parochial Jewish mother. Mahler did not marry Alma thinking she was his mother. If Mahler obtains relief by consulting Freud, it is, as he says, from "the magic word"—some intimation, possibly a Yiddish expression, that allows him to feel understood by a fellow Jew and therefore not alone in the world.

6. Puns

Rabbis in the Talmud speak Aramaic as their daily language, Hebrew on the Sabbath, and bits of Greek, Persian, Accadian, Syriac, and Latin as required. Often, in debate, they crack bad puns across two languages. At Tractate Sanhedrin 4b, for instance, the meaning of a biblical word, *totafot*, is debated. One sage opines that it is a composite of the Coptic word *tot* with the Phrygian *fot*. The rabbis kick these terms around for half a page, having fun with wordplay, just as Freud does.

A patient he calls the "Rat Man" is a fitness freak who exercises to excess and starves himself with diets. Anorexia nervosa is a recognized medical condition, but Freud ignores it. He takes the Rat Man's history and finds that his patient is upset that his fiancée is spending too much time with her American cousin Richard, whom everyone calls Dick. Rat Man wants to kill Dick. Freud reminds him that *dick* is the German word for "fat." Freud tells the Rat Man that he is trying to kill his own inner "dick" by extreme weight loss. The deduction is no more than a pun, and a superficial one at that, but it closes the case for Sigmund Freud.

These are just a few examples of the Jewish religious resources that Freud draws on. There are many more, and they spring to his lips in moments of crisis. The night after the Nazis march into Vienna in March 1938, the Psychoanalytic Society meets at Freud's apartment. Facing a roomful of traumatized Jewish shrinks, Freud reaches back into his Talmud and tells the story of Rabbi Jochanan ben Zakai and the Roman warrior Vespasian. Not long before the fall of Jerusalem in 70 CE, the scholar Rabbi Jochanan smuggles himself out of the city and surrenders to the Romans. Brought before the general, he tells Vespasian that he will be the next emperor in Rome. As a reward, he asks that his fellow rabbis be set free "to open a school at Yavneh to continue the study of Torah." Freud misidentifies the Roman general as Titus, but otherwise he knows the story well.

His disciples look around in consternation, fearing the old man has lost his mind amid the Nazi violence. Freud continues. "We are going to do the same," he says quietly. "We are, after all, accustomed by our history and tradition and some of us by personal experience, to being persecuted." Freud has recast his psychoanalysts as ancient rabbis, their loins girded to save the faith, and himself as Rabbi Jochanan, a figure as central to Judaism as Moses, Ezra, and Hillel. At this moment of existential crisis, Freud reaches deep into Jewish faith for a promise of salvation.

Three months on, once Marie Bonaparte bribes the Nazis to let Freud go and Ernest Jones secures British visas, Freud and his family leave for London, settling near Swiss Cottage, a district popular with Hitler refugees. Here, he becomes a magnet for the British intelligentsia, receiving teatime visits at Maresfield Gardens from H. G. Wells, and from Virginia Woolf and her husband, Leonard, his British publishers. Stefan Zweig arrives with Salvador Dalí. A "young Oxford philosopher" visits the Freuds one Friday afternoon in the summer of 1938. Martha tells him: "You must know that on Friday evenings good Jewish women light candles for the approach of the Sabbath. But this monster—unmensch—will not allow it because he says religion is superstition."[51] Freud confirms: "Yes, it is superstition." The visitor interprets this exchange as affectionate and thinks no more of it.

Three weeks into the Second World War, in agony from an ulcerated cancer in his mouth, Freud persuades his doctor to help end his existence. At Golders Green Crematorium, eulogies are spoken by Zweig and Jones. Zweig calls Freud "a spiritual hero . . . oblivious to the temptations of fame and vanity . . . a complete and responsible soul, dedicated to his mission, a mission that . . . enriches all of mankind." Without Freud, he says, "each of us would think, judge, feel, more narrowly, less freely, less justly." All true.

Receiving consolation visits at home, Martha announces that in more than half a century together she and Freud never exchanged a harsh word. But the Friday night after Freud dies, Martha lights Sabbath candles at the family table. And she continues to do so for the rest of her life.

Magnus Hirschfeld, after the First World War, buys Joseph Joachim's mansion on Beethovenstrasse and names it the Institute of Sexual Science.[52] Above the entrance, he posts a Latin motto: *Sacred to Love and to Sorrow.* He offers treatment for erectile dysfunction and venereal disease, as well as advice on contraception, gender identity, and genetic compatibility. In one year, he receives four thousand inquiries from men and women. He opens a special department for transgender patients. In an open environment, Hirschfeld himself finally comes out. At fifty, he takes a lover thirty years his junior. Karl Giese, of working-class background and limited education, calls Hirschfeld "Papa." An effeminate man who likes to be whipped, Giese deputizes for Hirschfeld in his absence. With the largest card index of sexual knowledge ever assembled, as well as a collection of artifacts featuring all known varieties of sexual conduct, Hirschfeld is the God of sexual knowledge. He buys the house next door.

Where he gets the money is unclear. Some of it comes from deals with pharmaceutical companies, makers of contraceptive jellies and virility supplements called Titus Pearls. Not all these remedies are tested. Some are useless. The institute's accounts show deficits. A filmmaker, Richard Oswald, arrives to direct the first film about homosexuality. Starring Conrad Veidt as a concert violinist who finds himself attracted more to his girlfriend's brother than to her, *Different from the Others* ends with a face-to-camera homily from Hirschfeld in which the title card shows him saying: "The persecution of homosexuals belongs to the same sad chapter of history in which the persecutions of witches and heretics is inscribed." Hirschfeld is credited as the film's medical adviser. The press dubs him "the Einstein of Sex." The Nazis call him "the apostle of sodomy." In Munich, he is beaten up by Nazi thugs and left for dead. In Vienna, shots are fired at one of his lectures.

Handing over his institute to the government, he sets off on a tour of the Soviet Union and Asia. In China, he falls in love with his interpreter, Li Shiu Tong (also known as Tao Li). Giese goes wild with jealousy but settles for a ménage à trois. At a party, Hirschfeld is pictured holding hands with Giese, who is wearing a dress. Above the institute, his sister rents rooms to gifted men and women: the philosophers Walter Benjamin and Ernst Bloch, the dancer Anita Berber, the writer Christopher Isherwood. In a city simmering with artistic and political ferment, the institute becomes a magnet for cultural tourists. Hirschfeld shows the French diarist André Gide cases of whips and thongs. The Soviet director Sergei Eisenstein, the Greek writer Nikos Kazantzakis, and the Bulgarian author Elias Canetti drop by. Outside, rent boys patrol the pavements. "Berlin meant boys," writes Isherwood.

Hirschfeld goes traveling once more with Tao Li. In Chicago, his lecture on homosexuality is illustrated with "beautiful revealing pictures." He visits Egypt and Palestine, where "the sobbing Hasidic youths along the Wailing Wall in Jerusalem" contrast with boys and girls on the beach in Tel Aviv, "the 'beautiful spark of joy' flashing from their eyes . . . they appear to have overcome all the repressions and unconscious feelings of erotic inferiority often found at this age."[53] He is the first to spot Tel Aviv as a gay magnet. On May 6, 1933, members of the National Socialist student organization turn up in military formation on Beethovenstrasse. On a word of command, they enter the institute and ransack it, throwing most of the library—twenty thousand volumes, thirty-five thousand photographic slides—onto a bonfire. The rest they put up for sale at auction.

Hirschfeld plans a new institute in Paris, only to be thwarted by his oldest enemy. The appalling Albert Moll writes to the dean of the Paris medical faculty, with a copy to the Nazi foreign minister, Konstantin von Neurath:

> The former local doctor, Herr Dr Magnus Hirschfeld, tells in Paris and also in Lyon, that he was forced to leave Germany because of the persecution of Jews and also for political reasons . . . According to my information Magnus Hirschfeld has left Germany for completely different reasons, not because he is discriminated against as a Jew, also not because he is a Social Democrat but because rumour has it that there had been misconduct in a totally different direction . . .[54]

The whiff of sodomy brings Hirschfeld's ménage to police attention. Giese is arrested "on account of an incident in a bathhouse."[55] Deported from France, he joins a Czech lover in Brno, committing suicide when the Germans occupy the town. Hirschfeld takes an apartment in Nice with Tao Li. On his sixty-seventh birthday, May 14, 1935, he dies of a stroke. A rabbi speaks at his cremation. Asked once if he is a German, a Jew, or a world citizen, Hirschfeld replies: "All three."

Albert Moll reaps no profit from his perfidy. The Nazis cancel his medical license and give him the middle name "Israel." Evicted from his home, he is taken in by a former housekeeper and dies on September 23, 1939, the same day as Freud. At his funeral, the cemetery priest refuses to read a eulogy to a former Jew. His housekeeper is murdered in Ravensbrück concentration camp. The Institute of Sexual Science is bombed to rubble in an Allied raid on November 22, 1943.

Tao Li ends up in Vancouver, Canada, where, at his death in October 1993, a neighbor finds several suitcases in a dumpster. They are all that survives of the Institute of Sexual Science. A German scholar, Ralf Dose, recovers them for a Magnus Hirschfeld foundation, the nucleus of Berlin's thriving museum of homosexuality. History begins to recognize Hirschfeld as a champion of gay rights, a scholar of sexual diversity, and a promoter of gender equality.

Freud lives close to me. I pass his bust every day outside Swiss Cottage Library, on my way to the swimming pool. His house at Maresfield Gardens is a museum where I have given talks. One of my children attended the Anna Freud nursery. The Tavistock Institute, just around the corner, is a hub of psychoanalytic industry. If I need a psychotherapist, there are more here than anywhere on Earth. Freud is alive and well in Swiss Cottage. Vanity and vicissitudes aside, the world now salutes his great inspirations of 1897: that the seeds of our discomfort are sown in childhood, that most misery is caused by sex, and that the best way to relieve distress is by talking it out.

EIGHT

1905

THE KNOWN UNKNOWNS

Troubled wives: Clara and Fritz Haber, Elsa and Albert Einstein.

S cientific discoveries come in two forms. Some are cracked by means of assiduous observation, gradual elimination, and a dash of inspiration. Others, extremely rare, expose a sudden, unimagined vision of the universe, beyond prior cognizance. As a future US secretary of defense will put it in another context: "There are known knowns. There are things we know that we know. There are known unknowns. That is to say, there are things that we now know we don't know. But there are also unknown unknowns. There are things we do not know we don't know."[1]

It was always likely, for instance, given the numbing properties of alcohol and other substances, that someone would work out how to administer a safe anesthetic. The emergence of ether, chloroform, and laughing gas in the 1840s is part of an inexorable process. Even the exhilarating revelation of penicillin by Alexander Fleming in 1928 is anticipated twenty years earlier in Berlin by Paul Ehrlich's development of the first synthetic antibiotic, itself the product of three decades of laboratory work.

The first decade of the twentieth century brings a rush of break-throughs that transform human health and comprehension. None, however, is as stand-alone and unforeseen as Albert Einstein's theory of special relativity, bursting on an unsuspecting world in 1905 and reversing its most solid self-perceptions. Einstein is the double unknown. His discoveries come from nowhere, overturning a 1900 statement by the Cambridge mathematician Lord Kelvin to the effect that "there is nothing new to be discovered in physics now. All that remains is more and more precise measurement."

Einstein's contemporaries appear pedestrian by comparison, no matter how brilliant their contributions. The near-forgotten Karl Land-steiner makes modern surgery possible. A scientist at the University of Vienna, Landsteiner enters the exciting new field of immunology. But instead of joining the main group, which is working on meningitis, Landsteiner applies his lonely mind to an everyday crisis in hospital emergency rooms. When a woman is brought in hemorrhaging from a miscarriage, or a factory worker bleeding to death from a machine accident, the blood they have lost cannot be replaced, since there is no way of knowing if the patient will accept a transfusion or if the red cells will clump together in an effect known as "agglutination," usually with fatal consequences. Since nobody knows what the "right" blood might be, lives are pointlessly lost.

Landsteiner has an intuition that the body has an immune system that protects it from hostile invaders and that this system rejects the "wrong" blood. If that is the case, how is one to know which blood is friendly and which alien? Blood must come in types. Could they be hereditary? Would a child have the same type as its parent? Landsteiner takes blood from everyone in the lab and puts it under a microscope. By November 1901, he has two blood types, antigen-A and antigen-B, neither of which can be given to a person of the other group. Soon, he adds a third group, C (later O), which has no antigen. Soon after, two colleagues convince him of the existence of a fourth type, AB, which has both antigens.

Landsteiner spends five years developing testing methods for different bloods. He receives little or no recognition until, in 1907, a young Jewish doctor at New York's Mount Sinai hospital tests a blood donor against a patient, finds them both to be O, and performs the first human transfusion using blood typing and cross-matching. Dr. Reuben Ottenberg is just twenty-five years old. The procedure is a universal lifesaver. In the carnage of the First World War, the lives saved by blood transfusion amount to millions.

Nobody remembers Landsteiner. A private man, son of a peacock journalist and close to his mother, who shepherds him into the Roman Catholic Church to improve his employment prospects, he is almost fifty before he marries. In 1920, starved of funding in Vienna, he moves to Holland and on to the Rockefeller Institute in New York. In 1930, he is awarded the Nobel Prize in Physiology or Medicine. Some years later, he seeks a court injunction to remove his name from *Who's Who in American Jewry*, arguing that his identification as a Jew would cause "irreparable injury to my private life and profession," it being "detrimental to me to emphasize publicly the religion of my ancestors." In June 1943, aged seventy-five, Landsteiner suffers a fatal heart attack in his lab. Humble and hardworking, he has always described his blood type breakthrough as "accidental."

Landsteiner is a double outsider, suspect to his peers and especially to his former fellow Jews, who distrust his methods. In a rare moment of limelight, in 1901 Landsteiner is savaged, in front of the entire German Society of Scientists and Doctors, by the great Paul Ehrlich, who is preeminent in the field of bloods. Forget blood types, says Ehrlich. Everything in nature has a purpose, but "what good is it to the goat if it has in its blood something directed against the red cells?" Ehrlich, for once, is wrong.

A Breslau Jew, unconverted, gregarious, and charismatic, Ehrlich is Landsteiner's antitype, a patriot who balances his German loyalty against a romantic Jewish nationalism awoken in him by the Russian biochemist Chaim Weizmann. Denied a university post for reasons of race and religion, Ehrlich conducts his research in a Frankfurt institute funded by forward-thinking German industrialists. His range is phenomenal. He stains bacteria with dyes to diagnose leukemias by categorizing white blood cells. Tasked by Wilhelm II to search for a cure for the cancer that has killed the emperor's mother, Ehrlich stains cancer cells and attacks them with chemical agents. By trial and error, he becomes the father of chemotherapy.

His assault on Landsteiner is an episode in a turf war over research funds. Ehrlich's dismissal of blood types as "irrelevant" is symptomatic of a Darwinian environment in which German-Jewish scientists are searching for what Ehrlich calls "the magic bullet"; the cure to a major disease.[2] Ehrlich, who receives the 1908 Nobel Prize, is lionized in a 1940 Hollywood film, *Dr. Ehrlich's Magic Bullet*, in which he is played by Edward G. Robinson, a Romanian Jew; the director is a German refugee, William Dieterle.

A year after the Nobel award, sustained by bottles of mineral water and expensive cigars, and assisted by a Japanese aide, Sahachiro Hata, Ehrlich synthesizes a compound that destroys the spirochetes of syphilis. He patents it as "606" because it is the 606th substance that he has tried on a hospital ward of incurables. Marketed as Salvarsan and Neosalvarsan, it is the first and only effective treatment for syphilis until the production of penicillin nineteen years later. Ehrlich is acclaimed at a 1913 London medical convention as the greatest living medical scientist.

But there is a backlash to his breakthrough. Lutheran pastors and nationalists unite to launch an assault on Salvarsan, claiming that Ehrlich has polluted the German family by making illicit sexual liaisons less susceptible to the risk of death. They accuse him of testing the drug on Frankfurt prostitutes, putting their lives at risk, and they allege that he has made himself "filthy rich." At a 1914 libel trial, Ehrlich, whose name means "honorable" and whose morals are irreproachable, is barracked from the public gallery by racist agitators and paid whores as he enters the witness box. Although one of his accusers is jailed, Ehrlich emerges demoralized. He suffers a stroke and dies at sixty-one. "The whole world is in his debt," laments the London *Times*.

Ehrlich is the prototype German-Jewish scientist of his time: diligent, methodical, focused, curious, principled, and patriotic. He creates an investment culture to feed new research, leads German science to a position of world leadership, and, in October 1914, lends his name to the "Manifesto of the 93" scientists, artists, and theologians who declare support for Germany's war aims. "It is not true that Germany is guilty of starting this war," states the manifesto. Signing it is the price Paul Ehrlich must pay for being allowed to survive as an independent scientist in the German Reich.

In May 1905, a Swiss government clerk confides in a friend that he is working on something "very revolutionary." The clerk is not referring to his day job in the patent office in Berne. Early each morning before he goes to work, and late into the night when he returns, Albert Einstein, twenty-six years old, is remapping the universe. In four papers, written between March and June, Einstein tears up everything the world thought it knew about space.

His own summary offers the best précis of the four papers: "The first deals with radiation and the energy properties of light and is very revolutionary." Einstein asserts that the speed of light is constant for all objects and observers, no matter how rapidly or slowly they might be moving in relation to the light source. This idea remains unproven for fourteen years until, in 1919, a British expedition in West Africa, led by Sir Arthur Eddington, provides photographic evidence of the sun's gravitational pull on other stars during a solar eclipse. Eddington's testimony results in Einstein being awarded a Nobel Prize in 1921 "for services to theoretical physics." A century later, an American observatory records two black holes colliding in space. "We have detected gravitational waves," declares the observatory's director. "So it turns out Einstein was right all along," reads a front-page headline in the *Guardian*.[3] Never again does Einstein employ the term *revolutionary*.

The second paper appraises atoms and molecules in a determination of the true size of atoms. Among other applications, it defines the behavior of particles in milk during the making of cheese. The third proves that bodies suspended in liquids must already perform an observable random motion that is produced by thermal motion. This paper resolves a riddle which has defeated scientists for eighty years, as to why tiny particles such as pollen grains jiggle around when suspended in a glass of water. Einstein has no access to a laboratory when he makes this supposition. Within months, a German researcher with a powerful microscope confirms Einstein's solution to "Brownian motion."

The fourth paper is only a rough draft at this point; it is an electrodynamics of moving bodies that employs a modification of the theory of space and time. Taking the experiments of Galileo Galilei in 1632, Einstein proposes that "the velocity of light is independent of the motion of the light source." This is the basis of his theory of special relativity. It would be the idea for which Einstein is most famous, were it not for an afterthought in September that year, which he shares with the same friend, Conrad Habicht:

> One more consequence also crossed my mind. Namely, the relativity principle, together with Maxwell's equations, require that mass be a direct measure of the energy contained in a body. Light carries mass with it. With the case of radium there should be a noticeable reduction of mass. The thought is amusing and seductive; but for all I know, the good Lord might be laughing at the whole matter and might have been leading me up the garden path.

This digression is Einstein's theorem $E = mc^2$, probably the best-known formula in the history of science. The paper that describes it fills just three pages. In Einstein's equation, the increased relativistic mass (m) of a body multiplied by the speed of light squared (c^2) is equal to the kinetic energy (E) of that body. By defining the source of energy in mass and inferring that it can be released from a split atom, Einstein provides the means for humanity to blow itself to bits. "Think what might happen in a town if the dormant energy of a single brick were to be set free, say in the form of an explosion," muses the Viennese physicist Hans Thirring. "It would be sufficient to raze a city with millions of inhabitants to the ground." He adds: "This, however, will never happen."

At the end of June 1905, Einstein submits the STR paper under the title "On the Electrodynamics of Moving Bodies" to the journal *Annalen der Physik*. The article appears in volume seventeen of *Annalen*, he earns a PhD in physics and a small pay raise at the office, but the year ends without anyone shouting *Eureka!* or recognizing that the world has been rebooted. "He was very disappointed," says a biographer. "According to his sister, his publication was greeted by an icy silence."[4] He writes to every German university in the hope of eliciting a job offer. Nothing doing.

Finally, in the spring of 1906, the German physicist Max Planck, a member of the *Annalen* board, publishes a paper commenting and expanding on the new theory of relativity. Planck sends his research assistant, Max von Laue, to Berne to form an opinion of Einstein. Expecting to meet a university professor, von Laue is astonished to be greeted by an inauspicious civil servant, albeit one of irresistible charm. Planck, when he meets Einstein, is won over by a shared passion for music. Planck, a pianist, joins Einstein on the violin and his own son Erwin on cello in an ad hoc trio in his Berlin living room. One of Einstein's university teachers, Hermann Minkowski, writes a paper evaluating the space-time concept as the world's fourth dimension. It then becomes known as Minkowski spacetime. Poor Minkowski dies soon after, from a burst appendix. In Salzburg that summer, Einstein addresses the leaders in his field with a speech that is called "one of the landmarks in the development of theoretical physics." "The next stage . . . ," says Einstein, "will bring us a theory of light that can be understood as a kind of fusion of the wave and emission theories of light."

He lands a teaching post at the University of Zurich and in 1911 becomes a full professor in Prague. While working "like a horse" on a general theory of relativity, he makes time to play a cycle of Mozart violin-and-piano sonatas in a public concert at Charles University, with the influential writer Max Brod. In 1913, Max Planck and the head of Berlin's Kaiser Wilhelm Institute for Chemistry, Fritz Haber, take a train to Zurich to offer Einstein a position at the Prussian Academy of Sciences. Eight years after his four papers, Einstein has finally arrived. Before long, his name is synonymous with genius the world over. His face, with its quizzical eyes, crinkly mustache, and crown of wild hair, becomes the most iconic of the century.

But not without resistance. Kelvin-like reactionaries resent the upstart, who cannot prove his bold ideas. Even Planck thinks that Einstein "might sometimes have overshot the target in his speculations, as for example in his light-quantum hypothesis . . ." He is moving far too fast for the rest of his field, propelled by forces unseen, anxiety among them. Who knows how long he can stay ahead of the game? Does anyone really understand him?

Einstein takes care to accommodate his critics. He is notably cordial toward the abrasive American Nobel Laureate Robert Millikan, who claims that "despite . . . the apparently complete success of the Einstein equation, the physical theory of which it was designed to be the symbolic expression is found so untenable that Einstein himself, I believe, no longer holds to it." Half a lifetime later, on Einstein's seventieth birthday, Millikan admits that: "I spent ten years of my life testing that 1905 equation of Einstein's, and, contrary to all my expectations, I was compelled in 1915 to assert its unambiguous experimental verification in spite of its unreasonableness since it seemed to violate everything that we knew about the interference of light." Where Newton was instantly comprehensible, Einstein confounds his contemporaries.

A pernicious opposition forms around the notion that Einstein is pushing a "Jewish science"; a form of casuistry, ungrounded in natural events or scientific method and acting, like the Talmud, more for the purpose of argumentation than for the betterment of humankind. The conductor of this campaign, Philipp Lenard, is a Heidelberg physicist and winner of the 1905 Nobel Prize in Physics, who is friendly with Einstein up to the First World War, at which point he announces that pure science should be reserved for pure Germans. Lenard claims that Einstein either made up his findings or stole them. In August 1920, he tops the bill of an anti-Einstein rally in the large hall of the Berlin Philharmonic. Einstein, hearing himself called "a scientific Dadaist," writes a rebuttal in one of the Berlin papers, challenging his opponents to debate at the German Society of Scientists and Physicians the following month in Bad Nauheim. The meeting turns into a bare-knuckle fight between Einstein and Lenard in front of five hundred peers. Lenard calls Einstein a Moscow agent and a plagiarist. Einstein's wife, Elsa, is so shocked that she suffers a nervous collapse. Einstein himself has to be walked around a nearby park by the Austrian scientist Felix Ehrenhaft to calm down. Lenard is shouted down by his peers and forced to resign from the society. "I will not allow myself to be made so upset again," vows Einstein. The following year in Paris, he declares: "If my theory of relativity is proven successful, Germany will claim me as a

German and France will declare me a citizen of the world. Should my theory prove untrue, France will say that I am a German, and Germany will declare that I am a Jew."

Lenard rises again early in 1933, pledging to purge German physics of believers in relativity. Joining the National Socialist Party, he is appointed chief of Aryan physics and takes steps to ensure that Thirring and von Laue are fired from their positions and others are sent to concentration camps. Lenard is decorated for his services, receiving the Eagle Shield of the German Reich. After the Nazi defeat, he dies, disgraced, in 1947, but his claim that Einstein's relativity is "Jewish" persists so doggedly at the fringes of science that books are still being written to refute it.

How Jewish is Einstein? The question retains its pertinence. Raised in the Bavarian town of Ulm, Albert startles his irreligious parents by refusing nonkosher foods and observing the Sabbath at the age of eleven. His religious phase, which lasts less than a year, leaves him with a love of Judaism, a faith in God, and a passion for the Psalms, which he quotes at the least provocation. As much philosopher as scientist, Einstein's worldview is formed by his heritage. "Judaism seems to me to be concerned almost exclusively with the moral attitude in life and to life," he writes:

> I look upon it as the essence of an attitude to life which is incarnate in the Jewish people rather than . . . the Talmud. . . . The essence of that conception seems to me to lie in an affirmative attitude to the life of all creation. The life of the individual only has value [insofar] as it aids in making the life of every living thing nobler and more beautiful. Life is sacred, that is to say, it is the supreme value, to which all other values are subordinate.[5]

This credo is the basis of his political pacifism and his hatred of all forms of racial discrimination. In an age of extremism and totalitarianism, he stands for personal freedom:

> A human being is a part of the whole called by us "Universe," a part limited in time and space. He experiences himself, his thoughts and feelings, as something separate from the rest—a kind of optical

delusion of his consciousness. . . . The striving to free oneself from this delusion is the one issue of true religion. Not to nourish it but to try to overcome it is the way to reach the attainable measure of peace of mind.[6]

Although he comes to reject religion as a tissue of "childish superstitions,"[7] he is the very antithesis of the Richard Dawkins–Stephen Hawking type of joyless atheist. Einstein says: "I believe in Spinoza's God who reveals Himself in the orderly harmony of what exists, not in a God who concerns himself with fates and actions of human beings."[8] He informs an American schoolgirl that "everyone who is seriously involved in the pursuit of science becomes convinced that some spirit is manifest in the laws of the universe, one that is vastly superior to that of man."[9] He is a religious man of no religion, a perfect Jewish paradox. In the book of Psalms he finds "the feeling from which true scientific research draws its spiritual sustenance but which also seems to find expression in the songs of birds."[10] Pantheism, say his scholarly biographers. Monotheism, say rabbis.

He is taught the general tenets of Christianity as a child at school, where he is alienated by prevalent norms of German discipline. His teachers, he says, were "like sergeants," and he has almost nothing to say about the Christian faith. His parents transfer him to a high school in Zurich, where his friends are fellow marginals: Habicht, Romanian Maurice Solovine, and a Serb, Mileva Marić, whom he gets pregnant; Habicht and Solovine are witnesses at their wedding. Scrupulous in academic ethics—Einstein does not use his PhD students as slaves or claim their work as his own—his personal code does not include marital fidelity. He is serially unfaithful both to Mileva and to his second wife, Elsa. A male primate, he attends to his own physical needs at the expense of women's, crushing Mileva's hopes of becoming a scientist.

His closest adult associates are Jewish men: his school friend Michele Besso, the physicists Max Born, James Franck, Paul Ehrenfest, Haber, and (later) Leo Szilard and Abraham Pais, the mathematician Paul Epstein, and the physiologist Georg Friedrich Nicolai (Lewinstein), lover of Einstein's stepdaughter Ilse. He enjoys making new friends and responds readily to friendly overtures. Early in 1921, Chaim Weizmann, leader of world Zionists, asks him to tour the

United States to raise funds for a Hebrew university in Jerusalem. Einstein, without hesitation, clears two months in his diary and packs his bags. "I am really doing whatever I can for the brothers of my race who are treated so badly everywhere," he tells Solovine.

In New York, Einstein is greeted by a mayoral deputation, and his motorcade is mobbed by Jews on the Lower East Side. Every seat in the Metropolitan Opera House, including the orchestra pit, is sold out for his lecture. Store owners in Cleveland shut up shop to catch a glimpse of him passing by. In Chicago, he plays the violin at a rich men's dinner party. In Washington, the United States Congress holds a debate on relativity. "I confess that I have nearly lost my mental faculties in trying to understand Einstein," sighs one senator. The president, Warren G. Harding, declares himself "puzzled." Einstein defies the Jewish anti-Zionists who control communal institutions to raise three-quarters of $1 million. Zionism, he tells Ehrenfest, "offers a new Jewish ideal that can give the Jewish people joy in its own existence again." He is sick and tired of the "Jewish weakness, always anxiously to want to keep the Gentiles [*Gojims*] in a good mood."[11] Anxiety is never far from the mind of this Jewish genius.

Visiting Palestine, he experiences "the greatest day of my life" inaugurating a public building in Jerusalem. He scorns the Hasidim swaying in prayer at the Western Wall—"a pitiful sight of men with a past but without a future"[12]—but back in Berlin, he makes a new friend in Martin Buber, a secularist who is infatuated by Hasidism. Einstein becomes "a regular visitor at the Buber house."[13] Buber, in his book *The Knowledge of Man*, quotes Einstein on the purpose of science: "What we strive for is just to draw His lines after Him." Einstein's words echo the physician-rabbi Maimonides that man's purpose on Earth is to complete the work of God's creation.[14] Like Maimonides, Einstein sees no division between God and science.

He has a rabbinic knack for elucidating complex propositions. Asked by a journalist to explain relativity, he says: "This is very simple. Matter tells space how to curve—and this is all it's about." When the hack pesters his secretary for more clarity, Einstein tells her to reply: "When you sit with a nice girl for two hours you think it's only a minute but when you sit on a hot stove for a minute you think it's two hours. That's relativity."

His key to understanding time and space is to tell a Jewish joke.

• • •

Among Einstein's friends, the closest one is his polar opposite. Fritz Haber of Breslau, a product of Ehrlich's hub of advanced science, is an ex-Jew, a Lutheran churchgoer. Blessed with a Teutonic forename, Fritz is a militant imperialist where Albert is a pacifist. Einstein is proud to be Jewish, Haber ashamed of it. Einstein unlocks outer space and nuclear destruction. Haber, providentially, enables the long-term continuance of life on Earth.

Differences aside, Haber and Einstein are intimate friends, perhaps the closest in either man's life. Haber is the academic activist who organizes Einstein's tenure in Berlin and finds him suitable accommodations. Einstein is the listening ear to which Haber turns twice in despair when his domestic world falls apart. Neither faith nor politics, ideology, or idealism can come between these friends. Haber is the only man who ever sees Einstein cry.

They meet first at a convention in Karlsruhe in 1909 and again in Brussels in 1911, at the Solvay conference organized by a Belgian industrialist. Haber, hearing Einstein deliver an important paper, recognizes that Einstein's career is not advancing as fast as it should. After fifteen years in Karlsruhe, Haber has finally landed the job of his dreams: director of the newly established Kaiser Wilhelm Institute for Physical Chemistry in Berlin, with an adjoining villa at 8 Faradayweg. The imperial institute is funded by private donors, chief among them the Jewish banker Leopold Koppel, who underwrites Haber's salary and ensures that he is "subject to no restrictions concerning his choice and pursuit of scientific projects."[15]

No sooner is Haber installed in his luxury home than he receives a visit from Einstein's cousin Elsa. Haber senses that Elsa is more than a cousin. He has what Einstein calls an "uncanny agility" in understanding relationships, as long as they are not his own. Elsa, divorced with two daughters, lives in a flat above her parents, who are Einstein's aunt and uncle. Einstein, reaching Berlin, gets involved with Elsa. He wants to leave Mileva but fears divorce might cost him access to their two sons. Haber offers to broker a separation agreement, a process that turns adversarial when Haber's wife, Clara Immerwahr, takes Mileva's side. Haber and Einstein find themselves aligned against their unhappy wives.

Clara, the first German woman to receive a PhD in chemistry, has given up most of her work to be a hausfrau to Haber, who shows no appreciation. He loads her with chores and sails off to America after the birth of their son, Hermann, a difficult birth that leaves Clara determined to have no more children. Haber is absent for five months. Suspecting him of sleeping with other women, Clara bans him from the marital bed. Haber pleads innocence; women, he writes, "are like butterflies to me. I admire their colors and glitter, but I get no further."

Clara sends a harrowing twelve-page letter to her Breslau tutor, Richard Abegg, calling Haber an egomaniac and accusing him of trying to destroy her. "All of Fritz's other human qualities except [the urge to work] are close to shrinking and he is, so to speak, prematurely aged," writes Clara. "Whatever remains of me fills me with the deepest dissatisfaction."[16] As Haber rises in science and society, Clara's attempts to resume her career are dashed on the assumption, palpably false, that she is riding on her husband's coattails. She starts to neglect her appearance and lose touch with friends as Haber works all hours to achieve the discoveries that will make Germany all-powerful. He practices science not for its own sake or the good of humanity but, first and foremost, in the national interest. Einstein is as far from him in his philosophy of science as it is possible to be, yet the two men continue to depend on each other for emotional support.

At the end of July 1914, two days before war breaks out, Mileva takes her two sons back to Zurich. Einstein, on the station platform, "bawled like a little boy," according to Haber, who escorts him home.[17] No other man will ever see the self-possessed Einstein in such disarray. At his most vulnerable, Haber is the only man he trusts.

War is what Fritz Haber has been waiting for, the chance to serve his kaiser. One of his Karlsruhe patents, registered together with an English assistant, Robert Le Rossignol, as early as 1909, now proves vital for Germany's economic defense. Haber has shown how to extract nitrogen from the atmosphere in the form of ammonia, which is an essential component of artificial fertilizers. With the chemist Carl Bosch at the chemicals company BASF, he perfects an industrial process to mass-produce ammonia, which is also in demand for the manufacture of explosives. Haber enables Germany "to make bread from the air." Without the Haber-Bosch process, it is estimated that Germany would have run out of food and munitions by 1915. "In war," declares Haber, "scientists belong to their Fatherland." He tells a Swedish colleague: "It is our ethical duty to take down our enemies with the use of all our strength and bring them to a peace that will make the return of such a war impossible for generations."[18] Haber, with every fiber of his being, wants Germany to win.

He climbs into uniform and goes to work for the Ministry of War, recruiting 150 brains into a chemistry unit that foreshadows America's Manhattan Project in the Second World War. Among his team are the organic chemist Richard Willstätter, the radioactivity expert Otto Hahn, and the nuclear physicist James Franck. All three are Jews, all three future Nobel Laureates. Having increased nitrate production from practically zero to twenty million tons a month, Haber puts his team to work on identifying a gas that can be used as a battlefield weapon. The use of poison gas is, he knows, illegal under the Hague Conventions of 1899 and 1907, but this is war, and Haber is a soldier. He assures his team that gas will bring an early end to the war, thereby saving German lives, and that if Germany does not use gas the French and British will surely do so first. There is another race on close at hand, as his rival Walther Nernst develops a gas grenade.

Willstätter, who wins a 1915 Nobel for work on plant pigments, refuses to cooperate in making poison gas. Under a different commander, he might have risked prosecution. Haber, knowing that Willstätter is mourning the death of his son from diabetes, gently reassigns him to developing a triple-filter gas mask for soldiers in the trenches. Haber's assistant, Otto Sackur, has a brain wave involving cacodyl chloride. Sackur calls the team to his bench for a demonstration. There is an explosion. Sackur is killed on the spot. Sackur is Clara Haber's closest friend, one of her Breslau doctoral supervisors. Accusing Haber of not exercising proper safety precautions, she blames him for Sackur's death.

From January 1915, all work at the institute is focused on chlorine gas. Haber argues that small amounts over a long period will kill more men than a big, short burst, a correlation known as Haber's rule. Under his direction, 1,600 large and 4,130 small steel gas cylinders are dug into a hillside outside the Belgian town of Ypres, where Allied forces outnumber the Germans. Haber patrols the line, instructing Stinkpionere units in how to release the chlorine gas. Secrecy is almost blown when, in March 1915, a German soldier defects to the Allies with a brand-new Willstätter mask, but the traitor cooperates so easily under interrogation that the British dismiss his intelligence as a double bluff. Allied generals refuse to believe that decent German officers would ever use gas. A northerly wind delays the attack by three bitterly cold weeks.

On the afternoon of April 22, 1915, when the wind turns, the code phrase *Gott strafe England* ("God punish England," a line by a Jewish poet, Ernst Lissauer) is passed down the trenches. Men of the Stinkpionere unscrew the cylinders and point the nozzles west. A yellow-green cloud of chlorine gas rolls over the Allied trenches. A French colonial regiment, new to the front, catches the first blast. Its men scramble choking onto no-man's-land, gasping for air, dying as they run. A Canadian soldier likens the sensation to "drowning on dry land." Amid the confusion, the Big Berthas open up, and masked German troops charge across four miles of front, trampling over the still-gasping bodies of asphyxiated Algerians. The Germans drive one mile deep into Allied lines on the first day of gas. Haber is up close and in the thick of it, observing the devastating effects. Some seven thousand Allied soldiers are killed or maimed in the poison attack.

Haber is recalled to Berlin and personally promoted by the kaiser from staff sergeant to the rank of captain. It is the proudest moment of his life, but not everyone congratulates him. The army high command, committed to honorable warfare, makes no secret of its disgust at stink bombs. The kaiser, regardless, sends Haber to lead a gas attack on the Eastern Front. On May 1, the night before his departure, Haber throws a party at home to celebrate his promotion. When the last guest has left, he has a noisy fight with Clara. Facing an early start, Haber doses himself with sleeping pills and heads to bed.

Clara waits until the house is quiet. Then she removes Haber's service pistol from its holster and goes into the garden. It is a mild spring night. Her son, Hermann, thirteen years old, is woken by two shots. The first must have been a test by Clara, to see if she could fire the pistol. The second goes into her chest. Hermann runs into the garden, but all he can do is hold his mother in his arms as she gulps her last breaths. Clara takes two hours to die. She is forty-four years old.

Haber, next morning, heads back to war, leaving Clara's sister to see to the funeral and arranging that no word of the "accident" leaks to the media. His conduct seems, by any standard, heartless. Any other officer of his rank would have been excused duty for a few days to bury his wife and take care of his son. But Haber is more Prussian than the Junckers, more dedicated to his nation than to his family. He does not care what the world thinks of his conduct while he is performing his patriotic duty.

Oddly, he has no shortage of defenders, chief among them the American historian of Germany, Fritz Stern, who is his godson. Stern, citing his father, Rudolf Stern, who was Haber's personal friend and physician, writes: "The oft-repeated assertion that Haber reacted coldly or indifferently to his wife's death is erroneous." His testimony, however, is neither impartial nor does it overturn immediate impressions of Haber's inhumanity.

James Franck is one of four witnesses who maintain that Clara's suicide is both a moral and a political act, a protest against her war-criminal husband. She learns at the party for the first time of the poison-gas attack and is heard condemning Haber's "perversion of science . . . corrupting the very discipline which ought to bring new insights into life."[19]

Eight other sources, however, tell a different story. Clara is depressed by the war, by her rotten marriage, by Sackur's needless death. She is melancholy, lonely, unfocused. There is a history of depression in her family; her sister, Lotte, will also take her own life.

Two witnesses report an incident at the party. Clara, going upstairs to check on her son, finds Haber in bed with a frisky Jewish admirer, Charlotte Nathan.[20] "Horrified by anything sensual," Clara is shocked by carnal activity in her own home. In this version of her motives, she takes her life out of personal shame and moral disgust at the man she married.

And what of Haber's reaction? There is none. He refers to Clara in one letter as "the poor woman," and in another he confides that, at work one day, "in a vision born of weariness, I see her head emerging between orders and telegrams and I suffer." This is the most emotion that Haber ever admits.

There is just one man who understands him. Einstein, like Haber, is under stress. Elsa is demanding that he divorce Mileva, and the war has complicated his ethical stance. Einstein, a pacifist, finds himself chief of the Kaiser Wilhelm Institute for Physics and a participant in the war effort. The death of Karl Schwarzschild, a young Jewish astronomer who finds brilliant proofs for relativity, hits him hard, and he berates Haber on several occasions for supporting the war. Still, their friendship deepens. Haber tells Einstein:

> It is not only in the field of mathematical physics that life depends on the knowledge of and acceptance of certain formal connections and not only in the field in which you work miracles is it usually impossible to achieve success without the formal laws. For myself I merely ask that you believe that I am pleased and happy to be useful to you, that I have too much respect for your person and achievement ever to make fun about something you do and that I am personally extremely fond of you [*ich Sie persönlich lieb habe*].[21]

It is almost a love letter.

In January 1917, Einstein is stricken with a stomach pain that he fears is cancer. Elsa moves him into an apartment in her building, nurses him back to health, gets him to divorce Mileva, and marries him. Haber, in October that year, pushes Charlotte Nathan into a Lutheran conversion and marries her at Kaiser Wilhelm Gedächtniskirche, the church of Berlin's elites. They are photographed on the front steps, Haber in his spiked brass helmet, Charlotte in a floppy black hat, and Haber's angry son, Hermann, who hates Charlotte, in a Homburg hat and black tie.

In the last months of the war, Haber, nominated by his friend Willstätter, is awarded the Nobel Prize in Chemistry for his prewar work on ammonia. His institute is now dedicated to protecting Germany from retaliatory Allied gas attacks. Haber hires toxicologists, among them Ferdinand Flury, a Würzburg professor, who conducts unpleasant animal experiments. Once the war ends, Haber, finding his name on an Allied list of possible war criminals, flees to Switzerland, out of reach of extradition. A British brigadier-general, Sir Harold Hartley, turns up at the institute to investigate its wartime activities. Finding that his gentle prewar tutor Willstätter is on the payroll, he accepts assurances that a last-minute bonfire of documents was entirely accidental and awards Haber and the institute a clean bill of health.

Willstätter urges Haber to join his campaign to ban weapons of mass destruction. Haber's reply is—in the light of Clara's suicide—cruelly revealing. "Eternal peace can't be assured though technical means," writes Haber. "A husband and wife can get along because of their spirit and self-discipline, not because you lock up every rod and poker."[22] In a 1920 lecture, he insists that "gas weapons [were] definitely no more inhumane than flying bits of metal."

In the postwar morass, he experiments in extracting gold from seawater and puts Ferdinand Flury to work on a pesticide that will protect crops without harm to animals. Flury synthesizes methyl cyanoformate and methyl chloroform into a compound named Zyklon A, patented under his own name in 1922. Dosage is calculated by Haber's rule.[23] Another Haber staffer, Walter Heerdt, produces an improved version of the chemical, Zyklon B. Zyklon B will be chosen by SS scientists as the most efficient means to murder millions of Jews at Auschwitz. A Haber aide, Bruno Emil Tesch, is hanged by the British in 1946 for supplying Zyklon B to the SS under an exclusive license.[24] Tesch claims he supplied it for fumigation purposes. Flury advises the Nazi leadership on which gas to use in euthanasia and how to maximize the destructive impact of V-1 bombers. He has the good fortune to be captured in 1945 by a controversial American toxicologist, Captain Robert A. Kehoe, who debriefs him, exempts him from prosecution, and allows him to return home, where he dies peacefully at the age of sixty-nine. Flury and Tesch are prime specimens of the culture of inhumanity ordained by Haber at his institute.

Einstein, despite all, maintains their friendship. When Haber urges him not to visit enemy nations on a postwar world tour, Einstein replies that he has no loyalty to Germany, only "to my dear German friends, of whom you are one of the most outstanding and most benevolent."[25] The two great scientists visit each other at home. "I remember sitting on Einstein's knee," relates Haber's daughter, "he was trying to explain his theory to me . . . the relativity. He was much younger than my father and also better with children."[26]

Haber's second marriage goes no better than the first. He has two children with Charlotte, but relations break down, either due to the

age gap, by Haber being absent at work, or—as Charlotte maintains—
by Haber siding with Hermann against her. An expensive divorce
in 1927, together with the stock market crash, leaves Haber finan-
cially ruined. "Ever since I separated from my second wife," he tells
Einstein:

> ... something inside me was broken. ... At the age of almost sixty
> I could not endure my marriage any longer and had to separate
> myself from my beloved children ... And it matters a great deal to
> me, my dear Albert Einstein, that you have a good opinion of my
> usefulness and it encourages me in my depressed hours or more
> exactly in the long days in which I am wholly filled with a sense of
> superfluity and mediocrity.[27]

Loneliness makes him work ever harder. Lise Meitner, a pathbreaker in
nuclear fission, passes the institute at night and sees, through a window,
the old man pacing up and down, all alone. She calls Haber a tragic figure, "divided within himself and extremely passionate, which as you
can imagine sometimes made things difficult for himself and for others."[28] Shadows are falling. Haber is shocked when Willstätter resigns
his Munich chair because the university is riddled with anti-Semitism.
"Late 1932, I think it must have been," his daughter says, "my father
called us in to tell us we were Jewish. We didn't know."

When Hitler becomes chancellor, Einstein is in America being
showered with honors and offers while Haber is in the South of France
recovering from a heart attack. Einstein accepts a chair at Princeton
University. Haber goes back to work in Berlin. At the institute door,
the janitor blocks his path. "The Jew Haber is not allowed in here,"
he announces.[29] Haber turns around, walks next door, and composes
a resignation letter. "I was German to an extent that I feel fully only
now," he tells Willstätter, "and I find it odious in the extreme that I can
no longer work enough to begin confidently a new post in a different
country."[30] At sixty-four years old, he has sold his soul to a Germany
that has turned its face against him.

Einstein, for once, shows no sympathy. "I can conceive of your inner
conflicts," he writes from America. "It is somewhat like having to give
up a theory on which one has worked one's whole life. It [Germany] is

not the same for me because I never believed in it in the least."[31] If Einstein no longer cares, who will save Fritz Haber?

Two saviors appear. Chaim Weizmann, the British-based biochemist, believes he can use Haber as a go-between with Einstein, with whom he has fallen out over the governance of the Hebrew University. Weizmann offers Haber a chance to share his dream. Deposed as leader of the world Zionist movement, he is setting up a research institute among the orange groves in Rehovot, funded by Israel Sieff, head of the Marks & Spencer stores. Weizmann has chosen Rehovot because it is near Yavneh, where Rabbi Johanan ben Zakkai regenerated Jewish scholarship after the fall of Jerusalem. There can be no better place for a Jew to practice science after Germany has fallen to Hitler. Haber, enthused, tells Einstein: "In my whole life I never felt so Jewish as now." Weizmann asks Willstätter to steer Haber "towards reaching a mutual agreement between Einstein and you to cooperate with me." He is looking to build a grand coalition of great Jewish scientists whom Germany is ruthlessly discarding.

In May 1933, after a second heart attack, Haber receives a counteroffer. Sir William Pope, convenor of the Chemical Warfare Committee at the Ministry of Munitions in London during the first war, invites Haber to make use of his laboratory in Cambridge, clearly intending to use him in the next war with Germany. Haber has a stepsister in England, the only person he can rely upon to look after him. He moves to Cambridge, only to find that his accommodations are dank, the food filthy, and the medical care inferior. Hermann calls him a fool for not taking up Weizmann's offer. Haber contacts Weizmann and agrees to accept any position in Palestine so long as it pays enough to support his ex-wife and children.

Einstein promises Haber they will see each other soon "under a milder sky."[32] As 1933 ends, Haber decides to move on. Sooner or later, someone in England is bound to reproach him for war crimes; when the next war comes, he will be interned as an enemy alien, just like his former assistant Le Rossignol in Germany. Worried about Hermann, he begs Weizmann to help find his son a scientific position. He turns his mind to water sterilization, an existential issue for Palestine, and vows that he will come to Rehovot "only . . . if it is not the visit of a sick man who is unable to meet people and confront issues." His Protestant work ethic remains paramount even as he contemplates the end of days. He writes to Willstätter, asking where he can obtain two drugs "for old age": morphine and cyanide.

On the last weekend of January 1934, Haber comes to London for lunch with Weizmann and his wife, Vera, at their hotel. They spend the afternoon together, and Haber pledges to donate his books, papers, and scientific equipment to Weizmann's institute, expressing a hope that they will meet next in an orange grove. He takes the boat train to Paris and travels on to Basel to meet his son, Hermann, and his wife Margarethe, together with Margarethe's brother, Rudolf Stern, who is Haber's physician. After a pleasant evening in the hotel, the party disperses to its rooms. Suddenly, the phone rings in Stern's room. Haber is having a heart attack. Stern cannot revive him. They bury Fritz Haber in Basel, Willstätter delivering a graveside eulogy. When the will is opened, there is an unexpected instruction. Haber wants Clara's remains to be removed from Berlin and brought to lie beside him. His love for her has never died.

Albert Einstein laments: "Now almost all of my true friends are dead. One begins to feel like a fossil . . ." He tells Hermann how, in happier times, in the Schlosscafé on Unter den Linden, Haber would complain of feeling unappreciated and Einstein would assure him: "Console yourself with me—your moral standing is truly enviable . . ." Einstein, the moral paragon of science, absolves his friend of sin. In another letter, Einstein writes: "Haber was of all my friends the intellectually broadest and most stimulating and the one ever readiest to help."[33]

Max Planck, organizing a Haber commemoration in Berlin, is warned by the Nazi minister of education that the meeting is "a challenge to the National Socialist state." Citing Haber's war record, Planck receives permission to hold a small gathering so long as none of the speakers is a state employee. Willstätter addresses what proves to be the last summit meeting of German science. Haber's name is soon erased from German chemistry books. Willstätter, thrown out of his villa by SS men, is arrested trying to cross the Swiss border; he succeeds in a second crossing and dies in exile. Max Born goes to England, James Franck to America. Planck's son, Erwin, Einstein's cello partner, is executed by hanging in a gestapo cell.

Hermann Haber becomes a patent attorney in Paris. When the Germans invade, he sails with Margarethe and their two children to New

York. On November 9, 1946, dogged by alcoholism and other issues, Haber's son commits suicide. He is forty-four years old, the same age as his mother at her death. Other members of Haber's extended family—Breslau cousins, nieces, and nephews—are gassed with the Zyklon B that he fostered.

Weizmann, true to his word, opens a Fritz Haber library in Rehovot. Browsing the archives, I am struck by the legibility of Haber's handwriting—unusual for a scientist—and by his practicality. Never a scatterbrained scientist, Haber makes sure, when accepting a dinner invitation, to check if it is black tie. He obtains directions. He never forgets to ask after the host's wife. James Franck reports: "Haber always knew what to say right away in the room, not later on the stairs. I've known even greater intellects—Albert Einstein and Niels Bohr. But I knew no one like Haber. This combination of—I'm tempted to say provocative—quickness in assessing a situation, along with good-heartedness and understanding, was quite remarkable."[34]

Other aspects are harder to fathom. His obsessive need for recognition, for instance. Einstein tells Elsa that "Haber's picture unfortunately is to be seen everywhere [at the institute]. It pains me every time I think of it. Unfortunately, I have to accept that this otherwise so splendid a man has succumbed to personal vanity and not even of the most tasteful kind."

Meitner finds that Haber "wants to be both your best friend and God at the same time." He craves love and control. Why he needs them is unclear. He has a Nobel Prize, optimum research conditions, and all modern comforts. "Dear Richard!" he writes to Willstätter. "It's nighttime, and I'm afraid to sleep."[35] He hears the march of jackboots, and he knows they are coming for him. Far into the future, whenever chemicals are used in war, Haber's name will be recalled as the "twisted mind that gave us chemical warfare."[36] Few will recognize the Fritz Haber whose recovery of nitrogen from the air feeds the world's ever-multiplying population. Fewer still can reconcile his contradictions: cultured man and mass murderer, kneeling Christian and needy Jew, devoted father and wife-abuser. Albert Einstein alone understands. In a beautiful compliment, Einstein predicts that one day "the age of Haber" will be compared to that of Isaac Newton. Haber's life, he sighs, is "the tragedy of the German Jew, the tragedy of unrequited love."[37]

NINE

1911
BLUES 'N' JEWS

An elusive Jewish sound: George Gershwin paints
Arnold Schoenberg, 1936.

One sweltering summer's afternoon on a brownstone stoop in the
Bronx or Harlem, a bunch of kids are messing around with a guitar belonging to someone's older brother when a light goes on in one

kid's head: they are speaking the same music. Half the kids are from African slave families freed in the aftermath of the American Civil War. The other half are fresh off the boat, refugees from Russian pogroms. The light is flicked on not so much by a catchy tune as by a common way of coping with heritage.

Blues, the morose music of ex–plantation slaves, strikes an intuitive chord with Jews, whose songs inhabit a dolorous minor key, steeped in past suffering. Blues are structured in twelve bars, broken into three groups: statement, obverse, and resolution. A blues C major scale has ten notes, with an additional E-flat and B-flat that augment and subvert the octave. To a European music teacher, these would count as "wrong" notes.

Ashkenazi Jews take music from itinerant influences, Baltic to Balkan, and adapt it to available instruments—violin, clarinet, accordion—known as *klei zemer* or klezmer. The klezmer scale, involving at least two flats in excess of the Western diatonic, is identified by a prayer name: Ahavah Rabbah or Mi Sheberach. Jews keep these names to themselves. They don't want academics chewing up their music. They favor a hazanic sob at inappropriate intervals, a tearjerk.

No one knows where or when the summer's day stoop conversation takes place, or if it occurs at all. All we can see is the result: a musical connection made between Jews and African Americans early in the twentieth century explodes into a 1911 firestorm of a million-selling song and the birth of the global music business. Jews are about to become the first American composers of world renown, and what they write is a fusion of African blues with their own minor-key temperament.

This is counterintuitive. It flies straight in the face of where music appears to be going. In Europe, the tendency has been to "civilize" folk music, a tendency that has required Haydn and Beethoven to prettify Scottish and Irish folk songs for drawing-room use and which is now setting abstract poetry to the increasingly arcane melodic forms of Debussy, Schoenberg, and Scriabin. The new American songbook does not belong in the drawing room. It throws a brick through a ground-floor window by coarsening the melody with "wrong" notes and the language with get-down-and-dirty street talk. "That's just the bestest band what am," jives Irving Berlin's "Alexander's Ragtime Band," the megahit of 1911. No pure rhymes, no *g*s at the end of gerunds. This is music that uses notes the way immigrants use the vernacular: whatever comes to lips and mind, regardless of the rule book.

Berlin, son of a penniless hazan (cantor) who dies soon after Irving's bar mitzvah, gets work as a "boomer" for publisher Harry von Tilzer, belting out new songs above the traffic on downtown street corners. He slips some songs of his own into *Ziegfeld Follies* but can't get any producer to accept the hybrid idiom of "Alexander's Ragtime Band" until Aaron Winslow tries it in *The Merry Whirl* and a singing waiter called Al Jolson lets it rip on the restaurant floor between soup and steak. By midsummer of 1911, Berlin's song sells half a million music sheets; by Christmas, a million.

Its composer cannot read music and never learns to play the piano properly, sticking to the black keys, which he calls "nigger keys," and working in F-sharp major until he finds a lever that mechanically changes the keys on his piano. "The key of C is for people who study music," scoffs Irving Berlin. In 1916, he asks the Irish operetta composer Victor Herbert if he should take lessons. Herbert advises him not to bother; it would only cramp his style. "I know rhythm," brags Berlin.[1]

He turns his hand to vaudeville: "Cohen Owes Me $97," about an old man who refuses to die until all his debts are in, and "Sadie Salome Go Home," about a burlesque dancer who needs to get her corsets on if ever she wants to marry. "Business Is Business, Rosie Cohen" is another yingle-jingle. With "Yiddle on Your Fiddle Play Some Ragtime," he defines the basis of the American songbook.

Tragedy halts his progress. In 1912, he marries Dorothy Goetz under a chuppah and goes on a honeymoon to the Caribbean, where Dorothy catches typhoid and within five months is dead. Berlin joins the army and goes to war, turning out songs all the while. Although he collects first editions and keeps a leather-bound set of Shakespeare in his hallway for all to see, he reads little and has few interests of any depth. His show writer Moss Hart finds him "deadly dull." With Irving Berlin, instinct is all. He composes the unofficial American anthem "God Bless America" and two tunes, "Easter Parade" and "White Christmas," which rebrand religious festivals for mass consumption. "There's no business like show business," cries Irving Berlin. His friend Jerome Kern comments: "Irving Berlin has no place in American music: he *is* American music." Some fifteen hundred songs bear his signature.

"Music never really interested me," declares George Gershwin. "I spent most of my time with the boys in the street, skating and, in general, making a nuisance of myself." The sound of a mechanical piano playing "Melody in F," by Anton Rubinstein, opens his ears. Rubinstein's odd, arrhythmic pauses, typical of a hazan's singing, intrigue the young George, who gets his parents to invest in an upright piano. "No sooner had it come through the window and been backed up against the wall than I was at the keys."[2] Quitting school at fifteen, he knows where to go. On West Twenty-Eighth Street, between Fifth and Sixth Avenues, every other business is a music publisher, most of them Jewish-owned. It's known as Tin Pan Alley, and the big players are former doorstep salesmen Isidore Witmark, Leopold Feist, Edward Marx, and Joseph Stern. George Gershwin becomes a song plugger for Jerome H. Remick & Co., playing a piano in the mezzanine, implanting earworms into passing trade. When he tries to sell Remick a song of his own, he is told, "You're here as a plugger, not a writer." The first music he gets into print, "When You Want 'Em, You Can't Get 'Em, When You've Got 'Em, You Don't Want 'Em," earns him all of $5. From here on, he is unstoppable, so prolific that some analysts suspect an attention deficit disorder.

His piano playing improves by leaps and bounds, helped on by a tubercular teacher, Charles Hambitzer. Gershwin learns to admire Liszt and Busoni, pasting their pictures into a scrapbook, but his heart is tugged by the fascinating rhythms of African Americans that he hears on the front stoop. George Gershwin's first hit is the Southern-style "Swanee." The music he hears most, because it is the most recorded, is St. Louis blues by an Alabama musician, W. C. Handy. When Gershwin finishes his most popular concert work, *Rhapsody in Blue*, he dedicates the first signed copy "to Mr. Handy, whose early blues songs are the forefathers of this work." Although he makes his fortune writing potboilers for Broadway with his brother Ira, his signature project, *Porgy and Bess*, has serious intent: to resemble "a combination of the drama and romance of *Carmen* and the beauty of *Meistersinger*." It will be the first authentic American opera, a deathless work whose power is drawn from two or three cultures. Irving Berlin would say: "The rest of us were songwriters. George was a composer."

The third Jewish commissar of the popular music revolution,

Jerome Kern, has little contact with African Americans during a fairly prosperous boyhood. A Savile Row–clad Anglophile, Kern composes 1,350 songs. Other than "Smoke Gets in Your Eyes," written for Al Jolson, ragtime becomes "an integral part of Kern's style more or less from the start."[3] His immersion in blues is manifest in his most enduring number, "Ol' Man River," from the 1927 musical *Show Boat*, a show that daringly broaches romance across the color bar. Kern's partner, Oscar Hammerstein, will hook up with Richard Rodgers to turn the Broadway musical into a distinctive American art form.

Across their differences what unites the early makers of American popular music is a social conscience. Irving Berlin, reading reports that black men have been lynched in Southern states, inserts in his musical *As Thousands Cheer* a solo number, "Supper Time," describing the children's anguish when their hanged father fails to return for his evening meal. Two stars of the show refuse to take a curtain call beside a black actor. Berlin, incensed, orders that no one will take a bow until they back down. The strongest response to a lynching, "Strange Fruit," sung by Billie Holiday, is the work—words and music—of a Jewish schoolteacher, Abel Meeropol, published under the WASPish pseudonym of Lewis Allan. Meeropol has good reason to cover up. He is an active member of the American Communist Party who writes hits for Frank Sinatra and Peggy Lee, and he adopts the two sons of Ethel and Julius Rosenberg after their parents are executed for espionage.

At this point in the American story, Jews and blacks are pretty much singing from the same page. An errand boy in New Orleans, Louis Armstrong (pronounced "Lewis"), is given his first trumpet as a reward for helping out the Karnofsky family at their store. "When I reached the age of eleven I began to realize it was the Jewish family who instilled in me singing from the heart," writes Satchmo. Ella Fitzgerald takes on the schmaltz song "Bei Mir Bistu Shayn" (Jacob Jacobs/ Sholom Secunda), bending the line way beyond belief. The ultimate Yiddishe Mamme, Sophie Tucker, does double acts with Mamie Smith.

American pop songs set the world dancing during the First World War, conquering Paris, London, and Berlin. Josephine Baker dances with a cheetah in the Folies Bergère, to the delight of Pablo Picasso. The French Sephardi composer Darius Milhaud infuses his *Création du Monde* with Harlem jazz. Gershwin repays the compliment with *An*

American in Paris. Kurt Weill inserts "Alabama Song" in *The Rise and Fall of the City of Mahagonny*, setting Berlin singing, "Oh, show me the way to the next whiskey bar."

In Manhattan, David Sarnoff and William Paley build the NBC and CBS radio networks. In Los Angeles, Louis B. Mayer, Harry Cohn, Samuel Goldwyn, Jack Warner, and Adolph Zukor open up movie studios. American Jews, immigrants or sons of immigrants, invent the industries of mass distraction. They are the tastemakers of the twentieth century.

George Gershwin is confused. Feeling he is not good enough to be making so much money, he applies to Maurice Ravel in Paris for lessons. Ravel refers him to the pedagogue Nadia Boulanger, who advises, simply, "Be yourself." This Gershwin cannot do. He cannot live with quick, slick fame. He aspires higher, to do something really hard. He cannot escape the fear that his fame is undeserved and undoubtedly ephemeral. Four or five times he tries writing a piano concerto, never quite getting there until he lets the piano run riot with jazz riffs for an experimental concert with the band leader Paul Whiteman. A train ride to Boston gives him rhythm and structure for *Rhapsody in Blue*. He does not have time for orchestration, leaving that chore to Whiteman's arranger, Ferde Grofé. The afternoon premiere at Aeolian Hall on February 12, 1924, is attended by Sergei Rachmaninoff, Igor Stravinsky, Fritz Kreisler, and Leopold Stokowski, all curious to see if a kid from Tin Pan Alley can write a classical concerto. Gershwin is sketchy about his intentions until the last minute. The slithering glissando that opens the piece is prompted by some rehearsal fooling around by the band's clarinet player, Ross Gorman. Gershwin immediately puts it in his score, telling Gorman, who is not Jewish, to make it sound "like a wail," klezmer-style. Whiteman is kept guessing which of the orchestral entries the composer has approved. Gershwin plays the piano part, signaling his intentions to the band leader. The city's two main critics are in the hall, and both pan the work. An impatient Olin Downes in the *New York Times* says the tuttis and cadenzas are too long; the whole rhapsody lasts no more than a quarter of an hour. The *New York Herald-Tribune*'s Lawrence Gilman dismisses the tunes as "trite, feeble and conventional." Whiteman takes *Rhapsody* on tour and on their return to New York records it with Gershwin, selling a million discs and mountains of sheet music. Grofé expands his instrumentation to symphony orchestra size. Gershwin, by now a millionaire, is hired as a soloist by the Philharmonic, and he is still not confident in his status as a serious musician. Follow-up Concerto in F lacks *Rhapsody*'s improvisatory vitality. Everything he does is a one-off, and he knows it. At first-night parties, he is at once the life and soul and a solitary misfit, playing the corner piano until the morning papers arrive. "When I don't play, I don't have a good time," he tells his mother.

No one knows what makes George Gershwin tick. His sister, Frances, describes a "very closed-in personality." A friend finds him prudish, tugging down Frances's skirt to make sure she is respectable. He appears to be a womanizer, always with a different girl on his arm, but massed ranks of hacks and snappers find no evidence of a lover. His biographers likewise fail to identify a meaningful relationship, beyond a rumor that he loves a married woman who will not leave her husband. Perhaps, like Beethoven, Gershwin pursues the eternally unattainable to avoid giving away much of himself. His brother Ira, who knows him best, offers charming anecdotes but no insight into George's character beyond this: "He was shy, reserved, a sweet guy." The pianist Oscar Levant, a fellow man-about-town, accuses him of narcissism: "Tell me, George, if you had to do it all over, would you fall in love with yourself again?" In the first age of mass media, in the heart of Manhattan and Hollywood, George Gershwin contrives to remain hidden in full sight.

What is he hiding from? One suggestion is that he is a repressed homosexual, dating women to cover up his closeted sexuality. The singer Michael Feinstein, an assistant of Ira Gershwin, raises this theory in a book, *The Gershwins and Me*. Feinstein thinks Gershwin is sexually "confused." Again, this is no more than supposition since— like Franz Schubert, to whom he is often likened—Gershwin remains firmly buttoned-up on the subject. The Jewish singer Kitty Carlisle, whom Gershwin dates in 1933 and supposedly asks to marry, "didn't reveal too much" when discussing him with friends.[4] Carlisle goes on to marry Moss Hart, who is Jewish and gay, just as she likes them.

There may be a clue to his sexual identity in the torch song "The Man I Love." Ira titles it "The Girl," only for George to change it to "The Man." Leonard Bernstein makes "The Man I Love" his party piece, camping it up for all he's worth. But George Gershwin never comes out. If he is gay, he keeps it undetected by his garrulous rival Cole Porter. We are left, as with Schubert, with the unsatisfactory conclusion that the composer of some of the greatest love songs is, if not asexual, then sexually inert. George Gershwin never drops his guard enough to love and live with another person of either sex. Which begs the question: What has he got to hide, other than, perhaps, the most elusive musical personality since Mendelssohn? He takes himself to a psychoanalyst in the hope that Dr. Gregory Zilboorg will "unlock his own mystery."[5] Zilboorg, a St. Petersburg Jew obsessed with the criminal mind, finds streaks of Russian melancholy over an eighteen-month analysis. And that's all we know.

In photographs, Gershwin's default look is bored. Sartorially suited bored, swimsuited bored, expensively bored, in-a-crowd bored, constitutionally out of things. When asked what he does, Gershwin says he writes American music. "True music must repeat *the* thought and inspirations of *the people* and *the time*. My people are Americans *and* my time is today." This is a broad mission but with a narrow remit. Gershwin's America is Manhattan and Hollywood. He hardly knows what lies in between. The country music of middle America, the hymns of Baptists and Quakers, the dances of Hispanic migrants, all pass him by. What Gershwin knows is Jews and blues. "All I've got is a lot of talent and plenty of chutzpah," he tells Jerome Kern.[6] Maybe that's a clue.

His music, Gershwin admits, sounds Jewish. The klezmer clarinet in *Rhapsody in Blue*; the aria "Summertime" that opens *Porgy and Bess*; an inversion of *Barechu*, the introductory trope for the Sabbath-morning service—"more Yiddish than colored," says the Hollywood composer Bernard Herrmann. "It Ain't Necessarily So" calls up the recitative chant of Talmudic learning. At the climactic confrontation between the cripple Porgy and the homicidal Crown, Gershwin inserts—for no obvious reason—a surge of Hasidic melody. The communal life of poor African Americans on Catfish Row recalls all too vividly the habits of immigrant Jews on the Lower East Side, living off their wits, trusting only in one another, resenting outsiders. *Porgy and Bess* is a masterpiece not because it is the first opera to present black lives without condescension but because it transcends the grim situation of one minority and applies it to all suffering humanity. There are no stereotypes in *Porgy and Bess*. Each character has a leitmotif, and the mention of New York gets a riff of its own, a phrase so conclusive that Kurt Weill borrows it in *Street Scene* and Leonard Bernstein in *On the Town*. Stephen Sondheim, who considers *Porgy* an unparalleled American masterpiece, finds its punch in the second word of its opening song. A lesser composer might have settled for "Summertime, when the livin's easy." Gershwin insists on "Summertime *and* the livin's easy," the unexpected conjunction setting us up for the opposite of easy. What's with the *and*? Could it be the standard "And it came to pass" of Torah translation?

Immersed in Yiddish culture, Gershwin records a piano roll of the theater song "Dos Pintele Yid." Visiting Berlin he seeks out, of all available entertainments, a Yiddish play by Sholem Aleichem, spoken in German. He tells the Yiddish theater star Boris Tomashevsky the "freygish" mode is his favorite composing style. *Freygish* is Yiddish for "questioning." There is a quizzical note to Gershwin's hits. America's foremost composer is fearfully insecure.[7]

Too famous to survive in the New York goldfish bowl, he moves to Hollywood in the early 1930s, works in the movies, plays with Pierre Monteux and the Los Angeles Philharmonic in the Hollywood Bowl, and takes up painting, showing great skill. He makes a portrait of his neighbor, the exiled composer Arnold Schoenberg, whom he pesters for lessons. Schoenberg, who sorely needs the cash, declines. "I would only make you a bad Schoenberg," he explains, "and you are such a good Gershwin already."[8] Gershwin, keen on Schoenberg's atonalities, turns up to film a rehearsal of Schoenberg's near-impenetrable fourth string quartet on a home-movie camera. He wants to know what makes music tick, what makes it last. "Do you think anything of mine will live?" he quavers.[9]

Savage headaches send him to the doctor. Tests are conducted at the Cedars of Lebanon Hospital, where the conclusion is "most likely hysteria."[10] A psychoanalyst, Ernest Simmel, decides his symptoms are psychosomatic. One night at dinner Gershwin puts a fork in his ear, unable to locate his mouth. On July 9, 1937, he collapses at home while going to the toilet. Two days later, after hours of brain surgery, George Gershwin dies. He is thirty-eight years old. His body is flown to New York for a full-pomp Temple Emanu-El funeral and burial at Westchester Hills Cemetery. The novelist John O'Hara issues a deathless aphorism: "George Gershwin died on July 11, 1937, but I don't have to believe it if I don't want to." America eventually accepts him as one of its immortals.

Not all of America, of course. The classical establishment deems him inferior to Aaron Copland, Samuel Barber, and Virgil Thomson. Olin Downes writes in the *New York Times*: "He never passed a certain point as a 'serious' composer." Leonard Bernstein refers to *Rhapsody* as "not a composition at all. It's a string of separate paragraphs stuck together."

It falls to Arnold Schoenberg, in a radio eulogy, to speak for the future. "Music was what made him feel, and music was the feeling he expressed," says the master of modernism in a lilting Viennese accent:

> Directness of this kind is given only to great men, and there is no doubt that he was a great composer. What he has achieved was not only to the benefit of a national American music, but also a contribution to the music of the whole world. In this meaning, I want to express the deepest grief for the deplorable loss to music.

Being Arnold Schoenberg is never easy, least of all for the man behind the name. Edgy, provocative, hotheaded, stubborn, insensitive, antisocial, and downright rude are just a few of the adjectives he attracts in the 1890s as a half-trained cellist with ideas miles above his station. No less forceful, on the other hand, is his innate charisma, a magnetic power to enthrall outstanding musicians and infuse them with his heretical thoughts. His first captive is Alexander Zemlinsky, the confused son of a former Catholic who works as a Sephardi synagogue beadle and his half-Muslim wife. The early works of Zemlinsky catch the ear of the dying Brahms, who predicts great things for the young man. Schoenberg, who joins his amateur orchestra, lifts him off the Brahms track into a modern mind-set. Zemlinsky is persuaded to give the younger man lessons in composition—he is the only teacher Schoenberg ever acknowledges—and introduce his sister Mathilde, whom the jobless Schoenberg promptly marries. Schoenberg completes a string sextet, *Verklärte Nacht*, which one critic astutely likens to Wagner's *Tristan* prelude taken with the ink still wet and smeared down the page. Schoenberg, by the turn of the century, is going way off what audiences expect to hear.

He has a stroke of luck, a chance meeting with the loveliest girl in Vienna. Zemlinsky has been giving lessons to Alma Schindler, a nubile late teenager with a taste for talent. She makes out with Alex on the piano stool, stopping just short of consummation, and then dumps him for a man twice her age, the director of the Vienna Opera, Gustav Mahler. Zemlinsky turns rejection into opportunity. When Mahler asks to meet Alma's young friends, he turns up, with Schoenberg, for coffee. Mahler likes Zemlinsky on sight and promises him a job at the opera. Schoenberg, on the other hand, is shabbily dressed and full of unsound opinions. Voices are raised, and Schoenberg storms out. "Don't come back!" yells Mahler. Two weeks later, he says to Alma, "Why don't those young guys come round anymore?"

Mahler gets his brother-in-law Arnold Rosé, concertmaster of the Vienna Philharmonic, to perform *Verklärte Nacht*. Schoenberg's next work, a string quartet, leaps neurotically all over the page. He writes a chamber symphony, "filled with joy at the expectation of success," only to be frosted by the audience. His next string quartet has a soprano singing Stefan George's poem "I feel the air from another planet." As the singer draws breath for her second solo, the musical line runs right off the tonal rails. "Kill the longing, close the wound," sings the soprano with a naked Freudian subtext. A riot erupts. Arrests are made. Vienna has a "scandal" on its hands. Schoenberg is the bogeyman of music, the lunatic who loathes Brahms, the enemy of the bourgeoisie.

In atonality, any note can be used without relation to what comes before or after. Schoenberg is an anarchist in the musical treasury. Before now, a work of music is governed by a signature key: A, or B-flat, or any other letter up to G. Holding the key, a composer knows how to write, and listeners know, more or less, what to expect. A composer can change the key to alter the mood, returning to the original key to offer resolution. It is a method that has kept audiences happy for centuries. The tonal system is as much the foundation of musical confidence as gold is of the world economy.

By dropping the key, Schoenberg unsettles the market. Where listeners expect notes to arrive in a comprehensible order, like words in a coherent sentence, his music strikes their ears like *xjktrup rjqaaa&cd*

mnylu%#v, as baffling as microbiology. Audiences react with alarm. Mahler stands up in one concert and threatens to punch a protestor in the nose. He is persuaded, in part by Alma, that Schoenberg is the future, as Klimt is in art and Hofmannsthal in poetry. But where Klimt's vague landscapes are greeted with puzzled looks and Hofmannsthal's verses with pleasure, Schoenberg's music provokes visceral fury. Only a truly open mind can hear the wan, extraplanetary beauty in his revolutionary new pieces, and few can believe how he got there.

Schoenberg has an upstairs neighbor, a depressive painter named Richard Gerstl. Schoenberg drops by, at first to keep Gerstl company and then to take lessons in painting. Gerstl, half-Jewish and unhappily swayed (like Ludwig Wittgenstein) by Otto Weininger's male-dominant theories of sex and society, is brushed off when he asks Mahler on the street if he can paint his portrait. He paints Schoenberg instead, an imposing portrait with a frown on his brow. His next sitter is plain-faced Mathilde Schoenberg, whom Gerstl paints several times looking severe and unapproachable, arms clasped across her chest. The Schoenbergs make Gerstl part of their social circle of musicians. In the summer of 1908, Schoenberg invites Gerstl to share their vacation in the lakeside resort of Gmunden. While Schoenberg is busy writing his second string quartet, Gerstl keeps Mathilde company. One afternoon, while out for a walk, Schoenberg catches them making love in a barn, naked. Aghast, Mathilde flees back to Vienna with Gerstl. Schoenberg's student Anton von Webern tracks them down, and Zemlinsky persuades his sister to come home. After Mathilde returns, Schoenberg orders Gerstl to stay away. The painter loses, at a stroke, all his friends. At the end of September, he paints a canvas of himself naked against a Picasso-blue backdrop. Weeks later, in exactly the same position, opposite the mirror, he jumps off a chair with a hangman's noose around his neck, all the while stabbing himself in the belly with a knife. A physician certifies insanity, and he receives a Catholic burial. Gerstl is twenty-five. His works are not seen in public for twenty years. Among them is a late nude of Mathilde, who visits him right up to the end. Schoenberg dedicates his rule-breaking second quartet "to my wife." Musical Vienna suspects that Mathilde's infidelity has tipped him into atonality.

This lubricious legend persists for about a hundred years until a British historian, Dr. Raymond Coffer, examines every Schoenberg manuscript of the summer of 1908 and proves, in a doctoral thesis,[11] that the second quartet is finished at least two weeks before the composer catches his wife and the painter in flagrante delicto. Schoenberg's atonality is not a violent response to betrayal but a slow-burning process that has evolved over a decade and has found expression just before the marital crisis. Schoenberg's second string quartet is the birth pang of modernism. It is the moment where music turns, and it can never turn back.

Others have been tempted and hung back. Richard Strauss in *Elektra* and Mahler in his tenth symphony go close to the atonal line, only to retract, knowing they have too much reputation to lose. Schoenberg, unknown outside the Vienna avant-garde, has the right combination of ambition, desperation, and detachment from mainstream tradition to go where no composer has gone before. Jewish to his roots, raised in the Matzah Island second district of Vienna, Schoenberg tries becoming a Lutheran in the hope of career improvement and, when that fails, nurtures an anti-establishment rage. His boorish conduct at Mahler's coffee table is typical of his attitude to power. He identifies key signatures as a Christian clamp on a composer's free expression. How satisfying it would be for a born Jew to break the key and revert to sounds that predate Christianity, the nontonal tropes of desert Jews.

He never puts it quite this way, nor does he present his new style as a useful strategy, rather "as an inner necessity of one's own development," but he is adamant that atonality is the only way forward. If the public "have taken leave of their senses," that is their loss.[12] The audience, in Schoenberg's view, is always in the wrong. "If it is art, it cannot be for all and if it is for all it cannot be art," he announces. Asked if he has given up melody forever, he says: "No, I'm just looking for a different kind of tune."

"I don't understand it," says Mahler of Schoenberg's music, "but he's young and maybe he's right."[13]

Schoenberg has put his livelihood on the line. With only two pupils, the neurotic Webern and the languid Alban Berg, he cannot feed his family, so he paints in his spare time and secures a gallery exhibition of his stark, staring art. Mahler acquires two paintings anonymously from the gallery owner. Schoenberg never knows the buyer's name.

In May 1911, Mahler, aged fifty, comes home to die in Vienna.

With Mahler gone, says Schoenberg, "Vienna is no more." In the early evening of May 22, he leaves the Grinzing Cemetery, his head bowed, his coat soaked by a spring shower. That evening at home, he makes two works of art: a painting entitled *The Burial of Gustav Mahler* with his own bald head bowed at the graveside, and the last of an atonal set of *Six Little Pieces for Piano*. Less than a minute long, the sixth piece tolls its sorrow in an empty soundscape, an Antarctic expanse of loneliness. Schoenberg is a castaway on his own continent.

Alban Berg issues an emergency appeal: "Arnold Schoenberg's friends and pupils consider it their duty to bring his extremity to the notice of the public. Shame prevents him from doing so himself . . . Our mouths are opened by the thought of this artist coming to grief for lack of the common necessities of life. Catastrophe has overtaken him with unexpected speed . . ."[14]

The 424 marks he raises from fifty donors pay for Schoenberg's move to Berlin, where the living is cheap and his notoriety is unknown. In October 1912, he submits *Pierrot Lunaire* for performance in a cabaret. The musicians play behind a screen, leaving the stage to the white-faced soloist, Albertine Zehme, who commissioned the work. Apart from a few hisses and one man who busts out laughing, *Pierrot* is received with the respectful enthusiasm that Berliners reserve for art that soars above their heads. A setting of twenty-one French poems, it is declaimed in a Sprechstimme, a novel kind of spoken music that owes its origins to German medieval drama but packs a contemporary impact. He is reviewed pejoratively in the *New York Times* and is mentioned in the London *Daily Mail*. He is a made man, almost, earning his living less from his music than from a published teaching manual, *Harmonielehre*, that goes into many editions. On the anniversary of Mahler's death he cries out, "Gustav Mahler was a saint, they martyred him," but he has no further need of a mentor. Schoenberg stands on his own merit. He is the composer everyone has heard of and no one wants to hear. Called up to the Austrian Army at the age of forty-two, he is bullied by a sergeant who demands to know if he is that dreadful modernist composer everyone talks about. "I must admit that I am," says Schoenberg. "Somebody had to be and, since no one else wanted to, I took it upon myself."

Chastened by war, he writes an oratorio, *Jacob's Ladder*, on a favorite theme of Mahler's: man versus angel. He finds himself back in Vienna, where he started. Atonality, he realizes, is not the solution. He is "on the way to something quite new." On a country walk in 1921 he tells a disciple, Josef Rufer: "I have discovered something that will ensure the supremacy of German music for the next hundred years."[15]

Atonality, he decides, is immoral—as flawed as a marriage without trust. There has to be order. In Schoenberg's new method, all twelve notes are equal, as in atonality, but they are laid out in a preordained row before the composer is permitted to write a single phrase. The row is a "scale" of any combination of twelve notes to which the composer must adhere, start to finish.

Schoenberg is not the first to toy with twelve notes. Mozart, who can do anything, uses all twelve notes in the finale of his fortieth symphony and again in the third movement of the forty-first. Josef Hauer, a Viennese theorist, has written a treatise on the subject: "We have twelve tempered halfsteps ('solar systems') with a calculated 479,001,600 melodic possibilities ('star paths'). Within the twelve tones none may be repeated or excluded—this is self-evident. Identical tones must be distanced from one another as far as possible."[16] Schoenberg and Hauer tussle over who got there first; inevitably, the more famous man wins. Schoenberg's row is stricter, structurally solid and texturally imaginative. It engages both ear and brain. Webern, its most fanatical adherent, applies the method with such rigor that every element in a score— pauses, dynamics, tempi, and which instrument plays what—is subjected to the rules of the row. Webern likes to make the second half of a row the exact reverse of the first, yielding a *cancrizan*, a canon that walks backward, delighting puzzle lovers. There is a cerebral payback to this system.

For Schoenberg, this is his book of Genesis:

To understand the very nature of creation one must acknowledge that there was no light before the Lord said: "Let there be Light." And since there was not yet light, the Lord's omniscience embraced a vision of it which only His omniscience could call forth. We poor human beings, when we refer to one of the better minds among us as a creator, should never forget what a creator is in reality. A creator has a vision of something which has not existed before this vision. . . . In fact, the concept of creator and creation should be formed in harmony with the Divine Model . . .[17]

If these are delusions, they are very Jewish delusions. Schoenberg is creating the world, out of the *nihilo* of war, with godly rules that must be obeyed for all time.

On February 17, 1923, he shares the new order with his inner circle. A year later, he achieves a twelve-note row in the fifth movement of *Serenade*, opus twenty-three, a capricious dance scored for string trio and mandolin, guitar, and two clarinets, with a bass singer. The serenade is premiered in a private Vienna home before being rolled out at a festival in Donaueschingen. It is the friskiest thing he has ever done, rippling with logical positivism and joie de vivre. In his fiftieth year, Schoenberg has saved the future of music and enjoys a second lease on life.

Mathilde dies in October that year, of adrenal cancer. On New Year's Eve of 1924, Schoenberg meets a woman twenty-four years younger than himself, the sister of one of his pupils. In marrying Gertrud, he is creatively revitalized. Doors that once slammed in his face swing open. Zemlinsky, now music director of the German Theatre in Prague, produces his mystic opera *Erwartung*. A second opera, *Die glückliche Hand*, is staged in Vienna. Finally and out of the blue, he is invited to Berlin, as professor of composition at the Academy of Music. Berlin offers financial security and immense prestige. It places him ahead of Stravinsky as the premier modernist and allows him to cultivate outstanding students.

His seven years in Berlin are the happiest of his life. Gertrud gives birth to three children and writes the libretto for a twelve-tone opera, *Von heute auf morgen*. Zemlinsky arrives from Prague with Otto Klemperer to found the Kroll Opera, crucible of radical opera. The Schoenbergs are nightlife celebrities, photographed in bars. He has the best teaching post in Europe. He even receives a commission from the immaculate Berlin Philharmonic Orchestra for a twenty-minute, twelve-note score, cast as a classic theme and variations.

At the first rehearsal, the conductor Wilhelm Furtwängler greets his musicians with "Bad news: gentlemen, today we are playing Herr Schoenberg's new work, *Variations for Orchestra* opus 31." He adds: "But there is good news: Herr Schoenberg this week is unfortunately not in Berlin." There is a presumption among musicians that, in a modern score, no one other than the composer can tell if they are playing all the notes, or even the right ones. The premiere, on December 2, 1928, has a mixed reception. Schoenberg hits back on state radio, attacking "the opinion of the majority." New art is never beautiful on first encounter, he argues, and the job of the composer is to listen to a higher calling. "Whoever God entrusted with the task of saying something unpopular is also given the chance to satisfy himself that there will always be others who understand."[18] His is the cry of the artist through history and of the Jew in the fevered atmosphere of pre-Nazi Germany.

Schoenberg has no illusions. In 1921, he was forced to abandon a family holiday near Salzburg in the face of local anti-Semitism. "Toward the end it got very ugly," he tells Berg. He sees himself as "possibly one of the first Jews in central Europe to be the victim of an actual expulsion."[19] Hypersensitive to racial denigration, he breaks off a friendship with the expressionist artist Wassily Kandinsky. "I have heard that even a Kandinsky sees only evil in the actions of the Jews and, in their evil actions, only the Jewishness," he charges. When Kandinsky attempts to placate him, he thunders:

> What is anti-Semitism to lead to if not acts of violence? Is it so difficult to imagine that? You are perhaps satisfied with depriving Jews of their civil rights. Then certainly Einstein, Mahler, I and many others, will have been got rid of. But one thing is certain: they will not be able to exterminate those much tougher elements thanks to whose endurance Jewry has maintained itself unaided against the whole of mankind for 20 centuries. For these are evidently so constituted that they can accomplish the task that their God has imposed on them: To survive in exile, uncorrupted and unbroken, until the hour of salvation comes!

The leader of modern music has found his inner Jew, bearing God's twin tablets of stone into the age of uncertainty.

He sets to work on an opera titled *Moses und Aron*, with twelve letters in the title to signify its twelve-note character, as well as to avoid its composer's fear of the number thirteen. Moses, in the opera, searches for the inexpressible: "O word, thou word, that I lack!" Schoenberg is the inarticulate leader who needs a brother to articulate his ideas.

When the Nazis seize power, Schoenberg is in Paris. Suspended from the Berlin Academy, his bank accounts frozen, he goes to the Liberal synagogue on rue Copernic and demands to be readmitted to the Jewish faith that he left in the 1890s. Told that there is no such procedure—anyone who is born a Jew remains one in Jewish law, regardless of conversion or defection—he demands a formal ceremony. On July 24, 1933, the synagogue certifies his reentry into the Community of Israel. The witnesses are the painter Marc Chagall and the scientist Dmitri Marianov, Einstein's son-in-law. Schoenberg wants art and science to unite in approving his Jewish identity. Prepared to give up his life as a composer, he forms a Jewish Unity Party, aiming:

> . . . to engage in large scale propaganda among all of Jewry in the United States and also later in other countries . . . to move the Jewish community to its very depths by a graphic demonstration of what lies in store for German Jews unless they receive help within two or three months. The immediate goal of my efforts is the commitment of all Jews in all countries to a monthly contribution of two marks per head for several months. As soon as the proceeds of this collection are secured, I shall attempt to open negotiations with Germany . . .

He will have to lease a plane, employ staff, and engage a film crew to record his speeches.[20] "I have prepared for fourteen years for what has happened now," he tells Webern. "I have definitely separated myself from whatever binds me to the Occident. . . . I am decided—if I am fit for such activity—only to work in future for the national state of Jewry."

Never having led anything larger than a performance of *Pierrot Lunaire*, Schoenberg now expects all the Jews in the world to join his party and empower him to negotiate on their behalf with Hitler. He has little policy beyond stating that "the ultimate Jewish homeland" is Palestine. "No true Jew could ever forget that Palestine is ours and that we have been deprived of it by mere force; that we will never consent to the claim of another nation to our promised land."[21]

He addresses a long appeal to the Reform rabbi Stephen S. Wise, cofounder of the National Association for the Advancement of Colored

People. Wise has the ear of President Franklin Delano Roosevelt, and Schoenberg needs him on his side. He begins:

> I wrote to Einstein in 1925 that I was less interested in the discovery of a Jewish music . . . than in militant ways of forcing a solution to the Jewish question and asked for an opportunity to discuss the matter with him in person, whereupon I had to undergo a very earthly treatment from this astronomer, whose eye ranges much too far to catch what lies closest—he neglected to reply . . .

This is not a promising overture. Schoenberg continues:

> Please don't misunderstand me: I have no political ambitions; my ambitions could have found complete fulfilment on music paper, had I any ambitions at all. I only insist on the quiet honour to be permitted to sacrifice my life for the existence of the Jewish people . . . I would be overjoyed if we could find an opportunity soon to talk about such and related matters provided, as I hope, that this would not bore you too much.[22]

His irony is lost on Wise. There is no record, either in his papers or in Schoenberg's, of a reply, let alone a meeting. Schoenberg complains to the writer Thomas Mann that Jewish leaders won't take him seriously because he, like Mann, does not belong to the political Left.

Having put Germany behind him, Schoenberg de-umlauts his name, replacing the ö with oe. Berg is perplexed: "Even if I regard his departure from the Occident humanly as possible . . . ," he tells Webern, "there remains for me the unshakeable fact of his musical works, for which there is only one description: German."[23] The man who secured the "supremacy of German music for the next hundred years" now identifies as a Jew. Adherents find it hard to keep up.

Needing to feed a young family and find a home, Schoenberg awaits an offer from the BBC in London, which turns out to be insubstantial. The only concrete proposition comes from a cellist, Joseph Malkin, who gives him a year's teaching contract worth $4,800 at two music schools in Boston and New York. Arnold Schoenberg leaves Europe on October 31, 1933, never to return. His East Coast career is short-lived. Dismayed at the lack of a school orchestra and fatigued by the five-hour train shuttle from Boston to New York, he sickens with bronchitis and is advised to seek a warmer climate. He writes to the Sydney Conservatorium in Australia, whose director, Edgar Bainton, rejects his application on grounds of his "modernist ideas and dangerous tendencies."

In September 1934, Arnold Schoenberg joins the University of California at Los Angeles (UCLA) for one-third of his East Coast salary. He never quite grasps the value of a dollar. Princeton University invites him to give a single lecture for $100, but the cost of getting there is so great he is left with barely enough change for coffee. A contemporary music enthusiast offers him $100 for an autograph. All he has to do is sign his name.

He rents a house in Brentwood between George Gershwin and Charles Chaplin, who become his tennis partners. Gershwin tells him that *Pierrot Lunaire* is his favorite work. Gertrud holds an open house on Sunday afternoons for fellow exiles, among them the brothers Mann, the playwright Bertolt Brecht, the film composer Erich Wolfgang Korngold, and the conductor Otto Klemperer, music director at the Los Angeles Philharmonic Orchestra. Try as he might, Klemperer cannot get Schoenberg into the Hollywood Bowl. Gertrud discontinues the Sunday hospitality because they cannot afford it. Zemlinsky, arriving in America, suffers a cerebral hemorrhage and three years of invalidity, dying in obscurity.

A synagogue commissions Schoenberg to compose "Kol Nidrei." Shunning the "cello-sentimentality" of the Bruch score, he writes a score infused with "the dignity of law."[24] The congregation hates it. He recasts a baroque harpsichord piece as a cello concerto for Pablo Casals, who plays it just once. He makes an orchestral setting of a Brahms piano quartet, finding few takers. "We were so poor," says his daughter Nuria. Chaplin arranges an introduction to Irving Thalberg, a cultured movie studio mogul. It is not a meeting of minds. "I almost agreed to write music for a film," Schoenberg tells Alma Mahler, "but [I] fortunately asked $50,000 which, likewise fortunately, was much too much, for it would have been the end of me." The film is *The Good Earth*, from the novel set in China by Pearl S. Buck. Gertrud reports: "The M.G.M.

company promised him to alter nothing (a promise which naturally they would never have kept) but the fee of $50,000 was, as we had hoped (!), too high and we got out of it with relief!"[25] A third version has Thalberg describing a hurricane scene to the composer, who interjects: "With so much going on, why do you need music?" Schoenberg is a complete stranger in paradise.

The news from Europe is dreadful. Berg dies of an infection. Webern flirts with Nazism. Schoenberg's brother Heinrich dies in Salzburg after being tortured by the gestapo. Schoenberg's music is banned in the old world, scorned in the new. When his richly textured violin concerto is premiered by Louis Krasner with Leopold Stokowski's sumptuous Philadelphia Orchestra, *Time* magazine warns America against this alien invader:

> For thirty years, bald, parchment-faced, Austrian-born composer Arnold [Schoenberg] has written music so complicated that only he and a couple other fellows understand what it is all about. This music, which sounds to the uninitiated not only queer but accidental, has been enjoyed by very few. But it has thrown the world of music into a Kilkenny cat fight. One cat camp maintains that [Schoenberg's] music, like Einstein's theory, sounds queer because it is way over the average man's head; opponents swear that [Schoenberg] is pulling everybody's leg, including his own, and that his miscalled music is a gibberish of wrong notes.

The review resembles a contemporary piece of Nazi musicology: "Schoenberg's tendency to negate all that was before him is the old tested Jewish tactics . . . at an opportune moment, to destroy the cultural values of the host peoples in order to set up their own as the only valid values."[26] Spot the difference?

Marooned on the Pacific coast, forsaken by the world at large, Schoenberg casts around for bits of paid work to sustain his growing family. He finds himself in front of a class of preschool teachers, trying to instruct them in the basic laws of music.

"Tell me," he inquires gently, "you teach the very youngest children, yes?"

"Yes, Mr. Schoenberg, that's right," chorus the teachers.

"So am I to understand there are human beings who know even less about music than you do?"[27]

It is not easy to be Arnold Schoenberg.

A man in a dark suit walks down the Street of the Prophets in Jerusalem carrying a large black case that might be a doctor's bag. Turning into an alley, he knocks at a door and enters a two-room hovel, typical of the neighborhood. A patriarch in a white galabieh robe sits at the table. The suited man sets down his case and opens it. When the old fellow is ready to sing, the visitor cranks a lever and makes a phonograph recording.

Abraham Zevi Idelsohn, a Lithuanian cantor, has arrived from South Africa via Berlin and London in search of a Jewish sound. Disliking the Germanification of prayer melodies by the Vienna and Berlin cantors Sulzer and Lewandowski, he visits three hundred synagogues in the Holy City in search of authentic melody. An Ashkenazi Jew who thinks his chants originated in temple times, he is shocked by the diversity and decides to document it. Imitating the Hungarian composers Bartók and Kodály, who roam Magyar plains and the Moroccan seaboard collecting folk songs, the Jewish ethnomusicologist sets out to conserve ancient tunes before the juggernauts of Zionism and Orthodoxy flatten the distinctions. Idelsohn records more than a thousand songs: motifs of prayer, celebration, lullaby, and mourning. He then finds himself in a position to pronounce on whether there is such a thing as Jewish music or not.

The world has two views on this subject. Richard Wagner holds the Jews to be irredeemably unmusical, capable only of imitation. Lord Byron, at the opposite extreme, thinks the Jews may hold the musical secrets of Solomon's temple. He writes a set of poems that are furnished with melodies by a London composer, Isaac Nathan. Byron's *Hebrew Melodies* include some of his most famous works: "She Walks in Beauty," "Jephtha's Daughter," "They Say That Hope Is Happiness." Nathan gets into debt and hares off to Australia, where he writes the dominion's first opera and is subsequently killed by a tram.[28] What is Jewish in music remains contentious. Gustav Mahler unsettles audiences with a klezmer tune in his first symphony. Ernst Bloch Judaizes

Shelomo for cello and orchestra. Schoenberg toys with Jewish tropes, and George Gershwin uses Yiddish doggerel until Ira gives him English words.

This, however, is a first-world problem. "The Jew, being of semitic stock, is part of the Oriental world, so Jewish music—coming to life in the Near East—is, generally speaking, of one piece with the music of the Orient,"[29] writes Idelsohn, infuriating Ashkenazi Jews by dismissing klezmer, Hasidic, and Zionist songs as "an amalgamation of non-Jewish and Jewish elements." His research among the old crooners of Jerusalem convinces him that the Jews of Yemen, a community isolated both from Arab neighbors and from the rest of the Jewish world, have traces of temple music, "uninfluenced from without and . . . spared the contact with Europe on the one hand and on the other with the Arabic-Persian art-music." He rolls out this theory in the introduction to the *Thesaurus of Hebrew Oriental Melodies*, a work that earns him a study grant to spend eight months in Vienna. There, he is introduced to Mahler's friend Guido Adler, the foremost musicologist of the day. Adler specializes in the study of Christian music up to 1600. Idelsohn, at one of his lectures, hears authentic Gregorian chant for the first time and recognizes it as a cousin of his Yemenite songs.

Before he can make more progress, Idelsohn is conscripted into the Turkish Army, serving in Gaza as a hospital clerk and bandmaster through the First World War. By the time he gets home, Jerusalem has been liberated by the British Army, Zionism is victorious, and his theories seem futile to everyone except Guido Adler, with whom he maintains a lively correspondence.[30] Idelsohn composes a five-act opera, *Jephtha*, takes in music students, and, failing to make enough of a living, leaves the country in 1922. In Berlin, he signs a contract with Polyphon Records for an album of *Hebräische Palästin Lieder*. Idelsohn is not keen on Zionist songs and does not know many of them, so, to fill the record, he invents "Hava Nagila" (you can hear his original recording online). The tune may belong to the Sadagura Hasidim of Bukovina, but it might also be a Romanian folk dance or just one of those airs that flutter from mouth to ear across the Balkans. In time, it becomes an Israeli anthem, played on El Al planes as they touch down on home soil. "Hava Nagila" exists to prove Idelsohn's point: the tunes most people think are truly Jewish are nothing of the sort.[31]

The Hebrew Union College in Cincinnati appoints Idelsohn professor of Hebrew and Liturgy. In 1929, he publishes his major study, *Jewish Music*, finally making the connection between the recordings on his cylinders and the tropes of early church music. A psalm intoned in Sana'a on the Jewish New Year[32] fits like a glove across a line of Gregorian chant. Yemenite Jews, descendant from First Temple exiles, are the *fons et origo* of all Christian music, according to Idelsohn.

His hypothesis outrages Christians and Jews alike. Idelsohn is accused of leaping to unfounded conclusions, trampling on hallowed traditions, lacking rigor. He is anathema to Orthodoxy, an enemy of Zionism, and incomprehensible to most readers. Admirers, who admit his methodology is "naïve," excuse him by saying "that he had no model, no established technique to guide him." Try as he might, Idelsohn can "not convince his fellow-scholars, Jewish or Christian, that a common *Ur-tradition* could be constructed."[33] He makes more enemies by describing living Jewish composers as "renegades or assimilants [who] have mostly corrupted the Jewish tradition with their attempts to modernise it."[34]

Dismayed by his reception, he is felled by a stroke and is left paralyzed, dying in South Africa in 1938. Dilettante or not, Idelsohn has redrawn the musical map of East and West. At the National Sound Archive in Jerusalem, where his cylinders are digitized, I call up at the click of a key a Yemenite cantor from 1910, singing a prayer so clearly that on the third line I pick up the trope and sing along. Idelsohn has excavated and conserved a musical past older than anyone has imagined.

Others follow his route. During the First World War, a German interpreter at a camp for French-African prisoners of war near Wünsdorf hears Arab songs that test his ear. He makes a recording of the POWs and changes his field of study from linguistics to ethnomusicology. With a PhD in Jewish music on the Tunisian island of Djerba, Robert Lachmann goes to work in the state library in Berlin until the Nazis throw him out. He migrates to Jerusalem in 1935 with a non-Jewish sound engineer, Walter Schur, and takes up where Idelsohn left off, recording every ethnic type of singer in cafés and prayer houses. Supplies of shellac for making recordings run out, and the Germans refuse to send more, but Lachmann is nothing if not ingenious.

He takes the metal lids from grocery tins and Schur adapts them for his recording machine. That works for a while. Then Lachmann asks a radiologist at Bikur Holim Hospital what happens to the X-rays of patients who die. Told that they are thrown away, Lachmann reclaims the celluloid and reuses it for recording. At the Jerusalem archive, I have played an X-ray of human ribs that emits a song of Balkan Jews.

Even more determined than Idelsohn, Lachmann records and catalogues more than a thousand new items in four years, much to the dismay of the Hebrew University, which abolishes his position as a research associate. Lachmann contacts the British-run Palestine Broadcasting Service and delivers twelve programs of *Oriental Music*, which he presents in German-accented English. Lacking any religious background, he approaches Jewish, Muslim, and Christian tropes with equal enthusiasm, fueled by an urge to foster dialogue across faiths. Priests, cantors, and muezzins jostle with secular instrumentalists in his studio. In no other country, declares Lachmann, is the need for understanding music as critical as it is in Palestine. "For the European, here, it is of vital interest to know the mind of his Oriental neighbour; well, music and singing, as being the spontaneous outcome of it, will be his surest guide provided he listens to it with sympathy instead of disdain."[35] His is the passion of a Wagnerian *liebestod*: a love that must end in death, "with self-destruction as its highest rapture."[36]

On a visit to London, he asks the BBC to broadcast his series, only to be told it is "outside its scope." After returning dejected to Jerusalem, he is hospitalized at Bikur Holim in September 1938 with chronic vascular disease and dies months later at the age of forty-six. His non-Jewish partner, Schur, is interned in Acre Castle as an enemy alien in 1939. Schur escapes in the clothes of an Arab woman and disappears from the record, an unsolved mystery. The age of discovery is over.

What remains is Lachmann's vision that "young Jewish or Arab composers may find one day a new way of expressing themselves, however imperfectly or clumsily, in a musical language somewhere, possibly, between the Western and Eastern." In the twenty-first century, no composer in Israel, Jew or Arab, can afford to be unaware of the other.

Obscure as Idelsohn and Lachmann might appear, they contribute to a significant shift in our perception of how music evolves, not in a straight progressive line but in a sideways crawl that keeps referring back to preclassical forms for confidence and redirection. They anticipate Schoenberg's atonality—itself a harking back to a pretonal age—as well as the period instrument movement and the increasing tendency of Western composers to research remote cultures, from Balinese gamelan to African nose-flutes. Most of all they establish that a musical DNA is central to Jewish identity.

And their path is still trodden. The American composer Steve Reich comes to Jerusalem to record Yemenite cantillation for his orchestral composition *Tehillim*. The Russian-born Mark Kopytman employs a Yemenite vocalist at the heart of his masterwork, *The Voice of Memory*, probably the most widely performed work of Israeli orchestral music. The Yemenite Israeli singer Ofra Haza is hired by Hollywood for the theme song of *The Prince of Egypt* and by the French director Patrice Chéreau for his historical drama, *La Reine Margot*. Achinoam Nini, an American-raised Yemenite Jew, teams up with an Arab-Israeli, Mira Awad, to represent Israel at the 2009 Eurovision Song Contest. The song they perform in front of two hundred million viewers is an appeal for peace titled "There Must Be Another Way." These are all legacies of the man with the black suitcase.

TEN

1917

DEAR LORD

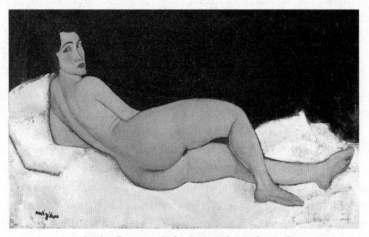

A look of reproach for Picasso's rival, Modi.

On Tuesday, February 7, 1917, ten men gather around a table to decide the fate of the Jews. The meeting starts on the dot of eleven thirty in the morning and is minuted by an unknown hand, supposedly that of a Whitehall civil servant. The location is 193 Maida Vale, a Victorian villa with a nameplate that reads MIZPAH. It is the home of Moses Gaster, Haham of the Spanish and Portuguese Jews. Herzl once stayed here, and, in the twenty years since, Gaster has advanced his cause. A black-bearded man of vast erudition and intellectual range, Gaster has written books and essays on Romanian literature, on the *Axiochus* of Pseudo-Plato, and on Samaritan archaeology. He renews the Spanish and Portuguese Jews' prayer book and constructs a curriculum for the schools of Romania. His command of ten languages, backed by an immense private library, gives him unchallenged authority in Jewish scholarship. Some consider him a genius; others accuse him of a lack of analytical depth. All agree on his besetting flaw: "A constant impatience tended at times to beget intolerance and to foster a conviction of infallibility. I never heard my father admit that he was wrong," reports his son, Theodor.[1] Gaster manages to fall out with every person of consequence in the Jewish community from the chief rabbi down, more over matters of dignity than principle. "He had not the essential humility of spirit," sighs his son. Lacking any sense of proportion in human relations, he is forever at odds with his bosses on the congregation's ruling council, the *Mahamad*. But obduracy in a good cause is a virtue, and, inspired by Herzl, Gaster never stops searching the horizons for a redeemer who might come unto Zion speedily in our days. Finally, at the start of 1917, Gaster thinks he has found him.

Colonel Sir Mark Sykes, MP, is a boys' own adventurer. Heir to thirty-four thousand acres of Yorkshire, a breeder of Arab horses, and a player of many sports, Sykes joins the Boer War in search of action and, finding none, goes traveling in the Bible lands, acquiring languages and useful contacts. His breezy travel books are bestsellers. In London, he catches the eye of the prime minister, Arthur Balfour, and is sent back to the British embassy in Constantinople to run an intelligence network. Elected to Parliament for Hull, Sykes forms a battalion from workers on his estate at the outbreak of war and is about to lead them into battle when the secretary of war, Lord Kitchener, orders him to Whitehall as a Middle East adviser. Sykes, calling on information from his spies, gives advance warning of Turkey's entry into the war on the German side in October 1914. He advocates British support for an Arab Revolt that would sabotage oil pipelines and desert railways, bringing down the Turkish economy. Once Turkey is defeated, he recommends that its resources be split between local tribes under the protection of world powers. Kitchener sends him out for a swing around the region, where he upsets the touchy guerrilla leader T. E. Lawrence, who calls him "a sadly unreliable intellect" but charms Arab sheikhs with his wit, knowledge, and authority in Whitehall. Sykes returns to

London with a blueprint that Lebanon and Syria should come under French influence while oil-rich Iraq, Transjordan, and Saudi Arabia would have Arab kings who are sympathetic to Britain. He has no plan yet for Palestine, but his boots are planted so firmly in Arab sand that in Whitehall he is nicknamed "the mad Mullah" and deemed to have "gone native." Sykes has not much time for Jews. In one of his books he writes: "Even Jews have their good points, but Armenians have none."[2] This is a familiar English cliché, echoed by George Orwell in chapter 13 of *Down and Out in Paris and London*.

Four days after Turkey enters the war, the Cabinet holds its first debate on Zionism. There is "very keen" support from the chancellor of the exchequer, David Lloyd George, a Bible-thumping Welshman, along with mild encouragement from the prime minister, H. H. Asquith, and polite opposition from the foreign secretary, Edward Grey. The strongest case for Jewish rule is made by Herbert Samuel, minister in charge of local government in England and Wales and the first Jew to reach Cabinet rank. Samuel writes a Cabinet paper, "The Future of Palestine," which argues that endorsing Zionism would "win for England the lasting gratitude of Jews throughout the world." He is immediately opposed by his first cousin Edwin Montagu, who has joined the Cabinet in the important post of financial secretary to the treasury. "There is no Jewish race now as a homogenous whole," writes Montagu to Asquith, prepared to put his body on the line to block a Jewish state. Samuel, however, is ahead after the first debate and, after meeting the Zionist leader Chaim Weizmann in December 1914, starts dreaming that "perhaps the Temple may be rebuilt."

Weizmann, forty years old and a British citizen since 1910, urgently seeks access to power. A biochemist with 120 patents to his name, he leases to the British government his acetone-making process as an aid in speeding up munitions output. It takes two years for a significant amount of acetone to be produced, and there is some resentment that Weizmann is being paid for the use of his patent. His access to Whitehall is further hampered by living in Manchester, where he teaches at the university and his wife, Vera, is medical health officer for the city council. Weizmann rallies support in Manchester from the Sieff family, who own the Marks & Spencer stores, and from C. P. Scott, owner and editor of the liberal *Manchester Guardian* newspaper. Scott sets up a breakfast for Weizmann with the Liberal leader David Lloyd George, who is delighted to make his acquaintance. "When Dr. Weizmann was talking of Palestine he kept bringing up place names which were more familiar to me than those on the Western Front," gushes the chancellor of the exchequer.[3] Weizmann moves his family to London in 1915 and is given an office at the Ministry of Munitions. He finds Lloyd George mercurial and cultivates Winston Churchill, First Lord of the Admiralty, who greets him with an immediate demand for thirty thousand tons of acetone. Churchill is launching a naval assault on the Turks at Gallipoli, which proves an epic disaster. There is no more Cabinet talk of Zion for a year until Colonel Sykes comes up with a comprehensive plan.

Sykes has been quietly redrawing the map of the Middle East, together with a French official, François Georges-Picot. They leave Palestine for last, knowing its sensitivity to three religions and all world powers. In February 1916, Herbert Samuel gives Sykes a copy of "The Future of Palestine" and makes a case for "using Zionism to advance British interests."[4] A Jewish state in Palestine could help protect the Suez Canal, and, if Britain were to support such a state, Jews in neutral countries would be impressed. If, on the other hand, the Germans or the Turks were to offer a Jewish state, that could harm the Allied cause. Sykes, never having had much to do with Jews, asks Samuel to put him in touch with "a reasonable" Zionist leader. Samuel gives the matter careful thought before recommending that Sykes should see, "at least in the first instance," Haham Moses Gaster, founder of the English Zionist Federation (EZF) and, by quaint coincidence, the English Folklore Society. Samuel's choice is dictated by two considerations. Gaster, he knows, is his own man, a British citizen, uncompromised (as Weizmann might be) by holding office in an international Zionist movement. Gaster is also a man whose discretion can be trusted. Samuel's wife, Miriam Franklin, has been best friends since childhood with Mrs. Gaster, Lucy Friedländer.

Sykes, never one to waste a minute, writes to Gaster, who replies feebly that he is laid up with lumbago and cannot make it to Whitehall for at least a week. Sykes, who waits for no man, hails a cab and, on April 11, 1916, rings Gaster's doorbell at 193 Maida Vale. The process has begun.

No record is kept of this first encounter. Sykes is thought to have proposed that Jews should rule part of Palestine under Anglo-French protection. What he wants from Gaster is an indication that world Jewry would rally behind the Allies if they endorsed Zionism. He is concerned that two million tsar-hating Russian-born Jews in America could tip Woodrow Wilson's White House toward the Germans. Gaster, ever the rabbi, replies with a discursive homily on the Jews, their historical sufferings, and the prayers they say thrice daily for a return to Zion. He assures Sykes that the Jews will unite behind a British-backed Jewish entity in Palestine. Sykes, duly enthused, puts the Haham in a taxi and sends him to the French embassy to win over Picot, who is unconvinced.[5] Sykes now informs the Cabinet that Britain needs the Zionists in order to "(a) calm their (anti-tsar) activities in Russia, (b) (cause) pessimism in Germany, (c) stimulate (Jews) in England, France & Italy and (d) enthuse in USA."[6] A devout Roman Catholic in an Anglican establishment, Sykes has enough of the outsider about him to get on well with the Jewish Haham. Both are bringing up large families. Sykes has five children with a sixth on the way; Gaster has thirteen. They are soon asking after each other's broods.[7]

Before more maps can be drawn, domestic politics intervenes. In December 1916, Asquith is toppled by Lloyd George in a Cabinet coup. Samuel, an Asquith loyalist, resigns. Edwin Montagu, his anti-Zionist cousin, stays. Lloyd George, on his second day as prime minister, puts Palestine at the head of his agenda, ordering the army to deliver a morale-raising victory in the Holy Land. General Edmund Allenby is sent out to Cairo. Sykes is told to get a move on with his Palestine plan. He asks Gaster to arrange a meeting of Zionist leaders. Gaster, whether on Sykes's prompting or his own initiative, writes the first draft of His Majesty's Government's policy on Palestine. Picot, meanwhile, is uneasy about Sykes's dependence on Gaster and widens his exposure to other strands of Zionist opinion. Sykes holds a secret meeting with Aaron Aaronsohn, a pioneering agronomist who, with his sister Sarah and some other friends, runs a pro-British spy ring in Palestine. (Sarah will be betrayed, tortured, and murdered by the Turks.) He also calls in Vladimir Jabotinsky, a Polish-Jewish firebrand who wants Jews to rule on both sides of the Jordan and offers to form a Jewish Legion to fight in British uniform. Several more Jews go through Sykes's swinging doors; Chaim Weizmann is still not among them.

When word reaches Weizmann that Sykes is consulting Gaster, he explodes like mishandled acetone. Weizmann knows the Haham and owes him a tip of the hat for sponsoring his original residence permit in Britain. But, anticlerical as Zionists are, he distrusts a man in canonical garb and is furious at being displaced. Calling Gaster "an absolute rogue,"[8] he begs Samuel to move heaven and earth to obtain him an introduction to Sykes before Gaster can convene his decisive meeting. Gaster, hearing that Sykes has held a meeting with Weizmann, pretends that he is being kept informed: "I hope to see Dr. W this afternoon and I shall probably hear from him the result of his visit to you last night,"[9] he tells Sykes. Weizmann, however, is two steps ahead. He gives Sykes a draft statement on Palestine that is clearer than Gaster's and proposes a final guest list for the critical meeting.

The meeting at Gaster's house on February 7, 1917, is stacked by Weizmann with his supporters. Present are Sykes, Samuel, Weizmann, and his publicist, Nahum Sokolow, secretary-general of the World Zionist Congress. Weizmann has also infiltrated the Marks & Spencer brother-in-law Harry Sacher, the EZF president Joseph Cowen, Herzl's lawyer Herbert Bentwich, and a brace of Rothschilds: Walter, head of the English bank, and James of the French branch; James's wife, Dorothy, is a gushing Weizmannite. Gaster has lost the meeting before it begins.

"Dr. Gaster opened the proceedings," record the minutes, "by stating in general terms that . . . what Zionists in England and everywhere desired was a British protectorate [in Palestine] with full rights to the Jews to develop a national life. The Jews in Palestine must be recognised as a nation."[10]

Walter, Lord Rothschild, an amateur zoologist who rides a coach drawn by four zebras around his estate at Tring, is the next to speak. He responds that while "he sympathised fully with the development of a Jewish state in Palestine under the British Crown, he was irreconcilably opposed to any form of [Anglo-French] condominium. Great Britain must annex Palestine." The London head of the Rothschilds' bank demands the imposition of Rule Britannia, which runs against the expressed interests of his Paris cousins.

Herbert Samuel speaks next, smoothly and diplomatically, favoring the creation of a Jewish state, which, he stresses with some anxiety, would not compromise the loyalty of Jews to the countries where they currently live. He believes the idea would be popular among the British electorate. In an aside quoted in the Rothschilds' papers, Samuel remarks: "Even today the Bible exercises a vast influence over important classes of Englishmen and has won their desire to assist at a Jewish return to Palestine."[11]

Sokolow pops up at Weizmann's elbow to opine that "many Jews of Russian origin" in America will rush to a new state in Palestine. "Jews of the whole world," affirms Sokolow, "desire that England should annex Palestine." Weizmann adds: "The Jews who go to Palestine would go to constitute a Jewish nation and be 100% Jews, not to become Arabs or Druse or Englishmen." Harry Sacher suggests that Jews in England would look in future to Jerusalem as Catholics do to Rome, "but would owe it no political obligation." The Frenchman James de Rothschild says "the support of Jews throughout the world was necessary and must be appealed to." Cowen thinks German Zionists will welcome British suzerainty in Palestine, and Bentwich says he would always trust the British government to come up with the very best constitutional remedy for the region.

Sykes says nothing until the last Zionist voice has been heard. Then he takes control. He opens by assuring everyone that he is attending "in a private capacity," a fiction that no one believes. British soldiers, he confirms, will soon conquer Palestine. A Jewish state in Palestine has "his full sympathy." He warns that there will be "within a generation or so a great Arab national movement" but that "the Arabs could be managed, particularly if they received Jewish support in other matters." His speech rings with imperial swagger. Could the Arabs be managed? There are 94,000 Jews in Palestine, against 589,000 Muslims and 70,000 Christian Arabs. These inefficient Turkish estimates include variable numbers of itinerant Bedouins and absentee sheikhs who own land in Palestine but never live there. Still, there is no disguising the fact that Jews are outnumbered by Arabs by a factor of about seven to one. Somehow, neither the Zionists nor Sykes see fit to mention this.

Russia, Sykes continues, would like to send its Jews to Palestine. Tsarist officials have told him privately that their only concern is that the territory would not be large enough for all the Jews they want to export. The French, he warns, will kick up a fuss when they hear that the Jews prefer British rule. Perhaps the Zionists could send someone to charm them? James de Rothschild nominates Sokolow, a Polish-born polyglot of refined committee skill. This is the moment Gaster realizes he has been cut out of the great game.

The meeting ends after two and a quarter hours with agreement on a draft declaration. Based on Weizmann's paper more than Gaster's, it designates Palestine as the Jewish National Home, grants "full and free right of immigration to Palestine to Jews of other countries," provides a charter for a Jewish development company, and ordains the Hebrew language "to be recognised as an inviolable right of the whole Jewish population." Other minorities are unmentioned.

As soon as they leave Gaster's house, Weizmann completes his putsch. Sokolow sees Picot the next day, assuring him that "Zionists and Jews generally have the greatest respect for and trust in France." The day after, Weizmann persuades Cowen to resign as president of the English Zionist Federation. Gaster is replaced on its board with three Marks & Spencer men: Sieff, Marks, and Sacher. Weizmann meets the new foreign secretary, Arthur Balfour. He breakfasts again with Lloyd George, who gives orders to "grab Palestine." Sokolov heads to Rome to see the pope. Russia has a revolution. America enters the war. Gaster is left fuming and excluded in Maida Vale.

"I feel in duty bound to state frankly that I take umbrage at the manner in which I have been treated," he complains to James de Rothschild:

> You perhaps are not aware in the first place that for the last nine or ten months it was I and I alone, unknown to anybody else except Mr Herbert Samuel, who has conducted the negotiations with Mr Samuel, Sir Mark Sykes and Mr Picot. They on more than one occasion have visited me in my house and I have seen the latter in the French Embassy. I may state at once that it appeared very strange to Sir Mark Sykes that another who knew nothing of all those private conversations and could therefore not take up the thread at the point where it had been left off by me, should suddenly take the place which I have occupied hitherto and apparently without any reason or justification. You are also certainly not aware that such a suggestion had come from Dr Weizmann on the evening previous to our meeting and that I then hotly resented it.

Gaster, like Asquith, is the victim of a kitchen coup, but where Asquith carries on as an effective opposition leader in Parliament, Gaster is left stewing in fury. He rages at Weizmann's ingratitude and persistently misspells his name in correspondence. Weizmann, for his part, all but erases Gaster from Zionist history. The riddle, to my mind, is why Weizmann, who is a moderate man of neither ruthless nor vindictive character, should act with such vehemence against a man of God who means him no harm. The closest I can find to a clue appears in Gaster's private papers, where he conjectures that political Zionism, dominated by Jews who have discarded their religion, cannot accept that an Orthodox rabbi might deliver its dream. "You are evidently under the impression," he lectures Rothschild:

> . . . that Jewish political life has nothing to do with Jewish religious life. They are intertwined, inseparably united. In Judaism also there is no difference between clerics and laymen—that is a Christian conception which does not apply. More than the layman has the Jewish rabbi been the true leader and guide of his people in all matters politic and religious . . . I have created the English Zionist Federation and I was the first President.[12]

Miserably for Gaster, the carnival has moved on. All eyes swivel to America, where President Woodrow Wilson's anti-imperialism inclines him to oppose a British-French carve-up of the Middle East. Louis Brandeis, whom Wilson is about to appoint as the first Jew on the Supreme Court, is called for advice. Brandeis, who has seen himself until recently "to a great extent separated from the Jews," has learned that his favorite Russian uncle was an ardent Zionist. He is introduced to a Herzl aide, Jacob de Haas, and, soon after, to the heroic figure of Aaron Aaronsohn, "one of the most interesting, brilliant and remarkable men I have ever met."[13] When the president calls, Brandeis assures him that the Jewish settlers in Palestine have nothing but the highest motives and can only help to bring democracy to the Middle East. Rabbi Stephen Wise visits the White House soon after with a similar message.

Opposition now flares in London. Two dignitaries whom Weizmann left off the Mizpah guest list write a letter to the London *Times* on May 24. The signatories are the wealthy leader of Liberal Judaism,

Claude Montefiore, and Lucien Wolf, a journalist who straddles posts at the Anglo-Jewish Association and the Board of Deputies of British Jews. Both have been trying for years to put a spike in the Sykes-Zionist romance, and this long and windy letter is proof of their failure. Allowing Jews to rule Palestine, they warn, "would prove a veritable calamity for the whole Jewish people. In all the countries in which they live, the principle of equal rights for all religious denominations is vital for them. Were they to set an example to Palestine of disregarding this principle they would convict themselves of having appealed to it for purely selfish motives." Their argument, which is not unreasonable, is regarded in some quarters as prophetic: if Jews mistreat minorities in their own state, they can expect to attract prejudice in other countries. The Wolf-Montefiore letter fires Edwin Montagu to have one last go at overturning Zionism. Montagu, in a Cabinet paper provocatively titled "The Anti-Semitism of the Present Government," argues that a Jewish state "would prove a rallying-ground for anti-Semites in every country in the world." He finds an ally in Lord Curzon, but Lloyd George has no tolerance for dissenters and duly dispatches Montagu to be secretary for India, sending him out on a slow boat to the far dominions.

The Cabinet, reviewing Palestine on September 3, 1917, decides to see where Woodrow Wilson stands. The president, facing State Department resistance to Zionism, replies that this is not a good time and passes the Balfour Declaration draft to Brandeis. Lloyd George, testing another option, floats a peace initiative with a faction of the Turkish government, offering to take Turkey off the carving platter and let it keep Palestine. The Turks are slow to respond. Brandeis, who has been privately assured by Balfour that "I am a Zionist," endorses the proposed declaration to President Wilson, who returns it to London for Sykes to present it to the Cabinet at the end of October. Weizmann, pacing a Cabinet office corridor outside, is clapped on the back by a cheerful Sykes. "Dr. Weizmann," exclaims the adventurer, "it's a boy!" On November 2, 1917, the British foreign secretary writes in an official capacity to the head of a London bank:

November 2nd, 1917

Dear Lord Rothschild,

I have much pleasure in conveying to you, on behalf of His Majesty's Government, the following declaration of sympathy with Jewish Zionist aspirations which has been submitted to and approved by, the Cabinet.

"His Majesty's Government view with favour the establishment in Palestine of a national home for the Jewish people and will use their best endeavours to facilitate the achievement of this object, it being clearly understood that nothing shall be done which may prejudice the civil and religious rights of existing non-Jewish communities in Palestine, or the rights and political status enjoyed by Jews in any other country."

I should be grateful if you would bring this declaration to the knowledge of the Zionist Federation.

Yours sincerely,

Arthur James Balfour

In these hundred and twenty-eight words, two thousand years of exile are ended. Jews are free to return to their land. Every Jew, even anti-Zionist, recognizes that a profound change has been made to their interior lives as Jews. Few can foresee the lasting consequences.

The declaration has been watered down. Instead of *the* national home for the Jews, it speaks of *a* national home in Palestine, and there is, in Weizmann's view, undue emphasis on minority rights, which he believes Jews are honor-bound to respect. His first reaction is to call the declaration "emasculated."[14] The act itself is an oddity. The foreign secretary would normally make a policy statement to Parliament rather than to a private citizen in a letter. And sending it to a banker rather than the head of a Jewish organization seems weird. Surely it would have been more appropriate to send it to Haham Gaster, or to Chief Rabbi Joseph Hertz, as spiritual heads of the Jewish community. But an old knee-jerk reaction has come into play. Ever since Disraeli's time, the British government has looked upon the Rothschilds as its useful Jews. Balfour sends the "Dear Lord" letter to Walter Rothschild as if by default. Rothschild can be trusted to maintain discretion for a week, after which the press will be informed.

Arab responses are muted, neutral. When Weizmann meets Emir Feisal in June 1918, the Transjordan Arab leader speaks of "the necessity for cooperation between Jews and Arabs." The pair sign an agreement, never to be implemented.

In the week of the Balfour Declaration, there is a second revolution in Russia. The year ends in a rush. Allenby has a breakthrough at Beersheba and heads north to Jerusalem on a route plotted for him by Aaronsohn. On December 11, the first morning of the Jewish festival of Chanukah, the commander in chief of the British expeditionary force dismounts from his horse and enters the city through the Jaffa Gate on foot, an act of notable humility. Lloyd George delivers the conquest of Jerusalem as "a Christmas present for the British people." Jews recite prayers of rejoicing. Marcus Sieff, a Marks & Spencer heir, is taken as a child to Manchester's Free Trade Hall to hear Weizmann speak. "Father said it was a joyous occasion but I saw that a lot of people were crying . . . He replied, 'they are weeping tears of joy.'"[15]

Thousands besiege the London Opera House in the Strand for a Great Thanksgiving Meeting. Lord Robert Cecil, for the government, cries that "Arabian countries shall be for the Arabs, Armenia for the Armenians, and Judea for the Jews." Sir Mark Sykes raises his voice to give credit where no one else will. "I should like to say," declares Sykes, "before I say one other word, that the reason I am interested in this movement is that I met one some two years ago who is now on this platform, and who opened my eyes as to what this movement meant . . . I mean Dr Gaster." This is the last time the two planners set eyes on each other.

The winners reap mixed rewards. Herbert Samuel is named the first high commissioner of Palestine, where, to appease Arab hostility, he is obliged to impose constraints on Jewish settlement. Weizmann will become the first president of the State of Israel. Nahum Sokolow remains head of Zionist organizations for the rest of his life. Edwin Montagu dies young. Aaron Aaaronsohn is killed in a plane crash in the English Channel in May 1919. Walter Rothschild retires to the study of exotic butterflies and birds, disturbed only by an occasional paternity suit. Sir Mark Sykes is sent to the Paris Peace Conference, where, in February 1919, he contracts Spanish flu and dies in his hotel, aged thirty-nine. "He fell a hero at our side," mourns Sokolow. Picot is sent as French ambassador to Argentina. Jabotinsky forms a maximalist wing of Zionism, in opposition to Weizmann's moderates.

As for Moses Gaster, he resumes his duties as Haham of the Spanish and Portuguese Jews, but not for long. A zeppelin drops a huge bomb on Maida Vale, demolishing four houses. Twelve people are killed, three dozen injured. Gaster, taking fright, moves his family to the coast at Brighton. Congregants accuse him of cowardice and seek grounds for his dismissal. The death of a prominent member provides due cause. A telegram is sent to Brighton, summoning Gaster to officiate at the funeral. Whether due to slow trains or sheer cussedness, he fails to attend. He is sent on leave by the Mahamad (the governing body of the Spanish and Portuguese Jewish community), ostensibly for health reasons. Three months later, his "resignation" is announced. "It was in fact his inability to compromise and his unwillingness to tie himself down even to meet a not unreasonable request, that resulted in his resignation of the post of Haham," writes his son Vivian.[16] "I always liked to go my own road . . . ," reflects Gaster. "I have never kowtowed, never turned to the right or to the left, and never asked what the Goy might say, or what the Jew might say. Everywhere I was anxious to help our people to its own emancipation, to self-realisation, to self-deliverance."[17]

Aged sixty-two and losing his sight, Gaster is left, Lear-like, in the wings. His congregation adds insult to indignity by stripping him of the honorific "Haham." Called—untitled—to the Torah in Manchester, Gaster pronounces a terrible curse on the synagogue. A crack opens in the ceiling. Worshippers beg his forgiveness. Gaster glowers at them through sightless eyes.

Zionism obliterates him from its narrative. No street in Israel is named after Gaster, not even in the town of Zikhron Ya'akov, which he helped found. On the site of Mizpah, at the bottom of the road where I live, and where he drafted the Balfour Declaration, efforts to install a blue plaque have been thwarted. The site is now a Church of England school. "Moses Gaster was transformed from a widely respected, influential and politically aware Zionist leader into a petty and peripheral individual,"[18] writes the modern historian James Renton. Gaster dies in 1939, survived by a large family and a lasting reputation in Romania. His meticulously revised prayer book remains in use in Spanish and Portuguese synagogues to the present day.

My aunt Fifi is born in Paris on August 2, 1914, my uncle René on June 5, 1920. In between, my grandparents do not see much of each other, or perhaps eye to eye about the war. Grandpère Nathan and Grandmère Berthe are first cousins, descendants of Grand Rabbin Klein of Colmar. Nathan is raised as a French patriot in Paris. Berthe, born in German-occupied Alsace, is the daughter of a rabbi in Frankfurt am Main. When Grandpère goes to war, Grandmère fears he may shoot her brothers, who are also his own cousins. She goes into labor. Grandpère does not see his baby for weeks. My grandparents are trapped in the fratricidal confusion of world war.

Their situation is mirrored in many Jewish families. Such as my father's, in London. His father, Michael, born in Mainz, is arrested on the first day of war and interned first in Crystal Palace, then on the Isle of Man. Deprived of a breadwinner, Grannie and her five children are reduced to penury. My father, hauled out of school at thirteen, is put to work as a tea boy in a trading firm on Finsbury Square. In the trauma of war, he forgets how to speak German, his mother tongue. Grandpa, released in 1918, clings to his German passport right through to the next world war.

In Germany, the kaiser pledges, "I recognise no parties or religions, only German brothers." Jews rush to fight for the kaiser. "All factions were to be united; everybody spoke one language; everybody defended one mother: Germany," writes the expressionist poet Ernst Toller.[19] Official photographs show a German Yom Kippur field service in occupied France and spike-helmeted soldiers bringing food to a Polish ghetto. Eminent rabbis—Leo Baeck, Joseph Carlebach, Siegfried Klein—serve on the front. "If this war were to bring us Jews nothing else but greater understanding from, and greater inner closeness with, our Christian fellow-citizens, then that would already be a prize that we German Jews would receive with special joy," declares Feldrabbiner Bruno Italiener.[20]

His credulity, widely shared, is shattered when, on October 11, 1916, the minister of war, Adolf Wild von Hohenborn, orders a Judenzählung, a Jew census, across the armed forces. Hohenborn says: "The War Ministry is continuously receiving complaints from the population that large numbers of men of the Israelite faith who are fit for military service are either exempt from military duties or evading their obligation to serve under every conceivable pretext."

The census results are disputed for years to come. Hohenborn refuses to publish the results, supposedly "to spare Jewish feelings."

His successor is too busy running a lost war to be bothered by ethnic concerns. In 1919, a right-wing agitator, "Otto Armin," flourishes what he claims are the true results: sixty-two thousand German Jews in the army, of whom just twenty-seven thousand see frontline action. This count is endorsed by Ernst von Wrisberg, head of the army section of the War Department, but two Jewish statisticians (one of whom is head of the Berlin Office of Statistics) are able to show that, of five hundred fifty thousand German Jews, a total of one hundred thousand served in the war, four-fifths of them at the front. Twelve thousand Jews died for the Fatherland. These facts are confirmed by the government, but the lie speaks louder. "The more Jews are killed," writes Foreign Minister Walther Rathenau, "the more obstinately their enemies will prove that they all sat behind the front in order to deal in war speculation." The libel that Jews dodged the draft will become a mantra in Adolf Hitler's stabbed-in-the-back narrative of Germany's defeat.[21]

The Judenzählung demoralizes Jewish soldiers. The "dream of community" is broken, writes the philosopher Ernst Simon: "We were foreigners . . . separately categorised and counted."[22] Simon becomes an ardent Zionist. His friend Martin Buber starts a magazine, *Der Jude*. The novelist Arnold Zweig embraces pacifism. Walter Benjamin and Gershom Scholem become fast friends at an antiwar demonstration in Berlin, where Scholem's socialist brother, Werner, is arrested. Ernst Toller and his friends are drawn to militant socialism. After Germany's capitulation, Jews lead revolutions. Werner Scholem is elected to the Reichstag, its youngest-ever member, for the Communist Party. Rosa Luxemburg, a Communist firebrand held in prison during the war, calls on the workers to topple Friedrich Ebert's social-democratic Berlin government. Ebert calls in the army. Luxemburg is hunted down by Freikorps paramilitaries, who drag her to a torture center at the Eden Hotel, smash her head, and throw her body into the Landwehr Canal. In Munich, the theater critic Kurt Eisner forms a Bavarian Soviet Republic, which proves briefly popular, if cranky; one minister tries to declare war on Switzerland, another on the pope. When Eisner is shot while about to submit his resignation, the intellectual Gustav Landauer invites the poets Toller and Erich Mühsam to join a Cabinet of anarchists. Landauer is ousted by Eugen Leviné, a Communist who grabs rich men's apartments and orders hostage executions. The army moves in. Leviné is put before a firing squad. Landauer, preaching human brotherhood to the officers who arrest him, is beaten to death in full public view. (Landauer's grandson is the American film director Mike Nichols.) Mühsam and Toller are sentenced to fifteen years' hard labor. Mühsam writes: "I am a Jew and will remain a Jew so long as I live. . . . I consider it neither an advantage nor a disadvantage to be a Jew; it simply belongs to my being like my red beard, my weight, or my inclinations." He is pardoned and released from his fortress jail on December 20, 1924, the same day as Adolf Hitler.

Albert Ballin tries to the last to have a quiet word with the kaiser. He has been trying since the war began, but every time he is admitted to the presence of Wilhelm II, a posse of Prussians surrounds him, snooping on his every word. Cut off from his British business partners, Ballin keeps some third-party channels open in the belief he can play a role in making peace. When the Americans enter the war, seizing thirty-five of his ships in New York harbor, Ballin tries to reach President Wilson for a constructive conversation.

His hopes fade when, on his sixtieth birthday, the kaiser forgets to send a card. Ballin realizes that Wilhelm has become a "shadow kaiser," manipulated by Juncker warmongers. A patriot to his core, he despairs for Deutschland. The Prussians turn to him only when, with German armies pushed back on the Western Front, someone must tell the kaiser that the war is lost. Ballin is asked by Generals Hindenburg and Ludendorff to break the bad news. He resists this act "of a very unpleasant nature"[23] at first, fearing he is being scapegoated as a Jew. The generals appeal to his sense of duty. A meeting is arranged on September 5, 1918, at a castle outside Kassel. Over lunch, the kaiserin warns Ballin that her husband has been unwell and must not be exposed to shocks. Ballin takes a walk with Wilhelm on the castle grounds. An aristocrat at a window sees Wilhelm strangely elated, Ballin dejected. A Prussian official walks with them, interrupting the conversation at any hint of defeat. Finding the kaiser "horribly misinformed," Ballin leaves Kassel "an utterly broken man."[24] In Hamburg, the sight of his teenaged godson trying on a uniform as he awaits call-up reduces the most powerful man in the shipping world to floods of tears.

On November 4, sailors mutiny in the port of Kiel. On the eighth, workers occupy the Hapag headquarters in Hamburg, threatening Ballin with violence. He calls a meeting of shipowners to secure food supplies during the coming turbulence. His wife, Marianne, harassed by revolutionaries in the streets, decides to sleep that night at a friend's house.

The following morning, Ballin is found by a servant, writhing in agony, a jar of sleeping pills at his side. He is dragged through the wild streets to a clinic, where his stomach is pumped. An ulcer bursts. Death is recorded at one fifteen p.m. on November 9, the exact moment when the Reichstag declares a German Republic. Ballin has done his best to maintain equilibrium. The kaiser sends condolences from exile. Accident or suicide? The evidence is equivocal, but Ballin has lately been saying: *"Lieber ein Ende mit Schrecken als Schrecken ohne Ende"*—better an end with anguish than anguish without end.

A philosopher ponders self-destruction. "If suicide is allowed, then everything is allowed," jots Ludwig Wittgenstein on January 10, 1917. "If anything is not allowed, then suicide is not allowed." Heir to a Viennese railway fortune, Wittgenstein is fighting the Russians on the Eastern Front. Obeying orders that range from the inhumane to the insane, he occupies his mind with the ethics of existence. What right have I to be alive, he wonders, amid so many pointless deaths? The question is never less than urgent. A friend notes that "all his life there had hardly been a day, in which he had not at one time or other thought of suicide as a possibility."[25] Afflicted by self-doubt, he considers himself "*de trop*"—unnecessary. If there is no purpose to his life, ergo it would be unethical to carry on living. On the other hand, he feels a higher calling to define, once and for all, the Foundations of Logic. To abdicate that command would amount to betrayal. Ludwig Wittgenstein does not live easy.

As an adolescent in Vienna, he is shocked by the suicide of Otto Weininger, a Jewish anti-Semite of Nietzschean fixations whose death at twenty-three is the making of his reputation as a madcap mind. The Weininger furor prompts the Wittgensteins to admit that their eldest son, Hans, who disappeared off a boat in Chesapeake Bay, took his own life. A second son, Rudi, will take cyanide seven months later. The home atmosphere is poisonous. Ludwig is sent at fourteen to a Realschule (high school) in Linz, where one of his classmates, six days older, is Adolf Hitler. Leaving school with low marks, Ludwig goes to study aeronautics at Manchester University. He discovers mathematics and philosophy by reading Bertrand Russell. Turning up unannounced at Russell's rooms in Cambridge, puppylike, he trails his idol around the campus. Russell, in 1911, declares him a genius. Wittgenstein deconstructs Russell's works. Free of material cares, he has a love affair with David Pinsent, a promising mathematician. His father's death in January 1913 prompts a return to Vienna but not for long. He flees with Pinsent to a fjord in Norway and winters there, alone in a wooden hut, reading Kierkegaard in the original Danish and immersing himself in questions of logic.

Despite being offered a medical exemption, he signs up for the Austrian Army at the outbreak of war, in a state of fatalistic euphoria. Wounded twice, he is decorated for "courage, calmness, sangfroid and heroism." His notes on the permissibility of suicide are written on a winter-white battlefield. He needs to make sense of nothingness. "He is morbidly afraid he may die before he has put the Theory of Types to rights . . . ," writes Pinsent. "He expected death because he had no right to live: he feared it only because he needed to produce some great work to give some meaning to the life he had already led . . . ," argues his biographer.[26] In May 1918, Pinsent's mother writes to inform Wittgenstein of David's death in a flying accident. Wittgenstein is redeployed, with his brother Kurt, to the Italian Front, where Ludwig is taken prisoner and Kurt shoots himself in the retreat. His brother Paul, a concert pianist, loses an arm in Russian captivity. The Wittgensteins are unlucky in war.

Ludwig emerges with a notebook for the century's most original philosophical work. His title, *Tractatus Logico-Philosophicus*, echoes Baruch Spinoza's *Tractatus Theologico-Politicus*, but there are few similarities to his fellow Jew or to any other. Wittgenstein's is a book of startling brevity: seventy-five pages, each line numbered with reference to seven aphorisms, of which the first reads: "*Die Welt ist alles, was der Fall ist*" (The world is everything that is the case). Each succeeding thought refers to its source: 1.1.67 and so on.

At once deceptively simple and impenetrably obtuse, Wittgenstein's investigation of the meaning of words is a clinical antidote to the political bluster that has brought the world to disaster. If the world can agree on the limits of understanding one single word, there need never be another war. Hence 5.6, *The limits of my language* mean the limits of my world. "The whole sense of the book might be summed up in the following words: what can be said at all can be said clearly, and what we cannot talk about we must pass over in silence" (*Man könnte den ganzen Sinn des Buches etwa in die Worte fassen: Was sich überhaupt sagen lässt, lässt sich klar sagen; und wovon man nicht reden kann, darüber muss man schweigen*). For some, it is a relief to know that there are things we can never know. Others maintain that Wittgenstein has solved all the major problems in philosophy.

Russell, the cleverest Englishman, likens Wittgenstein to Pascal in mathematics and Tolstoy in literature. The economist Maynard Keynes refers to him, only half ironically, as God. "If you ask philosophers—those in the English-speaking analytic tradition anyway—who is the most important philosopher of the twentieth century, they will most likely name Ludwig Wittgenstein," writes a twenty-first-century academic. "But the chances are that if you ask them exactly why he was so important, they will be unable to tell you."[27] A nonphilosopher can only stand back and admire Wittgenstein's rigor, his refusal to utter a word until it has been totally clarified.

His most famous proposition—"*Wovon man nicht sprechen kann, darüber muß man schweigen*" (Whereof one cannot speak, thereof one must be silent)—has the limpid beauty of a Schoenberg atonality, accessible at an entry level yet yielding, like Talmud, layer upon layer of added complexity. No matter how frustrating Wittgenstein's prose may seem—the first English text he approved is well-nigh incomprehensible—its originality commands awed attention. Throughout his life, he veers from high confidence to suicidal self-doubt. Having completed the *Tractatus*, he goes to work as a gardener in an Austrian monastery, then as a primary teacher in a mountain village. It is not clear if he seeks duty or penance (Catholicism is his religion of choice). He writes a spelling dictionary for schoolchildren, his only published work apart from the *Tractatus*.

In April 1926, he whacks a boy twice around the head, so hard that he knocks him out. There are calls for his arrest, but the police station is unmanned. By the time an officer arrives, the philosopher has fled. The boy, aged eleven, is slow-witted and sickly—he will die of leukemia at fourteen—but the village is in lynch mood, inflamed by Wittgenstein's oddity. From now on, he is alert to being Jewish. He calls himself a "Jewish thinker" and has dreams on Jewish themes.[28] In the Nazi years, he suffers loss of property and fears for his sisters in Vienna. Being Jewish is a state of insecurity. It entails a sacred obligation. *Duty of Genius*, the title of Ray Monk's Wittgenstein biography, expresses his indomitable will to realize a God-given mission.

He spends a year in Vienna after the village fuss, designing an ultra-modern house for his sister, refusing to sign off until the door handles are to his liking. Cambridge implores him to return. He settles there in 1929, remaining until his death from prostate cancer in 1951. His collected notes are published posthumously as *Philosophical Investigations*. His last words are: "Tell them I've had a wonderful life." Death, writes Wittgenstein (*Tractatus*, 6.431), "is not an event in life: we do not live to experience death." Weininger, he finally decides, is wrong. There must be a purpose.

On the heights of Montmartre, an Italian Jew lives each day as if it is his last. Amedeo Modigliani has suffered from tuberculosis since the age of sixteen. There is no cure. Anything he does as an artist needs to be done quickly. Life is to be lived in the moment, pleasures to be taken as they pass. A lantern-jawed man with olive skin and open features, Modi is serially promiscuous. He seduces the newly married Russian poet Anna Akhmatova ("I forgot to tell you I'm Jewish," he informs her in bed), the English critic Beatrice Hastings, the Welsh artist Nina Hamnett ("I am Modigliani, painter and Jew," he introduces himself), and any number of housemaids, shopgirls, students, and one-night-standees. He is short, handsome, sultry, well-endowed. "Don't I look like a god?" he cries one night in a crowded bar, dropping his pants. Tales of excess create a legend of an irresistible satyr with insatiable appetites. "All he did was growl; he used to make me shiver from head to foot. But wasn't he gorgeous!" says the model Kiki of Montparnasse. Modi, however, is no Don Juan who meets, shoots, and leaves. He likes women of valor and ambition, women who match fire with fire. He recites poetry, unusual for a painter, and, when sober, discusses philosophy.

He drinks to excess, always at La Rotonde and Le Dome, dressed in a gray corduroy suit and black hat. He uses hashish, apparently for sexual excitation. His supplier, Paul Alexandre, a young surgeon, rents him a studio space and buys as much Modigliani as he can afford. Modi gets by from one Alexandre check to the next. He manages without food, to the point of emaciation. A visit from his brother, a member of the Italian Parliament, results in a summons from Mama to come home for the Jewish holidays (my Livorno friends, the Nahons, see his father at the post office sending him cash). Modi's lifestyle is self-designed. He tells the Litvak sculptor Jacques Lipchitz that his will be *"une vie brève mais intense"* (a brief but intense life).

His friends are Jews, his lovers not. Modigliani is tribally, transgressively Jewish. He is the first Jew in two millennia to stand at the front line of world art and make naked graven images. Pablo Picasso, who owns several of his works, treats him with respect. They are friends, though not close. Modigliani, who wears a suit at night, deplores Picasso's paint-stained smock and sailor's shirt. Picasso drinks little and abhors drugs. Both start out in Paris with nothing, lending each other five francs here and there. But while Picasso goes from blue to pink to African periods and on to astonishing cubism, Modigliani sticks to what he loves: the female form. He paints women with a kindly eye, elongating necks and faces for gravity, toning down imperfections, presenting breasts and buttocks less as magnets of desire than as aspects of personality. He favors shades of yellow and brown. The face is often tilted to one side, pensive to the point of disapproval. A Modi portrait is unmistakable, and it is not what the market wants.

Where Picasso is besieged by collectors, Modi has neither patron nor dealer. He paints to live, but there is no living in it, least of all after Dr. Alexandre goes to the war. Modi is so desperately poor that he beds down with Chaim Soutine, sleeping on a filthy floor, surrounded by candles to ward off mites and bugs. Months go by in which he cannot sell a canvas. And then Zbo turns up. Léopold Zborowski, a Polish-Jewish poet, knows as much about the art market as he does about Antarctica. But he knows what he likes. Zbo is personable, persuasive, and persistent. He sells five paintings to a Polish tailor for five hundred francs. Zbo spends all the cash paying off Modi's debts and feeding him a square meal. Next day, the tailor comes by, saying his wife hates the paintings and he wants his money back. Zbo adds Soutine and Maurice Utrillo to his clientele, but he vests his faith in Modigliani and, at the start of 1917, promises him a solo exhibition, the first of his life. Modi does not know that Zbo has neither a gallery nor cash for such an undertaking, but he cuts back on the drink and paints enough to fill a hangar in six months. He has a gentle new lover, Jeanne Hébuterne, an art student with angry bourgeois parents. He paints Jeanne compulsively, although never in the nude. Jeanne is his chaste muse.

The third of December 1917 is the date set for Modigliani's opening at the Galérie Berthe Weill on rue Victor Massé in the ninth arrondissement. Berthe Weill, one of Picasso's first dealers, has turned down Modigliani many times before but is prepared to be convinced by Zbo that his time has finally come. A plump lady of fifty in thick-lensed granny glasses, Madame Weill is the only woman gallerist who dares to handle the avant-garde. She balks at Modi's demand to have, as her cover image, his most explicit nude—a long-haired young woman, her head inclined to the left, one small breast exposed and a clump of dark hair protruding at her pubic mound—but the artist knows best, and Madame gives up her Sunday to hang the image in her window on the exhibition's eve. Monday morning, a crowd gathers at the gallery window. A gendarme walks over from the *commissaire divisionnaire* across the road. The crowd grows. The cop delivers an order from the commissioner to take down the nude. Madame Weill refuses, declaring it to be fine art. The commissioner arrives in person. "These n-nudes," he splutters, "*ils ont des p-p-poils*" (they have h-h-hair).

There is a brief standoff. Madame continues to defend the integrity of art. The police chief says he will send in a squad and confiscate all her paintings. There can only be one winner. Modigliani's one-man show is shut down before it opens. Madame buys two works, out of the goodness of her heart. Zbo tries to sell four nudes to Lipchitz. "Where will I put all these triangles?" he protests, pointing at the pubes. The story of the exhibition that never opened is absorbed into the folklore of Paris art, forever repeated by licensed guides for the benefit of foreign tourists.

The closure does Modigliani no immediate harm. Collectors come calling at Zbo's, and, by April 1918, he has enough funds to send Modi and Jeanne to the South of France, together with the Soutines, to escape the end of war and add some sunshine to their work.

They spend a year in Nice and at Cagnes-sur-Mer. Jeanne gives birth to a daughter, Giovanna. Soon, she is pregnant again. Back in Paris, Modi is coughing badly and having blackouts. He tells Jeanne they will visit his mother in the spring and get married. They spend Christmas, with their child, in an unheated room. Modi, between demands for drink, sings a mournful dirge in Hebrew, possibly the Kaddish prayer for the dead. Zbo is flu-bound, unable to help. On January 22, 1920, Modigliani is taken by ambulance to the Charité hospital, where, on the twenty-fourth, he dies. Jeanne, eight and a half months pregnant, goes home with her father and throws herself to her death from a fifth-floor window. Modi is thirty-five, Jeanne twenty-one. They are buried in separate cemeteries. Years pass before her Catholic parents let her lie beside a Jew.

Lipchitz makes the death mask after Moise Kisling botches it. Zbo never recovers from Modi's death, loses all his art to bailiffs, and dies a pauper at forty-three. There is a brief exhibition on the Champs-Élysées and a flutter of buyers, but Modi's significance has yet to be discovered.

Jewish artists before Modi are confined to local fame: the Berlin portraitists Moritz Oppenheim and Max Liebermann, Simeon Solomon in London, Jozef Israels in the Hague, Léon Bakst in St. Petersburg. With Modi, horizons break open. As well as Soutine, Lipchitz, and Kisling, his Paris circle embraces Chagall, El Lissitzky, Max Jacob, Chana Orloff, Jacob Epstein, Marcel Janco; almost a school of Jewish artists. Epstein, his daily visitor, will be a sought-after sculptor. Epstein's pal David Bomberg (grouped with Mark Gertler, Jacob Kramer, and Isaac Rosenberg among the so-called Whitechapel Boys), teaches London's postmodernists Auerbach, Kossoff, and Metzger. Modi, without whom modernism would not look the same, leaves a long trail through a century of art.

Drunk or sober, he is concerned with purpose. His most-quoted saying might easily have come from Wittgenstein. "The function of art," says Modigliani, "is to struggle against obligation." Another encapsulates Freud: "I seek neither the real nor the unreal but the unconscious, the mysterious instinct of the human race." Eventually, his merit is matched by money. In May 2018, a long-faced *Nu couché (sur le côté gauche)* (reclining nude, on her left side), signed by Amedeo Modigliani, sells at Sotheby's in New York for an inconceivable $157.2 million.

On April 9, 1917, Vladimir Ilyich Ulyanov, known as Lenin, boards a train in Zurich, with his wife, Nadezhda Krupskaya, and thirty-one comrades. The police hold back a small pack of demonstrators who are protesting that Lenin, "going at the Kaiser's expense," is colluding with Germany to bring down the post-tsarist government and take Russia out of the war. His travel companions have been picked from diverse parts of a workers' movement that expends more energy on doctrinal factionalism than the overthrow of capitalism. The group includes several wives and two small children. It does not look like the battering ram of a revolution. James Joyce, living nearby, comments: "It sounds like a Trojan horse."

At ten past three in the afternoon, the train puffs out of the Hauptbahnhof. Stefan Zweig, also in Zurich, writes: "It was 3:10, and since then the world clock has kept different time." At the German border the party changes trains, occupying a green carriage with eight compartments, and a luggage van. There is one toilet. Lenin sits at a desk at the far end of the corridor, plotting revolution. The others spend a slow week vying for his attention, politicking, flirting, eating, drinking beer, kvetching, and queueing for the loo. They are a ramshackle, rather jolly band of would-be insurrectionists. Of the thirty adults in Lenin's sealed train, seventeen are Jews.

Russian Jews have been drawn to politics by the pogroms. Communism, however, attracts fewer Jews than other ideologies, Zionism and secular Bundism (trade unionism). In 1917, there are an estimated 300,000 Zionists in Russia and 34,000 Bundists.[29] The number of Communist Jews is, by party records, minute. At the start of 1917, there are 958 Jews in the party; a further 1,175 join during the year.[30] That half of Lenin's fellow travelers are Jews might be treated as a freak statistic, were it not for two supporting facts. At the secret sixth Congress of the Communist Party in July 1917, elections are held to the Central Committee. One in four of those chosen—23.7 percent—are Jews.[31] Three

months later, when the party seizes power, Lenin's seven-man Polit-
buro contains four Jews: Zinoviev, Sokolnikov, Kamenev, and Trotsky.
Lenin himself, it transpires, has a Jewish great-grandfather, Moshko
Blank.[32] The Jews with him on the train include Zinoviev (Gershon
Radomyslsky), Karl Radek, Moisei Kharitonov, Yelena Kon, and Olga
Sara Ravich. Among themselves, they do not agree on very much or
for very long.

Having crossed Germany, their carriage is hoisted on a ferry to neutral Sweden, where Lenin is pictured stretching his legs in Stockholm.
A regular train takes them northeast, toward the Arctic Circle, veering
south at the Russian frontier. On April 16, an hour before midnight,
the train pulls in to Finland Station, Petrograd (formerly St. Petersburg). Lenin has telegraphed his arrival time to *Pravda*. Soldiers and
workers crowd the arrival hall, cheering his proclamation of revolution. Lenin's slogan, "All power to the Soviets," is a call to bring down
Alexander Kerensky's "bourgeois" government and end the war.

Eighteen days after Lenin's arrival, the Finland Station throng welcomes another returning exile. "I went from the station straight to the
meeting of the Executive Committee of the Soviet," reports Leon Trotsky:

> The Bolsheviks moved that I be elected to the Executive Commit-
> tee, on the strength of my having been chairman of the Soviet in
> 1905. This threw the committee into confusion. The Mensheviks
> and the Populists began whispering to one another. . . . Finally it
> was decided to include me in an advisory capacity. I was given my
> membership card and my glass of tea with black bread.[33]

Where Lenin is "a leader purely by virtue of intellect,"[34] Trotsky can
turn an aimless rabble into a purposeful mob. The pair, once close, have
not spoken in years. Trotsky is not even a paid-up Bolshevik anymore.
But he has read Lenin's manual *What Is To Be Done?* and he knows
what to do. He asks his brother-in-law Kamenev (born Rozenfeld,
married to Trotsky's sister Olga) to arrange a meeting, and he proceeds
to convince Lenin that he alone—as head of the 1905 revolution—can
turn the minority Bolsheviks into a mass movement. Communism is
so fragmented that some Marxists are serving in the Kerensky Cabinet.
Lenin accepts Trotsky's proposal without rancor. "At those first meet-

ings of ours . . . ," says Trotsky, "Lenin gave one the sense of a terrific inner concentration under a surface of calm and 'prosaic' simplicity." Trostky is magnetized by Lenin's sphinxlike solidity. Lenin sees in Trotsky a man who can light the fuse of revolution.

Trostky, born Leiba Bronstein, is the fifth child of a landowning Jewish family in south Ukraine. Although his parents are barely religious, he is sent to a cheder to study Torah. At a Realschule in Odessa, he walks out of Christianity lessons and rejects God. By sixteen, he is a Marxist with a Jewish girlfriend six years his senior. At eighteen, he is jailed for organizing a labor union. He asks a rabbi to marry him to Alexandra Sokolovskaya under a chuppah so that they can claim the right to share a hut in the Siberian camps. Atheist as Leiba Bronstein might be, he is a very Jewish atheist. His marriage to Alexandra, which yields two daughters, ends with his escape from Siberia in August. "For several days after I had escaped, she concealed my absence from the police," he reports fondly. "Life separated us, but nothing could destroy our friendship and our intellectual kinship."

Still only twenty-two, Trotsky makes his way to London, where he wakes up Lenin at dawn with three coded knocks at the door. Lenin takes him to the library of the British Museum, where, like Karl Marx, he has a reader's card. In November, Trotsky moves to Paris, where a comrade, Natalia Sedova, finds him a room. They become lovers and have two sons. In January 1905, Trotsky returns with Natalia to St. Petersburg, where he forms a revolutionary Soviet and calls for "mass terror realised by the working classes."

His stronghold is stormed by tsarist troops before the year is out. Fifty-four revolutionaries are tried and sentenced to lifelong exile. On the way to Siberia, Trotsky effects a Houdini-like escape. He reaches Vienna, where foreign radicals are left alone. Trotsky sits in cafés composing articles for *Pravda*, a typical luftmensch (airhead) in his trademark pince-nez and goatee beard. Opposing Lenin on terrorism against banks, he is banned by the Bolsheviks. His friends in Vienna are Victor Adler, the Austrian socialist leader, and Adolf Ioffe, an Odessa physician who is being psychoanalyzed by Alfred Adler. He meets Rosa Luxemburg and Karl Liebknecht. When Austria's foreign minister is warned to expect revolution in Russia, he asks, "And who will lead this revolution? Herr Bronstein of the Café Central?" Trotsky absorbs some of Freud's language. Marxism, he writes, is "the conscious expression of the unconscious historical process."

Leaving Vienna as an enemy alien in August 1914, he goes first to Zurich, then on to France, Spain, and ultimately New York, where he sends his sons to a Bronx public school and tries to provoke a sweat-shop workers' strike. He lives in an $18-a-month worker's apartment "equipped with all sorts of conveniences that we Europeans were quite unused to: electric lights, gas cooking-range, bath, telephone, auto-matic service-elevator, and even a chute for the garbage." Dedicated as he is to revolution, Trotsky leaves his consumer paradise with regret. Setting out for Russia, he is detained as a German agent by British officers in Halifax, Canada. By the time he reaches Petrograd, he is in a violent mood. "I tell you heads must roll, blood must flow," he exhorts the Kronstadt garrison sailors. "The strength of the French Revolution was in the machine that made the enemies of the people shorter by a head. This is a fine device. We must have it in every city."

Alert to the lessons of 1905, Trotsky keeps a low profile, addressing pop-up rallies, urging patience to the unemployed. As spring turns to summer, Lenin succumbs to depression, muttering, ". . . they will shoot us down, one by one." During the party congress in July, held in the workers' enclave of Vyborg, Lenin goes into hiding, shaves off his beard, and flees to Finland. Trotsky is arrested. Rumors abound that a Cos-sack general, Lavr Kornilov, is heading in to conduct a massacre of cap-tured revolutionaries. Trotsky, released in September, is elected chair of the Petrograd Soviet, with headquarters at the Smolny Institute, a girls' school. Lenin returns, disguised in a wig. On October 11, Lenin asks the central committee to launch the revolution. In a 10–2 vote, Kamenev and Zinoviev dissent. Trotsky hedges, fearing insufficient support in the provinces. The mob takes to the streets, looting stores and attacking government buildings. Kerensky retaliates, sending troops to seize the party newspaper press. The Bolsheviks recapture it. Soldiers' wives and trade unionists take control of communications: telegraph offices, the railways, printing presses, the national bank. Military cadets defending the post office are one by one thrown from its roof.

Trotsky sits on the third floor of the Smolny, taking phone calls from his cadres. He asks Kamenev for a cigarette and, after two puffs, faints. Despite not having eaten for two days, he is the bridge that holds the revolution together. Ten naval ships sail into harbor, guns pointed at the Winter Palace. Before a meeting of Soviets, Lenin and Trotsky snatch some rest.

> Someone had spread a blanket on the floor for us; someone else, I think it was Lenin's sister, had brought us pillows. We were lying side by side; body and soul were relaxing like overtaut strings. It was a well-earned rest. We could not sleep, so we talked in low voices. . . . Then he started suddenly. "And what about the Winter Palace? It has not been taken yet. Isn't there a danger in that?" I got up to ask, on the telephone, about the progress of the operations there, but he tried to stop me: "Lie still, I will send someone to find out."[35]

Trotsky takes a call from Kerensky's allies, offering a coalition. He replies: "Our uprising has won. And now we are being asked to give up our victory, to come to an agreement. With whom? You are wretched, disunited individuals; you are bankrupts; your part is over. Go to the place where you belong from now on: the dustbin of history!" In the Bolshevik Revolution, Trotsky has all the best lines.

On October 26 (November 8 by Western calendars), Lenin forms a government, the Council of People's Commissars. He puts Trotsky in charge of internal affairs, securing their victory across the vast nation. Trotsky declines. "I brought up, among other arguments, the question of nationality. Was it worthwhile to put into our enemies' hands such an additional weapon as my Jewish origin?" He takes foreign affairs instead. Trotsky enters the foreign ministry, demanding access to the filing cabinets. Told that the keys have been lost, his sailor bodyguard seizes two or three senior officials and locks them in a cupboard. After a while, the keys reappear. Trotsky narrates such episodes of revolutionary justice with undisguised relish.

He dispatches Adolf Ioffe to talk to the Germans at Brest-Litovsk. A cease-fire is agreed to on December 2. Trotsky turns up to play for time, hoping the Germans will lose the war before Russia has to make painful concessions. He bamboozles the Germans in a Viennese dialect leavened with Jewish jokes and generally causes such confusion that Berlin delivers an ultimatum: peace treaty within two days or all-out war. Trotsky warns Lenin that the German terms are brutal, but Lenin needs the war to be over so he can consolidate the revolution. When the extent of Russia's territorial losses is made known—Finland, the Baltic states, and parts of Belarus and Ukraine—Lenin allows Trotsky to be scapegoated as the Jew who betrayed Mother Russia. In a *Pravda* article, Trotsky warns against the rise of Soviet anti-Semitism.

With the rest of the government, he moves to Moscow in March 1918 as tsarist, Menshevik, Polish, and British armies attack Russia. Bumping into Lenin a dozen times a day in Kremlin corridors, he is made commissar for military affairs. Lacking field experience, he picks a Jewish army doctor, Ephraim Sklyanksy, twenty-six years old, as his deputy. Traveling from one front to the next, Trotsky turns the Red Army into a ferocious fighting force by means of inspirational speeches and homicidal discipline. Leather-coated units of his Cheka secret police patrol the lines, shooting dissenters and deserters, as well as their families at home. "The game is won," declares Lenin. "If we have succeeded in establishing order in the army, it means we shall establish it everywhere else. And the revolution—with order—will be unconquerable."[36]

The civil war rages for three years. The writer Isaac Babel, who serves with the Red Cossacks, records the victimization of Jewish communities. The whites inflict pogroms of unspeakable cruelty, leaving behind piles of bodies. The reds defile synagogues and desecrate Torah scrolls. Commissars, often Jewish, prohibit the practice of religion. Rabbis who are caught performing weddings or circumcisions are shot or exiled. Work on the Sabbath is made compulsory. Schoolbooks denigrate God. Yet, in shtetls and kolkhoz farms, there are photographs of a *shochet* or *melamed* at work, keeping the faith against all odds. There may also be a Jewish party secretary who turns a blind eye. Isaac Babel, in one of the most-quoted passages of civil war literature, captures the dilemma of a yeshiva student faced with the new Russian reality: "Forget for a while that you have glasses on your nose and autumn in your soul. . . . Imagine for a second that you quarrel in city squares and stutter on paper. You are a tiger, a lion, a cat. You can spend the night with a Russian woman, and the Russian woman will be satisfied."[37]

The civil war keeps Trotsky away from Moscow, where for some the revolution is never over. In June 1918, the ideologue Moisei Volodarsky (Goldshtayn), a self-styled "counter-revolutionary terrorist," is shot dead by a radical socialist. On August 30, the Petrograd Cheka boss, Moisei Uritsky, is assassinated by a tsarist cadet. That same day, a socialist revolutionary, Fanya Kaplan, fires three bullets into Lenin. The Cheka secret police, led by Felix Dzerzhinsky, unleashes a wave of Red Terror that claims a hundred thousand lives. While Dzerzhinsky is a renegade Polish aristocrat, a majority of Cheka cops are Jews. So long as Lenin and Trotsky are in charge, Jews enjoy positions of prominence and responsibility in the Soviet state. Some are charged with missions considered too onerous for Russians. Yakov Yurovksy, commander of the Bolshevik squad that executes the last tsar and his family, is every bit as Jewish as his distant forebear, Gesia Gelfman.

Lenin, during an operation to remove an assassin's bullet, suffers a stroke and loses the power of speech. In Trotsky's absence from Moscow, Joseph Stalin cultivates Lenin's wife, Nadezhda Krupskaya, and controls access to the disabled leader. Zinoviev and Kamenev sign up as Stalin's yes-men. Kamenev is made Politburo chairman. Trotsky, aware of these power shifts, tells himself that "in routine work it was more convenient for Lenin to depend on Stalin, Zinoviev or Kamenev rather than on me." This is a fatal miscalculation on his part.

He is on a journey outside Moscow when Lenin dies on January 21, 1924. By the time Trotsky reaches the Kremlin, Stalin holds all the levers of power. The first resolution passed by the Politburo after Lenin's death is a measure denouncing "Trotskyism." Stalin, general secretary of the central committee, adopts a policy of Socialism in One Country, ending Trotsky's theory of global revolution. Trotsky is attacked in *Pravda* and allowed no reply. Sklyansky, his deputy, is sacked, then drowned in a lake in America. A year after Lenin's death, Trotsky is deposed as a minister. In October 1927, he is expelled from the party, seventeen months later from the country. His friend Ioffe commits suicide. Stalin goes on to liquidate all who had contact with Trotsky, from family members, to political allies, to passing acquaintances. Trotsky's first wife, Alexandra, is sent to her death in Siberia. His daughter is driven to suicide. His older son, Lev Sedov, dies in Paris of medical neglect, conceivably murdered on Stalin's orders; the younger, Sergei Sedov, is executed in 1937. Zinoviev and Kamenev are made to confess to their treason with Trotsky at Stalin's first show trial before being shot. Kamenev's two sons are executed, as is his ex-wife, Olga, Trotsky's sister. All are airbrushed from Soviet histories of Lenin's revolution.

Trotsky himself is hounded from one exile to the next. He stays for a while in Turkey, then moves to France, where he is deported to Norway, which also expels him. He is finally invited to live in Mexico at the home of the artist Diego Rivera, with whose wife, Frida Kahlo, he has a joyous late affair, rare in an otherwise uxorious existence. On August 21, 1940, a Stalinist agent in a pin-striped suit, Ramón Mercader, overcomes tight security to enter Trotsky's office and kill him with an ice pick.

Despite the opening of the Soviet archives, we still cannot quantify with certainty the relative importance of Lenin and Trotsky in the victory of the revolution. What Trotsky brought to the party is an unquenchable optimism to offset Lenin's frequent defeatism, a macabre sense of humor, a dazzling turn of phrase, and a capacity for improvisation. His confidence is as rigid as his tactics are flexible. He relishes argument and is rarely outdone in abuse.

Some of these traits might be regarded as Jewish. Trotsky, for his part, maintains that being Jewish is made irrelevant after 1917, superseded by supranational Marxism. He does not explain why Jewish citizens of the Soviet Union are made to carry an *E* (for *Evrei*, meaning Hebrew or Jew) in their identity cards. Trotsky feels no sentiment for the Jewish past, nor solidarity with the Jewish present. He clings to the belief that ethnicity, like hereditary privilege, can be overcome by ideology.

No one would have been more taken aback by the gritty endurance of Jewish religious life throughout seventy-five years of the Soviet Union or by the emergence of a State of Israel with initial Soviet support. The Jewish question never fades in Russia. Most personal of all, we can only speculate what Trotsky might have made of the decision of his great-grandson Vadim Sedov to rename himself "David," move to the land of Israel, and live there as a Hasidic Jew. An "unconscious historical process" ensures that the descendants of Leiba Bronstein, also known as Trotsky, now speak Hebrew as their mother tongue in a Jewish nation-state.

ELEVEN

1924

SCHOOLBOYS

The untold trials of Franz Kafka and Max Brod.

B erlin undergoes a personality transplant. Once as famed for its dullness as Washington, DC, the German capital becomes a creative hub after the war, a crucible of ideas, a talent magnet. With shots still ringing out in revolutionary streets, Bertolt Brecht arrives from Augsburg to a "shameless magnificence." Kurt Weill, a hazan's son from Dessau, discovers there is no better place to study. The journalist Joseph Roth, from Vienna, sleeps in the steam baths if he can't afford a room. The poet Else Lasker-Schüler beds down beneath a table in the Romanisches Café, "a waiting room for the talented" in the words of Erich Kästner, author of *Emil and the Detectives*. Walter Benjamin composes a celebrated essay on the café's prostitutes, arguing that there's not much difference between writers and whores. In the same café, Erich Maria Remarque writes part of *All Quiet on the Western Front* and Alfred Döblin conceives *Berlin Alexanderplatz*. Döblin, a doctor, treats poets for free.

Dawn, says the dramatist Carl Zuckmayer, is the city's defining moment: "that shimmering early morning after a wakeful, wild, drunken opening night . . . in the overcrowded train when you were still half dazed from nocturnal adventures and on your way to another rehearsal, trying to catch up on a bit of sleep standing up."[1] Berthold Goldschmidt, a music student from Hamburg, takes Sunday lunch with his teacher's mother, the impresario Luise Wolff. At her table, he meets great conductors grateful for a good meal: Furtwängler, Walter, Klemperer, Kleiber. "You hardly dared stay home of an evening for fear of what you might miss," says Goldschmidt. "After a concert or opera, there was cabaret. Then you looked at your watch and it was time to go to work."[2] The artistic hyperactivity exists above a stew of national despair, devastating stagflation, moral chaos, and threats of violence from right and left. It cannot last. Berlin is dancing on hot lava.

Its metamorphosis from Dullsville to Valhalla comes about apparently without planning or human agency. No one can say who makes Berlin buzz any more than they can identify one person who makes London swing. Still, no cultural revolution ever comes about without instigation, and this one appears, to a considerable degree, to be the work of one musician with a modest title—a petty official with unparalleled power.

Leo Kestenberg is a hazan's son from a Slovak town, who teaches in two Berlin conservatories. He is married and has two daughters. So far, so bourgeois. In his spare time, Kestenberg is an activist for the radical wing of the Social Democratic Party, recruiting members in working-class districts and preaching that great art can revivify deprived lives. He gives free evening classes in music appreciation, starts the People's

Theatre, and gets designers to make modernist furniture for poor families. Kestenberg is a one-man workers' educational association, the William Morris of Wannsee. Politically, he is unelectable. A portrait by his friend Oskar Kokoschka reveals why. Kestenberg, for all his fine qualities, is quite spectacularly ugly, and in a categorically Jewish way. He has a large nose, bulbous lips, and a high brow above a tubby body in a bulging three-piece suit. Kestenberg, on any platform, is a gift to caricaturists. Despite this, he is a power within the party.

On the day the kaiser abdicates, Kestenberg is seen in the Reichstag, negotiating with gangs of armed soldiers. The diarist Harry Kessler is impressed by his easy access to all sides in an inflammable situation. While others seek high office, Kestenberg enters the Ministry of Culture on December 1, 1918, as a Referent, or ministerial adviser. The title, deceptively meek, allows Kestenberg to take charge of all musical activity across Prussia, which is two-thirds of the German Republic. His friend Ludwig Seelig, lawyer for the theater workers' union, becomes Referent for the dramatic stage. Their writ runs from Cologne to Königsberg, the length of the Baltic Sea.

Kestenberg has a plan. The "masses," he argues, want new music, not old. Therefore, Berlin must be a crucible for young composers. There are plenty around, many fresh out of uniform and fizzing with radical views. Kurt Weill and Hanns Eisler, socialist Jews, found a November Group that includes a Russian, Wladimir Vogel, and an American, George Antheil. Kestenberg feeds his cubs indirectly by financing performing groups that perform contemporary works. His first target and greatest obstacle is the old imperial opera house on Unter den Linden, where the workforce refuse to work for his artistic director, the Jewish critic Paul Bekker, and elect the proto-Nazi reactionary Max von Schillings. Kestenberg lets Schillings know that he intends to blow the state budget on a new opera house, the Kroll, which will pursue a modernist agenda and lure away the Linden's audience unless he gingers up the output. Schillings, a wily operator with a soprano wife who gets all the good parts, spikes Kestenberg's attacks by putting on new operas by Busoni, Richard Strauss, Franz Schreker, and, crucially, Alban Berg, whose antiwar opera, *Wozzeck*, is a work of such difficulty that its conductor Erich Kleiber requires 125 rehearsals. Despite these concessions, Kestenberg is determined to get rid of Schillings. On the afternoon of the *Wozzeck* premiere, December 14, 1925, he faces a vote of censure in the Reichstag for his dismissal. That night, *Wozzeck* opens at the Linden to tumultuous acclaim. Berthold Goldschmidt, playing the celesta in the orchestra, remembers it as "the opening night of modern opera." Berg is deafened by the applause. "I was with him half the night," writes the philosopher Theodor Wiesengrund Adorno, "literally consoling him over success." Walter Benjamin, at a later performance, comments on a "metaphysically profound discovery" in the atonal singing.

Soon, the Kroll Opera is running reconceptions of Beethoven and Wagner operas alongside heady novelties: Weill's *Royal Palace*, Schoenberg's *From Today to Tomorrow*, and Hindemith's *The Daily News*. No opera house in the world would take such risks with unknown works, but nowhere else has Kestenberg's license to hustle in the future of art. Brecht, who meets Weill in a radio studio, founds their partnership with *The Rise and Fall of the City of Mahagonny*, an epochal representation of interwar Berlin. The pair are perfect antipodes. Brecht wears leather jackets, treats women like chattel, and proclaims, "*Erst kommt das Fressen dann kommt die Moral*" (First fill your belly, then you can preach morality). Weill—bespectacled, besuited, romantic—would rather go hungry than write a wrong note. They fight like wildcats over *The Threepenny Opera*, with Brecht changing his script almost until the curtain rises. The opera is an instant hit, its songs sold on the streets in Ullstein's *Musik für Alle* series, truly music for everyone. Kestenberg's vision of redemption through new art is fulfilled. Around eye-catching new operas, Berlin grows vibrant industries of film, fashion, leisure, and design. The city is the last word in chic—its flapper fashions upstage Paris, its movies are classier than Hollywood's, its nightlife is the envy of the world.

This dazzling revival is staged against the backdrop of a broken society, a shattered economy, and a collapsing currency in which a loaf of bread, affordable at breakfast, can cost the equivalent of a month's wages by suppertime. Berliners go shopping with suitcases full of notes. Sex is traded for food. A half-English violinist with £5 a month from her mother feeds a whole orchestra during the worst of times.[3]

Kestenberg, determined, presses on with the second strand of his reform. From 1921, he organizes annual music weeks—Reichsschulwochen—in schools in Berlin, Cologne, Breslau, Hamburg,

Darmstadt, Dresden, Munich, and Hanover. In 1924, he brings out a syllabus that upgrades music teaching from singing and choir sessions to a more challenging technical and intellectual engagement. Kestenberg's syllabus, titled "Memorandum on Fostering Music in Schools and Among the People," is so clear-sighted—starting with hand claps and working up to full orchestra—that its framework remains in use across Germany a century later. Taken up by the Czechs, the Poles, and the Hungarians, the Kestenberg Reform becomes the basis for international colloqiua on music in schools.

It arouses brute opposition from vested interests. The churches protest that, by reducing choir singing at schools, Kestenberg is undermining their services. He replies that they should invest in training their own choirs. Music teachers are enraged when Kestenberg wants to have them licensed and tested every few years and for private lessons to be charged on a national scale. These are sensible proposals, intended to cull charlatans and child abusers and improve instrumental teaching across the nations, but bad teachers will not go down without a fight. They turn to the Nazi Party, which turns its propaganda cudgels on Kestenberg as the Jew who is destroying German music. Caught in the crosshairs of a political war, Kestenberg is forced to retreat. After three years of exhilaration, he accepts that the Kroll Opera is unaffordable and, in 1931, shuts it down. The Nazis, sniffing victory, demand his head. On December 1, 1932, fourteen years to the day from his arrival at the ministry, Kestenberg is ordered by the right-wing chancellor, Franz von Papen, to take early retirement, effective that same day. He is fifty years old. Utopia is over.

A writer in Prague is facing a moral conundrum of such magnitude that, brilliant fixer though he is, he can find no practical solution. "It would be impossible to overrate the gravity of the problems," he sighs. The problems? For one, he has received a deathbed letter from his best friend:

> Dearest Max, my last request: Everything I leave behind me (in my bookcase, linen-cupboard, and my desk both at home and in the office, or anywhere else where anything may have

got to and meets your eye), in the way of diaries, manuscripts, letters (my own and others'), sketches, and so on, to be burned unread; also all writings and sketches which you or others may possess; and ask those others for them in my name. Letters which they do not want to hand over to you, they should at least promise faithfully to burn themselves.

The demand is unequivocal. Max is to burn every piece of paper he can find and do his best to track down the rest. That is the only way he can honor the poor man's dying wish.

But he can't. To do so would cut against everything he believes in, the core purpose of his life. With an act like this on his conscience, he knows he will never sleep again. Max has to find a way out, a loophole that will permit him to honor the spirit of his friend's instructions while disregarding the letter. "If, in spite of these categorical instructions, I nevertheless refuse to perform the holocaust demanded of me by my friend," he states, "I [must] have good and sufficient reasons for that."[4] Max Brod is in need of a Talmudic interpretation that will get him off the hook.

Brod is a theater critic and a fairly well-known writer. "Few works have so fully interpreted the spirit and emotions of the Middle Ages," says Stefan Zweig of Brod's bestseller *Tycho Brahe's Path to God*, a fictional account of the historic clash between the Prague astronomer Johannes Kepler and a senior Danish rival. A Salieri-Mozart scenario, *Tycho* demonstrates what happens when a solid performer comes up against an immortal genius. It is the story of Brod's life.

A man of many gifts, Brod is a capable composer and pianist who played a 1911 recital of Mozart sonatas at the Charles University with Albert Einstein as violinist. Meeting Einstein convinces Brod that, good as Brod may be at multiple endeavors, he is not and never will be a genius. In the light of this recognition, he decides to be the next-best thing: a mentor to genius. Each night at the theater, he is on the lookout for an exceptional talent.

Prague is a cauldron of conflicting cultures, Czech, German, and Jewish, each occupying a linguistic ghetto. The Germans, refusing to sully their ears with "uncultured" Slavonic sounds, have an opera house of their own, as well as newspapers and German-speaking cafés. The Czechs exclude Slovaks, Magyars, and Roma from their burgeoning cultural activities. The Jews, who try to stay on good terms with all sides, become everyone's scapegoats when the economy tanks, as it does from the start of the war. Still, there are some contacts across the linguistic divides.

Dvořák's son-in-law Josef Suk approaches Max Brod with a rec-ommendation that he should see an unusual opera by a provincial schoolmaster, Leoš Janáček, which has opened at the Czech-speaking National Theatre. *Jenufa*, the raw drama of a churchwoman who drowns a baby to protect her stepdaughter's marriage, overwhelms Brod, who describes it as his greatest theatrical experience since the war began. He is the first to review *Jenufa* in the German press; Janáček writes him a formal note of thanks. Brod replies, telling the composer to drop by for coffee if ever he is in Prague. Janáček, receiving the letter in Brno, jumps on the next train and lands on Brod's doorstep at six o'clock on a Sunday morning. He persuades Brod to translate *Jenufa* into German. "His glance bewitched me," recalls Brod. "Still more his words, whose holy naivety moves me to this day."[5] "You were the first, Dr Brod," writes the composer, "so fervent were your words about *Jenufa*."[6]

Janáček, decides Brod, is "the sort of man that God wanted." Brod has found his genius. In his German text, *Jenufa* is staged to tumultu-ous success in Vienna, Berlin, and New York. Brod translates four more operas and writes Janáček's biography before the composer starts to resist his influence. Both men, stepping back, appreciate their disparity. Brod is a metropolitan, German-speaking Zionist with a rakish sex life; Janáček is a rural Czech schoolteacher, immersed in Russian literature, frustratedly in love with a dull Jewish housewife. He is not, ultimately, the genius that Brod craves. The two creators tip hats to each other and go their separate ways.

Brod's next cause is a country bumpkin who is on his deathbed as his novel *The Good Soldier Schweik* appears in print in January 1923. Brod translates a chapter of Jaroslav Hašek in the German-language *Prager Tagblatt*. A little man's survival manual in the mayhem of war, *Schweik* appears, thanks to Brod, in sixty languages.

His third protégé is a rapid letdown, a Prague Jewish kid of tubby exterior and owlish looks who writes expressionist poetry. Brod brings Franz Werfel to his table at Café Arco, finds him a publisher in Vienna, and persuades Martin Buber to introduce his first collection. Great things are predicted. But in Vienna Werfel falls into the clutches of Alma Mahler, the composer's widow, who seduces and marries this "man-child," making him her plaything. Brod feels betrayed. Werfel will never be the Messiah.

Suddenly, he realizes that genius has for years been standing at his elbow. There are conflicting accounts as to when Max Brod first meets Franz Kafka, but from 1907 they are inseparable. On country hikes, the handsome, muscular Kafka outpaces little Brod, who has grown up with a curved spine. Kafka is tall, Brod short. Kafka wears a well-made suit of fine material; Brod is sartorially of a much lower cut. In all other respects, however, Brod has the advantage over Kafka. He has an engaging job, lots of friends, and girls to spare. Kafka, a lawyer in an accident insurance firm, is bored to his socks with his life and longs to share Brod's. He comes alive only after work, he writes: "I devour the hours outside the office like a wild beast. . . . I emerge from the crowdedness of my leisure hours scarcely rested." He joins Brod in the Café Arco for exhilarated conversation and spends the rest of the night writing in his bedroom. "He never spoke a meaningless word," says Brod. "In his presence the everyday world underwent a transformation, everything was new, new in a way that was often very sad, not to say shattering . . ."[7]

Once Brod recognizes Kafka's genius, Kafka looks to Brod as his reality check. They go swimming together in lakes and take a trip to Paris. Brod is keen on sex. Kafka, incapable of making love to any woman who might be fit to marry, seeks relief with prostitutes. "I passed by the brothel as though past the house of a beloved," he writes. Brod introduces him to a family friend, Felice Bauer, a "happy, healthy, self-confident girl" whom Kafka asks to marry him. Felice's concerns are aroused when Kafka warns her that he must sleep alone and describes the institution of marriage as "a scaffold." He suffers fears that are "alive as snakes." He breaks off the engagement, then renews it. Kafka can neither love Felice nor leave her.

Brod, a superficial analyst, concludes that Kafka is "tortured" by erotic desires. Kafka describes it otherwise:

Like a person who cannot resist the temptation to swim out into the sea and is blissful to be carried away—"now you are a man, you are a great swimmer"—and suddenly, with little reason, he raises himself up and sees only the sky and the sea, and on the waves is only his own little head and he is seized by a horrible fear and nothing else matters, he must get back to the shore, even if his lungs burst. That is how it is.

Duality is Kafka's game: he wants to have his cake and eat it. Through the cake run streaks of remorse and anxiety. Through the night of September 22, 1912, twenty-four hours after Yom Kippur, the Jewish Day of Judgment, he writes a story titled "The Trial" (or: "The Judgment") and dedicates it to "Miss Felice Bauer." Felice, alarmed by its paranoia, gets the message, marries a man who works in a bank, migrates to New York, and, in old age, sells Kafka's letters so the world can see how warped his genius truly was.

After Felice, Kafka woos three Jewish women, Julie Wohryzek, Grete Bloch, and Dora Diamant, and a Czech journalist, Milena Jesenská. Naïve as he tries to appear, Franz Kafka makes himself unknowable. He tells women that he is inhibited by conflicts with his overbearing father, who is forever going on about how his generation had it much harder and how his son does nothing worthwhile. Kvetch as he does, Franz is never estranged from his father. He tells stories that allow each of his friends to form a different version of Franz Kafka. He delights Brod by taking Hebrew lessons in preparation for a possible future life in Palestine; can anyone but Brod imagine Franz Kafka in khaki shorts, laying bricks on a Tel Aviv housing estate, or (Kafka's preferred option) carrying a tray as a waiter in a seaside café? Like so much else in Kafka, the self-image is simply surreal.

He writes and he writes, creating ever more versions of himself:

One works so feverishly at the office that afterwards one is too tired even to enjoy one's holiday properly. But even all that work does not give one a claim to be treated lovingly by everyone; on the contrary, one is alone, a total stranger and only an object of curiosity. And so long as you say "one" instead of "I," there is nothing in it and one can easily tell the story; but as soon as you admit to yourself that it is you yourself, you feel as though transfixed and are horrified.

This passage from *The Metamorphosis*, the only major work to appear in his lifetime, defines a state that becomes known as "Kafkaesque," an existential duality in which the narrator is both inside and outside his situation. The central character in *The Metamorphosis*, Gregor Samsa, wakes up to find himself turned into a horrible insect with six legs and a shell. He has no idea why. The opening sentence, *Als Gregor Samsa eines Morgens aus unruhigen Träumen erwachte, fand er sich in seinem Bett zu einem ungeheuren Ungeziefer verwandelt*, is the most famous in modern German literature. *The Metamorphosis* is praised by Rainer Maria Rilke, Robert Musil, Italo Calvino, and the dramatist Carl Sternheim, who relinquishes a literary prize in Kafka's favor. Brod sends it to his German publisher, Kurt Wolff, and wakes up one morning to find his friend acclaimed as a genius. This, he tells himself, is just the beginning. He presses Kafka for more: "I wrested from Kafka nearly everything he published either by persuasion or by guile," he writes. Kafka, elusive as a grass snake, keeps slipping away, one way or another.

On the night of August 12, 1917, Kafka wakes up in bed spitting blood, an event he has foretold in "A Country Doctor." Tuberculosis is usually received as a death sentence. Rather than recoiling in fright and horror, Kafka appears to welcome the diagnosis. "Today I have for tuberculosis the feeling a child has for the folds of his mother's skirt to which he clings." Yet he does not crave death. "The world—F[elice] as its representative—and my ego are tearing my body apart in a conflict that there is no resolving." Freudians interpret this diary entry as schizophrenic. Jungians consider it a mark of fine balance in his psyche. An American critic, Samuel Gilman, considers that Kafka is "becoming that which he fears he must become."[8]

Kafka appears sane and happy. He falls in love again, cherishes his friends, and works hard at his stories. After diagnosis, he spends two carefree months in the village of Zürau (Sirem), where his sister Ottla works on an agricultural estate. Ottla is his favorite relative. When she marries a Catholic and is shunned by their father, Franz takes her side, writing Hermann a hundred-page letter of complaint that he famously neglects to deliver.

He travels to magic mountains, to the seaside, and back to Prague. The tuberculosis comes and goes. He revisits all his sisters, growing attached to their children. In the summer of 1923, at a Baltic seaside resort, he meets Dora Diamant, daughter of a Hasidic family. In September, he moves to Berlin to live with her. Dora, twenty-five years old, works in an orphanage. Kafka, now forty, draws strength from her love. She begs her father's permission to marry, but his rebbe forbids the match. Brod, in Berlin for a fling with the actress Emmy Salveter, is moved by Dora's selflessness. "To have lived one day with Franz means more (to me) than all his work, all his writings," she says.[9] They live on bread crusts, burning manuscripts for winter fuel. Brod notes that Kafka is sleeping well for the first time in years. A letter arrives from Kurt Wolff closing his royalty account as no one is buying his book. Kafka writes to Ottla, asking for a loan. Ottla arrives with winter clothes for her brother. Like Brod, she is charmed by Dora. Each Saturday night, Kafka asks Dora to recite the Yiddish meditation *Gott fun Avrohom*, seeking God's help in the week ahead. In January 1924, he writes to Brod in the third person: "If only the ground beneath him were firm, the abyss in front of him filled in, the vultures around his head driven away, the storm in the skies above him abated—if all that were to happen, it might just be barely possible to go on for a while." His uncle, a physician, finds Kafka weighs less than a hundred pounds. In April, Dora accompanies Kafka to a sanatorium outside Vienna, where, on June 3, 1924, he dies.

A hundred people attend his funeral in Prague. Brod, holding Dora by the arm, follows the Kafka family down the gloomy walk from prayer hall to grave. As Brod delivers the eulogy, "a penetrating and painful cry" is heard from Dora, who falls to the ground in a faint.[10] Legend has it that Hermann Kafka turns his back on her as he recites the Kaddish. Hermann will soon join his son in the family grave; pilgrims from all over the world will find them eternally together. On the drive home, mourners see that the hands of the old town hall clock have stopped at four o'clock, the hour of Kafka's burial. Brod feels as if the light has gone out of his world. Franz, he says, has been "the mainstay of my whole existence."

That evening in the family apartment, Hermann Kafka signs a paper that grants Brod the right to bring his son's writings to publication. As Franz Kafka's literary executor, Brod goes through his room. He wants to fulfill his friend's last wishes—until he sees what they are. He finds two letters in a drawer. The first, quoted above, is a categorical instruction to destroy "everything I leave behind me." It is not open to negotiation or interpretation.

The second letter is written in pencil:

Dear Max,

Perhaps this time I shan't recover after all. Pneumonia after a whole month's pulmonary fever is all too likely; and not even writing this down can avert it, although there is a certain power in that. For this eventuality therefore, here is my last will concerning everything I have written: Of all my writings the only books that can stand are these: "The Judgment," "The Stoker," "Metamorphosis," "Penal Colony," "Country Doctor" and the short story "Hunger Artist" . . . But everything else of mine which is extant . . . all these things without exception are to be burned, and I beg you to do this as soon as possible.

Franz

Brod reckons this is the earlier of the two notes. It may even be a pencil sketch for the final letter. Whatever the case, it is superseded by the later document. He uses this letter to bend the law in his favor by means of Talmudic logic. If, in the penciled letter, Kafka allows *some* works to survive, that means he does not want *all* his work to be destroyed. Since *The Metamorphosis* and a few other stories have already been printed and cannot be erased, that means that the demand to destroy everything is unachievable and invalid. "Both sets of instructions to me were the product of a period when Kafka's self-critical tendency was at its height," he explains in a postscript to *The Trial*. "But during the last year of his life his whole existence took an unforeseen turn for the better, a new, happy and positive turn, which did away with his self-hatred and nihilism." In other words, Dora's tender love had engaged Kafka with the possibility that he might enjoy literary posterity.

Brod continues: "My decision to publish his posthumous work is made easier by the memory of all the embittered struggles preceding every single publication of Kafka's which I extorted from him by force and often by begging. And yet afterwards he was reconciled with these publications and relatively satisfied with them." Which is to say, Kafka did not know his own mind. Max knew best.

"My decision," concludes Brod:

> ... does not rest on any of the reasons given above but simply and solely on the fact that Kafka's unpublished work contains the most wonderful treasures, and, measured against his own work, the best things he has written. In all honesty I must confess that this one fact of literary and ethical value of what I am publishing would have been enough to decide me to do so, definitely, finally and irresistibly, even if I had had no single objection to raise against the validity of Kafka's last wishes."[11]

Under Talmudic law, a will that violates a moral precept can be set aside. Kafka has no moral right to deprive the world of his light, and his will is therefore invalid. "I . . . refuse," states Brod, "to perform the holocaust demanded of me by my friend." Using an emotive noun, Brod plucks Kafka's fame like a brand from the burning.

On April 26, 1925, *The Trial* is brought out by an avant-garde Berlin publishing house, Die Schmiede. *The Castle* goes to a Munich imprint in 1926. *Amerika* goes to Kurt Wolff. None generates great sales. Stocks of *The Castle* are pulped after sales stall at seven hundred copies. Kafka is a slow burner.

It takes a change in the world situation to establish Kafka's importance. The opening sentence of *The Trial*, written in 1912, acquires the force of prophecy as reports arrive in the 1930s of Stalin's Great Terror against loyal Communists and innocent citizens: "Somebody must have made a false accusation against Josef K, for he was arrested one morning without having done anything wrong." Josef K, set free after his first questioning, knows that sooner or later they will come for him again and that will be the end.

The Castle is home to a bureaucracy that operates without purpose. In both stories, as in *The Metamorphosis*, the hero is not responsible for his fate. Josef K no more knows why he is arrested than Gregor Samsa knows why he is a cockroach. Millions will go to the slaughter in Europe not knowing what they have done to deserve it. Kafka's three sisters are murdered. Ottla, dumped by her Catholic husband, chaperones a group of orphans to Auschwitz with an air of Kafkaesque fatalism, knowing she will never return. Kafka anticipates the Holocaust in images that Jewish survivors find oddly consoling. The Israeli novelist Aharon Appelfeld writes: "For a long time I was enthralled by the magic of Kafka. My reading of Kafka was that he was aligned more closely to the Kabbalah and to Hasidism than to the literature of the Jewish Enlightenment and modern literature."[12]

Kafka is open to infinite Jewish interpretations. Brod regards Josef K as a modern Job. My teacher, Baruch Kurzweil, attacks Brod from an Orthodox viewpoint for making a false Messiah of Kafka, "a Jew for whom Judaism is meaningless." Gershom Scholem and Walter Benjamin lampoon the Brod-Kafka duopoly as a kind of literary Laurel and Hardy. Benjamin, who overanalyzes Kafka, depicts him, here and there, as a Taoist storyteller; Elias Canetti calls him the most Chinese of Western writers; while Elie Wiesel aligns him with the Hasidic mystic Nahman of Breslav because, in one of Nahman's tales, a prince morphs into a rooster. Kafka is enthralled by Jewish mysticism. On a rest cure in Marienbad in July 1916, he sees the Belzer Rebbe, Yissachar Dov Rokeach, with his entourage. "It lures me," he tells Brod, "that look of calm, happy confidence." Kafka's companion in Marienbad is Georg Mordechai Langer, a Belzer Hasid who writes homoerotic poetry in Hebrew. Langer tells us that Kafka owns a book of Nahman stories, a collection of Chinese poetry, and a selection of Freudian psychoanalytic texts. He sees holiness in this "unknowable" Kafka, a man of more levels than anyone knows.

His impact on world literature is boundless. Jean-Paul Sartre adopts him as an existential positivist. Albert Camus owes his *Outsider* to *The Trial*. Samuel Beckett annoys James Joyce by telling him that the Irish have forsaken *Ulysses* for *The Trial*. J. M. Coetzee dreams of Beckett meeting Kafka on a beach. Graham Greene's *Ministry of Fear* originates in *The Castle*. George Orwell's *1984* is Kafka's world. Philip Roth is happy to be called "a Kafka *doppelgänger*." Kafka is revered by the magic realist Jorge Luis Borges, the narrative literalist J. D. Salinger, the political writers Günter Grass and Arthur Koestler, and the film comedian Woody Allen. The Czech writer Milan Kundera reveres Kafka for finding great beauty in dull, everyday existence. Yet almost any tag you pin to Kafka, the opposite is equally true. Always, his supreme achievement is his unknowability.

What he does not conceal, or disguise, or dissimulate, is his Jewishness. Kafka is Jewish to his core, Jewish in all his work: "Self-evidently," writes the essayist George Steiner, "of the Biblical and Talmudic legacy." Kafka's Jewish identity is proclaimed in his sense of family, his respect for social justice, his cultural curiosity, his multiple neuroses, above all in his prevailing anxiety—the awareness that something terrible is about to happen and there is nothing anyone can do to stop it. His anxiety is more than just a conditioned response to a history of Jewish persecution. It is a creative distillation of that legacy into something recognizable as genius. Anxiety is the engine of Franz Kafka's humanity.

"You may reproach Jews for their particular type of anxiety," he tells his Czech lover Milena Jesenská:

> Their insecure position, insecure within themselves, insecure among people, would above all explain why Jews believe they possess only whatever they hold in their hands or grip between their teeth, that furthermore only tangible possessions give them a right to live, and that finally they will never again acquire what they once have lost— which swims happily away from them, gone forever. Jews are threatened by dangers from the most improbable sides or, to be more precise, let's leave the dangers aside and say: "They are threatened by threats."

This is truly revealing, and Milena understands. She confronts Brod with her perception: "Are you saying, as it seems, that Franz is afraid of love but not of life? I think it is the other way round."[13] Kafka craves love. It is his fear of life that prevents him from committing to another living being.

Kafka meets Milena only twice; their love is conducted in letters. Trusting Milena as much as he does Brod, Kafka leaves her his diaries. Milena, a woman of fierce integrity, resigns from the Czech Communist Party over Stalin's show trials and is tortured by the gestapo under German occupation. Dora Diamant, forbidden by Brod from writing about Kafka, flees with her husband to the Soviet Union, escaping when he is arrested and finding her way to London, where she dies in August 1952.

Max Brod, gatekeeper to Kafka's genius, tends his friend's flame for forty years, latterly among indifferent café dwellers in Tel Aviv. His decision to overrule Kafka's wishes and publish his works will command a Supreme Court judgment in August 2016, when the National Library in Jerusalem, over the claims of Brod's designated heir, successfully demands the right to Brod's papers, with Kafka's among them. Brod is being punished beyond the grave in a Kafkaesque trial of rights. The moral precept in the case—lawyers quote the Talmud (Gittin, 16b)—remains unresolved.

On October 1, 1923, Richard Wagner's family welcomes Adolf Hitler to Bayreuth. Siegfried Wagner puts his hands on Hitler's shoulders. "You know," says Siegfried, "I really like you."[14] Five weeks later, Hitler leads a Munich beer-hall putsch and lands in Landsberg Prison. Siegfried's wife, Winifred, provides him with him the stationery on which he composes *Mein Kampf*. At a juncture where Hitler is no more than a shabby street ranter, he is granted cultural legitimacy by Germany's Holy Family. Winifred is smitten by "this German man who, filled with the most ardent love of his Fatherland, sacrifices his life for his ideal of a purified, united national Greater Germany." Wagner's son-in-law, the racist English historian Houston Stewart Chamberlain, proclaims, "Germany in the hour of her greatest need brings forth a Hitler." Hitler writes from jail that Bayreuth is "on our line of march to Berlin." There "first the Master and then Chamberlain forged the spiritual sword with which we fight today."[15] The 1924 Bayreuth Festival is a jamboree of proto-Nazi propaganda. That prompts Siegfried to worry about his box office.

Steeped in the anti-Semitism of both parents, Siegfried holds Jews in low regard, the more so once the Jewish journalist Maximilian Harden threatens him with exposure as a homosexual. Siegfried visits Berlin regularly to meet boys. The war has left Bayreuth half-broke, and hopes of fresh funding from the car maker Henry Ford, a promoter of Jewish conspiracy theories, are dashed when Siegfried and Winifred visit him in America. The dollars they raise in America come from Wagner societies, many of whose members are generous and Jewish. Siegfried is shocked. "If the Jews are willing to help us that is doubly meritorious, because my father in his writings attacked and offended them."[16]

With the mark worthless and the best Wagner singers working abroad, Siegfried is wondering how he can ever afford another festival when he receives a letter from the rabbi of Bayreuth. Rabbi Dr. Benjamin Falk Felix Salomon is concerned at signs of racialism at the 1924 festival. He asks Siegfried for reassurances. Siegfried responds warmly by return.

The correspondence between Siegfried and the rabbi, unknown until 2001, is strikingly frank. The rabbi berates Siegfried for befriending Nazis and promoting racial hatred. Siegfried replies: "In the last few days I have been criticised anonymously for entertaining Ludendorff and Hitler on the one hand and engaging with Jewish circles on the other. As head of our local Jewish community, you deserve an explanation." *Deserve* is a strong word, signifying respect.

Siegfried goes on: "We oppose the Marxist spirit, regarding it as the source of all our misery. But we have nothing against Jews of a nationalist inclination." He then makes a tortuous distinction between Jews who embrace "German" values and those who defile them. "The greatest misfortune for the German people is the mixture of the Jewish and Germanic races. Those who emerge from it are neither fish nor fowl. I prefer to deal with a pure-bred Jew than with one of those half-natures." He reminds the rabbi that his father had Hermann Levi as conductor of *Parsifal* and Heinrich Porges as chorus chief, and Josef Rubinstein made the piano score, "so you can see that my father did not practise anti-semitism in life, rather that he fought against the spirit of what I would call 'the Heinis.'" What he means by this offensive term is ostentation and mixed-race Jews. "Can you take this from a German?" he demands.

The rabbi can and does. He replies with an attack on Chamberlain and other Wagners "who wear the swastika," meaning Siegfried's wife, Winifred. He reminds Siegfried that Jews have lived in Germany for two thousand years. "How little you understand of Judaism and the thinking of German Jews," rails the rabbi. "How do you think that people rooted for countless generations in our German homeland, families whose sons have fallen for our German fatherland, feel about the distinction between Germans and Jews?"

Siegfried replies that "it is important to me to continue cultivating peaceful and friendly relations with well-intentioned Jews." The exchanges continue. Rabbi Salomon warns Siegfried in 1925 that "certain national circles want to misuse Bayreuth for their own purposes."

Siegfried sends him tickets for the festival and allays his fears that Adolf Hitler has been given access to rehearsals. "I can assure you there has been no such invitation," declares Siegfried. "[As for] the festival, anyone can come, be it Hitler or Harden. You personally are warmly invited to the general rehearsals." Siegfried unexpectedly brackets Hitler with a gutter journalist; while calling Hitler "a splendid fellow," he orders that the 1925 festival is kept "free from political influences." Hitler, grouching that Siegfried is "somewhat in the hands of the Jews," stays away from Bayreuth for the rest of the 1920s, except to attend Chamberlain's funeral. The rabbi seems happy.

On Siegfried's death in August 1930, Hitler demands that his papers are sent to Berlin to protect Winifred from embarrassing gay scandals. They fall into Soviet hands in 1945 and eventually reach the National Holocaust Museum in Washington, DC. To read these friendly exchanges between a rabbi and the head of the Wagner family is nothing short of astonishing. Rabbi Salomon and his wife are Siegfried Wagner's personal guests at Bayreuth. The Jew-hater's son has discovered a German–Jewish symbiosis.

After Siegfried, Winifred ("fanatically with us," says the propagandist Joseph Goebbels) turns Bayreuth into a swastika fest, as symbolic of Nazi power as the Nuremburg rallies. Hitler attends every year from 1933 to 1939. The rabbi of Bayreuth is fired in 1936, and his 177-year-old synagogue is burned down. Dr. Benjamin Falk Felix Salomon escapes with his wife to London, where he is killed in a German air raid in 1940.

While Berlin turns from militarism to modernism, Frankfurt switches from financial hub to a cell of radicalism. The Frankfurt School is founded in 1924 as the Institute of Social Research at Goethe University. Its director, Carl Grünberg, is a Marxist historian who comes from an Orthodox family in Bessarabia. His successor, Max Horkheimer, shares a similar background. Seed funding comes from Felix Weil, Marxist son of a Jewish grain merchant. The faculty is almost entirely Jewish: the philosopher Herbert Marcuse, the social scientist Friedrich Pollock, the economist Henryk Grossman, the psychoanalyst Erich Fromm, and the musical polymath Theodor Wiesengrund

Adorno. Informally linked to the School are Walter Benjamin and the film theorist Siegfried Kracauer. A more bristling pack of Jewish Marx-wranglers exists nowhere else on Earth.

The Frankfurt School teaches a Critical Theory that, rooted in a thought of Wittgenstein's, rejects "objectivity" as a way of establishing whether black can be agreed to be black, and white white. The amount of hot air generated by this hypothetical engine provides underfloor comfort for academic campuses the world over and launches a thousand doctoral theses. The beauty of Critical Theory is that it can be applied to anything, from cooking to cricket to clitoral stimulation. What is more, it can be disputed but not refuted. Like the Talmud, CT exists to be argued over for its own sake. The Frankfurt School is its supreme yeshiva.

It enjoys growing esteem in Germany and France until, under Hitler, Horkheimer is obliged to lead his CT flock to New York, dispersing them between Columbia University and the New School for Social Research. Here, Erich Fromm applies a Freudian form of CT to demonstrate that socialist humanism is the ultimate, unparalleled best way to live one's life. His book *The Art of Loving* is a massive bestseller in 1956. Marcuse, scorning capitalism and materialism as "unnecessary," writes *Eros and Civilization*, a 1955 money-spinner. Famous as these titles are, their impact is sadly ephemeral. It is impossible to mention Fromm and Marcuse today in intelligent company without a wince of irony. Their fad is overtaken by the 1960s. The rest of the Frankfurt School is repatriated by Adorno in 1949, only to be mocked to perdition by 1968 student revolutionaries. After his lectures are disrupted by demonstrators, Adorno dies of a heart attack. Although the institute survives, it has long been damned as a dodo, except by a few Marxist nostalgists.[17]

There is, however, a second Frankfurt School, less renowned and more durable. The Freies Jüdisches Lehrhaus is the brainchild of a soldier who comes out of four years of war with a book he has written on the back of postcards home. Franz Rosenzweig's *The Star of Redemption* has a resonance unparalleled among Jews since Samson Raphael Hirsch's *The Nineteen Letters*. *The Star* postulates a triangular relationship between God, the world, and the individual, expressed through triple "miracles" of creation, revelation, and redemption. In this model, no single element fully determines any event. War happens not because

God necessarily wills it but as a function of the triple link. Two triangles interlock into a mystic Star of David, mark of Jewish redemption.

Like Martin Buber, Rosenzweig fosters an I-you dialogue between God and the individual. Beyond Buber, he describes prayer as therapy. Faith, he writes, cannot banish death, nor can it diminish the fear of death. But "by teaching [a person] to live again, we have taught him to move towards death; we have taught him to live, though each step he takes brings him closer to death." To men crawling home from the killing fields, Rosenzweig represents the survival of reason. His Judaism is a distillation of Jewish experience down the ages. Being Jewish, he writes, is all you need to be a Jew. This existential idea rises so high above sectarian divisions of Orthodox and Reform that both can embrace it. Rosenzweig proposes that rather than learning from Torah how to lead a good life, we should learn from life—"from a world that knows nothing of the Law or pretends to know nothing"—how to find Torah. He is the most exciting and accessible Jewish thinker since Schechter, using his own life story as a pathway to faith.

Son of an assimilated middle-class family from Kassel, Franz switches from medicine to Hegelian philosophy at university. With his research attracting serious attention, he picks a fight with a distant cousin, Eugen Rosenstock, who has converted to Lutheranism. It is the evening of July 7, 1913, and the cousins agree that whoever loses the debate will accept the other's faith. Rosenzweig, ignorant of Judaism, loses the argument "step by step" as the night wears on. At dawn he concedes defeat. Jesus will be his future. Before leaping into the font, he asks to spend the High Holidays at prayer. In his family temple at New Year, he feels nothing. For Yom Kippur, he goes to Berlin, not to one of the grand edifices of official Jewry but to a *shtiebl*, a prayer room for ultra-Orthodox Jews from Eastern Europe. "I seem to have found the way back," he informs his mother.[18]

Judaism, for Rosenzweig, is all a matter of feeling. He discovers the Sabbath—"a miracle"—but follows the rules in a manner quite unlike submissive Orthodoxy. He tells his fiancée, Edith Hahn:

I'm sure you understand why I neither can nor must take too solemn a view of kosher eating. I look forward with pleasure to it since we will do it together in our house! But I can't be solemn about it or find "educational value" in it . . . Just see the emotional sclerosis of many Orthodox Jews, the sclerosis of their Jewish feelings![19]

On war service in the Balkans, he meets Sephardi Jews, descendants of the Spanish expulsion. "Their Jewish knowledge is nil, but the Jewish way of life is entirely natural to them."[20] He corresponds intensively with Rosenstock and his Gentile wife, Gritli. After the war, he turns his postcards into a book, marries his fiancée, Edith, and finds a garret for them to share. At a Passover meal with an Orthodox Frankfurt rabbi, Nehemiah Nobel, he floats the idea of a Lehrhaus, an adult institute teaching traditional Judaism as contemporary lifestyle. While Nobel raises funds, Rosenzweig finds another backer.

Salman Schocken has made a fortune reinventing the department store. Inclined to art deco, he hires the architect Erich Mendelsohn to create modernist palaces of consumerism with undulating contours and gleaming black exteriors, opening them in medium-sized towns all over Germany. Shopping at Schocken is an antidote to provincial ennui, an uplift for drab lives. When Schocken himself goes shopping, it is for antiquarian Jewish books and manuscripts, an esoteric magpie hobby. Rosenzweig is the first intellectual to pay respect to the businessman's private collection. Schocken, who already finances Martin Buber's journal, *Der Jude*, and pays a salary to the Hebrew novelist S. Y. Agnon, agrees to fund Rosenzweig's Lehrhaus.

Rosenzweig recruits a stellar cast, headed by Buber, Nehemiah Nobel, and Ernst Simon, with occasional lectures from Bertha Pappenheim, Agnon, Gershom Scholem, and such Frankfurt Schoolers as Fromm, Leo Löwenthal, and Kracauer. Scholem, the pioneering scholar of medieval Jewish mysticism, arranges Hebrew lessons for his symbiotic friend Walter Benjamin, the penetrating essayist on German literature. The Lehrhaus draws eleven hundred student registrations by its fourth year. Leo Baeck, the Berlin Reform leader, grants Rosenzweig the title "rabbi," which he never uses. Envious of his success, his Christian cousin Rosenstock sets up the Academy of Labour in Frankfurt, offering evening classes to blue-collar workers.

Then, tragedy strikes. In February 1922, Rosenzweig is diagnosed with a neurodegenerative disease that, he is told, will kill him within a year. He responds with hope: if he must die, so be it, but he will get a lot done first. Edith gives birth to a son—"it helps to make up for everything," he says. He finishes a Bible translation with Buber. Edith takes dictation. As he loses the power of speech, he points to letters on a board. When he can no longer move a finger, "she recited the alphabet, letters were combined into words and words into sentences."[21]

Friends rally. The atheist Erich Fromm attends Sabbath prayers at his home to make up a minyan of worshippers. Orthodox rabbis authorize his German Bible. Leo Baeck orders seven thousand sets for Reform schools. Paralyzed, Rosenzweig brings souls together until his dying breath and beyond (he is a primary influence on the postmodern Orthodoxy of Lord Jonathan Sacks). Rosenzweig is the guiding angel of the Schocken Verlag library, which issues ninety-two titles. The department-store magnate, empowered by Rosenzweig's positivism, acquires English-language rights to Franz Kafka's works and takes over the liberal Tel Aviv newspaper *Haaretz*. A fresh breeze blows through parochial Jewish letters.

On December 10, 1929, having survived almost eight years from his diagnosis, Franz Rosenzweig informs a visiting doctor in alphabet language, "I am improving." That night, he dies, aged forty-two. His influence lives on.

In February 1932, Berthold Goldschmidt, aged thirty, is hailed as "the white hope of German opera." After a brilliant premiere in Magdeburg, his opera *The Magnificent Cuckold* is booked for Berlin the following year. On February 1, 1933, Goldschmidt enters the Linden opera and sees brown uniforms. "I had never met a Nazi until then. I didn't think I knew any. But suddenly here they were. The double-bass player who never got promoted. The most difficult stage hands. An unhappy makeup artist. They were now in charge."

Kurt Weill asks the stage designer Caspar Neher to drive him to Paris. Bertolt Brecht goes to Prague. Leo Kestenberg, hearing Hermann Göring rant against Jews on the radio, buys a second-class rail ticket to Prague, where Max Brod meets his train. He founds the International Society for Music Education and, in 1938, is approached to manage an orchestra of German exiles in Tel Aviv. Kestenberg's first season with the Palestine Symphony Orchestra features Schoenberg's intractable

Orchestral Variations, played beside a Hebrew sacred service by Karel Salomon and a concerto grosso by Paul Ben-Haim. "I learned from Busoni that every concert programme must have its own artistic personality," says Kestenberg, still dreaming of rebuilding Berlin in the sand dunes.[22]

Goldschmidt stays on in Berlin for a couple of years. He has a girlfriend, blond and bisexual, whose brown-shirt brother says he will kill her if she sleeps with a Jew, so she does. Unable to stage his opera, Goldschmidt writes a set of variations on a Palestine shepherd's song for Jewish audiences. A summons to the gestapo settles his future.

An SS man demands to know how he makes a living. Goldschmidt explains that he makes music with Jews and gives private piano lessons. "What are you teaching at the moment?" demands the officer.

"Schumann's *Kinderszenen*," he replies.

"I love that piece," says the Nazi. "What do you charge?"

"Three marks a lesson."

"Really? I'm paying five for my kid."

"You're being ripped off." Goldschmidt shrugs.

"Listen," says the Nazi, leaning forward. "You're a decent fellow, Goldschmidt. Take my advice: leave this country as soon as possible. It won't go well for people like you."

A week later, Berthold Goldschmidt is in London.[23]

TWELVE

1933
FOUR MURDERS

Rabbi Akiva Posner's Chanukah candles defy
the swastika flag, Kiel, December 1932.

One Friday night in June, a couple sit down to dinner at a small
hotel at the northern edge of Tel Aviv. They are given the best
table, on a sea-facing balcony. Victor Arlozorov, thirty-four years old,

is a person of consequence, head of the Political Department of the Jewish Agency and, in effect, foreign minister of a future Jewish state. Cofounder of the Mapai party with the abrasive David Ben-Gurion, he steers a midway line between Chaim Weizmann's diplomatic pragmatism and Ben-Gurion's radical activism. Russian-born, his earliest memory is the sound of a Cossack rampage. Evacuated to the philosophers' town of Königsberg, he acquires German culture and earns his PhD with a paper on the Marxist theory of class war. Half-blind behind pebble lenses, eloquent in five languages, Arlozorov makes small talk with British colonialists, charms European diplomats, and engages in meaningful dialogue with Arab regimes. He recently hosted the Jordanian king at a dinner in Jerusalem's King David Hotel. Arlozorov is known as Vitaly to Russian friends, Victor to Germans, Chaim in Palestine. He has an aura of authority. People cross a busy road to shake his hand. In the pressure cooker of Zionist politics, he has no venomous enemies.

That Friday evening at Pension Käthe Dan, other diners report a certain tension between Arlozorov and his beautiful wife, Sima. They have been arguing about eating out rather than taking the Sabbath meal with Victor's mother as usual. Victor is just back from a seven-week secret mission in Germany and has been in meetings since his return. Sima wants him to herself, but first Victor must make his excuses to his mother and drop in on his child by a previous marriage. It is after eight thirty p.m. before they sit down to eat, and privacy is hard to come by. Frau Käthe Dan, the pension's owner, flutters around their table, and everyone else in the room is watching them. Pinchas Rosen, a future justice minister, comes over for a chat. Sima finds Victor fretful, out of sorts. At nine thirty p.m., she gets up and says she needs a walk.[1] Both are on their second marriage. Victor knows when to concede.

The paved road ends at Pension Dan (today's Dan Hotel). Victor and Sima stroll north along the seashore beneath a quarter moon. They pass the Muslim cemetery (beside today's Hilton Hotel) and stumble on in pitch darkness toward the Yarkon River. They hear the voices of other couples—out for a stroll, like themselves, or looking for a spot where they can make love—but they see no one. Sima, nervous, says, "Let's go back." Victor presses ahead. Two men brush rudely past Sima. At the Yarkon, Sima's and Victor's moods improve at the sight of a clump of new houses, lit by electricity. They turn back toward home. At the cemetery, they are accosted by the two men who jostled Sima earlier. One shines a flashlight at Victor. "*Kama Hasha'ah?*" (How much would be the hour?) demands the man, in cumbersome Hebrew. Arlozorov tells him it's about quarter past ten. The second man pulls a pistol and shoots him twice in the chest.

"Help!" shouts Sima.

This is what Sima tells the police five hours later. Other witnesses hear her cry, "*Man hat Chaim geschossen*" (They shot Chaim). In a third version, she says: "Jews have killed a Jew!"

Courting couples hear the shot and come running. "They shot Dr. Arlozorov," cries Sima. "I am his wife. Take him to Hadassah" (the hospital). Four men carry Victor to the nearest building, a tannery, and lay him on a pile of sacks, blood pulsing over his festive white shirt. One runs off in search of a telephone. An ambulance arrives. The nearest medical facility is a private clinic on Balfour Street. Word spreads. A crowd gathers. The elderly mayor of Tel Aviv, Meir Dizengoff, barges in. At ten forty-five, Arlozorov is transferred to Hadassah. A surgeon arrives, but there are no blood supplies. A call goes out to the crowd for donors. An operating theater is prepared, and the patient is connected to a transfusion. The moment he receives blood, at twelve forty-five, Victor Arlozorov dies. The cause of death is blood loss, *anemia acuta corporis.*[2] He dies not so much from the bullets as from delays in treatment.

"Who killed Arlozorov?" clamors the crowd. At three a.m., Sima gives a statement to a senior British police officer, Harry Patrick Rice. Colonel Rice, deputy inspector of police and prisons, shows her a dossier of possible suspects, one of whom she half recognizes as an anti-Mapai political agitator. The colonel returns to the murder scene the following night to test the visibility, which is better than expected. It encourages him to believe that Sima will make a positive identification. Rice is so frustrated by the lack of forensic evidence that he orders sniffer dogs to be trained, the first such unit in the country. A reward of £500 is offered by the British government for information and £1,000 by the Jewish Agency.

On the Monday, Rice arrests three members of Vladimir Jabotinsky's Revisionist Party, a breakaway Zionist faction that fights the British and the Arabs. The named suspects are Abba Ahimeir, leader of the Brit Biryonim vigilante group, and two Russian immigrants, Avraham Stavsky and Zvi Rosenblatt. At a lineup in Jaffa jail Sima picks out Stavsky as the man with the flashlight. She asks him to say, "*Kama Hasha'ah?*" informing Rice that he is deliberately distorting his voice. Stavsky, twenty-seven, and Rosenblatt, twenty-two, are charged with capital murder. Ahimeir is held without charge.

The assassination cleaves the Jewish community in Palestine down the middle. Mapai accuses the radicals of cold-blooded murder. Jabotinsky calls Ben-Gurion a British puppet. Ben-Gurion gives pretrial speeches in which he declares Stavsky to be guilty. So acrid is the enmity between the two parties that forty years will pass before their leaders shake hands.

Then Sima changes her story, telling a Jewish policeman that she saw two Arabs with a donkey on the dunes. Perhaps they killed Arlozorov? Abdul Majid Buchari, an Arab facing a long sentence for an honor killing, confesses in January 1934 to the murder of Arlozorov. Sima, however, fails to pick him out of a lineup, and he retracts his statement, saying he was bribed by Stavsky. Rosenblatt is cleared after the girlfriend who fingered him is found to be a Romanian secret agent.

Stavsky goes on trial, defended by Horace Samuel, the former British commissioner's cousin. He claims to have been in a Jerusalem restaurant that night. Two judges find him guilty; a third dissents:

> The Court, by majority, finds that at Tel Aviv, on the night of June 16/17, 1933, with premeditated intent to kill, the accused Abraham Stavsky, did take part in the premeditated killing of Dr Haim Arlosorov by following him, waiting for him, stopping him and directing the light of an electric torch upon him and being close by during the commission of the offense.[3]

Stavsky is sentenced to hang.

The chief rabbi of Palestine, Avraham Hakohen Kook, cries:

> Innocent blood is about to be shed in Jerusalem. I attest on the basis of my inner conscience that Abraham Stavsky is innocent of the murder charge. The absolute truth, known to me, rests with

the one judge who voted for acquittal. Whoever has a divine spark within himself, Jew or non-Jew, must protest and must do his utmost to rescue Stavsky.[4]

Rav Kook's appeal, sent to every Jewish leader from Albert Einstein to Stephen Wise, infuriates Ben-Gurion. The Mapai newspaper *Davar* calls Rav Kook a charlatan. Kibbutz laborers picket his yeshiva. The rabbi repeats that "no Jew participated in this murder." Stavsky puts in an appeal. On the eve of the ninth of Av, a day of Jewish mourning, the Court of Appeals overturns the verdict. Stavsky is carried shoulder-high to Rav Kook's yeshiva and on to the Wailing Wall. He devotes his life to the Revisionist cause, dying from a Mapai bullet in June 1948 as he tries to land the *Altalena* arms ship on the Tel Aviv shore, a few yards up from where Arlozorov died. Zvi Rosenblatt lives to the age of seventy-one, issuing lawsuits against anyone who connects him to the murder. Abba Ahimeir, released in 1935, becomes the teacher of Benzion Netanyahu, father of a future Israeli prime minister. Abba nurtures a paranoid mistrust of Ben-Gurion and Mapai. Thirty-five years later, in the course of a romantic involvement with his niece, I hear that the false accusation still rankles. The death of Arlozorov corrodes Israeli politics from that day to this.

Who killed Arlozorov? If not the Revisionists, might it have been Mapai? The armed wing of the Jewish labor movement, the Haganah, has been known to kill opponents. In June 1924, an ultra-Orthodox homosexual Dutchman, Jacob de Haan, is gunned down by Mapai gunmen near Jerusalem's Shaare Zedek hospital as he leaves evening prayers. De Haan is suspected of secret dealings with Arabs. In January 1948, the Revisionist Yedidyah Segal is kidnapped, tortured, and killed by the Haganah at a house in Haifa. A Haganah murder of six Polish Christians in Jerusalem in the spring of 1948 has recently come to light.[5] These are ruthless executions undertaken on Ben-Gurion's orders. There is, however, no known case of the Haganah killing one of its own. Ben-Gurion might want Arlozorov or other moderates out of his way, but he never asks anyone to remove them, knowing that none of his aides would obey such an order. Ben-Gurion is a risk-averse politician. The hotheads belong to Jabotinsky's ultranationalists. Murder, in Zionist history, is owned by the Revisionists, starting with the assassinations of the British minister of state Lord Moyne and the United Nations mediator Count Bernadotte and culminating in the 1995 assassination of the Israeli prime minister Yitzhak Rabin.

Half a century on, Sima and other survivors are interviewed by Shabtai Teveth, a *Haaretz* journalist who acts as an apologist for Ben-Gurion. Teveth opens a new line of inquiry by looking into Arlozorov's German past. As a teenager, Victor gets to know his sister Lisa's best friend, Magda Friedländer, a jolly, round-faced blonde. Magda has a Jewish stepfather and a Christian mother. She hangs out with Jews and, according to Lisa, longs to live in Palestine. Magda likes Victor. He gives her a Star of David necklace. They are boyfriend and girlfriend until Magda catches Victor with another girl. Victor has a baby with his new girlfriend, Gerda Goldberg. Magda meets a middle-aged businessman, Günther Quandt, a German nationalist who refuses to let her Jewish stepfather, Friedländer, attend the wedding. Victor migrates to Palestine, where Gerda dumps him for a brawnier pioneer, Zvi Luft. Victor seeks consolation with another former girlfriend, Sima Rubin, who is pregnant by another man. Victor, unbothered by bourgeois morality, brings Sima to Palestine, where she bears him two more children, in a volatile marriage marred by Victor's frequent absences and Sima's difficulties in adjusting to heat and dust.

In Berlin, Magda grows bored with Quandt. One night at a dance, she sees Victor Arlozorov, back in town on political business. Magda divorces Quandt and joins the Nazi Party because that's where the action is. In November 1930, she seduces Joseph Goebbels. Adolf Hitler attends their wedding. Bubbly Magda becomes the favorite wife in the Führer's inner circle, giving birth to six blond kids, in addition to Harald, her son by Quandt. Goebbels, a brutal orator and political operative, is crippled by a lack of physical confidence, stemming from a deformed right foot and twisted features. Magda plays on his insecurities. Hearing that he consorts with actresses on his office casting couch, Magda takes lovers of her own. Hitler has to intervene twice to save their marriage.

Now that Hitler is in power, Victor Arlozorov is the only man on the Zionist Executive who knows what needs to be done. He tells the leadership they must extricate as many German Jews as they can before Hitler carries out his threat to kill them. Ben-Gurion is only interested in German Jews if they can be brought to Palestine.

There are two immediate impediments. The British now require every immigrant to show visible means of support, a minimum of £1,000, and the Nazis are refusing to let Jews take any money out of the Reich. The economist Arlozorov comes up with a plan. He proposes that German Jews put their cash into a trust fund, Paltreu (Palästina Treuhandstelle zur Beratung deutscher Juden), which will buy German goods for sale abroad and pay the revenues to immigrants as they reach Palestine, thereby showing proof of assets to the British and saving Germany from a run on the mark. If the Nazis agree to this scheme, Arlozorov will offer to call off the international Jewish boycott of Germany. It's an ingenious political maneuver and one that requires strict secrecy on both sides; the Nazis can't be seen negotiating with Zionists, and Jabotinsky will bring down thunderbolts on any Jew who deals with the Nazis. Arlozorov is brave enough to give it a try.

At the end of April 1933, he sails for Trieste. Moving incognito via Vienna and London, he reaches Berlin on a sunny day in May. His first problem is how to meet the men in power. He has no contacts in the New Germany. Berlin is bedecked in swastikas. On a stroll with journalist Robert Weltsch, he sees in a bookshop window a photographic display of Hitler and his inner circle. Beside Joseph Goebbels, he spots a familiar face. According to Weltsch, Victor falls to the ground in a dead faint. Revived by a passing doctor, he tells Weltsch that he knows Magda Goebbels and he must see her.[6] Weltsch warns him off, but Arlozorov says she is his best and only chance. If he can spend a few minutes with Magda, he will manage to reach the right Nazis to engage with his offer.

There is no record of their secret meeting, or of Magda's apparent agreement to meet again, when Victor returns from Warsaw, where a Zionist Congress is being held. At the Congress, Arlozorov is savaged by the Jabotinskyists for his moderation. Back in Berlin, he receives word from Magda that a second meeting is too risky. Her ex-husband, Quandt, has been arrested by the gestapo, and she fears he might spill the beans about her Jewish background. Goebbels gets her out of this situation by allocating her a radio slot on May 14 to give a talk on "The

German Mother." Hitler is among her listeners. Victor sends his sister Lisa a photograph of Goebbels with the caption "Magda's Bridegroom." Behind closed doors, he reaches outline agreement on Paltreu with the Reichsbank governor, Hjalmar Schacht, soon to be Hitler's minister for economic affairs.[7] The deal is Victor's greatest achievement, enabling sixty thousand Jews to leave Germany for Palestine with some of their assets over the next five years. It may also be the cause of his death.

Goebbels finds out that his wife has been seeing a Zionist leader behind his back and that she was once—may still be—his lover. He needs to shut this down before Hitler hears of it. He has a motive to murder Arlozorov. He also has the means.

Two Nazi agents, Theo Korth and Heino Grönda, have been sent to Palestine on a Goebbels mission to recover a stash of gold buried in 1918 near the Arab town of Jenin by a retreating German sergeant, Karl Todt. The agents meet at the German consulate in Jerusalem on April 5 and set out for Jenin, picking up bits of Hebrew from a phrase book. When they fail to show up in Jenin, the consul, Dr. Wolf, asks Berlin what has become of them. There is no reply. They have either left the country or they have gone to ground, awaiting instructions.

On May 12, Goebbels records in his diary a violent row with Magda. Is this the day he orders Arlozorov's death? Agents Korth and Grönda are well trained, and are acting on his orders and his alone. If they are the hit men, it is conceivable they might identify the target with an awkward "*kamah hasha'ah*" and even more feasible that they should use a dictionary phrase instead of the colloquial "*ma sha'ah*." The only flaw in this theory is the inefficiency of the execution. German hit men would have made sure the victim was dead.

Teveth's book, published in 1982, prompts the prime minister, Menachem Begin, to hold a public inquiry into the Arlozorov murder. There is no conclusive outcome. The case remains unsolved to this day, though new clues come to light from time to time. Schacht's role remains occluded. Sacked by Hitler in January 1943 and sent to concentration camps, Schacht is acquitted of war crimes at the Nuremburg trials and never discusses Paltreu for the rest of his life; he dies in 1970.

Goebbels remains propaganda minister throughout the Third Reich. He and Magda poison their six children in the Führerbunker in the last hours of the Reich, an act so inhuman that even hardened

Nazis recoil. The couple then take their own lives. Magda, it becomes apparent from a later memoir by her mother, might actually have been Friedländer's natural daughter, making her half-Jewish. Had Hitler known this, Goebbels would have lost his job and Magda her life. Had Arlozorov lived, Jewish–Arab and Jewish–German relations might have taken a markedly different course. In modern Tel Aviv, the highway from the commercial center to the sea is named Arlozorov Street, ending at the spot where he was shot.

On the evening of August 30, 1933, a professor is writing at his desk on the first floor of the Villa Edelweiss, a pension in the Czech resort of Marienbad, when two bullets are fired through the open window. He dies within hours. The killers, Rudolf Eckert and Franz Zischka, cross the border into Germany, where they are hailed at a Nuremburg Rally. Their victim, Theodor Lessing, is a philosopher who, until now, has provoked more hatred from Jews than from Nazis.

Lessing's most celebrated book, *Der jüdische Selbsthaß* (*Jewish Self-Hatred*), defines a state of mind in which Jews blame themselves for their misfortunes, a tendency that stems from collective guilt for the sin of the Golden Calf, the destruction of two temples, and the loss of the Holy Land. Lessing holds East European Jews responsible for most Jewish woes, lampooning their indecorous services and disparaging their choice of commerce above any productive occupation. He accuses them of "uglification," scorning the way they dress and their resistance to integration. They are a major cause of anti-Semitism, he decides. Also in his firing line are the descendants of Moses Mendelssohn, who rushed to get baptized as soon as he was dead. His writing, spiced with gallows humor, is full of self-contradiction. He chooses the scurrilous Maximilian Harden, the racialist Otto Weininger, and the assassinated German foreign minister Walther Rathenau as three prototypes of self-hating Jews. Lessing cannot see that he himself is one of those Jews who cannot bear to be what he must be.

The sickly child of a wealthy physician, beaten at home and at school, Lessing concludes that if a child is hated by adults, there must be a reason for it: self-hatred. As a professor in Hannover, his first marriage ends when he uncovers his wife's affair with one of his students, clearly another case of self-hatred. He starts wondering if he is, like Rathenau, a repressed homosexual. In wartime, his essays on the senselessness of conflict are banned by the censor. Lessing turns anti-intellectual, blaming *luftmenschen* (airheads) like himself for Germany's woes. He fights for women's rights and noise abatement, any cause that will get him attention. He particularly hates the sound of piano practice that floats from neighbors' windows. Scandalously, he sets up home with Ada, a divorced journalist, marrying her shortly before their child is born. Far from being a rebel, he craves respectability and cultural recognition; he is a cousin of the playwright Carl Sternheim and the poet Karl Wolfskehl.

Through Ada, his journalism loses its academic stuffiness, and he acquires a column in Sunday newspapers, tilting at big targets such as Thomas Mann and President Hindenburg. Although accustomed to backlash, he is shocked by the hostility to his self-hatred book, suddenly overwhelmed by a fear for Jewish survival. "Now, for the first time," he writes to Martin Buber, "I am alarmed by the weaknesses of our kind. What should be done with this race of ghetto heroes who feel incapable of standing naked in front of a mirror?"[8] The essayist Kurt Tucholsky, in a deathbed note, leaves a wry response to *Jewish Self-Hatred*. "I am proud of being Jewish," says Tucholsky. "If I wasn't proud, I'd still be Jewish. So I'd rather be proud."

Lessing's justification, he writes, is "always punishing myself more sternly and despising myself more severely than anyone else could."[9] His duty is speaking truth to power. His downfall is a warning that Hindenburg, seeking reelection in January 1932, is running as a Trojan horse for a Hitler takeover. "One might say 'Better a zero than a Nero,'" jibes Lessing, "but behind every zero lurks a future Nero." The Nazis go berserk on reading this. Goebbels incites a crowd to shout: "Hang him!" Lessing wonders: "Is this all that will remain of me, a sentence from a Doctor Goebbels speech? That would be terrible." On January 16, 1933, the Nazi clairvoyant Erik Jan Hanussen turns up in Hannover with a prediction that someone in the town will soon meet a violent death. Lessing flees to Prague, where he sees posters in German offering eighty thousand marks for his capture. "My blood froze," he writes.

Germany, he estimates, is losing more than just its Jews. "So we Jews are leaving our native land. With us are the armies of the fathers,

Abraham, Jacob, Moses . . . With us, too, the German guardian spir-
its, Goethe . . . Schubert . . . Dürer."[10] Lessing is the first to understand
that Germany will be culturally devastated. Goebbels, the day after his
assassination, tells a newspaper: "That miserable creep has been wiped
out." Thomas Mann confides to his diary: "I'm afraid of such an end." It
is understood that Goebbels will go to great lengths to erase enemies.
Murder is now an instrument of state policy. If Goebbels can order
Lessing's obliteration, why not Arlozorov's?

Hermann Steinschneider cannot believe his time is up. He has diced
with every kind of danger, often by sleeping with the wives of powerful men and keeping their secrets as insurance. Steinschneider gets
away with it because he is a stage star with charm to spare and politicians who owe him money. Nobody calls him Steinschneider. His stage
name is Erik Jan Hanussen, and there are few bigger names on a Berlin
newsstand. Hanussen sells magazines like no one else. He sees into the
future, and his predictions come true. Nazis or no Nazis, he has nothing to fear. It is widely believed he has hypnotized Hitler.

On March 24, 1933, his credit runs out. Four SA men call at his luxury home and take him down to the prison on General-Pape-Strasse.
On the ride, Steinschneider chats with his captors, two of whom he has
met before on social occasions. In the interrogation room, he offers a
deal: top secrets in exchange for freedom. The mood changes. He is
hauled out of jail by Sturmbannführer Wilhelm Ohst and dragged back
to the SA car. Ohst is Göring's linkman with SA chief Röhm. He also
runs missions for their mutual enemy, Goebbels.

It is the middle of the night when the prisoner is returned to
General-Pape-Strasse, thrown down a flight of stairs, and shot three
times, in the stomach, the neck, and the back of his head. His corpse,
torn apart by wolves, is found two weeks later by foresters in the woods
outside Berlin. The Goebbels press reports: "The body of a Jew was
found in an evergreen grove on the road from Bayreuth to Neuhof. He
had been shot dead. His face was unrecognisable. At the morgue, the
body was identified as Hermann Steinschneider who, under the name
of Hanussen, had a certain vogue in Berlin as a clairvoyant." The *New*

York Times headline reads: "Seer Who Told Hitler's Rise Found Slain; Hanussen Was Adviser to European-Royalty."[11] Nazi bosses and the world's press find themselves asking the same question: Who the hell was Hanussen? The facts are not hard to find.

A synagogue caretaker's son in Vienna, Herschel Chaim Steinschneider joins a circus in his teens and masters elementary escapology. In the occult fad that sweeps Europe after the war, he stars in a silent film, *Hypnose*. Not yet twenty years old, he finances a second film, *The Mysterious Death*, before leaving Austria under allegations of theft and fraud.

In Berlin, under a Danish name, he tells people's futures onstage by means of mind reading and hypnosis. Hyped by the gutter press, he fills big theaters and gives private séances for wealthy women. Exactly how and when he meets Hitler is undocumented. An American spy report dates their first encounter to the early 1920s, when the unformed Führer takes "regular lessons in speaking and in mass psychology" from this master manipulator. Hermann joins Hitler's inner circle and keeps the others sweet by lending them untraceable amounts of cash. His theater act gains a patina of political punditry, always chillingly accurate. He seems to anticipate what the Nazis will do next.

In 1931, he buys a printing press and launches a gossip magazine. His girlfriends wear furs, and he employs a valet. When Hitler comes to power, he is thirty-three years old and the only Jew in Berlin with nothing to fear, although he prudently sends his ex-wife and twelve-year-old daughter to an Italian resort. In the first three weeks of Nazi rule, Hermann loses none of his swagger. Then he makes a fatal error. On February 24, he predicts that "a great German government building is on fire . . . The Führer's enemies have set it on fire. A dastardly crime! We must stamp out the vermin who try to steal victory from the Führer and set up Bolshevism in its place."[12]

On February 27, the Reichstag goes up in flames. How did Steinschneider know? The word is he was called in to hypnotize the arsonist Marinus van der Lubbe before he struck the match. Göring, who arrests five thousand Communists for the crime, is made to look stupid by Steinschneider's prediction, as is Berlin's SA commander, Karl Ernst, who is the actual organizer of the fire. Ernst owes Steinschneider a fortune. He has good reason to want him out of the way. It is Ernst's deputy Ohst who arrests Steinschneider and puts him in a Göring jail, where other grudge-bearers can give him a kicking.

No one knows who administers the fatal blow, but, unusually under the Nazis, this political murder has judicial consequences. Ohst is arrested in January 1934 and again in June before he is dismissed from the SA and left to his own devices. Ohst is the only suspect still alive when Steinschneider's widow finally gets the West German police to reopen the case in the 1960s. His boss, Karl Ernst, is long gone. After Hitler acts as best man at his wedding in June 1934, Ernst is arrested en route to his honeymoon, taken to an SS barracks, and shot. Another Steinschneider SA pal, Count Wolf-Heinrich von Helldorf, vanishes from Berlin just before the murder.[13] He judiciously switches to Goebbels's staff but, implicated in the July 1944 plot against Hitler, is hanged in the most horrible fashion.

Erika Steinschneider, the victim's daughter, keeps the case alive until her death in October 2016. Three film directors—Otto Wilhelm Fischer, István Szabó, and Werner Herzog—retell the story. The most recent book is titled *El mentalista de Hitler*. That a Jew could fool the Führer for so long is fascinating. The response to his disappearance confirms Hitler's perpetual sense of insecurity. Arlozorov, Lessing, and Steinschneider look like a settling of personal accounts by Goebbels and Hitler, a prelude to mass murder.

The typical Nazi murder is marked by exemplary cruelty. Erich Mühsam is arrested in March 1933 as he is packing to leave the country. He is taken to the Sonnenburg concentration camp, where his glasses are smashed underfoot, his teeth knocked out, and clumps of hair pulled from his head. The former Cabinet minister is subjected to daily beatings. When he asks permission to send a letter to his wife, the camp commandant grabs his hands, breaks both thumbs, and orders him: "Now, write a letter." At the Oranienburg camp, he is caged with a chimpanzee, which, instead of mauling him, is soothed by the poet's voice.

On July 9, 1934, Mühsam is ordered to commit suicide. "They want me to hang myself—but I will not do them the favor," he tells fellow prisoners. The next morning his corpse is found hanging from a beam in the latrines. "Mühsam had been beaten to death before he was hanged," a prisoner confirms. His widow writes: "I have seen Erich dead. He looked so beautiful. There was no fear on his face; his cold hands were so gorgeous when I kissed them goodbye."

Zenzl Mühsam leaves Hitler's Germany for Stalin's Russia, taking with her all of Erich's unpublished writings. These papers are confiscated by the Soviet state and never seen again. Zenzl is put on trial for Trotskyist and counterrevolutionary acts. She spends the next twenty years in Siberia.

THIRTEEN

1938
CITIES OF REFUGE

Leo Szilard relives the day he got Einstein
to write to the White House.

Four days after the Anschluss, two SA men knock at Egon Friedell's
door. Friedell, a former cabaret artist–turned–cultural historian,
is a barometer of Viennese mood. As a Jew and a satirist, he knows
what to expect. As his housekeeper stalls the Nazis at the door, Friedell
opens a third-floor window and, calling out to the people below to
stand aside, jumps to his death. He is fifty years old.

That month, March 1938, hundreds of Jews commit suicide, many of them as whole families together, according to an American embassy report. Terror scars the city. In the Taborstrasse of the second district, ultra-Orthodox women are made to remove their head coverings, throw them on a bonfire, and dance until they drop. The chief rabbi, Israel Taglich, is thrust to his knees to scrub pavements. In the Prater park, Jews are made to lie on the grass while jackboots stamp on their hands. The cabarettist Felix Grünbaum is beaten to death. The novelist Leo Perutz evades the same fate by showing his Iron Cross. The playwright Carl Zuckmayer claims he is a film writer "and the Führer loves films." Baron Louis de Rothschild is hauled off a plane, his passport ripped to pieces. He is taken to the gestapo headquarters at the Hotel Metropole until a ransom is extorted from his bank. SS lieutenant Adolf Eichmann, a self-styled "Jewish expert," likes to tease victims with Talmudic quotations. He schedules psychological tortures for Jewish holy days. Sixty-seven thousand Jews are arrested.

The world's indifference to Vienna's terror encourages the Nazis to intensify anti-Jewish action in Germany. In June, a temple in Munich is torn down; in Nuremberg, another is set on fire. Neville Chamberlain's Munich surrender reinforces Hitler's sense of inviolability. The November shooting of an official at the German embassy in Paris is the trigger for a Kristallnacht orgy of arson, arrests, and assaults. Fourteen hundred synagogues are desecrated. A rabbi of my family is beaten up in the streets of Munich as he pulls Torah scrolls from the flames. After the beating, he is dragged to a gestapo jail. Next morning, his wife comes banging at the gate with a bundle. "Go away," she is told, "don't you know what the gestapo is?"

"My husband needs his shawl and phylacteries for his prayers," says the young woman. "Make sure he receives them."

Twelve days later, as she lights the Sabbath candles, the rabbi stumbles home. "I did not recognise him, shaved bare of hair and beard and with a frightened look on his face."[1] Traumatized by their ordeals, heads of family decide to migrate. Michael Blumenthal, a future US Treasury secretary, sees his father come home "after six weeks in Buchenwald, a shrunken and broken man. One day he was back, a small, pitiful figure sitting in his old living room chair, a gaunt sixty pounds lighter . . . I remember two Sundays when eager buyers trooped through our apartment on the Kurfürstendamm to look for bargains among the household effects being sold at whatever price."[2] Those with friends and family abroad can often obtain visas. The less fortunate queue for days outside consulates. The gates of mercy are slamming shut. Britain cuts Palestine entry to fifteen thousand Jews a year over the next five years. America imposes a pitiful quota of a few thousand for the whole of Europe; Canada admits a few hundred. Brazil bars Jews. Australia is inhospitable. A conference of thirty-two countries called by President Roosevelt at Évian in Switzerland resolves that no one wants Jews, signaling that Hitler can do as he pleases. It takes an exceptional individual to swim against the onrushing tide.

In Vienna, a new Chinese consul-general, Dr. Feng-Shan Ho, cannot bear to watch the collapse of German civilization without rendering some service to humanity. Dr. Ho, a Munich-trained political economist, decides to create a haven for Jews. China is under invasion by Japanese forces. China's ruler, Chiang Kai-shek, is generally pro-German; his son is a lieutenant in Hitler's 98th Jaeger Regiment in Vienna. The ambassador in Berlin orders Dr. Ho not to waste his time on Jews. But Dr. Ho has an idea. He knows that the city of Shanghai is in near anarchy, under four or five different jurisdictions. The French control an elegant concession in the south and west, the British police two northern areas, and China hangs on to whichever parts the Japanese have not yet occupied. Shanghai is home to untold millions, with room for more. Dr. Ho starts to issue Shanghai visas to Viennese Jews, at first hundreds, then thousands. The visas are worthless in lawless Shanghai but a visa constitutes proof to the Nazis that an emigrant has someplace to go. Shanghai becomes Shangri-La.

The exact number of lives saved by one Chinese official is unknown. In the twelve months after the Anschluss, Dr. Ho distributes almost five thousand visas, at a rate of four hundred a month. In 1939, as war looms, he redoubles his efforts, sending batches of visas to Jews in other countries, including an entire yeshiva in Lithuania. Shanghai takes in eighteen thousand Jews, four thousand of them with Dr. Ho visas. This one man, operating without backup and against his government's policy, saves innumerable Jewish lives.[3] Imagine if there had been more like him.

• • •

The Jews who reach Shanghai are not the first. The city has a nineteenth-century Sephardi community of Baghdad and Bombay traders, the Sassoons, Kedouris, Ezras, and Abrahams. These clans have left their mark on the Bund waterfront, with art deco office blocks and the spectacularly decadent Cathay Hotel, home to the monocled Sir Victor Sassoon, who spends his happiest days on the race course. Anglophile to a fault, at four o' clock the Iraqi Jews take tea poured from silver teapots. Sir Victor pays for the Ohel Rachel Synagogue on Seymour Road.

The French Concession is home to refugees from Russia's pogroms and revolutions. Their occupations are motley and their faith vestigial, to the despair of the rabbi of the Ashkenazi Ohel Moshe Synagogue. The Russian Jews run fur stores, hardware stores, truck networks, and smuggling rackets. One of their wild men, Morris "Two-Gun" Cohen, becomes a Chinese general.

The new wave of Viennese refugees is collected at the port by charity workers and driven to run-down Hongkew, where temporary *heime* have been set up. The newcomers are issued "blankets, bedsheets and a tin dish, cup and spoon, fed from communal kitchens and given some useful good advice," writes Michael Blumenthal. "The collective will to make life bearable was surprisingly vibrant and strong. Debris was cleared and houses made liveable. Little stores and restaurants sprang up. There were synagogues, schools, a hospital, theatres, concerts and sports for the young. Everyone spoke German and the atmosphere resembled a German quarter, part Vienna and part Berlin."[4] American Jews send relief funds. Newspapers appear in six languages.

On December 8, 1941, the Japanese seize control of the entire city, and, in February 1943, they corral the Jews into a ghetto for "military necessity." Despite German pressure, the Japanese refuse to kill their Jews. Japanese guards speak warmly of the New York Jew, Jacob Schiff, who backed their side in the 1905 Russian war. "Why do the Germans hate you so much?" a Japanese commandant asks a learned rabbi. "Maybe because we're orientals," comes the reply. Although conditions are cramped and food meager, members of my family look back on the Hongkew ghetto without fear or rancor. Along with most foreigners, they are asked to leave Shanghai when the Communists take control. Among those who remain, Ruth Weiss, a Viennese teacher at the Hebrew school, is allowed to join the Communist Party, and

Dr. Jakob Rosenfeld becomes commander of Mao's medical corps. On the wall of the Ohel Moshe Synagogue, preserved as a museum, a plaque states proudly that China is the only country in the world that knew no anti-Semitism. The raucous streets around the synagogue, a Chinese friend tells me, are still known to older inhabitants as Little Vienna.

Two high school chums from Cleveland have an idea for a comic strip and take it to New York. The first issue, dated April 18, 1938, sells so well that the hero gets his name on a series. An American icon is born. Jerry Siegel, one of the creators, sees his father die of a heart attack after being beaten up in his store. Joe Shuster has a newspaper route. The character they create, Clark Kent, is a journalist with the *Daily Planet*, with an alternative life as Superman, a red-caped invincible being from outer space. All Clark Kent has to do is rip open his button-down office shirt to expose his T-shirt, and he is able to lift cars off the street and hurl them head-high.

Superman is created by Depression-era kids of immigrant parents who have been crushed by the rough side of American life. The monosyllabic moniker "Clark Kent" denotes successful integration. Kent's girlfriend, Lois Lane, lacks any distinguishing features. Superman is a revival of the medieval Golem of Prague, who avenges attacks on the Jews. "What led me into creating Superman in the early thirties?" says Siegel. "Hearing and reading of the oppression and slaughter of helpless, oppressed Jews in Nazi Germany . . . seeing movies depicting the horrors of privation suffered by the downtrodden . . ."[5] A year behind Superman, Bob Kane (Kahn) and his pal Bill Finger create Batman, the next all-American superhero. In 1940, Joseph Goebbels warns the German people that Superman is a Jew.

A young man in London, frustrated by committees, forms a one-man European rescue operation. Solomon Schonfeld is twenty-six years old, a reluctant rabbi, ordained after his father's early death. He would have preferred to read literature at university, but he heads off to complete his studies at a yeshiva in Slovakia, and he returns to lead the Adath

Yisroel community with a nagging fear for the Jews in central Europe. When the Nazis enter Vienna, he springs into action.

Blue-eyed, blond-bearded, six feet tall, and with a taste for cricket and English poetry, Solomon Schonfeld does not look like an ultra-Orthodox rabbi. A quicksilver wit, with a voice like thunder when roused, he wears an immaculate black coat and, on formal occasions, a gleaming top hat. Among the timid Anglo-Jewish clergy, he stands out like Apollo.

Schonfeld's guerrilla activities are, of necessity, undocumented. I rely on anecdotal evidence from his supporters, who are themselves kept mostly in the dark. No one can tell me, for instance, how Schonfeld finds his way into the impenetrable Home Office; other Jewish leaders cannot get past the lobby. My guess is that an old schoolmate inveigles him into the immigration control section. Over a cup of tea, his roars of laughter rolling down Horse Guards Parade, one of the officials asks, "How can we help you, Dr. Schonfeld?"

"Well, it's like this," says the rabbi. "You see, I've become for my sins the pastor of an orthodox flock in Stoke Newington and I find to my dismay that we lack the sacerdotal experts we need to help us fulfil religious duties."

"How so?"

"I need qualified, rigorous people to lead services, chant from the Torah, make fringes for our garments, supervise kosher facilities, conduct circumcisions and the like. We simply haven't got such people in this country . . ."

"And where would you find them?"

"Vienna," cries Schonfeld.

On the strength of a conversation like this (I hear his voice booming in my ear), Schonfeld heads to Vienna with five hundred visas for religious officiants and their families. Weeks later, he is back at the Home Office.

"How can we help you, Dr. Schonfeld?"

"There's something that slipped my mind," he confesses. "You see, these religious specialists have rather large families and I'm having to start a school for their children. I've got premises but where do I find teachers for specialist subjects like Mishna, and Rashi, and Talmud?"

"Would that be Vienna, Dr. Schonfeld?"

"You took the word right out of my mouth."

A second trip plucks more brands from the burning, and he keeps going back. Arriving back in London, Schonfeld knocks at the doors of his congregants, telling each family how many refugees he expects them to take in. "But, Dr. Schonfeld . . . ," they protest. "No buts," he shouts. Once, when a bus he has hired breaks down, he persuades all the taxi drivers at Victoria Station to carry refugees to their new homes for free. After Kristallnacht, he concentrates on children, working with other organizations on the so-called Kindertransport. When the Nazis arrange for one train to depart on the Sabbath, Schonfeld, with the blessing of the Reform rabbi Leo Baeck, refuses to let the children board until after nightfall. On the paperwork, each arriving child is supposed to have a relative already in the UK. Where no such relative exists, Schonfeld invents one. He is inflexible, infuriating, irresistible.

He calls my father late one night. "I need fifty pounds." We are not a wealthy family, and that's a big sum.

"What's it for?" says my dad.

"Rescue."

"I haven't got that kind of money . . ."

"Consider it a loan." When my dad dies, we find more such requests in his desk drawer.

One Friday night, he sits with my uncle Mark and others, polishing documents for refugees. As it is a matter of life and death, the Sabbath prohibition on written work is suspended. Sometime after midnight, Uncle Mark gets up. "Solly," he tells the rabbi, "we are breaking the laws of God and the law of the land and my nerves are shot to pieces. I need a cigarette."

Schonfeld freezes him with a coral-blue glare. "Mark," he shouts, "*shabbes!*" Under no circumstances will he permit the Sabbath to be broken for the indulgence of a smoke.

From January 1939 to the outbreak of war, twenty-two thousand refugees are admitted to Britain from Germany, Austria, and Czechoslovakia, many under Schonfeld's auspices. He is sleepless, tireless, tenderly compassionate. His jacket pocket jangles with half crowns that he dispenses as pocket money to the most distressed children. Every Sabbath, he walks ten miles between Stoke Newington, Highgate, Hampstead, Hendon, and Edgware, visiting his synagogues and schools, radiating good cheer, escorted on the hike by handpicked teenaged boys and girls, whom he questions along the way about their studies, their ambitions, and their beliefs.

He has no time for a private life until the coming of war puts his rescue efforts on hold. In January 1940, in a private ceremony in the home of Chief Rabbi Joseph Hertz, he marries the chief's daughter, Judith. The aging Hertz calls him "my Cossack." This does not stop Schonfeld attacking Hertz's United Synagogue and his unbearded rabbis for their perceived religious laxities. He thrives on conflict and crisis. These are his finest hours, evacuating his schools to the countryside when the Blitz begins, ensuring that no refugee is uncared for. Asked by his children in later life to recount his adventures, Rabbi Dr. Solomon Schonfeld changes the subject. "It is He who gave me these tasks," he says, "and I would not want to appear to take credit for what He's done, just in case He doesn't ask me again."

One man, ten thousand lives.

In Berlin, a German businessman with dual nationality is under no immediate danger. Wilfrid Israel, head of a landmark department store on Alexanderplatz, is an international entrepreneur of impeccable respectability who frequents gay clubs after dark. He puts his double life to the service of saving others. "His over-civilized, prim, finely drawn, beaky profile gave him the air of a bird in a piece of Chinese embroidery" is how the English writer Christopher Isherwood describes him in *Goodbye to Berlin*. "He was soft, negative, I thought, yet curiously potent with the static potency of a carved ivory figure in a shrine. I noticed again his beautiful English and the deprecatory gestures of his hands, as he showed me a twelfth-century sandstone head of Buddha from Khmer which stood at the foot of his bed."[6]

Israel's, the family department store, changes its name under the Nazis but not its management. Wilfrid lets the wives of Nazi leaders buy on credit and does not always send the bill. Ordered to fly a swastika flag on some Nazi holiday, he refuses.[7] He is arrested twice and beaten, saved by being a British citizen, born in London, the great-grandson of Chief Rabbi Nathan Adler. Concerned for his Jewish staff, among them Martin Buber's son and Rabbi Leo Baeck's nephew, Wilfrid goes to Palestine to find them homes. In Berlin, he befriends a foreign ministry aristocrat, Adam von Trott zu Solz, and a British spy, Frank Foley. Trott is a conduit to the anti-Hitler opposition. Foley, head of the MI6 station, issues visas to anyone Wilfrid sends to him. Son of a railway worker, Foley has no time for embassy toffs and Foreign Office protocol. He is out to help the helpless, some of whom will join his network. A scientist, Paul Rosbaud, needs visas for his Jewish wife and child. In exchange, he obtains for Foley Germany's nuclear and rocket-building plans. Rosbaud, brother of the renowned conductor Hans Rosbaud, spies for Foley through to the end of the war.

Fearless and inconspicuous, Foley drives to the gates of concentration camps to demand the release of men who, he claims, enjoy British protection. After Kristallnacht, as consular queues spill into the street, he refuses a spell of home leave to get more Jews out of Berlin. His wife, Kay, offers a bed in their Lessingstrasse home to people at risk, including Rabbi Baeck. "Often we heard how wives were called to the Gestapo headquarters to collect their husbands' belongings," writes Kay. "When they got there, they were handed an envelope containing ashes . . . I don't know what the Nazis would have done if they had discovered we were hiding Jews."[8]

Lacking diplomatic immunity, Foley could have been made to disappear without international consequences. He stays in Berlin until the day war breaks out, moving first to Norway, then home, tending his networks all the while. His name comes to light at the Eichmann trial in Jerusalem in 1961. "There was one man who stood out above all others like a beacon," says a witness, "Captain Foley, Passport Officer in the British Consulate in the Tiergarten in Berlin, a man who in my opinion was among the greatest among the nations of the world." In January 2019, a bust of Foley is installed in the lobby of the Foreign Office in Whitehall by the foreign secretary, Jeremy Hunt, who extols Foley's lifesaving exploits. He confides that Foley "happens to be the father-in-law of my cabinet colleague, James Brokenshire. Others [whom he saved] include the grandparents of an SIS officer who is serving today."

In Berlin, Wilfrid Israel's store is ransacked on Kristallnacht, and he is urged to emigrate. He replies, indicating Leo Baeck: "I will go when the rabbi goes." "I will go," declares Baeck, "when I am the last Jew alive in Germany."[9] Baeck, who stays with his community to the bitter end, sends Wilfrid to London to arrange accommodation for Kinder-transport children. At home among the Anglo-Jewish hierarchy and well connected in commercial circles, Wilfrid is a tireless organizer. "I have tried to live according to my principles and I have tried to make a supportive contribution with all my power," he tells Albert Einstein.[10] Unlike the general run of department-store owners, his friends are artists and intellectuals.

At risk of his life, in the final week of August 1939, Wilfrid returns to Germany one last time, to escort a trainload of children. Unable to find a home in London for one boy, he takes him under his own roof. In wartime, he maintains contact with German dissidents and advises the Churchill government. At the end of March 1943, he flies to Lisbon to push ahead with schemes for rescuing children from Vichy France. Flying home five weeks later, his plane is attacked by eight Luftwaffe fighters, operating on false intelligence that Churchill is on board. Wilfrid, forty-two years old, is declared "lost at sea." Einstein condoles with his grieving mother: "Never in my life have I come in contact with a being so noble, so strong and as selfless as he was—in very truth a living work of art."

Days before Christmas 1938, a London stockbroker is about to go skiing in Switzerland when a letter arrives from a friend in need. Martin Blake, a teacher at Westminster School, tells Nicholas Winton that he has hundreds of children on his hands in Prague. The children have been displaced from the Nazi-occupied Sudetenland, and the challenge is to get them out before Hitler grabs the rest of the country. Winton arrives in Prague on New Year's Day 1939. Setting up office in a hotel dining room on Wenceslas Square, he focuses on getting travel passes for unaccompanied minors through the bureaucracy of third-party countries. He is a devil for detail and relishes the work, imploring his employer for an extra week's leave. On January 12, he sees twenty children, converted to Christianity by their desperate parents, flown out to London by a missionary organization.

Winton does what brokers do best: he makes connections. At a party, he meets a Swedish woman who agrees to take thirty children. On a train, he chats with a motorcycle salesman who turns out to be a former British MP. Back in London, Winton secures the Home Office's agreement that orphans will be admitted on a deposit of £50. From his Hampstead living room, he raises funds and attention. Press cameras are waiting when 130 children from Prague arrive at Liverpool Street Station. In all, he extricates 669 children, the oldest in her late teens, the youngest a three-year-old boy. Then he reverts to obscurity, driving an ambulance in France before joining the RAF.

Nicholas Winton does not act alone. He gives particular credit to a schoolmaster, Trevor Chadwick, who faces down the gestapo in Prague over every single child, and to a few other volunteers. It takes half a dozen English men and women to save 669 children. Winton, as the one who organizes foster homes and follows up on their care, is the most visible. If only there had been more like him—and like Feng-Shan Ho, like Solomon Schonfeld, Wilfrid Israel, Frank Foley, and Trevor Chadwick.

The endings are not always happy. Although some Kindertransport children grow up to lead brilliant and valuable lives—they include a Labour MP, a groundbreaking filmmaker, and a mathematician of genius—many are haunted by a nagging guilt. "Why me?" agonizes one elderly survivor. "Why was I put on the train when most of my class went to the gas? Have I done enough to justify being saved?"[11] Another, finding his parents alive after the camps, rejects them for having sent him away. The psychological damage to the transported Kinder is often incurable. The three-year-old boy on the final train is so traumatized that he spends his entire adult life in British mental institutions.[12]

On the last train out of Prague on March 14, 1939, Max Brod carries Franz Kafka's papers in a bulging suitcase. The train departs at eleven at night. Brod awakes at dawn on the Polish border, to see German troops sealing off his former country. Making his way to Tel Aviv, he is immediately offered the job of dramaturg, or artistic consultant, to the Habimah Theatre. He sets to work commissioning writers, analyzing productions, composing incidental music for new plays. There is nothing in the theater he cannot do.

Sharing a three-room apartment with his wife and two other families, he fears for the safety of the Kafka suitcase and offers it to the

National Library. Unable to obtain a positive response, he appeals to the publisher Salman Schocken to store the case in the iron safe of his Balfour Street mansion in Jerusalem. Schocken, flattered, agrees that only Brod will have a key to this drawer; deviously, he makes a second key for himself. Deceits and equivocations will dog Kafka's legacy until, controversially, in August 2016 the Israeli Supreme Court consigns the suitcase to the National Library.

In Tel Aviv, on summer afternoons, wearing a three-piece suit and tie, Max Brod might stroll beside the sea with his old pal, music teacher Leo Kestenberg, often with a student or two skipping beside them to learn from their exchanges. These are years of high tension, with the Italians bombing Tel Aviv, the Germans advancing to the Egyptian border, and the Palestinian leader, Haj Amin al-Husseini, urging Hitler in Berlin to make common cause in the destruction of the Jews.

Brod and Kestenberg speak only of art: What can be done to raise the human spirit once this madness is over? How can humanity be rescued? Kestenberg has developed his own style of teaching, never touching the piano during a private lesson. If the student does not meet his expectations, he announces that they are going for a walk. On the seafront or in a grove of trees, Kestenberg expatiates on Goethe, Wagner, and the infinite varieties of the eucalyptus tree, an Australian impostor that sucks too hard at the water sources of the Holy Land. Kestenberg is knowledgeable about many esoteric subjects. When they get back to the piano, the student finds that the Chopin he or she plays sounds quite different.[13]

A British parliamentary delegation visiting Tel Aviv is taken to a building site where new homes are being prepared for refugees from Hitler. An MP sees the laborers' lips moving as they pass bricks down the line. "What are they saying?" he wonders. Drawing closer, he hears, *"Bitte, Herr Doktor,"* *"Danke, Herr Doktor."*

Joseph Stalin has two favorite poets, both Jews. In April 1934, Boris Pasternak runs into Osip Mandelstam on Tverskoy Boulevard in Moscow. Mandelstam insists on reciting to him, out loud and in broad daylight, his latest poem, "Stalin Epigram." The closing couplet reads: "And every killing is a treat / For the broad-chested Ossete." Pasternak tells him: "I didn't hear this, you didn't recite it to me."[14]

That night, Mandelstam is arrested. The poet Anna Akhmatova sees secret policemen from the NKVD ransack his flat. She calls a friend deep inside the Kremlin. Pasternak appeals for help to the editor of *Izvestia*, Nikolai Bukharin. The phone rings in Pasternak's apartment. "What do they say in literary circles about Mandelstam's arrest?" demands the voice of Joseph Stalin. Pasternak stutters, stumbles, equivocates. Stalin rebukes him: "If a poet friend of mine was in trouble, I would do anything to save him." He assures Pasternak that Mandelstam will not be executed. "I have wanted to talk to you for a while," adds Stalin.

"About what?"

"About life and death," says Stalin, hanging up.

Mandelstam is exiled for three years to Voronezh, in southwest Russia. Pasternak wonders: "How could he write a poem like that when he's *a Jew*?" In the Great Terror, the fear is greatest among Jews. Mandelstam returns to Moscow just as Stalin is liquidating the last of Lenin's Bolsheviks. In March 1938, Bukharin is shot, and the poets lose their protector. Mandelstam is sent to Siberia. He is made to stand naked in the snow during registration. Typhus sets in. At his death on December 27, 1938, Mandelstam is forty-seven years old.

Pasternak outlives Stalin, only to be crushed by Khrushchev, who forces him to turn down the Nobel Prize in Literature, for the Revolution-era romantic novel *Doctor Zhivago*. Pasternak learns that he has been betrayed by the woman who was his model for the heroine, Lara. On his deathbed, in May 1960, he is ravaged by anxiety. "Who will suffer most because of my death?" he cries.

In Stalin's Russia, German refugees suffer most. The conductor Kurt Sanderling lies in bed at night, listening to NKVD boots stomping through his building. Once the boots pass his door, he feels tremendous relief, only to be tormented by guilt for his joy at having been spared when neighbors and friends are taken, never to be seen again.[15]

Martin Buber's daughter-in-law Margarete flees to Moscow with Heinz Neumann, her second husband. Neumann is arrested in April 1937 and shot. Margarete is sent to a labor camp, where she shares a hut with Zenzl Mühsam, Carola Neher, and other Weimar dreamers. Under the Hitler-Stalin pact, Russia returns German escapees to the Nazis. Margarete is sent to the Ravensbrück concentration camp, where she befriends Milena Jesenská, Kafka's lover. Milena dies of kidney failure. Margarete writes an autobiography titled *Under Two Dictators*. Between Stalin and Hitler, she concludes, there is not much to choose.

Budapest, 10 percent Jewish overall, 20 percent in the inner city, is profligate with its talent. It strews its best and brightest around the world as the dictatorship of Admiral Horthy imposes a *numerus clausus* (fixed maximum number) on Jews entering universities and public service, choking any chance of advancement. Three Jewish brothers by the name of Korda (born Kellner) head to London, where they kick-start the British film industry with *Henry the Eighth*, the best film of 1933. Alexander Korda, the eldest, makes a star of Charles Laughton, signs up Laurence Olivier and Vivien Leigh, and masterminds the postwar thriller *The Third Man*. The second brother, Vincent, wins an Oscar for art direction for *The Thief of Baghdad*, directed in Hollywood by the third brother, Zoltan. More than filmmakers, the Kordas are talent magnets. All that newcomers need to get a screen test is two words of English: "Mister Korda." Alex founds Denham Studios, just outside London, marries Merle Oberon, and is knighted by King George VI in 1942. He stakes a fortune on bringing *Anna Karenina* to the screen, suffers an unmitigated flop, and continues to make thoughtful moneylosers: *The Four Feathers*, *The Winslow Boy*.

Budapest Jews—Andre Kertész, Robert Capa, László Moholy-Nagy, Gilberte Brassai—invent documentary photography. The marketing is done through picture agencies—Magnum, Hulton, Rex, Camera Press—set up by their ex–Budapest friends. Capa takes the most arresting war picture of all time: a Spanish volunteer, hit by a hail of bullets, captured as he falls. "It's not enough to have talent," crows Capa, "you also have to be Hungarian." Budapest yields America's next crop of orchestral conductors: Eugene Ormandy, Fritz Reiner, George Szell, Georg Solti, Antal Doráti. Hollywood fills with Hungarian producers, directors, actors, composers: Adolph Zukor, George Cukor, Bela Lugosi, Zsa Zsa Gabor, Miklós Rózsa. A Hungarian Jew, Biro, invents the ballpoint pen, another (disputedly) the zip fastener. The emigrant ingenuity is boundless, spiced with paprika wit.

While Budapest Jews might be expected to excel in the arts, their impact on science is unforeseen and, literally, earth-shattering. Hampered by Horthy's laws, four Jewish teenagers go to Berlin to study. John von Neumann, before the age of thirty, will compose the mathematical formulation of quantum mechanics. Eugene Wigner, a future Nobel winner (with Maria Goeppert Mayer and J. H. D. Jensen) for contributions to the theory of the atomic nucleus, works on group theory. Jolly Edward Teller becomes "the father of the hydrogen bomb." Leo Szilard, the one who wins no prizes, saves the world.

A contemplative character who likes nothing better than sitting in a field for hours, staring at a blue sky, or spending the whole morning in the bath, Szilard grows up with the German name Leo Spitz in a prosperous suburb, disconcerting his parents with his aversion to water and physical exercise (both markers of autism). "I was born a scientist," he would say. "I believe that many children are born with an inquisitive mind, the mind of a scientist, and I assume that I became a scientist because in some ways I remained a child."[16] A kind of naïveté clings to his utterances, some of them oracular. At sixteen, he warns his parents that there is going to be a world war. Pressed into uniform, he fights for his country, only to be barred at the Budapest Technical School by the slogan "You can't study here, you're Jews." Officials stamp his exit visa vindictively with a blue cross, the mark of a Communist revolutionary. Applying to enter Max Planck's class in Berlin, he says, "I only want to know the facts of physics. The theories I will make up for myself." He approaches Einstein for a tutorial in statistical mechanics, inviting his best friend Wigner to attend, together with von Neumann. Einstein takes a shine to Szilard, signing off on his doctoral thesis, "On the Extension of Phenomenological Thermodynamics to Fluctuation Phenomena." Szilard walks Einstein home after lectures, each challenging the other to think the impossible. Together, they invent an electromagnetic pump for refrigerators, with the idea of improving domestic food safety. The pump proves too noisy in the home, which deters the market leader, General Electric. The inventors sell seven patents to Sweden's Electrolux company.

Szilard's sixth sense starts twitching, and he sleeps with two packed

313

suitcases beside the door. In Berlin, he has a relationship, of sorts, with his landlady's daughter, a singer called Gerda Philipsborn, who has studied with the conductor Bruno Walter. Gerda, three years his senior, has good shorthand and handles some of his correspondence. She is a curious young woman with private means. She supports a youth village in Palestine, visiting it in 1932, and then travels on to India, where she teaches at a Muslim school, the Jamia Millia Islamia, and takes a vow of poverty. Szilard talks of joining her, but nothing comes of it. Gerda dies in 1943; Szilard carries her picture in his wallet ever after.[17]

A medical student, Trude Weiss, nine years his junior, is smitten with him. Trude is pretty, with coal-black eyebrows, dark eyes, and a lively mind. Szilard offers her career advice but will not commit. In March 1933, while other Berlin scientists wait to see what Nazism means, Szilard loads his two bags onto a train, heads to Vienna, then Geneva, and then on to London, where he takes a room at the Imperial Hotel, a gloomy pile near the British Museum. For the next eighteen years, he lives only in hotels.

Einstein urges him to recruit refugees for a Jewish university in England. He joins the economist William Beveridge at the Academic Assistance Council, telling everyone he meets that Germany will win the next war on the scientific front. On September 12, 1933, he wakes up with a cold and misses a lecture by the leading British physicist, Lord Rutherford. A report of the lecture in the London *Times* enrages him. Rutherford has announced that there is no imminent prospect of creating energy by cracking the atom "and anyone who looked for a source of power in the transformation of the atoms was talking moonshine." Szilard knows in his gut that Rutherford is behind the times. He recalls:

> I was wondering about this while strolling through the streets of London. Walking along Southampton Row, I had to stop for a streetlight and, at the very moment the light turned green, it occurred to me that Rutherford might be wrong . . . It suddenly occurred to me that if we could find an element which is split by neutrons and which would emit two neutrons when it absorbed one neutron, such an element, if assembled in sufficiently large mass, could sustain a nuclear chain reaction.[18]

It is one of the eureka moments in the history of science, the dawn of the atomic age. "As he crossed the street, time cracked open before him and he saw a way to the future, death to the world and all our woes, the shape of things to come," writes a Szilard biographer.[19] Szilard himself muses: "It might become possible to . . . liberate energy on an industrial scale and construct atomic bombs." The kind of machine he needs is the refrigerator pump that he made in Berlin, reconceived on a gigantic scale. In the middle of 1934, after an intense discussion with his visiting best friend Wigner (whom he calls "Wigwam"), Szilard files a patent for a nuclear chain reactor.

Moving to ever-grimmer hotels, he works that summer in a medical lab at St. Bartholomew's Hospital, bombarding an iodine compound with neutrons. His results prompt Enrico Fermi at the University of Rome to attempt a larger sample. Fermi, three years his junior, wins the 1938 Nobel Prize in Physics for "demonstrations of the existence of new radioactive elements produced by neutron irradiation and for his related discovery of nuclear reactions brought about by slow neutrons," much of it based on Szilard's work. Anxious about security leaks, Szilard assigns his next patent to the British admiralty. Trude, hoping to marry him, takes a medical position in London, only for Szilard to tell her—truthfully or not, there is no way of knowing—that he is seeing other women.

Trude obtains a pediatric internship in New York. Unpredictable as ever, Szilard decides to follow in mid-1938, taking a room at the King's Crown Hotel at 420 West 116th Street, close to Columbia University. He sees the world closing against him—Hungary, Germany, Austria; now Czechoslovakia, soon Italy. Fermi, alert to Mussolini's anti-Jewish laws, takes his Jewish wife, Laura, straight from his Nobel ceremony in Stockholm to a new life in America. He and Szilard try without success to convince Americans of the importance of the nuclear chain reactor and of the real threat the Germans might build one first. Fermi works on the top floor of Columbia's Pupin Hall, Szilard in the basement. They see little of each other.

In January 1939, the Danish physicist Niels Bohr, who is half-Jewish, lands in New York with explosive news: the Germans have achieved fission with uranium, and Otto Hahn and Fritz Strassmann in Berlin have split the atom, although they haven't understood the full potential of this work. Hahn has shared the data with his lab partner, Lise Meitner, exiled in Sweden. Meitner begs Bohr not to reveal her as his source, fearing for her brother-in-law, who is in Dachau. In February, Meitner publishes an article claiming her share in Hahn's discovery. The nuclear race is now on. Fermi tells the *New York Times* it will take twenty-five to fifty years to make a bomb.[20] Szilard, in his basement lab, is almost there. Fermi says "Nuts!" when told this.

With a Canadian assistant, Walter Zinn, Szilard prepares to irradiate uranium with neutrons that have been slowed down by passing through paraffin wax. A flash on the screen would mean that "the large-scale liberation of atomic energy was just around the corner." Szilard and Zinn start the experiment and stare at the screen, waiting for something to happen. The screen stays blank. Szilard emits a sigh: part frustration, part relief. This means there will be no bomb.

Zinn notices that the screen is not plugged in. They connect the screen to a power source and start again. "We saw the flashes," writes Szilard. "We watched them for a little while and then we switched everything off and went home. That night there was very little doubt in my mind that the world was headed for grief."[21] Before bed, he phones Teller, interrupting him as he plays a Mozart sonata. "I have found the neutrons," says Szilard.

At a scientific conference in Washington they brief Fermi. The *Washington Post* reports: "Physicists here debate whether experiments will blow up 2 miles of the landscape." Germany swiftly forms an *uranverein*, a uranium society, whose task is to locate and collect sources of the vital element for its nuclear project. In America, Fermi infuriates his Hungarian colleagues by deciding to test all the elements that will *not* yield a nuclear reaction before he starts work on those that might. Szilard erupts in frustration. He wants to attempt a massive, decisive test with five hundred pounds of uranium. But Fermi has a Nobel Prize, and his word carries more weight. In Budapest, Szilard's mother dies, but he has no time to return home or pause for mourning. He must stop the Germans from being the first to the bomb, and, above all, he must get America to wake up before it is too late. There is only one man who can help him make that happen.

Albert Einstein is in Princeton, where the living is easy. He goes for walks with great brains (the mathematician Kurt Gödel is a favorite stroller), sails his boat on Lake Carnegie, and, in the evening, takes his violin and plays Mozart. He has a lovely new instrument, made for him by a local furniture craftsman, Oscar Steger, a cellist in the Harrisburg Symphony. Inside the body of the violin he can read: "Made for the Worlds [*sic*] Greatest Scientist Profesior [*sic*] Albert Einstein. By Oscar H. Steger, Feb 1933/Harrisburg, PA." It is a mellow instrument, and it gives Einstein much pleasure. He holds Wednesday-night music soirées at home and plays in public with the virtuoso Toscha Seidl, at a fund-raiser for Jewish refugees. Music is his personal refuge, "a reflection of the inner beauty of the universe itself." At sixty, Einstein wants to put the cares of the world behind him. Leo Szilard is not going to let him do that.

On July 11, in Pupin Hall, Szilard informs Fermi that he now knows how to split an atom. All he needs is the backing. That day, Wigwam visits the King's Crown Hotel, and Szilard bombards him with information, as if he were a chunk of uranium waiting to be split. They decide to visit Einstein without delay. A call to Einstein's office informs them that the professor is on vacation, in "Dr. Moore's cottage" in Peconic, Long Island. Next morning, Szilard climbs into Wigner's 1936 Dodge coupe, and they drive out to Long Island. A wrong turn adds two hours to the journey. On the streets of Peconic, they ask for Dr. Moore's house. No one has heard of it. Wigner is ready to give up and go home. Szilard says, "Let's ask a child." He leans out the window and asks a passing kid, "Do you know where Einstein lives?"

"Sure," says the kid, "everyone knows Einstein."

They find the professor in a white T-shirt and rolled-up trousers, just back from a jaunt on his dinghy. He calls for tea on the lawn, happy to spend time with old pals from Berlin, chatting away in his German mother tongue. Szilard rolls out his results and explains the workings of a nuclear chain reactor and its capacity for world destruction.

Einstein gives a shake of his famous head. *"Daran habe ich gar nicht gedacht,"* he says. *I never, ever thought of that.*

All things considered, he decides the best course of action is to write to his friend Queen Elisabeth of the Belgians, a fellow violinist whose country holds most of the world's uranium in its African colony, the Belgian Congo. He formulates a letter to the Belgian ambassador in

Washington, which Wigner suggests they should run past the State Department, giving them two weeks to approve the letter before they send it to the Belgians. Szilard is left wondering if he is the only man alive who can smell the earth burning beneath his feet. He calls a friend, who connects him to a Lehman Brothers financier, Alexander Sachs, an economic adviser for President Roosevelt's New Deal. Sachs does not take much convincing. He says forget Belgium, talk to the president of the United States. Szilard drafts a letter in Einstein's name. It runs to four and a half pages and is comically impenetrable. He sends it to Einstein, who summons him to Peconic for revisions. Wigner is in California and cannot join them. Szilard has never learned how to drive. He asks Einstein if he can bring Edward Teller as his driver, promising that "his advice is valuable [and] I think you might enjoy getting to know him. He is particularly nice."[22] Teller drives a 1935 Plymouth.

Einstein receives them on his porch on August 2, wearing an old robe and slippers. They agree on the essence of the letter and wrangle over how many pages should be devoted to the fission of uranium. They are scientists, not men of action. Szilard goes home to produce two final drafts, one long, one short. Before he knows what he is doing, he drafts ten commandments by which a scientist should live their life. Szilard's first commandment reads: "Recognise the connection of things and the laws of conduct of men so that you may know what you are doing." The fourth commandment is "Do not destroy what you cannot create." At the summit of his creative life, a moment of life and death, Szilard reaches for the ultimate Jewish source of order and law.

That week, Einstein sends the letter to the White House. It begins:

> Sir: Some recent work by E. Fermi and L. Szilard, which has been communicated to me in a manuscript, leads me to expect that the element uranium may be turned into a new and important source of energy in the immediate future. Certain aspects of this situation which has arisen seem to call for watchfulness and, if necessary, quick action on the part of the Administration. I believe therefore that it is my duty to bring to your attention the following facts and recommendations:
>
> In the course of the last four months it has been made probable—through the work of Joliot in France as well as Fermi

and Szilard in America—that it may become possible to set up a nuclear chain reaction in a large mass of uranium, by which vast amounts of power and large quantities of new radium-like elements would be generated. Now it appears almost certain that this could be achieved in the immediate future.

This new phenomenon would also lead to construction of bombs, and it is conceivable—though much less certain— that extremely powerful bombs of a new type may thus be constructed. A single bomb of this type, carried by boat and exploded in a port, might very well destroy the whole port together with some of the surrounding territory. However, such bombs might very well prove too heavy for transportations by air.

Einstein goes on to warn that Germany is racing ahead. One of Hahn's team, the physicist Carl Friedrich von Weizsäcker, is the son of a state secretary in the German Foreign Office. As a result of his tip-off, the German government has taken control of uranium sources in Czechoslovakia. America has no time to lose. It needs to accelerate experiments on nuclear chain reactors and to get scientists and industrialists on the same page.

The outcome of this letter is so historic that in 1946 Einstein and Szilard are brought together by a film crew to reenact its inception on the porch. The initial response is sluggish. It is August, after all. Sachs keeps calling the White House but does not manage to speak to anyone in or around the Oval Office. When he finally penetrates the inner circle, he is told that there are no appointments available with the president for at least two months. It is October 11 before Sachs enters the White House with Einstein's letter, augmented by Szilard's longer memorandum. Before he can be admitted to the Oval Office, he is required, as a matter of protocol, to brief a military and naval attaché on the purpose of his visit. It takes all Sachs's courtesy to suppress his impatience. Roosevelt, a year ahead of an election, does not seem overjoyed to see him. Sachs reads out Einstein's letter, followed by Szilard's detailed synopsis and a summary of his own. The president, his eyelids drooping, declares that it would be "premature" for the US government to do anything at this stage. Sachs, aghast, draws deep on their long personal friendship and asks if the president might be free to see him for breakfast the next morning before he returns to New York.

That night, sleepless, Sachs leaves his hotel room four times to sit on a park bench and ponder what he must do to grab the president's attention and activate his power. A story from his school days comes to mind, of Robert Fulton, an American inventor who offered Napoleon a steamship that could reach England in all weathers. Napoleon refused to believe a ship could sail on steam and sent Fulton away, changing the course of history.

Sachs tells the story to Roosevelt over breakfast. The president gets the point, calls for a bottle of rare Napoleon brandy, and fills two glasses. "Alex, what you are after is to see that the Nazis don't blow us up," he says.

"Precisely."

He snaps his fingers for the military attaché. "This requires action!" says the president.[23]

Things happen when the president of the United States requires action. Within ten days, an Advisory Committee on Uranium holds its first meeting, under the chairmanship of a bureaucrat, Lyman J. Briggs, but with Sachs, Wigner, and Szilard on board, as well as a couple of uncomprehending military men. In November, the committee concludes that a nuclear chain reaction could "provide a possible source of bombs with a destructiveness vastly greater than anything now known." Roosevelt demands more action. Briggs puts in an order for fifty tons of uranium oxide and four tons of pure graphite. Things stall. In February 1940, Einstein and Szilard ask Sachs to jog the president's memory. Uranium and graphite arrive at Columbia in brick-shaped blocks. Fermi and Szilard are hired by the National Defense Research Committee at $4,000 a year. They start looking for suitable test sites.

Szilard brandishes solutions while worrying himself sick over moral accountability:

Those who have originated the work on this terrible weapon and those who have materially contributed to its development have, before God and the World, the duty to see to it that it should be ready to be used at the proper time and in the proper way.

I believe that each of us has now to decide where he feels that his responsibility lies.[24]

He proposes that, once Hitler is defeated, the bomb should be placed under international control—a wildly impractical idea, and one that will be regarded in Washington as subversive, if not treasonous.

In September 1942, General Leslie R. Groves is put in charge of the renamed "Manhattan Project." A competent engineer, of limited scientific knowledge, Groves takes against Szilard at sight, deciding that he is either a German spy or Communist, or both. Groves petitions the secretary of war to have Szilard "interned for the duration." Secretary Stimson's refusal only makes Groves angrier. Something visceral prejudices him against Szilard, who is saved because he is working at the University of Chicago while Groves is desk-bound in New York. The big bang that he wants is set up in a squash court beneath Stagg Field, a disused sports stadium at the heart of the campus. It takes seven days to stack the uranium and graphite bricks into a pile. On December 2, 1942, in a temperature of 10°F (−12°C) and a biting wind, the test is ready to roll. At 2:20 p.m., Fermi gives the order to partly withdraw a cadmium rod, to release neutrons. Szilard stands at his side. For half an hour, they watch the dials and listen to the clicks of the neutron counter. The results are inconclusive. They call for a larger counter, and the count goes off the scale. Fermi raises a hand. "The pile has gone critical," he says.

This is the moment to end the experiment. The result is achieved, ready to be written up and analyzed. But Fermi, awed or paralyzed, cannot give the order. Minutes tick by, one after another. The counter can count no more. For all anyone knows, they could be about to vaporize the university, to blow up Chicago. Finally, at 3:53 p.m. Fermi tells Zinn to lower the cadmium control rod, and the neutron counts begin to drop. The theory has been proven to everyone's satisfaction. Fermi pulls a bottle of Chianti from behind his back and pours the wine into paper cups. Szilard shakes his hand. Szilard writes: "I doubt that [Fermi] ever understood that some people live in two worlds like I do. A world . . . in which we have to predict what is going to happen and another world in which we try to forget those predictions in order to be able to fight for what we would like to happen."[25] The pair never see eye to eye for more than a fleeting moment.

Szilard leaves the drinks party, declaring that "this would go down as a black day in the history of mankind."[26] Wherever he goes, he is tailed by the FBI: "Subject is of Jewish extraction, has a fondness for delicacies and frequently makes purchases in delicatessen stores . . . occasionally speaks in a foreign tongue, and associates mostly with people of Jewish extraction." Six agents watch him eat breakfast. Groves keeps trying to have him arrested. In the thick of the experiments, he is granted American citizenship. He keeps bothering colleagues with questions of conscience as well as those of science. In August 1943, Groves fires him from the Manhattan Project and bars him from talking to its scientists. Without his patents, the project stalls; Groves is forced to rehire him.

Building of the bomb shifts to Los Alamos in New Mexico, under the direction of Robert Oppenheimer, a troubled New Yorker who admits to having been "a member of every kind of Communist organisation" and to be sleeping with two Communists—one of them his wife—at the same time. Oppenheimer hires Fermi, Teller, Wigner, and most of the Chicago team, but not Szilard, whose moral doubts are confusing other scientists. Szilard takes his exclusion lightly, telling anyone who cared to listen that "nobody could think straight in a place like that. Everybody who goes there will go crazy."[27] Oppenheimer's deputy, Isidor Isaac Rabi, rates the project's chances of success at fifty-fifty.[28]

Szilard keeps up the moral pressure on Einstein, who, in March 1945, writes to Roosevelt, asking him to give Szilard "his personal attention." But Roosevelt dies before they can meet. On July 16, 1945, a nuclear device is successfully tested in the New Mexico desert. America has won the race for the means of mass destruction. On August 6, at eight fifteen a.m. local time, the US Air Force drops an atomic bomb on Hiroshima, killing ninety thousand people; three days later, a second bomb is dropped on Nagasaki. On August 15, Japan surrenders. Otto Hahn, held captive in England with his Berlin nuclear team, is so shaken by the devastation that he requires "considerable alcoholic stimulant" to calm him down. Weeks later, Hahn receives the Nobel Prize in Chemistry "for his discovery of the fission of heavy nuclei." He is refused permission to travel to Stockholm for the ceremony. Lise Meitner says: "Hahn fully deserved the Nobel Prize in Chemistry.

There is really no doubt about it. But I believe that Otto Robert Frisch and I contributed something not insignificant to the clarification of the process."[29] Like Szilard, Hahn devotes the rest of his life to the pursuit of peace.

With tenure at the University of Chicago and a brief that covers all the sciences, Szilard, approaching fifty, abandons nuclear science to work with molecular biologists on cloning a human cell. He is relieved to have job security but puzzled by some facets of the American way of life. Staying with Trude, who is a professor of preventive medicine at the University of Denver, he is given to understand that if she were found with a man in her room she would face a morals charge and possible dismissal. Szilard, the least marriageable of men, at last makes Trude Weiss his wife in a New York register office in October 1951. Although they do not live together for some years, they appear to be happy ever after.

In his determination to save the world from the bomb, Szilard asks Congress to take nuclear funding from military hands and give it to civilians, and with Einstein, signs petitions to ban further tests. He warns in a radio talk of a superbomb, based on cobalt-60, in the explosion of which "everyone would be killed." On NBC television, he debates "Is Disarmament Possible and Desirable?" with Edward Teller, each accusing the other of showing too much trust in either the Americans or the Russians. Szilard spends two hours with Nikita Khrushchev in Moscow, and stays on in the city for several days, waiting in vain to hear that the Soviet leader has come around to his view on the abolition of nuclear weapons.

All his friends collect prizes. Szilard receives none. "I am thinking of keeping a diary," he remarks, "not with the intent to publish it, merely to record the facts for the information of God, in case God does not know my version of the facts." Like Heine, he expects God to smile at his little joke. After his death, Trude will publish a book entitled *Leo Szilard: His Version of the Facts* (MIT Press, 1978).

Diagnosed with incurable bladder cancer, he takes control of his own radiation therapy at Memorial Sloan Kettering Cancer Center in New York, applying unorthodox doses. To general surprise, he cures himself of cancer. What kills him, eventually, is the tubby residue of a high-fat Budapest diet. A coronary thrombosis takes him in his sleep on May 30, 1964. Trude says, "God would never have got Leo if he had been awake."

Such is his polemical zeal that Leo Szilard is remembered less as the inventor of the nuclear reactor than as the progenitor of nuclear nonproliferation, an idea that keeps the world safe after 1945. Year by year, one after another, he signs the world's scientists to his cause. A story about nuclear confrontation he writes in 1949 is read by Andrei Sakharov, maker of the Russian H-bomb. It converts Sakharov into a human rights activist who accepts internal exile in the hope of stopping the bomb. "Sakharov," write his biographers, "was especially attracted to Leo Szilard, one of the main instigators of the American A-bomb who became one of its chief opponents."[30]

The greatest achievement of Leo Szilard is to stop the world dropping his bomb.

FOURTEEN

1942

BLACK DAYS

You must remember this: Budapest in *Casablanca*.

On June 1, 1941, the morning of the Shavuot festival, Baghdad's Jews awake to find red paint on their doors. The cause is soon apparent. A mob armed with pistols, knives, swords, and scimitars comes, shouting, "Kill the Jews!" Over two days, the world's oldest

Jewish community, dating back three thousand continuous years, is subjected to a murderous, unrestrained pogrom. Iraq is in an interregnum as a pro-German prime minister topples the monarchy and the British, who control the oil fields, await orders to release their troops from barracks.

The Arab rioters are tanked up with Nazi propaganda and egged on by the grand mufti of Jerusalem, Haj Amin al-Husseini, Hitler's ally. In the two-day *farhud* (a Kurdish word for dispossession), women are raped, babies are maimed, and houses are ransacked and set on fire. Children hide in cellars. Some run to the roofs—where Baghdadis sleep in summer beneath the stars—to hurl bricks onto the mob's heads and hold the onslaught at bay.

At least 150 Jews—perhaps as many as 800—are killed. By the time the British Army quells the revolt, Baghdad is not the same. The *farhud* shatters the Jews' sense of belonging. Over the next decade, 120,000 Jews leave Iraq, nine-tenths of the community, joining close to a million Jewish refugees from Syria, Egypt, and Yemen as the Middle East enters an endless conflict.

On January 20, 1942, fifteen men turn up for a meeting at a Berlin suburban villa beside a frozen lake. The Wannsee Conference is convened by Heinrich Himmler's deputy, Reinhard Heydrich, with a view to coordinating a Final Solution (*Endlösung*—Göring's term) to the Jewish Question. It is the darkest date in the history of the Jews since their expulsion from Spain was ordered on March 31, 1492. Heydrich is a mass murderer who, by some quirk of international bureaucracy, holds the title of president of Interpol. He orders Adolf Eichmann to secure the participation of all relevant civil and military authorities at his meeting. Half the men around his table have PhDs from German or Austrian universities, a high-water mark of Western civilization. Heydrich himself is a classical violinist of good pedigree.

The attendees include the gestapo chief Heinrich Müller, Judge Dr. Roland Friesler of the Ministry of Justice, Dr. Josef Bühler for the Polish territories, Dr. Alfred Meyer, gauleiter of Westphalia, Dr. Wilhelm Stuckart of the Ministry of the Interior, and a round-spectacled man, Martin Franz Julius Luther, who represents the German foreign ministry. Martin Luther's copy of the minutes is the only one that survives; it becomes Exhibit A at the Nuremberg trials.

Delayed twice due to the Pearl Harbor attack, the meeting is under pressure to deliver results. Eichmann gets off on the wrong foot by booking the wrong house, 56-58 Am Grossen Wannsee, instead of Interpol HQ, 16 Am Kleinen Wannsee. Heydrich is not pleased. He opens the session with a cold statement of intent that "Europe would be combed of Jews from east to west." He continues: "There is now a further possible solution to which the Führer has already signified his consent—namely deportation to the east." He leaves no doubt that this involves forced labor and death. Eichmann recalls later that they all talked, off the record, of "elimination and annihilation," but his brief is to keep the record ambiguous.[1]

Heydrich speaks for an hour and takes questions for thirty minutes, mostly concerning the status of mixed marriages and half-Jews. The meeting is over in ninety minutes. So pleased is Heydrich with the progress that he takes Müller and Eichmann into a side room to clink cognac glasses. He tells Eichmann to restrict the minutes to participants only, adding a memorandum that enumerates the total of Jews. "Approximately 11 million Jews will be involved in the final solution of the European Jewish question," says the memo. The figures are inaccurate. Reliable estimates place the number of Jews in Europe at 9.5 million in 1939, shrinking to 3.8 million by the end of the war.

On February 24, Hitler announces: "My prophecy will come true that Aryan mankind will not be destroyed by this war but that the Jew will be eradicated." Wannsee is the green light for that process. In a follow-up letter to participants, Heydrich names Eichmann as his liaison with all departments. Eichmann notifies police stations across the Reich to prepare for Jewish roundups. On March 6, he informs the gestapo of a planned deportation of fifty-five thousand Jews, mostly from Prague and Vienna. An order is given to the Lublin SS leader, Odilo Globocnik, to use the Majdanek, Treblinka, Sobibor, and Belzec camps for the liquidation of all Jews in his sector. On March 25, Slovakia's puppet government agrees to deport twenty thousand young Jews. In April, Eichmann travels to Auschwitz to test the capacity of the Deutsche Reichsbahn to deliver hundreds of thousands of Jews to the new gas chambers. He observes men, women, and children being herded to their deaths, hears cries of pain and desperation, smells the smoke of burned flesh. "I was the one who transported the Jews to the camps," Eichmann affirms at his trial in Jerusalem in 1961. "I carried out my orders."

Adolf Eichmann makes the transition from minute-taking bureaucrat to operational mass murderer with no apparent difficulty. During and after the Holocaust, he leads what appears to be a contented life with his wife, Veronika, who bears him four sons. Like Heydrich, he plays the violin. The Israeli court that convicts him of genocide will find him innocent of ever killing anyone with his own hands. Eichmann does his killing at the desk, by written directive to the relevant departments. Israeli psychologists who examine him fail to resolve the dichotomy between this courteous individual and the operational director of genocide.[2] "Here was a man who didn't look very different from you or me," reflects the historian Deborah Lipstadt, "in fact, he looked sort of innocuous when they brought him into the glass booth. And it caused people to sit up and take notice and see the perpetrator and understand that you can't say the perpetrator is 'other' . . . You have to understand what makes it possible for a seemingly normal person to become the doer of such evil."[3]

At Nuremberg, Nazi leaders present themselves as men of high moral values. The British journalist Gitta Sereny, who attends the trials, tells me their indignation is genuine. They do not accept any wrongdoing. Sereny goes on to conduct book-length interviews with the Treblinka commandant Franz Stangl—"not an obviously evil man"—and the slave-labor chief Albert Speer, sharing with me her dismay at how unremarkable they seem and, in Speer's case, how intelligent and charming.[4] This disarming ordinariness in Nazi murderers prompts the philosopher Hannah Arendt, reporting on the Eichmann trial for the *New Yorker* magazine, to coin the term "the banality of evil." Arendt, personally riven by her long affair with the pro-Nazi philosopher Martin Heidegger, is attacked for her bland typification of Eichmann and for her swift exit from the trial before the most tragic survivors enter the witness box. But historians who fault her can find no better phrase.

Eichmann, guilty of crimes against humanity, is hanged at Ramle jail in June 1962, his body burned and his ashes scattered far out in the Mediterranean. Biographers continue to wrestle with his split personality. David Cesarani, who attacks Arendt's term, reads Eichmann as "typical more than aberrant," alarmingly "a man of our time." Normal people in certain circumstances "can and do commit mass murder."[5] Eichmann, in Cesarani's view, is everyman. But is that satisfactory? Eichmann has become a generic term for committers of genocide, but the idea that each of us has an inner Eichmann does not lead to any greater understanding of the human element in the greatest crime in history.

It takes a poet to see through the firewalls, placing himself in the skin of both killers and victims. The Czernowitz writer Paul Celan emerges from forced labor to find that his mother has perished in Auschwitz. In May 1945, in Romania, his head filled with horrors, the twenty-four-year-old Celan writes his signature work, "Todesfuge" ("Death Fugue"). The poem sees Auschwitz in bifocal images—from the prisoners' side and the guards'. Much in the poem is elliptical, ambiguous, unexplained. Celan offers nothing simple or obvious. The opening phrase *black milk* may refer to the filthy coffee substitute the prisoners are fed or to the ashes from the crematoria that they inhale. "We are scooping a grave in the air" may refer to bodies unburied. Here's the opening stanza:

> Black milk of morning we drink you at night
> we drink you at dawn and at noon we drink you at dusk
> we drink and we drink
> we are scooping a grave in the air
> there is room for us all.
> There's a man in the house who plays with snakes and who
>   writes,
> who writes when it's nightfall to *Deutschland* your golden hair
>   Margarethe
> your ashen hair Sulamit . . .

The "man in the house" is a Nazi. He's writing a letter home to his girlfriend, who has blond hair. The prisoner thinks of his girlfriend, Sulamit, whose hair is in ashes. As the cadence speeds up—you need to hear Celan recite it on YouTube[6]—the decisive line tolls: "*der Tod ist ein Meister aus Deutschland*" (Death is a master from Deutschland).[7]

Celan repeats the line twice, ineradicably. Germany is renowned for great masters, he implies: Bach, Goethe, Beethoven, Wagner. But the true German genius is Death. The Nazis bring this master from Deutschland. *Der Tod ist ein Meister aus Deutschland.*

Celan moves in 1948 to Paris, where he studied before the war. He marries a French aristocrat and makes his living teaching German and translating Maigret detective stories. All his poems are written in German, his mother's tongue, and that of her murderers. In 1958, receiving a literature prize in Germany, Celan explains that he writes in the German language, which "had to go through terrible silence, go through the thousand darknesses of fatal speech. It went through and did not provide any words for what happened." Impenetrably, he adds: "But it went through this happening. Went through and was allowed to come back into light, enriched by it all."[8] Does he really believe that? His actions suggest otherwise.

On April 20, 1970, depressed beyond words, Paul Celan throws himself into the River Seine from the Pont Mirabeau, unable to live with a language that "did not provide words."

At Bletchley Park, where cryptographers have cracked the Enigma code and are reading the enemy's signal traffic messages, the chief of the German and Italian section, Walter Ettinghausen, picks up a message from a vessel in the Aegean Sea, saying it is transporting Jews from the Greek islands to Piraeus, "*zur Endlösung.*" A native German speaker and an Oxford don, Ettinghausen translates this phrase as "for the final solution." He understands immediately what it means. He passes the message upward to Downing Street but says nothing to anyone about it, not even to his brother, Ernest, who works in the same unit. Code breakers at Bletchley are sworn to secrecy. Hitler must never know that Enigma has been broken. So Ettinghausen keeps to himself the knowledge that the Germans are wiping out all Europe's Jews, including members of his family. His colleague Rolf Noskwith decrypts a signal that all passengers aboard a Jewish refugee ship in the Black Sea have died. He, too, maintains his vow of silence, at acute emotional cost. Three decades will elapse before any of the Bletchley team starts to speak.

• • •

Faith, miraculously, survives. Three rabbis in Auschwitz are forced, by fellow Jews, to put God on trial for murder. They convene a court, hear evidence, take notes. After much deliberation, they return a verdict. God, they declare, is *chayav*. Guilty. Silence grips the barracks. Then one of the rabbis announces: "And now it's time for the evening prayer." The story is thought to be a myth until, in 2008, the writer Elie Wiesel affirms that he was present at such a trial.[9] The Jews, in Auschwitz, do not let God off the hook.

In the Kovno ghetto in Lithuania, a rabbi is asked for rulings in situations of unspeakable horror. A pregnant woman is shot dead: May a surgeon violate the sanctity of the corpse to save the baby (he may; he does; he saves it)? Can the morning blessing thanking God for not making one a slave still be recited when all are enslaved (it can, it must: spiritually, we are free)? Most troubling of all, on the eve of deportation a man asks if he is permitted to commit suicide to assure himself of a Jewish burial at home among his ancestors. Rabbi Ephraim Oshry, twenty-seven years old, draws deep on Jewish sources before advising the man that suicide is, in any context, unacceptable. It constitutes a desecration of God's name. The deportee must live his life to the last second, trusting always in salvation. Oshry writes: "I cite proudly that in the Kovno Ghetto there were only three instances of suicide by people who grew intensely depressed. The rest of the ghetto dwellers trusted and hoped that G-d would not forsake His people."[10]

The French philosopher Emmanuel Levinas is puzzled by such acts of faith. He demands to know how it is possible for people to carry on believing in God and practicing religion in the midst of intolerable cruelty:

> Is it not proof of a world without God, a world where man is the only measure of Good and Evil? The simplest, most obvious response would be atheism. This would also be the reasonable reaction of anyone whose idea of God up to now is a kind of nursery deity that dishes out prizes, inflicts punishment or pardons sins—a God who, in His goodness, treats men like eternal children. But I have to ask people: what kind of poor demon, what weird magician

have you put in your heaven, which you now claim is empty? And why, under that empty sky, do you continue to search for a world that is rational and good?

Elie Wiesel, a teenager in Auschwitz, confronts God with His actions: "In the concentration camp I had cried out in sorrow and anger against God and also against man, who seemed to have inherited only the cruelty of his creator."[11] At the crematorium, "for the first time I felt revolt rise up in me. Why should I bless His name? The Eternal, Lord of the Universe, the All-Powerful and Terrible, was silent. What had I to thank Him for?"[12] Wiesel, like many others, wrestles with this dilemma for the rest of his life.

Otto Dov Kulka, a child prisoner, many years later dreams of seeing God inside Crematorium II:

> I saw—the terrible grief of God, who was there. . . . He was alive, shrunken, hunched forward with searing pain . . . a figure on the scale of His creatures, in the form of a human being who came and was there—also, as one of His creatures . . . as a response to "the question they were forbidden to ask there. . . ."[13]

The forbidden question, never to be asked or answered, is: Where is God in Auschwitz?

The Hungarian writer Imre Kertész lives by a further paradox: "God is Auschwitz but also He who brought me out of there, who obliged, even compelled me to give an account of all that there happened, because He wants to know and hear what he had done."[14] Kertész overcomes a frequent urge to commit suicide by reminding himself of his stubborn duty to keep pointing the finger at an unforgiven God. Israel Meir Lau, an infant in Auschwitz and future chief rabbi of Israel, emerges defiant. "They took our families," he tells a memorial meeting. "Do not let them take our God." Leo Baeck, who stays with his community in Berlin to the last, preaches that the Holocaust is man's failure, not God's. In March 1945, in the final weeks of the war, he is in the administration block at Theresienstadt when an SS chief arrives. "Herr Baeck," rasps Adolf Eichmann, "are you still alive? I thought you were dead." "Feeling certain that I had little time to live,

I wasted none with him," writes Baeck, who, in the ensuing confusion, survives.

Ultra-Orthodox rabbis interpret Auschwitz as God's rage against German Jews who turned away from His commandments. "It is no wonder that the Almighty has lashed out in anger," cries the Satmar rebbe Joel Teitelbaum. But this punishment theology is contradicted by the fact that those who suffer in the greatest numbers are not assimilated German Jews but the devout communities of Poland and Hungary. Other Hasidic rabbis take the view that it is pointless to attempt to read God's motives. "There is no rational explanation and no elucidation based on Torah wisdom whatsoever for the Devastation, nothing but the knowledge that 'thus it arises in [God's] Mind!' and 'It is a decree before Me,'" says Menachem Mendel Schneersohn of Chabad-Lubavitch.[15] Judaism believes that there are limits to man's understanding. The moral mind can probe no further.

The Viennese psychiatrist Viktor Frankl, an opponent of both Freud and Jung, emerges from Auschwitz with a thesis that he titles "The Unconscious God." Humans, he says, need both faith and a means of understanding. Frankl ascribes his own survival to what he calls self-distancing, imagining as a slave laborer on a winter's day that he is "standing at the lectern in a large, beautiful, warm and bright hall . . . about to give a lecture on 'Psychotherapeutic Experiences in a Concentration Camp.'"[16] Frankl's unconscious God refers to "a hidden relationship with a hidden God," a relationship in which both sides maintain their privacy and their mystery. His more widely read response is delivered in a manuscript that he dictates in nine days, under the working title *Trotzdem Ja Zum Leben Sagen: Ein Psychologe erlebt das Konzentrationslager* (*Despite Everything Say "Yes" to Life: A Psychologist Experiences the Concentration Camp*). The book, retitled *Man's Search for Meaning*, sells ten million copies. What Frankl takes away from the Holocaust is the theory that man's primary need, after food, drink, and shelter, is the desire to understand the world around him. Despite everything, Frankl continues to believe in God.

Atheists emerge unchanged. "I entered [Auschwitz] as a non-believer and as a non-believer I was liberated and have lived to this day," writes the Italian chemist Primo Levi. Freed in January 1945, Levi writes a scientific "Auschwitz Report" with a medical colleague and follows it with the first draft of *If This Is a Man*, a record of inhumanity cast in precise, unemotional Italian, all the more chilling for the absence of adverbs. The publishing house Einaudi turns it down on the advice of two fine writers, Cesare Pavese and Natalia Ginzburg. A small publisher takes it up, selling barely fifteen hundred copies. The book opens with a poem, challenging us to decide what is a man. In it, Levi, the nonbeliever, strikes a contradiction by quoting from the Shema, the Jewish credo, Deuteronomy chapter 6:

> I commend these words to you.
> Carve them in your hearts
> At home, in the street,
> Going to bed, rising;
> Repeat them to your children.

Levi obtains recognition with later works, *The Drowned and the Saved*, *If Not Now, When?*, and most movingly, *The Periodic Table*, a work that aligns episodes of his life's story with elements of the natural world. Levi takes great pains with his text, striving for accuracy and comprehension. He is exceptionally meticulous with the German editions, aimed at the perpetrators and their families. He is the scientific witness, par excellence. On April 11, 1987, Primo Levi plunges to his death from the third floor of his house in Turin, the house where he was born and which he only left to be carted off to Auschwitz. At his funeral, the rabbi of Turin calls his death a "delayed homicide."

I shall never forget the moment I receive the news, droning from the kitchen radio amid the breakfast clatter. It stuns me like the roof caving in. Levi's careful prose, seeing Auschwitz through scientific microscopy, seems to me the clearest factual path to a possible understanding. But Levi, recording his memories coolly and without malice, is ultimately overwhelmed. If he cannot live with the Holocaust legacy, what hope is there for the rest of us?

The philosopher Walter Benjamin, arrested as he enters Spain in September 1940, swallows morphine pills at Portbou, from fear of being returned to German-occupied France. The physicist Arnold Berliner, editor of the scientific journal *Naturwissenschaften* and an early friend of Gustav Mahler, takes his life in his Berlin apartment on hearing he is about to be summoned for deportation. A Jewish player in the Berlin Philharmonic orchestra does the same. The playwright Ernst Toller hangs himself in a New York hotel room. Fritz Haber's son kills himself at the Brooklyn Bridge. The essayist Kurt Tucholsky gulps pills. The Berlin theater critic Alfred Kerr takes poison on returning to Germany in 1948. It is estimated that ten thousand German Jews die by their own hand during, or as a result of, the Third Reich.

Among cultural suicides, none is more dispiriting than the death of Stefan Zweig in faraway Brazil. An early wanderer, leaving Austria and his first marriage in 1934 and settling in England, Zweig fears he may be interned in wartime. In October 1939, he marries his secretary, Charlotte Altmann, and books passage for New York, where his American publishers lay on a celebrity welcome. Zweig is the world's bestselling nonfiction author, reliably prolific, turning out a new book every other year. He is also a respectable novelist. His latest, *Beware of Pity*, is by far his best. Zweig dislikes the New York literary circuit, an amalgam of monoglot Americans and jealous Europeans. He takes a house upstate, in Ossining, to work on his memoirs. When isolation palls, he books a cruise to Rio de Janeiro, where he is lionized by a press unaccustomed to celebrity book tours. He writes a book, *Brazil: Land of the Future*, and seems happy enough until summer heat drives him and his wife to the uplands, to a town called Petrópolis, which vaguely reminds Zweig of Salzburg, out of season. Lotte, luxuriating in the foliage of a subtropical garden, types his next book. In November 1941, Zweig turns sixty, a dreaded birthday. Three months later, on February 21, 1942, Lotte types the last page of his autobiography, *The World of Yesterday*. It is a seminal portrait of fin de siècle Vienna, a culture teetering on the edge of a precipice, searingly truthful in some of its social insights, slippery and evasive about Zweig's personal life and unseemly habits. Like every memoirist, he wants the world to think the best of him.

The next day, a Sunday, the Zweigs go for a walk and retire early to bed. When they fail to appear by Monday afternoon, the housemaid and her husband enter the bedroom. They find Stefan Zweig lying on his back, in a sweat-patched dark shirt with a knotted tie, hands clasped across his stomach, a glass on the bedside table, an empty pill-box of barbiturates nearby. Lotte lies on her side in a kimono, her head on Zweig's left shoulder, her hands upon his. The police are called. Photos of the suicide flash around the world.

Zweig has left a note in a prominent place, with instructions to his publishers to append it to his memoirs. It is a classic self-epitaph for a writer who favors elegance above substance:

> Before parting from life of my own free will and in clear mind, I am impelled to fulfil a last obligation: to give heartfelt thanks to this wonderful land of Brazil which afforded me and my work such kind and hospitable repose. My love for the country has increased every day and I would not have asked to rebuild my life in any other place after the world of my own language was lost to me and my spiritual homeland, Europe, destroyed itself.
>
> But to make a new beginning at sixty requires unusual powers and my strength has been exhausted by years of homeless wandering. So I think it is better to end my life at the right time, upright, as a man for whom cultural work has always given the purest happiness and personal freedom—the greatest gift on earth.
>
> I send greetings to all my friends: May they live to see the dawn after this long night. I, all too impatient, go ahead.
>
> Stefan Zweig, Petropolis, 22. II. 1942[17]

His protestations ring hollow. Zweig is in good health, and Lotte, though asthmatic (she coughs a lot at night), is just thirty-three years old. Stefan may be tired of running, but Lotte has a mother, a brother, and a niece to whom she is devoted. Coming from a rabbinic family, she is well aware of the stringent religious taboo against suicide. It appears that Zweig took his pills first, leaving Lotte to make her decision at her leisure. He makes no mention of his wife in the suicide note. Does he, perhaps, not expect her to join him?

His message is diplomatic toward his Brazilian hosts and more than a little condescending to his fellow writers, informing them that he, as ever, is ahead of the pack. Thomas Mann, reading this, is irate. "He can't have killed himself out of grief, let alone desperation," mutters Mann. "The fair sex must have something to do with it . . ." Other exiles succumb to despair. Zweig, sitting on a mountain of royalties and with a lovely young wife to attend to his needs, has given up.

Zweig's true reasons are buried between the lines. He has a history of depression and has threatened to kill himself several times before, most violently on the occasion when his first wife wants to have a baby. Zweig informs Friderike that a child would distract her from her duties to her husband and forbids her to conceive. He is rumored to indulge peculiar sexual habits. His ego is monstrous, matched only by his urge to inhale the air of genius, to mingle with the greatest musicians, artists, and writers, men who occupy a pantheon he can never hope to attain. He crams his study with artifacts of geniuses—a lock of J. S. Bach's hair, a desk at which Beethoven wrote—and he is close to heaven when the German opera composer Richard Strauss approaches him for a libretto after the death of his regular partner, Hugo von Hofmannsthal. They continue to communicate after Zweig goes into exile, until Strauss gets into trouble with Goebbels. When that contact is cut off, Zweig is a lost soul. In exile, there is no genius to greet him as an equal. In Petrópolis, he has no canapés and champagne. Zweig has nothing left to live for. But that is still not the full cause of his suicide.

The clinching phrase in his note is: *after the world of my own language was lost to me.* A writer's home is his mother tongue. Take away a language and they can learn another, but they will still dream in the original and still long to belong to their mother's pantheon of immortal writers. Zweig, in exile, is doubly bereft. Not only is he unable to reach German readers, he has come to believe the language itself is lost. German, once the vernacular of science and philosophy, has become the colloquy of killers. Its writers are banished; their books burned. The world of yesterday is fading to black.

Zweig can just about imagine "the dawn after this long night," but he wants no part of a future in which civilization can only be contemplated in a foreign tongue. The German language will be relegated down the table of ideas and intelligent discourse, behind English, Russian, and French. Europe, whatever its political status, will be void of an essential component. Stefan Zweig, so lacking in self-knowledge, sees further ahead than fellow writers, and what he sees he wants no part of. After the Holocaust, there will be nothing worth writing about, and what needs to be written will be inexpressible. Wittgenstein's phrase—*Wovon man nicht sprechen kann, darüber muß man schweigen* (Whereof one cannot speak, thereof one must be silent)—rings with the force of a Mosaic commandment. If a writer cannot speak, he gives up the right to live, the more so when his language is *lost*.

Theodor Wiesengrund Adorno, a man as slippery as Zweig, nails the German language to a cross upon his return to Frankfurt, a city occupied by American forces, populated with refugees in transit camps and ex-Nazis who have resumed their lives as if nothing has happened. Adorno, a clumsy writer who can write a whole page of German without recourse to a verb, coins a crisp epigram. "After Auschwitz," says Adorno, "writing a *Gedicht* would be barbaric—*there can be no poetry after Auschwitz.*" His saying is much misquoted and misunderstood. Adorno, a social scientist, is not concerned with poetry. He believes the German language is dead.

Monday morning at nine a.m., shooting starts on a new movie at Jack Warner's lot. Forty-eight days have been allocated, the budget is $878,000, and the director is a pro who never overruns. It is May 25, 1942. The first scene on the day's list shows two lovers in Paris as the German Army rolls in. A Montmartre café has been constructed on stage twelve. Cameras and lights are working, but there is a problem with sound. Shouting ensues. Nobody knows what's going on. The story is so inchoate it will require a voice-over introduction: "With the coming of the Second World War, many eyes in imprisoned Europe turned hopefully or desperately toward the freedom of the Americas."

The two leading actors sit in makeup. They have met only once before, at lunch a few days ago, when both bitch about how they would rather be in some other film. The director has a reputation for pushing actors further than they like and keeping them past midnight until he is satisfied with a scene. He has made a shining star of Errol Flynn and a nervous wreck of many more. In the Hollywood hierarchy, a director is bottom of the pecking list, just above the writers, until the moment that cameras start rolling, at which point they can be an absolute dictator for seven or eight weeks. This director has many reasons for being in a bad mood. He is being well paid—$3,200 a week—but he feels undervalued, and he knows he is not the producer's first choice for this project. The producer, Hal Wallis, is supposed to be his best friend. A director can trust no one in this industry. What is more, he has not been consulted about casting or story. He has just finished shooting *Yankee Doodle Dandy*, a vacuous biopic, and he is now meant to take charge of a political romance whose script is only half-written and half of whose cast is held up on other films. The director's first recorded act that morning is to sack the soundman. This is not a happy shoot by any stretch of Jack Warner's limo, and Jack Warner is nowhere to be seen. He is at the launch of the brainless *Yankee Doodle Dandy*, tipped as the year's box-office hit.

The two lead actors of *Casablanca*, Humphrey Bogart and Ingrid Bergman, have nothing to say to each other, no off-screen chemistry. "I kissed him, but I never knew him," says the Swedish actress. Bogart has been grumping around in gunman roles, with the occasional cowboy for light relief. The second male lead, the classical actor Paul Henreid, is about to crash his career with a performance of paralytic frigidity. The composer Max Steiner, who has an Oscar for *Gone with the Wind*, is ordered to rewrite his entire score around a smooch song, "As Time Goes By." It's just another bloody morning at the spinning wheel of the dream industry. No one imagines that this is the start of the most durable movie of all time, the one people will demand to see on special birthdays, and some on their deathbeds.

In the absence of a coherent script or much conviction, the director must create order from chaos. Michael Curtiz, raised in an Orthodox home as Manó Kaminer, forced by anti-Jewish prejudice to leave Budapest, has made his name in Hollywood as a brilliant angle man, noted for economy of camera movement and an ability to picture a story in his mind, frame by frame, as if he is drawing it on a board. He is a slave driver with few interests, who arrives on set at seven in the morning and puts in a seventeen-hour day. He drives actors like cattle, reducing box-office stars to quivering wrecks to get the effect he wants. "When I see a lazy man or a don't-care girl, it makes me tough," he explains. "I am very critical of actors, but if I find a real actor, I am the first to appreciate it."[18]

With no tongue for gossip and little taste for drink or drugs, Curtiz is never asked to Hollywood parties. Other than clay pigeon shooting with Hal Wallis, he has no recreations other than dropping in to a

Hungarian hangout on Sunset Strip on his days off, where he shoots the Danube breeze with hometown buddies in his Magyar tongue. Curtiz's English never rises above basic. "Bring on the empty horses" is one of his directorial howlers. He depends on his wife, Bess Meredyth, a bedridden alcoholic ex-scriptwriter, to decipher the script he is directing; he phones her twice a day during coffee breaks. When he puts the phone down, he calls out one of the female extras. "He was always going behind a flat," says an assistant director. "On *Casablanca* as on every other picture. The girls were always extras. There were a couple of girls who were always on call because they were famous for their behaviour."[19]

Casablanca is born from *Everybody Comes to Rick's*, a play by a New York couple, Murray Burnett and Joan Alison, who visit Vienna in 1938 to help Jewish cousins smuggle out their valuables. They go on to the South of France, smelling something more scary than the coffee, and they write a script with a café at its heart, a café that represents a haven of sanity on a continent of terror. Unable to get the play staged, they sell it to Hollywood, where it is butchered by the screenwriting Epstein twins, Julius and Philip, and doctored by Howard Koch and other hands. All that survives of the original *Rick's* is the café.

Nobody at Warner has ever been to Casablanca in Morocco. On early clapboards, CASA BLANCA is spelled as two words—a white house. The enterprise is more and more ethereal. When Bergman asks the writers which man she should love more—Bogart's Rick Blaine or Henreid's Resistance hero—the answer she gets from the script room is "I dunno."

The story opens on two Germans shot dead in a street. A monocled gestapo officer (Conrad Veidt) asks the French police chief (Claude Rains) to arrest two suspects at Rick's café. Rick (Bogart) tells the Frenchman that he sticks his neck out for no one. The door swings open; Ilsa (Bergman) swans in. She was Bogart's lover in Paris. Now she's trying to get the freedom fighter Henreid out of Casablanca. Using short scenes and terse dialogue, Curtiz builds seat-gripping momentum. Bogart, the wisecracking café owner, is not the kind of guy to let his heart rule his head. "Here's looking at you, kid" is his idea of foreplay. Curtiz hires Magyar pals as extras. S. Z. Sakall, the plump headwaiter, is straight out of Budapest central casting. Julius Epstein reckons that the story has "more corn than the states of Kansas and Iowa combined."

From this cornfield, Curtiz achieves transcendence. No scene in *Casablanca* can withstand close structural analysis, least of all the byplay with the black pianist and the love song from Paris (no one ever says, "Play it again, Sam"), leave alone the schmaltzy finale in which Bogart heads into the desert with the French cop: "Louis, I think this is the beginning of a beautiful friendship." Even on a belch of Coke and popcorn, it is hard to suspend disbelief if you watch the film one scene at a time. Curtiz, however, never lets the eye linger on a single scene. He builds a *Boléro*-like momentum that powers right through the irrationality to a slowly revealed larger purpose.

Casablanca becomes a metaphor for a world at war. People are trapped in a sweaty spot, facing a trade-off between survival and sacrifice. We are asked to identify with the choices facing Bogart and Bergman: to live for love or give it up and save the world. Curtiz tilts our hearts toward the nobler destiny. The lovers, we feel, make the right decision. At a time when the war could go either way, *Casablanca* preaches idealism. "This time," says Henreid to Bogart, "I know our side will win." The loser in love offers his rival a share in a better world. A forest of PhD theses on the film spares me the need for further homiletics.

All agree that the visual signature is Curtiz's, and his alone. Paul Henreid says: "He had an instinctual visual flair . . . Every now and then he would stop the camera and say, 'There is something wrong here. I don't know what it is.'"[20] His masterstroke is this: *Casablanca* surmounts its fake location—there's no sniff of hashish and kebabs in Rick's café—by superimposing a very different venue, one that feels like home to this Hungarian Jew who never fits the Hollywood spec. Rick's café, reenvisioned by Curtiz, is down by the Danube. The piano plays day and night, and the owner plays all comers off against the middle, earning his take from deals made at his tables. This Buda-café is a refuge from all forms of local instability, from a regime that restricts Jews but is open to bribes, from personal relationships crumbling under social change, from men with guns and women with grievances, from politics beyond comprehension. Rick's is a respite, temporary but secure, from the hubbub of a world gone mad and if the ending is as flimsy as a desert mirage—Curtiz demands rewrites to the final day—it has a feel-good glow that sends us into the night feeling ever so slightly uplifted and wanting to see the film again.

Casablanca goes $130,000 over budget and comes in a week late, rare for Curtiz. Released in November 1942, it makes $3 million on first run and wins Academy Awards for Best Picture and Best Screenplay. In December 1943, General de Gaulle asks for a copy to be shown to Free French Forces. Bogart visits North Africa in 1943 on behalf of the Hollywood Victory Committee.

The movie will inspire a Bugs Bunny parody, the Marx Brothers' *A Night in Casablanca*, and tribute titles from Neil Simon and Woody Allen. The Italian semiotician Umberto Eco finds "Homeric depths" in its narrative and "a myth of sacrifice." Semioticians sometimes know best. At the box office, *Casablanca* makes $6.8 million by 1955.

Michael Curtiz, for the first and only time in his career, collects an Academy Award for Best Director. Humbled, he grabs the microphone stand by the neck and says shakily, "So many times I have a speech ready but no dice. Always a bridesmaid, never a mother." The quip joins his lexicon of comic malapropisms.

The team breaks up. Bergman falls in love with Robert Capa, another Budapest Jew. Bogart marries Lauren Bacall, a Jew from the Bronx. Hal Wallis falls out with Jack Warner after the studio owner clings to the producer's Oscar statuette. Curtiz screws himself a pay raise out of Warner but soon quits to go freelance. Sam Goldwyn Jr. says of him: "Work was everything. When he left on Saturday, he was waiting to come back to work on Monday."[21] Curtiz tells a reporter, "I work because I don't want to be kicked out."[22] He tells another, "It doesn't exist—friendship—here."[23] An eternal refugee, he longs for home. "I was walking in the streets of Hollywood, when all of a sudden it seemed as if the palm tree lined pavement slid from beneath my feet and I was walking around the deck of a huge ship gliding back towards Hungary," he writes to a friend. "My nostalgia for Pest threw me back . . . could I be buried in Pest?"[24]

Living alone in a tiny apartment in Sherman Oaks, Curtiz dies of cancer in April 1962, days after delivering *The Comancheros* for John Wayne. At Forest Lawn cemetery, his coffin is carried by Jack Warner, Cary Grant, Danny Thomas, and Alan Ladd. Hollywood never figures out what it is that makes *Casablanca* tick or why it stands the test of time. But Hollywood without *Casablanca* would not be Hollywood. And the displacement anxiety of Michael Curtiz is crucial to the making of its legend.

A schoolboy refugee from Vienna writes to Eleanor Roosevelt appealing for her help in getting a college scholarship. The letter is fed by the White House to the Washington bureaucracy, and the boy is accepted at a Presbyterian college in Missouri, then at Kenyon College, Ohio. Nobody notices he has not finished high school and is only sixteen years old. In 1942, aged nineteen, Carl Djerassi is in his third year of college and working in the laboratories of a Swiss-based company in New Jersey, developing an antihistamine that will be registered as his first patent.

The son of a Bulgarian Sephardi and an Austrian Ashkenazi, both medical doctors, Djerassi has no time to lose. He marries at twenty to lose his virginity, and quickly divorces in Mexico. Colleagues fear that Djerassi is too fast and too brilliant at too many things. Any time he spares from science, he devotes to the study of his Viennese cultural heritage.

That same year, 1942, a crackpot chemist, Russell Earl Marker, boards a train for Mexico to test his theory that the female sex hormone, progesterone, can be synthesized from plants. Marker, raised in a Maryland log cabin, quits the Rockefeller Institute after being told by the biochemist Phoebus Levene that he is barking up the wrong tree. He quits his post at Penn State and sinks all his savings into researching the giant Mexican yam, *cabeza de negro* (*Annona purpurea*). This yam's roots weigh up to a hundred pounds. In Mexico City, Marker hooks up with a lab that he finds in a telephone directory, and his theory is soon proven right. By means of the Marker degradation, progesterone can be extracted from the yam in large quantities. Marker, aware that American doctors are beginning to use progesterone injections for women who suffer frequent miscarriages, glimpses a commercial application.

In Massachusetts, the biologist Gregory Pincus is seriously disgruntled. After creating a baby rabbit by in vitro fertilization, he earns a "Dr. Frankenstein" tag in a *New York Times* report and is accused of detaching parenthood from human love. Whether because he is a Jew, or due to his sudden notoriety, Harvard refuses him tenure. Having grown up on a Russian-Jewish commune in rural New Jersey, Pincus prefers bucolic surroundings and joins Clark University in Worcester, Massachusetts. Here, he founds the Worcester Foundation for Experimental Biology. His concern, he says, is to understand "why does an egg start to develop and why does it continue to develop?" But "Goody" Pincus co-opts the town's rabbi, Levi Olan, onto his board. He is aware that he is heading into uncharted moral territory.

Sex is an explosive subject and, at this time, anything but safe. To have sex without tempting fate, a man must withdraw his penis from the vagina before ejaculation or wear a rubber sheath. A woman can insert a synthetic diaphragm, which, smeared with spermicidal cream, may stop fertilization, but this is far from foolproof. The Roman Catholic Church, which forbids contraception, recommends a "rhythm method"; sex only during the infertile phase of the menstrual cycle. Sex is fraught with the fear of an unwanted pregnancy. Women who become pregnant have few options for safe abortion. Single mothers face social opprobrium. Babies born out of wedlock are commonly given up for adoption. There is little charity, Christian or human, to an unwed mother. Sex is one of the Church's control mechanisms. Take the fear out of sex and chaos could result. Pincus, an eclectic Jew, is walking blindfolded into a minefield.

The first pioneer drops out in a year. Marker, falling out with his Mexican lab, takes his Marker degradation back to the US. In 1949, aged forty-seven, he is bored with yams and spends the rest of his life in Pennsylvania, making replicas of antique silver objects.

The Mexican lab owners call in a Budapest Jew from Cuba to pick up where Marker left off. George Rosenkranz, an expert in venereal disease, finds that Marker has deleted his workings. There is no PhD chemistry program in Mexico to provide him with assistants. By chance he runs into Djerassi, seven years his junior and familiar with Mexico after his divorce. Djerassi signs on as associate director. Having successfully synthesized cortisone, he applies the same process to progesterone. In five months, he achieves the breakthrough. The path to the contraceptive pill is powered by three Jews: Rosenkranz and Djerassi on the chemical track and Pincus (with his Chinese assistant, Dr. Min Chueh Chang) on the biological.

At a 1951 dinner party, Pincus meets a birth-control advocate, Margaret Sanger, who is funded by an elderly heiress, Katharine McCormick. Covering his back, Pincus recruits gynecologist John Rock, a Boston Catholic who takes Communion every morning and defies the Church by offering his patients birth control. Rock, in his sixties, does not want to die without making an improvement in women's lives. Word arrives from Mexico that the Djerassi team has perfected a compound, norethisterone, that is more active than human progesterone. Pincus is one of four peers to whom the substance is sent for testing.

Rock and Pincus conduct clinical trials on fifty women in Massachusetts, followed by five hundred women in Rio Pedras, Puerto Rico. Some are taken from asylums (did they run this past the rabbi or the priest?). The pill achieves almost 100 percent success in suppressing pregnancy. In 1957, the US Food and Drug Administration approves norethynodrel (Enovid), initially as a treatment for menstrual disorders. In 1960, it is licensed for prescription as a female contraceptive, though only to married women in certain parts of the United States. It takes several lawsuits and much protest before the Pill, as it is known, is made available in 1972 across America to all women without regard to marital status. Pope Paul VI issues a 1968 encyclical, *Humanae Vitae*, condemning contraception as a violation of the Church's teachings. Protestant churches are more relaxed from the outset, and Orthodox rabbis gradually permit the Pill to married women.

There are widespread reports of side effects. The Pill contains too much estrogen. Cases of thrombosis, phlebitis, migraine, and jaundice are recorded. Some women lose their fertility. Safety concerns will persist for decades, along with hundreds of lawsuits. The Pill is one of the biggest talking points in the mass media. It sets off the sexual and feminist revolutions of the 1960s, empowering women to make choices about their bodies and freeing them to engage in meaningful careers and less constricting relationships. Men are forced to reform timeworn habits and prejudices, at home and at work. Equality of the sexes becomes a realistic possibility. The roles of men and women will never be the same again.

Of the three inventors, Pincus displays a Talmudic turn of mind. "Pincus can interrupt a critical problem to take ten phone calls and then switch his mind back to the problem in a second," says a colleague. "Recognizing people and human frailties as they exist, he has freed himself from emotional turbulence."[25] Where Djerassi focuses on making an artificial hormone, Pincus poses a hypothesis: In what situation might a married woman be permitted not to get pregnant? Clearly, if she is pregnant already. Ergo, all science has to do is simulate a state of pregnancy and the woman is then free to use contraception.

Pincus dies of bone cancer in 1967, leaving Djerassi to strut alone as the Face of the Pill. He becomes fabulously rich, buys a ranch in California, amasses the world's largest collection of art by Paul Klee, and turns to writing novels and plays. Djerassi foresees a future in which sex becomes "purely recreational,"[26] just for fun, isolated from the act of procreation, which will take place in a laboratory between frozen eggs and frozen sperm.

"How many acts of sexual intercourse would you guess occur every 24 hours?" he asks a British journalist:

> I often do this with my students, and they say a billion. I say: "No, no, no, you're dreaming. There are six billion people. Well, you need two for sexual intercourse, so there are only three billion. And some of them are five years old, so they're out." So then they say a million. Well, now you're underestimating, because you're sitting here and you're not having sex. It's actually 100 [million], every 24 hours. And they produce about a million conceptions, about half of which are unexpected. Of the 500,000, half of them are unwanted. As a result, every 24 hours, 150,000 abortions occur; of these, over 50,000 are illegal.[27]

Djerassi dies at ninety-one, in 2015. Rosenkranz reaches the age of one hundred and two at his death in 2018.

In Jerusalem, they still talk of the beggar woman who sits in cafés claiming she is a princess of Egypt. Else Lasker-Schüler is so poor she cannot fit a bed in her rented room; she sleeps upright in a chair. She rails day and night against her landlady, who makes her clean her room. She, who is of royal birth, whose poems are recited on state occasions. Some say she is mentally ill. They are quite wrong. Else is the most lucid poet since Heine, "the greatest lyric female poet that Germany ever possessed," in the words of Gottfried Benn. How she happens to be in Jerusalem in 1942 is haphazard, but here she sits, and the poems flow.

> Come to me at night in seven-starred boots
> Late into my tent, clothed in love
> Moons will rise out of dusty chests of light.
>
> We will rest our love like two rare beasts
> In the tall reeds, beyond this world.

A descendant of rabbis, Else is married off at twenty-four to a Berlin chess fanatic, Berthold Lasker, whose brother is world champion. The marriage fails, and she becomes pregnant by a man she meets "in the street." The baby, Paul, is the love of her life. In 1901, she marries Georg Levin, a penniless young writer, whom she renames Herwarth Walden. A monocled poseur, Walden opens a gallery with works by expressionists, among them Oskar Kokoschka and Otto Nebel. Else publishes two volumes of poems, *Styx* and *The Seventh Day*, but she is unsuited to conjugality. "I know you and you know me," she tells Walden after ten years together. "We can no longer astonish each other, and I cannot live without surprise."[28] Her next volume is titled *My Surprise*. When she cannot afford rent, she sleeps with little Paul underneath a table in the Café des Westens. Friends raise a collection.

Of her next three lovers—the poets Gottfried Benn and Georg Trakl and the artist Franz Marc—two fall in the First World War. Else invents a new persona—she becomes Yussuf, Prince of Thebes:

> I scatter in space
> in time
> in eternity
> and my soul glows
> in the twilight shades
> of Jerusalem.

Between the wars, she is a Berlin institution, dressed in exotic robes, perpetually homeless, so hungry that "I feed off my fingertips like asparagus heads." Paul falls ill with tuberculosis. Albert Einstein raises a fund for his medical care. Else sits at her son's bedside for weeks, holding his hand until, in December 1927, he dies: "You will always die, for me, with the parting year, my child, when the leaves crumble and the branches are thin."

She channels her grief into *Arthur Aronymus*, a play in which Jewish girls in Westphalia are about to be burned on the scaffold until peace and harmony breaks out between Christians and Jews. Part *La Juive*, part *Nathan the Wise*, the play has an irresistible lyricism and a spirit of optimism that runs counter to the times. Rowohlt publishes a prose version, which Franz Werfel calls:

> . . . a wholly wonderful work . . . It is the most Jewish and at the same time the most naïve work of art that one can imagine . . . Ironically enough, it is also the most *German* work that I know. None of the so-called "national poets" of today could write anything even remotely as close to the true nature of Germany and its people.[29]

Else gives a public reading at the Schubert-Saal on the Nollendorfplatz in November 1932. "When is it going to be staged?" a journalist demands. The Prussian Academy of Arts awards Else a thousand marks. She sends it back with an open letter to the academy's president, Heinrich Mann, denouncing its inbuilt prejudice against women writers.

She does accept the Kleist Prize and, with it, the recognition that she is not a freak but a genius, a member of the literary elite. *Arthur Aronymus*, "a story from my father's childhood," is scheduled for performance in Darmstadt but overtaken by events. In April 1933, Else is assaulted by SA men and knocked to the ground outside her rooming house. Not bothering to go inside and pack a bag, she takes a train to Zurich and sleeps for six nights on a park bench. Brought before the magistrates, the plight of a Kleist Prize winner arouses a public outcry, and the canton grants her a residence permit. *Arthur Aronymus* is premiered at the Schauspielhaus Zürich but is taken down after just two shows, possibly under pressure from Berlin.

Dreaming of an ethereal Jerusalem, she makes two trips to the Holy Land before deciding, in 1939, to remain—a decision she instantly regrets. No one cares here for poetry, she sighs. "Even King David would have moved on. I live, forgotten, in poems" (*im Gedicht*).[30] At her café table, she bewails the plight of street children, Arabs, and Jews, and rails at bigwigs who ignore their needs. "So long as there is one hungry child, God will abolish synagogues," she declares. "I believe I am speaking in God's name."

No one listens. Ignored by her well-established Hebrew University acquaintances Buber and Scholem, Else is lonely and isolated. Other than the kindness of the novelist S. Y. Agnon, who invites her home for Sabbath meals, and Max Brod, who asks her to revise *Arthur Aronymus* for the Habimah Theatre, she is an outcast once more. A stipend from the publisher Salman Schocken fends off starvation. The Swiss refuse to readmit her.

In letters to Leo Kestenberg, she names her habitat "Misrael." "The Jerusalem of God is dead," she tells Ernst Simon, whom she reimagines as her lover in a poem, "Ich liebe Dich." "I am lost and out of reach and I cannot reach anyone. My life has ended in a prison."[31] Unstable on her feet, propping herself against trees and walls, she is pissed on by a passing dog. "I am no longer worth anything," she writes.

The Hebrew poet Leah Goldberg, who has seen her in Berlin's Café des Westens, finds Else in exile. "We went to Zichel's Café. Upon entering I saw Else Lasker-Schüler sitting at one of the tables. The café was almost empty. She sat in her usual place, grey as a bat, small, poor, withdrawn . . . This dreadful poverty, the terrible loneliness of the great poet." But Else can still dream. "Jesus Christ sat in the moon in the night," she writes. "He came in a dream to me, very close to my bed and said: 'Jerusalem is not lost. It lives in your heart.'"

One freezing day in January 1945, Else Lasker-Schüler falls in the street and is taken to Hadassah Hospital, where she dies, aged seventy-five. On the Mount of Olives, a rabbi recites her last poem over her open grave: "*Ich weiss dass ich bald sterben muss*" (I know that I must soon die). The poet, always a prophet, tempers fate with resignation. Leah Goldberg shivers. "Was I not also bound to be poor, solitary and virtually outcast like her, had I not been untrue to myself every single day, had I not been unfaithful to the truth, to purity, to poetry? Was her terrible sitting [in the café] not a symbol for all those lives of injustice that we, the others, who often write in resounding rhymes, have led?" Goldberg, who lives with her mother in a two-room Tel Aviv flat one street back from the sea, escapes to Café Kassit on Dizengoff Street, sitting alone at her *stammtisch* (regular table in the café), refusing company.

In a new society founded on physical labor, the café dweller is a contrarian, a figure of European decadence. The newspaper *Davar*, for which Leah writes, calls them *batlanim*, idlers. Leah Goldberg is no idler, however. Wreathed in cigarette smoke, she makes translations of world classics for the Working People publishing house. Her Pasternak reads better in Hebrew than in any language except, perhaps, Russian. "'*Batlanim*' actually met there after an exhausting day of work," she whispers. "All of us used to 'steal some time' in order to write poems. . . . In the evening, instead of laying down to sleep, we allowed ourselves to be *batlanim*, sit in the café, converse, and argue."[32] She teaches comparative literature at the Hebrew University. In the summer of 1969, when I register for the course, she is in Switzerland, recovering from cancer surgery. Months later, she dies, aged fifty-eight. In one of her drawers, they find a last poem: "*Machar ani amut—tomorrow I shall die.*" Like Else Lasker-Schüler, Leah Goldberg looks God in the eye and dares Him to blink.

FIFTEEN

1947
NEW YORK, NEW YORK

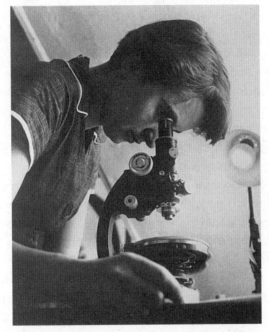

Cracking the human code: Rosalind Franklin
at work on the secrets of identity.

I t's a wonderful town. With Europe in ruins and the boys coming
home, America's biggest city is the creative hub of the free world.
"New York, New York" is the theme song of *On the Town*, a Broad-

way show created by the choreographer Jerome Robbins to music by Leonard Bernstein and a script by Betty Comden and Adolph Green. Four first-generation Americans, they speak the same language: Jewish. Elsewhere on Broadway, Rodgers and Hammerstein are closing *Carousel* after two years, and Kurt Weill is presenting *Street Scene*, the closest thing to a New York opera before *West Side Story* and with the best sextet since *Così fan tutte*. Weill, Busoni's best Berlin pupil, has made it big in pop. Everyone wants to record his "September Song," from Bing Crosby, to Sarah Vaughan, to Frank Sinatra.

New names abound. Arthur Miller makes his stage debut with *All My Sons*. Norman Mailer's *The Naked and the Dead* tops the bestseller list for sixteen weeks. Irwin Shaw writes the next big war novel, *The Young Lions*. At the New School, Elia Kazan and Stella Adler run a drama workshop with Tony Curtis and Marlon Brando as students. Mark Rothko and Barnett Newman are the gallery stars of abstract expressionism. Robert Moses exercises an iron grip on urban planning, for better and worse. Still, the city works. In the year's smallpox scare, it vaccinates six million residents in a month.

Edwin Land invents the Polaroid instant camera—sixty seconds from shutter click to a printed photo—founding a new cult of intimate snapshots. Peter Goldmark, a Budapest Jew who is Columbia's chief television engineer, is fed up with turning over symphonic records every four minutes, "like having the phone ring at intervals while you're making love." He develops a record that revolves at thirty-three-and-a-third rotations a minute and only needs changing every half hour. A CBS producer, Goddard Lieberson, turns the LP into a money-spinner. Four students of the Bronx High School of Science this year, all Jewish, will win Nobel Prizes. Three others will win Pulitzers. E. L. Doctorow becomes the city's supreme historical novelist. New York has never been newer or more Jewish.

Amid the talent boom, no one is less reticent than Leonard Bernstein, a Harvard-trained musician who shoots to fame on a Sunday afternoon, conducting the New York Philharmonic in a radio concert after Bruno Walter falls ill that day. He makes the front page of the *New York Times* ("Young Aide Leads Philharmonic, Steps In When Bruno Walter Is Ill") and, at twenty-five, is a made man. A protégé of Serge Koussevitzky at the Boston Symphony, Bernstein is an eye-catching gymnast on the podium, a dazzling pianist, and a fertile composer of symphonic and theatrical scores, straddling highbrow and low. Lithe, good-looking, ferociously intelligent, and inexhaustibly gregarious, he is a magnet to both sexes, flaunting his lovers, mostly male, without fear or much favor. Lenny prances around like all three sailors in *On the Town*. Nobody calls him Leonard.

As much as his gay abandon, he flaunts his Jewish roots with wanton swagger. Aaron Copland, a generation older, keeps his head down and his gay connections quiet. Copland writes award-winning "Amurrican" music for Hollywood Westerns and pretends in *Appalachian Spring* that he is some kind of Puritan fresh from the *Mayflower*. Copland has studied in Paris with Nadia Boulanger, washing away the last of his Jewishness in a font of neoclassicism. Only one work, the violin sonata *Vitebsk*, hints at his shtetl origin. Lenny, in his first symphony, splashes tropes from his bar mitzvah reading and calls the work *Jeremiah*. His second symphony, *The Age of Anxiety* (after W. H. Auden's poem), takes a Jewish topic. The third symphony is *Kaddish*. He raises two fingers to Gentile America. He is Jewish, out, and proud, and to hell with WASPs and glass ceilings. In life as in music, Lenny speaks with a Jewish cadence, throwing in Yiddish words at rehearsal, talking to his audience as if it is family. No classical musician has done this before. He acts as if being Jewish is the norm for a great composer, as it is for a comedian, a tailor, or a financier.

His symphonies do not gel. They are grab bags of half-formed ideas, written helter-skelter to missed deadlines, and leaving musicians and audiences uncomfortable at their excess. His violin concerto, *Serenade after Plato's Symposium*, would be insufferably presumptuous were it not, quite possibly, a Harvard in-joke. Crackling with irreverence and adventure, Lenny never takes classical music at its own pretensions. When the dean of Chichester commissions a Psalm setting for chorus and orchestra, Bernstein insists on having it sung in the original Hebrew in an Anglican cathedral. So there. Of all his concert works, *Chichester Psalms* is by some measure the most uplifting.

In 1947, Lenny visits Palestine, bonding with its philharmonic orchestra of German refugees and its kibbutzim of Russian pioneers. He returns during the independence war to play piano in a desert clearing to sand-caked Jewish fighters. "They will never let their land be taken from them; they will die first," he informs Koussevitzky. "The bombs fly, but the newspapers exaggerate."[1] Bernstein leaves Israel a new Jew, neither nationalist nor socialist, nor particularly religious, but one who has shaken off the historical cringe.

"Sweetie," he addresses Copland, "the end [of Copland's third symphony] is a sin. You've got to change. Stop the presses! We must talk—about the whole last movement, in fact . . . By the way, I do it awfully well, and I'd love to do it in the States."[2] Filled with his own hot air, he undermines Copland's confidence and rubs his friend's nose in the reality that all Lenny has to do is stand in front of an orchestra and everything comes up roses. While Copland struggles to conduct, Lenny is a fearlessly coherent interpreter of new music great and small. He is the shining light of a generation that speaks culture with an American accent.

Brimming with the joys of spring, Bernstein returns from Europe to an America that has turned against him. The State Department, acting on an FBI report, confiscates his passport. Boston rejects him as Koussevitzky's successor. "A prisoner in my own country,"[3] a baton without a band, he is required to swear a loyalty oath: "I am not now nor ever have been at any time a member of the Communist Party . . . knowingly engaged in activities which supported the Communist movement . . . adhered to the so-called Communist Party line." In the hiatus, awaiting clearance, he marries Felicia Montealegre, a Catholic actress from Chile who converts to Judaism. They bring up a model family of Manhattan respectability. This is prime composing time. He writes jazz riffs for Benny Goodman—aware that Copland has written him a concerto—and tackles, in the wittiest of his stage works, Voltaire's *Candide*, in which "all is for the best in the best of all possible worlds." Its hilarious aria "I am so easily assimilated" is a blatant parable of Jewish peregrination. Its overture is the most concentrated stretch of orchestral exhilaration he ever achieves.

He next turns his attention to the New York melting pot. *West Side Story*, created with his *On the Town* team, plus the writer Arthur Laurents and the lyricist Stephen Sondheim, is an all-Jewish, almost-all-gay scenario about Puerto Rican immigrants playing out Shakespeare's *Romeo and Juliet* story. Bernstein composes one of the great stage love songs in "Maria," captures his nation's contortions in "America," and writes a Schoenberg twelve-note row in the "Cool" fugue. This is a composer who can do anything when the mood is on him. "Somewhere" (there's a place for us) is Bernstein's "Summertime," the moment he reaches Gershwin's mark and surpasses it. Copland will never come close.

West Side Story is bombproof. It survives the disaster casting of opera singers Kiri Te Kanawa and José Carreras in Bernstein's recording, a host of smoochers and crooners in lesser productions, and a spate of twenty-first-century protests whenever non-Latinos are cast in the main roles. In the year of its premiere, Bernstein is named music director of the New York Philharmonic Orchestra, the top job for an American conductor. At Carnegie Hall, he performs America's first cycle of Mahler symphonies, launches new composers, embarks on cultural diplomacy to Russia, gives Saturday-morning music lessons from Carnegie Hall on television, and leads the nation's mourning at the assassinations of President Kennedy and his brother Robert. His signature piece is Charles Ives's *The Unanswered Question*. "Isn't it a flagrant piece of elitism?" he challenges a Harvard audience in a lecture on musical syntax. No conductor has ever connected so extensively with the next generation and the liberal intelligentsia. After a dozen years, his mercurial curiosity subsides, and he grows bored with leading an often murmurous orchestra. America has changed. Richard Nixon is president, and the Vietnam War hangs heavy in the sky.

He wanders to Europe, winding up at the Vienna Philharmonic, which has war criminals on its honors board and unrepentant Nazis among its players. Helmut Wobisch, the horn player and orchestral fixer, is not just an ardent Nazi but an SS man. Bernstein is wondering whether or not to shake his hand when he receives a letter from Georg Solti, a Hungarian refugee who has recorded Wagner's *Ring* in Vienna. "Dear Mr. Bernstein," writes Solti from London, where he is music director at the Royal Opera House, "As another Jewish conductor I understand your feelings surely better than anyone else . . . I am aware of Wobisch's political past [but . . .] despite everything he is probably one of the most trustworthy members of that orchestra." To force Wobisch out would not only "be bad for the orchestra but that both you and I might well find any replacement totally unacceptable for political and human reasons."[4] Solti is warning, as one Jew to another, that there are no shades of gray in Vienna: all are Nazis and there is nothing for a Jew to do but hold one's nose and make the best of it. Neither has any thought of pulling out. Their shameless expediency reveals a collective lack of moral courage or judgment.

Lenny grows to trust the Vienna Philharmonic so completely that he conducts the finale of a Haydn symphony by facial gestures alone, both hands clasped behind his back.[5] He speaks to the Viennese in a mixture of English and Yiddishized German. He founds festivals in Germany and Japan. He wants to be loved everywhere, and he likes to be around when history is being made. On Christmas Day 1989, six weeks after the fall of the Berlin Wall, he conducts Beethoven's ninth symphony in the Berlin Konzerthaus, changing one word, *freude* (joy), in the chorus to *freiheit* (freedom). Cue headlines.

As his celebrity grows, his personal conduct becomes gross. He greets new acquaintances by sticking his tongue in their mouth. His devoted daughter Jamie confesses in a memoir that he tongue kisses her. When she is twenty, he encourages her into bed with a German pianist he fancies for himself. He leaves Felicia for a male lover, returning when she is mortally ill. "You're going to die a bitter and lonely old man," she says. Lenny, widowed, tests the tolerance of all around him. There is nothing pretty or purposeful about his actions, although there is always a suspicion that he is looking to expose hypocrisy. It is as if he is trying to say: *I am the Jew you've always been warned against, how do you like that?* Self-disgust is his signature act. Is it Jewish self-hate? Or a kind of penance? Lenny, for whatever perverse reason, turns his sometime golden boy persona into something warped and loathsome.

This man who is as much at home on Broadway as in Berlin's Philharmonie, as eloquent at Harvard as at children's concerts, a media performer who never plays to the camera yet controls it completely, this man who has all the gifts, squanders them, one by one. To meet him late in his life can be an ordeal. Ringed by young men who leap to his whims, wreathed in cigarette smoke and with a tumbler of whiskey at his elbow, he is a picture of debauchery, reeking—in the actual, olfactory sense—of bodily corruption. He is too fat for his trousers and too smug to be liked. Yet the force of his personality is undimmed. All I have to do is open a score of Mahler's ninth symphony or quote a Hebrew phrase and the eyes come alive, the gravelly voice crackles with wordplay, and one feels a deep sorrow for this wreck of a man. At his final concert, with the Boston Symphony, he loses bladder control and leaves the stage in a paroxysm of emphysema. Death arrives weeks later at the age of seventy-two.

Yehudi Menuhin dubs him New York's finest. He is the face of midcentury Manhattan and the most Jewish musician of his time. He attends Yom Kippur at the Orthodox Fifth Avenue Synagogue and receives a rabbinic Jewish burial in Brooklyn, with Mahler's fifth symphony placed upon his heart. What is the meaning of it all? In the course of a firefly life, he has recast the Jew in the public eye as a person who does not apologize for his faith and will not be mistaken for a wishy-washy humanist. Lenny is God's Jew, farts and all. Barely five and a half feet tall, he stands two sizes larger than life, a stub of a man who can enter a crowded room and leave no one unaware. In the words of Chaim Weizmann: "Jews are just like everyone else. Only more so." That's Lenny Bernstein.

In a double-fronted house on a main drag in Brooklyn, a Hasidic sect confronts a fragile future. Their rebbe is confined to a wheelchair by multiple sclerosis, diabetes, and a stroke. The house of Chabad-Lubavitch, a movement that sits midway between Hasidic mysticism and Lithuanian rationalism, is muted by Holocaust shock. Every family is in mourning, "for there is no house where there is not one dead."[6] The rebbe's youngest daughter, Sheina Horenstein, has been gassed with her husband in Treblinka. As in all communities, a curtain of silence falls on the horror so that each family bears its loss without collective consolation. God is kept out of the frame. There is no Holocaust theodicy. Later, when others raise memorials to their martyrs, Chabad holds back. A resolution has been taken by its incoming rebbe not to commemorate the past but to save souls for the future. This decision will have a greater impact on Judaism than any movement since the dawn of Reform.

Chabad is new to America, its arrival arising from circumstances that seem almost miraculous. The story, which takes decades to emerge, is that the sixth rebbe, Yosef Yitzchak Schneersohn, is plucked from Poland by a secret unit of German Army intelligence. At the start of the war, the rebbe is trapped in Warsaw during the Jewish New Year. Warsaw is bombed, then starved, by the Germans. Hasidim in America, fearing for the rebbe's safety, contact Senator Robert F. Wagner of New York, who approaches the US secretary of state, Cordell Hull, for humanitarian assistance. America is not at war with Germany, and the State Department maintains good contacts in Berlin with a number of agencies. A DC official knows a guy who works for Hermann Göring, a former Columbia student called Helmuth Wohlthat. This man's job is seizing Jewish assets across the Reich, but he is happy to hear from the Americans and can see personal advantage in doing them a favor. High-ranking as he is, Wohlthat can do nothing on his own and dares not share his information, since no Nazi in Berlin wants to be caught helping a Hasidic rebbe. He takes his problem to the most secretive man in Berlin, Admiral Wilhelm Canaris, head of the Abwehr (military intelligence). Canaris has a free hand to conduct covert operations in German territories and abroad. But he is starting to worry that Hitler is going off the rails. "This means the end for Germany,"[7] he tells staff after the invasion of Poland, "our children's children will have to bear the blame for this."[8] Having seen the SS burn a synagogue with two hundred Jews inside, Canaris shares his dissidence with a handful of other Wehrmacht patriots. He is the only man with the means and the daring to extricate a rebbe from the clutches of the SS, and Wohlthat is right in thinking that Canaris would welcome contact with the Americans.

For special operations, Canaris keeps several half-Jews on his staff. For the rebbe rescue, he assigns Major Ernst Ferdinand Benjamin Bloch, a decorated First World War hero with a Jewish father and a face frighteningly disfigured by a bayonet wound. Canaris orders Bloch to go to Warsaw, find the rebbe, and get him out. Bloch is allowed to take two aides—Sergeant Klaus Schenk and Private Johannes Hamburger, both half-Jewish.

They drive to Warsaw, check in with the Abwehr office, change into civilian clothes, and enter the ghetto, calling "Shalom" to passersby. Bloch finds a Hasid who admits to knowing the Chabad people. Hearing the Germans are looking for him, the rebbe goes deeper into hiding. It is the end of November 1939 before Bloch tracks him down in a ruined building. The rebbe sends out a son-in-law, Rabbi Shmaryahu Gurary. Bloch conveys his mission. The rebbe sends back conditions.

He wants to take an entourage twice the size Bloch envisaged and will require kosher food for the journey (how does a Nazi obtain kosher sandwiches?). The rebbe is also determined to take out his precious library, some forty thousand volumes dating back to the movement's founder. Bloch tells Sergeant Schenk that the rebbe is "totally divorced from reality."[9] He secures seventeen visas from the US consul in Warsaw. Canaris is concerned that Joachim von Ribbentrop's foreign ministry may read the diplomatic signals and blow the whistle. He tells Bloch to move quickly.

Two weeks before Christmas, Bloch and his men turn up in uniform and start loading Jews onto a truck. At the sight of an SS patrol he yells, "Get in, you pigs!" The truck moves out with the rebbe at the front sitting next to Bloch, whom he questions about his Jewish soul. Stopped at a checkpoint, Bloch leaps out and castigates the SS for not saluting him properly. At the next barrier rifles are pointed at the rebbe's head while an SS officer demands to know on whose authority Bloch is taking Jews out of Warsaw. Bloch reels off the names and ranks of all the SS chiefs he knows until the black-cap bows to rank.

They finally reach a railway station, where the ticket inspector queries why these Jews are traveling first-class and, of all places, to Berlin. The train is crammed with Nazis. The swastika flies at every station along the way. In Berlin, Bloch escorts the Hasidim to an overnight stay at a Jewish organization. Next morning, he picks up a couple of diplomats from the Latvian embassy and takes them on board a train with the Hasidim, heading northeast. At the Latvian border, he bids farewell to the rebbe, whose followers dance with joy and relief on the other side. In Riga, the rebbe's mother undergoes abdominal surgery, and the rebbe himself falls and breaks his arm. It is February 1940 before the group boards a ship to Sweden and on to the United States, mission accomplished.

Bloch and Canaris will die within days of each other in April 1945, Bloch fighting the Russians in Berlin and Canaris humiliated and hanged for his part in an anti-Hitler plot. Wohlthat rides out the war as an economic attaché in Tokyo, finishing his career with a nomination to the World Bank. Their rescue story remains secret until the twenty-first century when an American historian, Bryan Mark Rigg, publishes two books about Jews in the Wehrmacht. In 2009, Chabad applies for Bloch and Canaris to be honored by the Yad Vashem institute as "righteous among nations." The approach is received with confusion: Could the remembrance center for victims grant an honor to Hitler's head of military intelligence? Ten years on, the request is still pending.

In New York, the rebbe turns a mansion on 770 Eastern Parkway into the headquarters of Chabad-Lubavitch. There is a new language to be learned, a cultural adjustment to be made. The senior son-in-law, Rabbi Gurary, is put in charge of the yeshiva and the ordination of rabbis. The younger son-in-law, Rabbi Menachem Mendel Schneersohn, takes charge of education. One or the other is destined to be the next rebbe, and there is friction between their followers. Gurary has played a pivotal role in springing the rebbe from captivity while M. M. Schneersohn is regarded with suspicion for his Western clothes and education. He has studied philosophy, mathematics, and physics at the University of Berlin, moving on to mechanical and electrical engineering at ESTP in Paris, one of the *grandes écoles*, graduating in 1937. He also attends courses at the Sorbonne, taking in the major streams of European thought. It is unheard-of for a potential rebbe to attend university. Once in New York, instead of devoting his life to the study of Torah, M. M. Schneersohn goes to work as an engineer in the Brooklyn Navy Yard, supervising electrical wiring on Liberty cargo ships. "I did my share for the war effort of the United States, which gave me shelter," he says.[10]

On lunch breaks, he reads *Ripley's Believe It or Not!* and *Dick Tracy* over his workmates' shoulders. Comic strips begin to appear in Chabad children's magazines. In summertime, he sets up study camps from one coast to the other, reaching out across a continent where Reform and Conservative synagogues are losing their grip and half of all young Jews leave the faith. The official history of Chabad (there is no other, since external historians are denied access) records that Menachem Mendel Schneersohn is the choice of the sixth rebbe as his successor. But there is no statement to this effect from the ailing rebbe and the choice of a new rebbe is dependent, in any event, on acclamation by a majority of Hasidim. Gurary's claims are considerable: he is the senior candidate, and his Talmudic expertise is unchallenged. What Schneersohn brings is personal charm, profound humility, and a prospect of renewal. The rebbe dies on January 28, 1950. A year later Menachem Mendel Schneersohn becomes the seventh Chabad-Lubavitcher rebbe.

His opening words, *"bati legani"* (I have come into my garden), are taken from his predecessor's last address. He emphasizes continuity, but his plans are radical. Judaism has never been an outreach religion. It deters would-be converts from other faiths and washes its hands of children who drop out. Each person has free choice; if he or she decides to defect, no one will step outside the lines to bring them back. Menachem Mendel Schneersohn overturns this attitude. Faced with millions dead in the Holocaust and millions more marrying out in the American melting pot, he presents a strategy to reclaim a legion of strayed souls.

"One must go to a place where nothing is known of Godliness, nothing is known of Judaism, nothing is even knowing [*sic*] of the Hebrew alphabet, and while there, put one's own self aside and ensure that the other calls out to God!" he tells followers in his opening address.[11] He sends young couples in their twenties to university towns in the middle of America to attract students who have never tasted what it is to be Jewish. Typically, the *shluchim* (emissaries) put on a Friday-night dinner with gefilte fish, chicken soup, brisket, and plenty of wine, vodka, and chat. Cheered by the glow of a good meal, students return to Sabbath services in the Chabad house and are gently introduced to religious requisites: lighting Sabbath candles, laying *tefilin* at morning prayer, eating kosher food, placing a *mezuzah* on the doorpost, giving charity, observing marital respect, studying Torah.

Contrary to Orthodox norms, couples are equal partners: the wife's role is as vital as the rabbi's in providing a safe environment. *Shluchim* are also trained to respect non-Orthodox communities, offering help with classes and kosher food. Chabad *shluchim* go where other rabbis fear to tread. Without compromising their practice, they offer Abrahamic hospitality with no missionary pressure. Students who meet at Sabbath dinner get talking, fall in love, get married, and start communities. The rebbe keeps tabs on all his ambassadors, alert to their requests. Emissaries in a midwestern town tell him that the Reform rabbi would like to see the rebbe with a personal issue. An audience with the rebbe is usually reserved for Chabad followers and VIPs, but the request is, surprisingly, granted. On his return to the Midwest, the Reform rabbi is asked what the rebbe said.

"I told him that, after twenty years here, my wife and I want to go and live in the Holy Land."

"Absolutely not," said the rebbe. "You must stay and serve your community."

"But I am Reform, hardly Jewish in your eyes."

"You are still a rabbi," said the rebbe. "You must stay."

His inclusivity is attractive, and the benefits start to flow. Wealthy Jews who have lived far from Orthodoxy fund Chabad schools across America and, as the campaign goes global, around the world. The rebbe dispatches *shluchim* to Morocco, instructing them to learn indigenous tunes, fluent Arabic, and respect for Sephardi traditions. Emissaries are sent to Brazil and Argentina. Judaism gets a global boost. Jews can now travel almost anywhere with the knowledge that they can find a kosher meal at Chabad. I have spent Sabbath with Chabad in Shanghai, where the rabbi is Moroccan, and heard the Purim reading in Beijing, where there are two Chabad houses, one for Russian speakers. I have danced at a Chabad wedding at the poshest hotel in Venice, eaten sushi with Chabad in Tokyo, and prayed for the rebbe's health in Melbourne, Australia. In Kathmandu, on top of the world, Chabad puts on a Passover seder each year for fifteen hundred gap-year travelers, most of them Israelis. The murder of Chabad *shluchim* by Islamic terrorists in Mumbai, India, in November 2008 arouses universal sympathy for the young victims and awe at their self-sacrifice.

The rebbe's mantra is that Judaism begins not with a declaration of faith but with undertaking one small custom or commandment, be it lighting a menorah at the minor festival of Chanukah or washing hands before a meal. Unlike rigid Orthodoxy, Chabad does not flinch from Sabbath guests in "immodest" blouses and ripped jeans. Orthodoxy is exposed to new members who have, in their recent life, partaken of forbidden flesh. Young Chabad rabbis speak from the pulpit of their former lives as beach bums.

Each night from ten o'clock into the small hours at 770 Eastern Parkway, Menachem Mendel Schneersohn sees visitors for *yechidus*, one-on-one consultations. Aside from *shluchim*, these might include a businessman seeking advice on a new venture and parents discussing marriage partners for their children. The rebbe replies in Yiddish, English, French, German, Russian, and Polish. He listens with intensity and reveals degrees of empathy, sobbing when a couple bewail their childless status. The rebbe, too, has no children. To each visitor, he gives a dollar bill, asking them to donate it to a charity.

In 1964, Robert Kennedy visits the rebbe before making a run for the Senate, with Franklin Delano Roosevelt Jr. and Governor W. Averell Harriman as his wingmen. The rebbe is keen on the Kennedys, remarking that JFK's Peace Corps has much in common with his own corps of young *shluchim* in remote parts of the world.

Every Israeli prime minister comes to pay homage. There is a photograph of the austere Yitzhak Rabin, socialist and atheist, dancing awkwardly with the rebbe in the foyer of 770. Menachem Begin, an observant Jew, calls on the rebbe before he sees President Jimmy Carter in the White House. Benjamin Netanyahu, as ambassador to the United Nations, presents his credentials at 770 before he meets the secretary-general. Arriving in Israel late one night, I see Ariel Sharon on an airport bench, waiting for his driver. He recognizes me from a press conference and beckons me over. I ask where he is flying in from.

"New York," says Sharon.

"United Nations?"

"No, the rebbe. I visit when I can."

The rebbe never visits Israel, arguing that if he ever set foot on holy soil, tradition would forbid him to leave again. His distance from the Jewish state does not preclude him from making interventions in Israeli affairs. On the eve of the 1967 war, he proclaims that soldiers who don *tefilin* before battle will come to no harm. After the victory, he announces that it would be against Jewish law for Israel to give back territories it had conquered. He orders the restoration of a Chabad prayer house in the Old City of Jerusalem and demands a tightening of Israeli citizenship rules to exclude non-Orthodox converts. His long-distance decrees are hotly resented, most obviously by secular Israelis who disdain rabbis, but even more powerfully by the Israeli religious establishment.

The venerable yeshiva leader Rav Elazar Menachem Man Shach issues a stream of attacks on Chabad, defining it acidly as "the world religion that is closest to Judaism." Hasidic rabbis in London warn their followers against "men of Chabad who make great efforts with their false doctrines and slick tongues to trap pure-hearted people in their nets."[12] For all its positive aspects of outreach and moderation, hardline Orthodoxy regards Chabad as a separatist cult, one that flirts at times with dangerous delusions.

In 1977, the rebbe suffers a heart attack and is revived on the spot by the inventor of the defibrillator, Dr. Bernard Lown, himself a Lithuanian rabbi's son. Fifteen years later, the rebbe suffers a stroke while praying at his predecessor's tomb. The Chabad movement is confronted with a dilemma. In the absence of an obvious or likely successor, some begin to acclaim the rebbe as immortal and proclaim him the *Mashiach*—the God-sent Redeemer of the Jewish people. Shach denounces these moves as heretical, irrational, and a threat to the Jewish people. At the rebbe's death in June 1994, many followers persist in the belief that he is still alive. It looks for a while as if Chabad will split between false Messianists and pragmatic realists, a schism of potentially disastrous consequences. But so strong is the rebbe's will that 770 Eastern Parkway continues to function as globally as before, a group of shadowy controllers now forming a leaderless autocracy. Chabad, a charismatic movement without a leader, just carries on growing. A quarter of a century after the rebbe's departure, there are four thousand *shluchim* in Jewish communities in eighty countries, their presence demonstrating how irrevocably Schneersohn changed the face of the faith. His official Chabad biographer calls him "the most influential rabbi in modern history." He may well be right.[13]

The refugee town of Nahariya, just south of the Lebanese border, receives a visit in May 1947 from Kurt Weill, whose refugee parents have settled there. Weill gives his father his new setting of the Friday-night Kiddush and proceeds to reorchestrate the Zionist anthem "Hatikvah." He takes his parents to lunch with Chaim Weizmann—"the greatest honour one can get here"[14]—and is shown around his scientific institute. Each morning, he swims in the Mediterranean, sending beach snaps back to his on-off wife, the singer Lotte Lenya. She writes that, despite playing to full houses, *Street Scene* is about to shut down because its overheads are too high. Brecht writes from California, asking if they might work together again. Weill declines. Those days are over.

• • •

In paradise, there is much unhappiness. Erich Wolfgang Korngold, Hollywood's highest-paid composer, takes themes from his movies *Another Dawn* and *Anthony Adverse* and turns them into a violin concerto. Once hailed by Gustav Mahler as a child prodigy, Korngold dedicates his concerto to Alma Mahler, in an attempt to recover his highbrow status. Jascha Heifetz, the greatest living violinist, plays the concerto's world premiere, on February 15, 1947, in St. Louis, Missouri. Six weeks later, it reaches Carnegie Hall, where two snooty critics are sharpening their pencils. Olin Downes in the *New York Times* attacks this "Hollywood concerto," deciding that "the facility of the writing is matched by the mediocrity of the ideas." In the *Sun*, Irving Kolodin calls it cruelly "more corn than gold." Korngold never recovers. Six months after Carnegie Hall, at the age of fifty, he suffers a massive heart attack. He lives a few years more, a sun-kissed semi-invalid, cursing the cardinals of classical music.

Others face tougher tests. In May 1947, the House of Representatives Un-American Activities Committee (HUAC) opens an investigation into alleged Hollywood Communists at the Biltmore Hotel in Los Angeles. Its first target is a tubby, bespectacled man whom the press has named "the red composer-in-chief." Hanns Eisler, a German refugee, has scored eight movies and been nominated for two Academy Awards. He is the author of a technical study titled *Composing for the Films*, cowritten with the social theorist Theodor Wiesengrund Adorno and published by Oxford University Press. He has a portfolio of pithy cabaret songs and some mildly atonal piano music. He lives quietly in Lotusland, where his friends include Brecht, Chaplin, and Schoenberg. The problem, it transpires, is not so much his friends but his immediate family.

Eisler's brother, Gerhart, is alleged to be the head of the American Communist Party. Their firebrand sister, Ruth Fischer, a former member of the German Reichstag who once called for Jewish capitalists to be hung from lampposts, turns coat in America and denounces her two brothers as dangerous Communists, along with Thomas Mann and his children Erika and Klaus. No intelligence agency would take such charges at face value in normal times, but America is entering its McCarthyite paranoia, and Ruth Fischer's mendacity adds fuel to its fire. Richard Milhous Nixon, counsel to the HUAC investigations, declares that "the case of Hanns Eisler is perhaps the most important ever to have come before the Committee."[15]

Sentenced to one to three years in jail for filing false visa information, Gerhart Eisler skips bail and flees the country. That leaves Hanns to face the committee alone in late September. "Are you now or have you ever been a member of the Communist Party?" he is asked. "No," replies Eisler. "My purpose is to prove that Mr Eisler is the Karl Marx of Communism in the musical field and he is well aware of it," blusters a witness. "I should be flattered," says Eisler. Unable to break him, the committee recommends deportation. "I'm not a hero," protests Eisler mildly, "I'm a composer."

The culture industry rallies to his cause. Albert Einstein seeks asylum for Eisler in European countries. Martha Gellhorn, Ernest Hemingway's wife, publishes a pamphlet attacking McCarthy's "kangaroo court." Picasso and Jean Cocteau sign a petition in France. Bernstein and Copland put on a solidarity concert in New York Town Hall. Kurt Weill drums up support. To no avail. In March 1948, on the steps of a TWA aircraft taking him into a second exile, Hanns Eisler says:

> I leave this country not without bitterness and infuriation. I could well understand it when in 1933 the Hitler bandits put a price on my head and drove me out. They were the evil of the period; I was proud at being driven out. But I feel heartbroken over being driven out of this beautiful country in this ridiculous way.

He lives out his remaining years in East Germany, never confident of Communist approval, living just long enough to see Nixon defeated for the US presidency by John F. Kennedy. In his mind, the HUAC witch hunt was chiefly motivated by anti-Semitism.[16]

Arnold Schoenberg, mortified by news of Eisler's expulsion, writes to his attorney asking if he must now sever contacts with anyone who ever had Communist connections. Unsettled and over seventy, Schoenberg has recovered from a near-fatal heart attack, which he describes musically in a string trio. He presents *A Survivor from Warsaw*, a breathtaking twelve-tone oratorio based on eyewitness accounts from the ghetto, and he is turning to the next score when Alma Mahler tells him, with mischief aforethought, that Thomas Mann has written a novel that traduces his character. In *Doctor Faustus*, Schoenberg's distinctive twelve-note method of composing is attributed to a fictional character, Adrian Leverkühn, an unpleasant fellow in an advanced stage of venereal disease. Schoenberg, to Alma's joy, is incensed. The two men are near-neighbors. Mann sends a courtesy copy of *Doctor Faustus*, inscribed "to Arnold Schoenberg, the real one." This drives Schoenberg even wilder with rage. He sends Mann a satirical encyclopedia entry in which Leverkühn is credited with his invention and Schoenberg is dismissed as an impostor. Mann, embarrassed, agrees to insert a note in all translations and new editions acknowledging Schoenberg's ownership of the twelve-note method. Schoenberg, slowly placated, is concerned for his place in the history of music. "I can count only on posthumous fame, and that I should not still have to defend," he writes.[17]

And there the matter should have rested. But Schoenberg dislikes the wording of Mann's acknowledgment in the English edition and discovers, probably through Alma, that the novelist has been secretly educated in the twelve-note method by the parasitical Frankfurt professor Theodor Wiesengrund Adorno, a musical dilettante whom he despises. Schoenberg rekindles the row in a letter to the *Saturday Review of Literature*, accusing Mann of taking "advantage of my literary property" and defaming him as a syphilitic lunatic. "I am now seventy-four and I am not yet insane, and I have never acquired the disease from which this insanity stems," he asserts. "I consider this an insult, and I might have to draw consequences." Mann writes to the *Review*, retorting that Schoenberg is suffering "delusions of persecution." The row entertains literary bystanders for several weeks until the two great men decide to shake hands. As book storms go, this is a few blows short of a hurricane.

But it leaves a trail of wreckage. Schoenberg, distressed, lacks the composure to produce another major work. Thomas Mann has touched a nerve with "delusions of persecution"; the north German Lutheran accusing him, in effect, of acting like a hysterical Jew with "all-too-understandable hypersensitivity." Schoenberg knows what Mann is getting at and so does Mann. Two Paradise fugitives from Hitler's persecution are locked in a German–Jew confrontation from which Schoenberg cannot, will not, does not back down. He still dreams of being crowned leader of the Jewish people. "Here I am, Arn[old] Sch[oenberg]; the President of the G[overnment] in Exile of the Jewish Nation. We are on a ship which I received through the generosity of Pr[esident] Tr[uman], the Am[erican] Government and the Am[erican] People . . . ," reads a proposed broadcast script in his private archive.

On the last composition he ever begins, a commission for the cellist Gregor Piatigorsky, Arnold Schoenberg inscribes at the top of the page, "*Ich bin ein kleiner Judenbub*" (I am a little Jewish boy).[18] It is with these words that he leaves the world on July 13, 1951.

Within a couple of years his twelve-note method becomes compulsory for contemporary composers, practiced by all who claim to be modern and progressive, especially in postwar Europe. Even his archrival Stravinsky converts to Schoenberg's style. "Those who have not passed through Schoenberg and Webern," proclaims the dominant French modernist Pierre Boulez, "may be considered redundant."[19]

Solomon Schonfeld buys an officer's cap at the army surplus store, fits it with the self-invented badge of a "Chief Rabbi's Emergency Corps," and talks himself onto military transport to Soviet-occupied Poland, a near-impossible feat. He is looking for children whose parents hid them with neighbors, in barns, in monasteries. At one convent, the Mother Superior insists she has no Jews. Standing in the courtyard, Schonfeld throws back his head and bellows "*Shema Yisroel . . . !*" From every level of the building, children's voices chant the rest of the credo: "*. . . Adonai eloheinu, Adonai echod!*"

Poland is no more Jew-friendly after the war than before. Jews who return to reclaim their homes are attacked in pogroms. Schonfeld's car is shot at in an ambush. "The Almighty must have more work for me to do," he says. "He's not ready for me to leave." In two trips to Poland, he collects a thousand orphans and brings them to England, teaching them "Daisy, Daisy, give me your answer do" (from the song "Bicycle Built for Two") on the Channel crossing. Immigration officials turn a blind eye until a woman turns up, claiming a child as hers. "But you said they were orphans, Dr. Schonfeld," chides the Home Office. "Would you, sir, part a lone child from its mother?" retorts the rabbi.

He starts a Jewish Secondary Schools Movement, turning orphans into Englishmen and Englishwomen. Two of my sisters work as his teachers. I, my children, and four of my grandchildren attend his schools. At my first Yom Kippur in synagogue, he leads the Ne'ilah service, bellowing at the Almighty to keep the gates of forgiveness open. I remember thinking, as a child, that no power on Earth or in heaven could withstand this man. If Dr. Schonfeld says "Stay open!" it stays open. This, to me, is the force of genius.

A few years ago, my phone rings. A woman asks if I am Norman Lebrecht and would I confirm my date of birth? "Then you are the one," she says. Here is what she tells me:

I was plucked from Poland after the war by Doctor Schonfeld, the only survivor of a large family. In London I met another lone survivor and Doctor Schonfeld married us. We knew no one. People in synagogue shied away from asking what had happened to us.

The day came for me to give birth. I entered the Bearsted Maternity Hospital on Lordship Road. In those days husbands were not allowed in the delivery room. I never felt more alone. All through labour I sobbed. The matron came in and told me there was a lady in the next room who had just given birth to a boy and who was asking if she could sit with me for the rest of the labour.

The caller pauses.

"She came in and held my hand until my child was born."

Another pause.

"That lady was your mother. I needed you to know."

A young Englishwoman heads to Paris in February 1947, frustrated by male chauvinism at the universities of Cambridge and London. Rosalind Franklin is twenty-six years old, daughter of a prominent Jewish family and strikingly uninterested in conventional goals for women. She is onto something big. It lies, for the moment, tantalizingly beyond her grasp.

With a PhD in physical chemistry, specializing in the structure of coal, she joins the Paris laboratory of Jacques Mering, a Russian-born

Jewish scientist with a string of adoring young interns and a wife somewhere in the background. Franklin, smitten but reserved, studies Mering's application of X-ray diffraction to natural substances. After three years with no discernible romance, she returns to London more fashionably dressed but no less obsessed with her grail. She has no time for men. An attempt to match her with an unattached Jewish Marxist, Ralph Miliband, aborts on their first date.

The physicist John Randall, one of the secret wartime developers of naval radar, gives her a three-year post at King's College London to work on X-ray diffraction, redirecting her researches to DNA fibers, which look promising. DNA—deoxyribonucleic acid—is a molecule that contains the genetic instructions for building life-forms. Randall's deputy, Maurice Wilkins, a bespectacled New Zealander, is head of the DNA team. He is on leave when Franklin arrives. She takes charge of the new X-ray equipment. On his return, furious, he accuses his boss of acting like Napoleon and gives Franklin the cold shoulder. Although Wilkins is first to identify a helical structure for DNA, it is Franklin who observes a vital distinction between two forms of DNA, A and B. Wilkins shares the findings with a pair of Cambridge researchers, James Watson and Francis Crick. In May 1952, Raymond Gosling, a PhD student working under Franklin's supervision, takes an image known as "Photograph 51," revealing the structure of DNA for the first time. Photograph 51 is shown, without Franklin's consent, to Watson. She catches another scientist reading papers in her office. When Watson and Crick's breakthrough letter about the structure of DNA is published in the journal *Nature* in April 1953, Franklin arranges to spend time in Israel with her cousins, one of whom, Herbert Samuel's grandson, works at the Weizmann Institute. Attracted by its compactness and idealism, she is tempted to join the faculty but decides against it on learning that women scientists have the right to take time off after childbirth, a concession that strikes her as profoundly unserious. She is further deterred by "extreme Orthodox Jews and their way of life, and [by] . . . the brash attitudes she found in Tel Aviv."[20] Tel Aviv, she writes home, "would make anyone anti-Semitic."

Hitchhiking south to Eilat, she fights off a truck driver's rape attempt. To a cousin who asks why she does not marry, Franklin volunteers that the only men she has ever liked are married. Joining

Birkbeck University in London, she persuades the Stalinist crystallographer John Desmond Bernal (who is half-Jewish) to obtain an Israeli visa and take a research trip. But Birkbeck, she finds, is riddled with "narrowmindedness and obstruction at those who are not Party members." Communism takes precedence over scientific merit, and she is once again shunted aside from the main DNA agenda.[21]

Nine years on, Watson, Crick, and Wilkins share the Nobel Prize for their work on DNA. Rosalind Franklin is unmentioned in their citation; she died of ovarian cancer in 1958, at the age of thirty-seven. Watson, in his memoir *The Double Helix*, depicts her as dowdy, spinsterish "Rosy." Bernal, in his review of the book, points out that "Rosy" (as she hated to be called) "was the first to recognize and to measure the phosphorus atoms in the helix . . . thus showing . . . the helix to be a double one."[22] In March 2000, King's College London belatedly acknowledges her contribution with the Franklin-Wilkins Building. In *Photograph 51*, a stage play running at London's Old Vic in 2014, Franklin is played by Nicole Kidman. In 2017, her grave at the Willesden Cemetery is listed as an English Heritage site.

As well as suffering sex discrimination, Franklin detects another form of prejudice. "I was," she tells her sister, "always consciously a Jew."[23] Watson, as he ages, utters opinions that are widely deemed to be racist and sexist. He claims that Africans are of lower intelligence than Europeans, the Latins are more priapic than other men, that women are less effective at math, and, in a 2007 *Esquire* magazine interview, that "some anti-Semitism is justified." Rosalind Franklin was not imagining it.

The war is over and memories of the Great Terror are fading when Joseph Stalin orders a purge of the Jews. As with the first Terror, which Stalin set off with the murder of a Bolshevik rival, Sergei Kirov, he singles out a public figure for state assassination. Solomon Mikhoels is the lynchpin of the Moscow State Jewish Theatre. His Yiddish King Lear is a marvel of the Moscow stage,[24] his madness at Cordelia's death unbearably affecting.[25] He is the prototype Tevye in Sholem Aleichem's shtetl play (later reborn on Broadway as *Fiddler on the Roof*). Mikhoels is a major player in Soviet culture, a friend of the filmmaker Sergei Eisen-

371

stein, the composer Dmitri Shostakovich, and the poet Osip Mandelstam. He is "quite unlike anybody else," records Mandelstam's widow.[26]

During the war, Mikhoels has been the public face of the Jewish Anti-Fascist Committee, formed to raise political support and cash donations from American Jews. He takes *King Lear* to New York, where he meets Albert Einstein and Yehudi Menuhin. His committee raises $45 million for Stalin's war effort.[27] Emboldened, Mikhoels puts forward a plan to create a Soviet Jewish state around the old Black Sea homeland of Odessa and sends the idea to the Politburo, arguing that it would afford relief and rehabilitation to Holocaust survivors. Stalin, suspecting a plot by foreign Jews to infiltrate the Soviet Union, orders the arrest and torture of friends of Mikhoels. On reading their "confessions," on November 21, 1947, he orders the actor's murder.[28]

On a trip to Belorussia to judge plays for the next year's Stalin Prize, Mikhoels is joined by a theater critic and NKVD informer, Vladimir Golubov-Potapov, who suggests they go out after dinner to a friend's dacha near Minsk. There, Mikhoels is injected with poison. As he fights back, he is hit on the head with a blunt object and, for good measure, shot. His body, together with the critic's, is dumped on a nearby road, run over by a truck, and left in the snow. Stalin tells his daughter that Mikhoels died in a road accident. He orders a magnificent funeral. Then he starts rounding up Jews by the dozens and hundreds.

A deputy foreign minister, Solomon Lozovsky, is top of the list, followed by the foreign minister's Jewish wife, Polina Molotova, and members of the Anti-Fascist Committee. The Moscow State Jewish Theatre is shut down. Lozovsky is subjected to a show trial and, on August 12, 1952, is executed, together with twelve Jewish intellectuals, in a Night of the Murdered Poets. They include Peretz Markish, Itzik Feffer, and David Bergelson, all legends of Yiddish literature. The pseudonymous novelist Der Nister is sent to his death in the Gulag. The pioneering biochemist Lina Stern, winner of the Stalin Prize and the first woman elected to the Soviet Academy of Science, is brutally interrogated and exiled to Siberia. Yiddish culture is all but extinguished. The murderer of Mikhoels is awarded the Lenin Prize "for exemplary execution of a special assignment."

Stalin next turns on his medical team. Seven of his nine doctors are

Jews, among them Mikhoels's first cousin Miron Vovsi. A front-page article in *Pravda* whips up public outrage:

> Participants in the terrorist group, exploiting their position as doctors and abusing their patients' trust, deliberately and viciously undermined their patients' health by making incorrect diagnoses and then killed them with bad and incorrect treatments... Wearing the noble and merciful calling of physicians, men of science, these fiends and killers dishonoured the holy banner of science . . . Participants of the terrorist group . . . were bought by American intelligence, recruited by a branch-office of American intelligence—the international Jewish bourgeois-nationalist organization called "Joint." The filthy face of this Zionist spy organization, covering up vicious actions under the mask of charity, is now fully revealed.[29]

Only Stalin's death, eight weeks later, prevents a full-scale Soviet pogrom. Nothing much has changed in Russia since the tsars. When a ruler fails, he kills the Jews.

> *1940s Tel Aviv joke: Two ex–Berlin professors in three-piece suits are taking a postlunch stroll beside the sea when they catch sight of a colleague struggling in a riptide. "Help!" shouts their friend, "I am sinking . . . !" "Really," cries one of the professors, "vot are you sinking?"*

A sixteen-year-old Bedouin boy counting his sheep in the desert north of the Dead Sea comes up one short. Fearing the animal has fallen into a cave, Muhammed edh-Dhib throws a stone into a crevice and hears something smash far below. He clambers down and finds clay jars strewn around the cave. Each jar contains a scroll. The scrolls, the boy sees in daylight, are old—very old. And possibly valuable. He pulls out some more.

Muhammed's account may be a tissue of memory and fantasy, but the scrolls emerge with speed. With two cousins, Muhammed sends samples to Bethlehem in March 1947. A Christian trader buys one scroll, another dealer three more. The cousins bring back seven Jordanian pounds, about $300 in 2019 values. In May and June, they sell three more. Word of the discovery reaches collectors. Through one of the barbed-wire fences that divide the Holy City, an Armenian dealer in East Jerusalem shows a scrap of parchment to a professor of archaeology at the Hebrew University. Professor Eliezer Lipa Sukenik, who is just back from a sabbatical in the United States, is overcome with emotion. The scroll is not just ancient, it is unquestionably important, in that its text varies from that of the Bible. The Armenian says they should go to Bethlehem two days later to see a man about the scrolls. The roads are unsafe as the British prepare for withdrawal from Palestine and Arab insurgents open fire on Jewish traffic. Overcoming his wife's safety concerns and his own doubts about the scrolls' authenticity, Sukenik takes a bus with the Armenian to the birthplace of Christianity. Three scrolls are placed on a table before them.

"My hands shook as I started to unwrap one of them," records Sukenik:

> I read a few sentences. It was written in beautiful biblical Hebrew. The language was like that of the Psalms, but the text was unknown to me. I looked and looked, and I suddenly had the feeling that I was privileged by destiny to gaze upon a Hebrew Scroll which had not been read for more than 2,000 years.

A mathematics teacher, self-trained in archaeology, Sukenik has been excavating sites in Galilee since the First World War. He uncovers intricate floor mosaics in early synagogues, dazzling *chalutzim* with evidence that their ancestors once prayed in this land. Sukenik's son Yigael accompanies him on digs when he is eleven years old and old enough to wear an adult rucksack. His father founds a department of archaeology at the Hebrew University and organizes digs at the walls of Jerusalem. Sukenik lays no claim to being a decoder of ancient hieroglyphics, but he can recognize early Hebrew. His ability to read a Dead Sea scroll is proof that Jews in the first century wrote Hebrew the same way as they do in the twentieth, just the kind of evidence that Zionists need to underpin their right to the land. There is a distinct political purpose to the new fad for biblical archaeology.

Of the Dead Sea scrolls he is shown in Bethlehem, Sukenik recognizes one as the book of Isaiah and the others as communal documents that did not make the final cut of the Hebrew Bible. He names them the War Scroll and the Thanksgiving Scroll and defines them as *sefarim genuzim*—hidden books from the greatest *genizah* on Earth. "My supposition is that these are damaged sacred scrolls that can no longer be used and which have been put, as in Cairo, into a *Genizah*." The dealer says there are more scrolls, dozens more. The Bedouin are digging them out, but access is restricted because the region is sitting on a time bomb that everybody knows is about to explode.

The day Sukenik visits Bethlehem is a Saturday, November 29, 1947. In New York that afternoon, the United Nations will be meeting to determine the future of Palestine now that Britain has given up the mandate. The conflict between Arabs and Jews is irresolvable. The Jews want to admit thousands of Holocaust survivors who are languishing in displaced people's camps across Europe. The Arabs want to protect their land and rights. The UN has drawn up a map that partitions the territory in favor of the Arabs. The Jews reluctantly accept it. The Arabs reject it out of hand and swear to liberate every inch of territory, throwing the Jews into the sea. Sukenik knows he must leave Bethlehem by nightfall or his life will be forfeit. But he cannot leave without the three scrolls, which, in his view, are worth more than a mere vote at the UN. They establish, beyond contention, that Jews once owned this land and have never given up the right of return. Sukenik hands over £35 British, a sum advanced to him by the Hebrew University president, Judah Magnes.

Night is falling in the Judean Hills, and the United Nations is about to meet at the former World's Fair building in Flushing Meadows. There are fifty-six UN members. A two-thirds majority is required to endorse the partition plan. The Jewish Agency, which acts as a government in waiting for the Jews in Palestine, has sent twenty officials to New York to lobby at the UN. They are working against sanguinary Arab rhetoric—the Egyptian ambassador has told the assembly that the lives of a million Jews in Arab lands would be put in jeopardy by the creation of a Jewish state—and a slick diplomatic effort by the United Kingdom, which is damned if it is going to leave Palestine in the hands of the Jews. The British team is "held to be the ablest of all the delegations."[30] A month before the meeting, twenty-three ambassadors are committed to vote for partition and thirteen against. This is far short of the numbers required to declare a Jewish state.

At the heart of the lobbying offensive is a German-born Jew, Walter Eytan (formerly Ettinghausen), an academic who spent the war with his brother Ernest at Bletchley Park, cracking German codes. Attired in suit, tie, and (as I remember him) immaculate white cuffs, Walter is the antithesis of the Ben Gurion–type *chalutz* in crumpled blue shirt and uncombed frizzy hair. Intent on building a professional foreign service for the unborn state, he stays out of the limelight in the agency's New York office, barely attending the General Assembly. This perfect British civil servant relishes the opportunity to tweak the tail of the mangy imperial lion. He recalls in a 1990 interview for the UN archives:

> I belonged to no political party and I have not belonged to a political party since. I saw myself as a civil servant and so everybody was on more or less good terms with me. Everybody more or less trusted me. I did the organizing work for the delegation. That is to say, I hardly ever went to a meeting of the General Assembly. We had a meeting of the whole delegation in the morning which I was responsible for organizing. And then we had a debriefing session in the evening when the people all came back from Flushing Meadows . . . they usually came back with requests. I would then sit down until whatever time at night it required and prepare all this so I could equip the delegation with it.

Every vote counts, Luxembourg's as much as China's. Stalin, to general surprise, declares Soviet support, and President Truman is expected to do the same. Albert Einstein writes to the Indian prime minister Nehru, who declines. The French waver. Guatemala comes good from the Zionist point of view, amid British whispers that their ambassador is taking kickbacks from American Jews and there is an American intelligence report that he has a Jewish girlfriend. Walter Eytan, behind dark blinds, tallies each piece of information and conceives fresh strategies for undecided delegations. The direct approaches to ambassadors are made by Moshe Shertok and Abba Eban, future foreign ministers.

"The whole debate for the whole of the two months at the UN really did not so much turn on the idea of partition," says Eytan,

... but on whether or not there should be a Jewish state. No one was really interested in an Arab state because the Arabs had said they didn't want one. The debate was not for or against an Arab state or for or against partition as such, as an ideal. Whether or not there should be a Jewish state was the real topic of debate at the General Assembly.[31]

Down to the last minute, it is touch-and-go.

In Bethlehem, Eliezer Sukenik has to go. Having paid for three scrolls, he learns that four more have been sold to a Syrian archbishop. He carries his purchases, which include two of the clay jars, onto the last bus to Jerusalem. Reaching home, he has a few minutes to peruse them before, like everyone else, he gets swept up in the excitement of the United Nations vote. Everyone, it seems, is going out into the streets and cafés to listen on loudspeakers to the live radio broadcast of the General Assembly vote that will determine whether the Jews will get a state of their own. The time for speeches and arguments is past. All that counts is the show of hands.

The tension positively crackles on archival film of the General Assembly session, visible on YouTube. "You all know how to vote," says the chairman, Oswaldo Aranha of Brazil. "Those who are in favour will say yes. Those who are against it will say no. And the abstainers, always they know what to say." Nervous laughter shudders around the room.

"Some people were pursued by us until the last minute," testifies Suzy Eban, Abba's wife. One Latin American ambassador is found hiding in a cubicle in the men's room. He is cajoled out to vote in favor. Finally, the voting begins:

Afghanistan? Loud no.

Argentina? Long silence. The chairman calls again: Argentina? Abstain.

A groan goes up in Tel Aviv's Dizengoff Square. Argentina is meant to be a supporter. Men and women are taking down the results, as if they are football scores. The tally continues.

Australia? Yes.

Belgium? Yes.

Bolivia? Yes.

Brazil? Yes . . .

France? Yes.

Greece? No . . .

And all the way down to . . .

Yugoslavia? Abstain.

A tally is made and checked. United Nations Resolution 181 (II) is adopted by thirty-three votes in favor to thirteen against, with ten abstentions. One member, Siam (later Thailand), has failed to turn up. It is the first time a vote of the international community has created a new state. The Jews will have a home of their own.

In Tel Aviv, cafés are reported (not altogether credibly) to be pouring free champagne. "Like everyone else in the yishuv I was glued to the radio, with pencil and paper, writing down the votes as they came through," writes Golda Meir, acting head of the Jewish Agency's political department, at fifty years old:

> Finally, at about midnight our time, the results were announced . . . I went immediately to the compound of the Jewish Agency building which was already jammed with people. It was an incredible sight: hundreds of people, British soldiers among them, holding hands, singing and dancing, with truckloads of more people arriving all the time . . . From the balcony of my office, I spoke for a few minutes.

In her memoirs, she recalls addressing her remarks to Jordan's King Abdullah, with whom she has been holding secret talks. "The partition plan is a compromise," she announces, "not what you wanted, not what we wanted. But let us now live in friendship and peace together."[32] An alternative record has her saying: "For two thousand years we have waited for our deliverance. Now that it is here it is so great and wonderful that it surpasses human words. Jews, *mazel tov!*"[33] There is a quaver in her gravelly voice.

Twenty-four years later, as prime minister of Israel, Golda shares with me her sense of disbelief on that wild November night: "That I, who saw my father barricading the house against a pogrom, have lived to see the birth of a Jewish state. Tell me, is that not a miracle?" In the kitchen of her prime ministerial house, speaking in Milwaukee-accented Hebrew, she chats with a journalist young enough to be her

grandson who does not know why he has been invited. It is the fiftieth anniversary of her arrival in Palestine on the US ship *Pocahon-
tas*, and she gathered her surviving fellow passengers, who include her
niece Judy (her memoirs say press are banned from the event; I must
be an exception). Immovable in her opinions, Golda can be irresistibly
personable behind a pair of bushy black eyebrows and large, restless
hands, a genius of one-on-one persuasion. In a messy political landscape, her personal integrity is spotless. The publisher George Weidenfeld recounts that she keeps refusing to let him pay her the size of
advance he usually gives world leaders for their memoirs.[34] Golda has
no small talk. Her favorite position is back to the wall. "Israel's greatest
weapon," she likes to say, "is *ein bereirah*, we have no choice."

The morning after November 29, Arab militias open fire on buses
in different parts of the country, the kind of bus that Sukenik rode the
day before. "There is an area in Jerusalem which is called the commercial center," says Walter Eytan. "That very night or the next day
the Arabs came and burned it down and finished it. That was within
24 hours. That was their first sign that they were not going to knuckle
under." Before long, Jerusalem is under blockade. "We were really cut
off," says Eytan. "It was very interesting to be a besieged city with nothing to eat and nothing to drink and no electricity, with extraordinary
consequences. It went on for months."

Salman Schocken catches the last flight for New York, where
he supplements his bibliomania collecting coins and gramophone
records. Gershom Scholem breaks off his studies of Kabbalah to join
the Haganah defense forces as guardian in chief of the national library.
"Who knows what will happen or what direction the Jews will take in
their own state?" he wonders. "I live in despair and can be active only
in despair."[35] He is working on a theory debunking the six-pointed Star
of David as an authentic Jewish symbol.

Sukenik, ignoring privations and gunfire, is immersed in scrolls.
He is determined to publish his texts ahead of the Syrian Christians
and the American Baptists who are converging on Qumran. "Sukenik
moved faster," writes the scrolls scholar Géza Vermes, "and by 1948
released a preliminary survey of his own material and also photographs, with his own decipherment and commentary, of texts which
belonged to the rival camp.

"Both Sukenik and the leading American orientalist, archaeologist and biblical scholar of the mid-century, W. F. Albright, unhesitatingly accepted the authenticity of the Scrolls and dated them to the end of the pre-Christian era," continues Vermes. "Albright coined the phrase 'the greatest manuscript find of modern times.'"[36] A Hungarian-Jewish Holocaust survivor who is studying for the priesthood in a Belgian Catholic seminary, Vermes grows "more and more excited." He writes the first PhD thesis on the scrolls, translates the standard edition, and becomes the paramount authority on the Jewish identity of Jesus. The scrolls have pierced a personal unconscious for Vermes; in time, this disaffected Jew returns to Judaism, marries a Buber disciple, and becomes professor on the faculty of Oriental Studies at Oxford. His edition of *The Dead Sea Scrolls in English* sells half a million copies.

In Palestine, the war stutters sporadically for eighteen months with terrible losses on both sides. Around a million Arabs are driven into exile. Around a million Jews are expelled from Arab countries. The *yishuv* loses four thousand fighters and twenty-four hundred civilians. Among the casualties is Sukenik's son Matityahu, a lone pilot who fights off an Egyptian naval assault on Tel Aviv. "Don't weep, don't grieve," writes Sukenik's elder son Yigael Yadin. "When Matti took off yesterday to chase away the enemy ships from the shores of Tel Aviv, he knew very well what awaited him. He was not frightened by the risk. . . . Just be proud that he was one of us."[37]

Yigael Yadin, ending the war as deputy chief of staff, is promoted to commander in chief of the redesignated Israel Defense Forces at the age of thirty-two. In June 1954, he is shown a small advertisement that appears in the *Wall Street Journal*: "Dead Sea Scrolls for Sale: Biblical manuscripts dating back to at least 200 BC, are for sale. This would be an ideal gift to an educational or religious institution by an individual or group. Box F 206."

These are the Syrian archbishop's scrolls. Yadin, whose father died the previous year, buys them through an American intermediary and brings them to Jerusalem. The Hebrew University builds the Shrine of the Book to display the seven scrolls. Yadin retires as commander in chief at thirty-five to write his PhD on the War Scroll. He devotes much of the rest of his life to archaeology, achieving world fame with his excavation of the Masada mass-suicide site.

Ten more caves are investigated at Qumran, yielding more scrolls, including parts of Psalms and Leviticus. Their publication is delayed until the 1990s by Christian fears that variable texts might undermine fundamentalist teachings of the Bible. The Jews have no such fears. The scrolls testify to their historic presence in Palestine; they are Exhibit A in any trial of entitlement to the Land of Israel, the title deeds of renewed statehood.

On Friday, May 14, 1948, an hour before the start of the Sabbath, David Ben-Gurion declares the foundation of the State of Israel. It is either the end of Jewish history or the start of a new dichotomy.

SIXTEEN

2018

BUBBLES AT BREAKFAST

The sun sparkles off the Mediterranean Sea beside the Carlton Hotel. The breakfast room is packed with techies, inventors, and investors, Indians and Chinese, squinting into the sun for the deal of the century. Israel in 2018 is a hub of ideas and innovation, a small state living expansively from its wits. Among recent Israeli patents are a camera inside a pill, which delivers noninvasive endoscopy; a possible cure for multiple sclerosis; the Waze navigation app; a warning system for driverless cars. Israel is known the world over as a land of ideas.

It is also a state of haves and have-nots, a nation that forsook its founding ideals of social equality and the dignity of labor. The gulf is widening all the time between the few who sell start-ups to Silicon Valley for incomprehensible sums and the many who struggle to afford hummus for their lunchtime pita. The gap is not just economic. Ultra-Orthodox Jews live in self-made ghettos. Arabs and Jews are more segregated than ever. An underclass of underpaid African migrants and Filipino domestics sustains a leisure society. A tent city springs up around Tel Aviv's railway terminus, occupied by wage-earners who cannot afford to rent rooms. There is no disguising these schisms and no solution in sight.

In the Carlton breakfast room, there is vodka on tap for Russian oligarchs and champagne on ice for new-struck deals. It is impossible to reconcile this feast of plenty with the sand dunes from which the town sprang barely a century ago, or the *alte-zachen* men that I remember collecting old pots and clothes for resale in the flea markets, or the short-sleeved women I saw sitting on the bus, going to work with Auschwitz numbers tattooed on their arms.

After a breakfast omelette with a finely chopped side salad, I take myself out into fresh air to revisit the spot where Arlozorov was shot. I lay a pebble on the wall of the apartment building where Leah Goldberg died. From there, I descend the street named after *Daniel Deronda*'s translator until I hit the avenue they still call "King George," after the English monarch who ruled when Balfour made his declaration. There used to be a shop on the corner that sold only homegrown foods and homemade goods, an emporium of utopian self-sufficiency. The balladeer Arik Einstein wrote a song about it. Up King George, past a homeopathic pharmacy, a shopping mall, the museum to Jabotinsky's Revisionism. I approach my favorite bookshop, hoping that this is one of the rare afternoons when it is open. It is. Mr. Pollak greets me as a fish greets plankton.

I head into the back room where he keeps the libraries of erstwhile residents, a polyglot colloquy of books united by a streak of genius. And not a little anxiety. Many of the spines have a similar title: *The Jewish Question, La Question Juive, Die Jüdische Frage, hashe'elah hayehudit, еврейский вопрос.* No one has yet come up with an answer. When I first browsed here in the 1960s, it was assumed the question had been solved, if not by the existence of a Jewish state then by Jewish assimilation in America and Europe.

Half a century on, that is no longer the case. Israel, mighty as it may seem, is threatened with extinction by Islamic nations that are creeping ever closer to having a nuclear bomb, just as Leo Szilard once warned. Jews, in the lands of their dispersion, have to post guards at the gates of schools and synagogues for fear of anti-Semitic attacks. A visitor finds it harder to pray in an Istanbul synagogue than to fly from the airport. The sense of otherness is back. Jews, we are told, are different. They have no sense of irony, a divided loyalty. The Jewish Question reopens. What is to be done about the Jews? As the anxiety rises, so, too, does the flood of invention. This story is not over yet.

I leave Pollak's with a play script that has Max Brod's bookplate inside it, some late poems of Leah Goldberg, a memoir of the Dreyfus affair, and a study of Jews in German uniform. Plus a bag of cheap paperbacks in tatty covers. And I'll be back for more. The book is our hope and our salvation. It may contain an idea no one has thought of before. A flash of genius. A world unimagined. A world remade.

ACKNOWLEDGMENTS

Among many people who helped shape this book, I must first thank the following institutions and their librarians for access to unpublished material:

Library of Congress

Free Library of Philadelphia

National Library of Israel, National Sound Archive, Jerusalem: Dr. Gila Flam

New York Public Library, Performing Arts Division

Bibliothèque Nationale de France, Département des Manuscrits, Paris

United Nations Oral History Archive

University of Cambridge, Genizah Research Unit: Dr. Ben Outhwaite

University College London, Moccatta Library

University of Southampton, Hartley Library: Karen Robson

Weizmann Institute, Rehovot, Israel: Sheridan Gould, Navit Kopelis, Merav Segal, Lior Hecht-Jacoby, Judy and David Dangoor

Arnold Schoenberg Institute, Los Angeles and Vienna: Nuria Schoenberg-Nono, Leonard Stein

US National Holocaust Museum in Washington, DC

Bletchley Park Collections

Other material has been drawn over many years from the private archives, researches, and personal memories of a wide circle of family and friends, chief among them: Patrice Klein, Jocelyne Schischa, Naftoli Schischa, Shimon Schischa, Margarita Bar, Chanoch Erntroy, Stuart Lebrett, Isaac Abraham, Romeo Vecht, Steven Englander, Aviva Astrakhan, Gidon Remez, Erna Weiss, the late Fifi Klein, Brunette Adler, Ruth Kivity, Aharon Lizra, George Whyte, Caroline Whyte, Gilbert E. Kaplan, Lotte Klemperer, Anna Mahler, Eleanor Rosé, Berthold Goldschmidt, Peter Diamand, Ladislav Sip, Jaroslav Seda, Jonathan Carr, Gitta Sereny, Ernest Ettinghausen, Harry Karet, Tom Roboz, Belle Schulhoff, Yehudi Menuhin, Vera Frankel, and Miron Grindea.

Further documents and links have been provided by Professor Robert Eschbach, Rabbi Isaac Abraham, Rabbi Shlomo Odze, Dr. Malcolm Miller, Hellmut Stern, Wolfgang and Susanne Herles, the late Fred Barschak, Jonathan Carr, and George Weidenfeld.

I owe my immersion in Jewish studies to the late Rabbis Solomon Schonfeld, Joseph Dunner, S. Z. Oyerbach, Joshua Neuwirth, Louis Jacobs, Yeshayahu Leibowitz, Immanuel Jakobowitz, Raphael Lowy, and Michael Weizmann, and to the happily alive Rabbis Abraham Levy, Israel Elia, Joseph Dweck, Shlomo Levin, Ivan Binstock, Alexander Grunfeld, Yehoshua Engelman, Alan David, and Professor Uriel Simon.

My cultural instincts were awakened by the late Richard Grunberger, Walter Stanton, Baruch Kurzweil, Leah Goldberg, Jacob Talmon, Herbert Frieden, Gad Levi, Géza Vermes, Betty Freeman, Ernest Fleischmann, Klaus Tennstedt, Isaac Bashevis Singer, Yehuda Haezrahi, Yossi Banai, Ken Davison, and Dieter Pevsner.

I am grateful to Simon Schama, Simon Sebag Montefiore, and the late David Cesarani and Walter Laqueur for conversations that touched on key ideas in this book. Also to David Biran, Sylva Darel, Jane Gelfman, Dr. Isabella Ginor, Ivry Gitlis, Lord Grade, Dr. Jeff Graham, Daniella Grunfeld, Michael Haas, Ida Haendel, Lea Harris, Professor Jehoash Hirshberg, Victor Hochhauser, Robert Lantos, Sylvia Laqueur, Cochava Levy, Yasmin Levy, Gerry Mizrahi, Leon Nahon, Dr. Irene Polonskaya, Menahem Pressler, Steve Reich, Rabbi Jeremy Rosen, Professor Edwin Seroussi, and especially the late Tatiana Hoffmann, Ricci Horenstein, Alexander Ivashkin, RB Kitaj, Noam Sherriff, Nathan Milstein, Paul Myers, Peter Mayer, Arnold Wesker, Alexander Chancellor, Rafi Unger, and Hagai Pinsker.

For hospitality and help in relevant locations, I owe thanks in manifold degrees to Lori Kaufman, Yoram Youngerman, Oded Zehavi, Yehezkel Beinisch, Sheng Yun, Aviva Cohen, James Manishen, Luis Sunen, Moshe and Dafna Kahn, Jonathan and Dafna Kahn, Debbie Leuchter, Allan Kozinn, Pini Dunner, Steve Rubin, Esther Klag, Ann

Foden, Asma Siddiqi, Aythen Sohrabe, Declan Cahill, Joanne Franks, Nicholas Pilavachi, Roger Wright, and Veronica Wadley.

My agent Bill Hamilton and editor Sam Carter have been pillars of support, indispensable as and when it mattered. At Scribner, Colin Harrison, Sarah Goldberg, and Kathleen Rizzo applied three extra pairs of eagle eyes.

Nothing would be possible without Elbie, who walks with me hand in hand through life, nor without our daughters Naama, Abigail, and Gabriella; their husbands, Simon, Bernard, and Gideon; and, one by one, their children. A work of history is not written in isolation.

NOTES

Introduction: Thinking Outside

1 The historian Cecil Roth, a cousin by marriage, wrote a well-meaning but error-strewn potboiler of famous Jews who contributed to Western civilization.

2 *The Times*, October 10, 2018.

Chapter 1: 1847: The Visitor

1 Letter from Frankfurt, dated June 2, 1837.

2 Bakunin, *Oeuvres*.

3 Letter to Moses Moser, December 14, 1825.

4 February 1844, in *Deutsch–Französische Jahrbücher*.

5 New York Public Library collection, transcribed by David Conway and shared with the author: *Heute fruh haben sie die Juden emanzipiert, das macht mich stolz, zumal da vor ein paar Tagen Eure lumpigen Posener Ordnungen hier untergemacht worden sind, nach Recht und Billigkeit! Die Times fuhlte sich vornehm, und meinte, in England sey es doch besser fur uns, und nachdem gestern eine Menge Juden[-] hasser: Mr. Finn und Mr. Bruce, und der Rosche Inglis gesalbadert hatten, schloss Robert Grant, der die Bill einbringt, indem er fragte, ob sie glaubten, dass sie da seyen, um die Prophezeiungen zu erfuellen (denn darauf stitzen sie sich), und sagte er hielte sich an das Wort: "Glory to God and good will to men," und darauf waren ayes 187 und noes 52.*

6 Conway, 6.

7 Conway, 178.

8 Mace, 38.

9 Psalm 130, 4.

Chapter 2: 1851: The Wars of the Jews

1 Malcolm L. Miller, "Samson Raphael Hirsch and the Revolution of 1848," http://web.ceu.hu/jewishstudies/pdf/02_miller.pdf.

2 Ruth Gay, 139.
3 Blidstein, 173.
4 Susannah Heschel, 32.
5 Jakob J. Petuchowski, in LBY 1977, pp. 139–40.
6 http://seforim.blogspot.co.uk/2009/08/meir-hildesheimer-historical.html.
7 Ferguson, 169.
8 http://traditionarchive.org/news/_pdfs/0035-0053.pdf.
9 Smith, 35.
10 Smith, 45.
11 Murai, "'The Esquisses.'"
12 Chyet, 13.
13 Katz, 144.
14 Hyman, 75.
15 Hyman, 113.

Chapter 3: 1863: Brought to Book

1 Ritterband, np.
2 Rosenzweig, 340.
3 Glendinning, 433.
4 Cheyette, PhD thesis.
5 http://www.british-history.ac.uk/survey-london/vol21/pt3/pp99-100#fnn94.
6 Receipt dated September 1860, in Eliza Davis Collection, University of Southampton.
7 Baumgarten, "The Other Woman."
8 Gasson and Baker. Cf: http://discovery.ucl.ac.uk/1560268/1/Gasson%20and%20
   Baker_article.pdf.
9 William Michael Rossetti, quoted by Rebecca Mead in "George Eliot's Ugly Beauty"
   in the New Yorker, September 19, 2013, https://www.newyorker.com/books/page
   -turner/george-eliots-ugly-beauty.
10 Henry James, quoted in Mead above.
11 Haight, 470.
12 Himmelfarb, 65.
13 Deutsch, xi.
14 Braswell, no page found.
15 Haight, 471.
16 F. R. Leavis, "Gwendolen Harleth," LRB vol. 4, no. 1, January 21, 1982.
17 Dekel, 783–98.
18 Bayoumi and Rubin (eds), The Edward Said Reader. First published 1979 in Social
   Text, issue 1, pp. 7–58.

NOTES

Chapter 4: 1875: Carmen, *Quand-même*

1 Letter of November 8, 1885, in *Letters of Sigmund Freud*, 181.
2 Freud, *Interpretation of Dreams*, 259.
3 Lawrence Letters, 55.
4 Bernhardt, 258.
5 Tierchant, 174.
6 January 14, 1898. Bibliothèque Nationale de France, Département des Manuscrits, Paris.
7 Gottlieb, 154.
8 Baldick, 345.
9 Huret, no page number.
10 Laurie Levy, "You're a Real Sarah Bernhardt," *Midcentury Modern*, May 8, 2017, https://midcenturymodernmag.com/youre-a-real-sarah-bernhardt-70ca0a0150b.
11 Curtiss, *Bizet*, 235, 245, 251.
12 Curtiss, *Bizet*, 273.
13 Curtiss, *Letters*, 132.
14 Lazarus, 63.
15 Lazarus, 65.
16 Painter, 89.
17 Schmidt-Reiter, 160.
18 Foschini, 70.
19 Proust, 1176.
20 Painter, 314.
21 Proust, *Letters*, 32; ending modified by Curtiss, *Letters*, 132.
22 Carter, 400.
23 Thiriet, 359.
24 Finn, 169.
25 Thiriet, 30.
26 Bowie, 68–69.
27 Attributed in Talmud Berachot to R. Eliezer, son of R. Yosi the Galilean.
28 Jain.

Chapter 5: 1881: The Tsar's Hamburger

1 Blake, 749.
2 *Illustrated Sunday Herald*, February 8, 1920, 5.
3 Reinharz, 259.
4 Wynn, 111.
5 December 2, 1881, the date of the pogrom.
6 Mendes, 328–29.

7 Sanders, 92.

8 Kosak, 42.

9 Heschel, *The Earth Is the Lord's*.

10 Quoted in Shindler and other translations.

11 Davitt, quoted in Elon, *Israelis*, 51–52.

12 Interview in the *New York Times*, May 18, 1903. Quoted in Klier, 207.

13 Pak, 91.

14 *New York Times*, June 19, 1877, 1.

15 Birmingham, 320–21.

16 Naomi Wiener Cohen, 208.

17 Rose, 132.

18 Zimmermann, 70.

19 Marr, 30–32.

20 Rose, 152.

21 Zimmerman, 110.

22 Hilmes, 145.

23 Peter Gay, *Freud, Jews and Other Germans*, 216.

24 Skelton, 601.

25 Skelton, 592.

26 Skelton, 603.

27 Rose, 121.

28 Gay, 214.

29 Fellman, 69.

30 Mandel, 14.

31 Mandel, 8.

32 Fellman, 71.

33 Wilson, quoted in Kark and Oren-Nordheim, 28.

34 Wikipedia: "Esperanto."

35 Conversations with NL, 1995–2010.

36 Account given to me in Wengen by I. B. Singer, July 1983, and confirmed by Israel Zamir, Warsaw, August 2013.

37 White.

38 JC, June 2, 1882.

39 Bermant, 149.

40 Lesebuch, 143.

41 Soshuk, 36.

42 Letter of October 20, 1882.

43 Letter to Rashi Pin, quoted in Be'eri, 38–39, and Morris, 49.

44 Elon, 94.

45 Elon, 95.

46 Gordon, 130.

47 Karp, 65.

48 Slezkine, 117.

49 Cecil, 36–37.
50 Cecil, 44.
51 Cecil, 43.
52 Gerhardt, 56.
53 See Wikipedia: "History of the Hamburger."
54 Schor, 82–83.
55 Schor, 75.
56 Schor, 169.
57 Karp, 74.
58 Chyet, 280–81.
59 Chyet, 176.
60 Gurock, 23–24.

Chapter 6: 1890: Two Beards on a Train

1 Goldstein, 22.
2 Sassoon, 217.
3 Schechter, 111–12.
4 Bentwich, 306.
5 Bentwich, 60.
6 Bentwich, 83.
7 Dr. Ben Outhwaite, University of Cambridge Genizah Research Unit, interview with NL.
8 Bentwich, 111.
9 Adler, 29.
10 University of Cambridge Library, Genizah collection, MS Or. 1102.
11 Bentwich, 140.
12 Stefan Reif in *JHS*, Vol. XXXII, 293.
13 Schechter, 5–6.
14 Letter to Mathilda, *JHS*, loc. cit.
15 Cambridge University Library, Add.6463(e)3416.
16 Ben Outhwaite in *JHS*, Vol. IIL, 34.
17 Reif, 279–316.
18 Schoeps, 54.
19 Schoeps, *Herzl*, 82 (from *Neue Freie Presse*, January 5, 1895).
20 Beller, 32.
21 Stewart, 183.
22 Schoeps, *Herzl*, 86.
23 Herzl, *Diaries*, entry for November 21, 1895.
24 Ibid., March 10, 1896.
25 Ibid., October 29, 1898.
26 Ibid., October 31, 1898.

27 Schoeps, *Herzl*, 173.
28 *Jewish Chronicle* obituary, November 13, 1908.
29 Romeo Vecht family archives.
30 Stewart, 366.
31 Zweig, 91.
32 Gay, *Godless*, 122.
33 Bentwich, 311–15.

Chapter 7: 1897: Sex in the City

1 Dose, 25.
2 Moll, 6.
3 Freud Museum, London, from the text of a picture caption.
4 David Biale in Gilman, 274–75.
5 Jones, 273.
6 Freud-Jung Letters, 453–54.
7 Schnitzler, *Youth*, 71.
8 Schnitzler, *Youth*, 255.
9 Freud, *Letters*, 251.
10 Freud, *Letters*, 339–40.
11 Arthur Schnitzler, *Tagebuch, 1920–1922* (Vienna: VÖAW), 1993, entry from June 16, 1922.
12 Letter to Georg Brandes, May 8, 1899.
13 Yates, 32.
14 Gay, *Freud*, 93.
15 Masson, 264–66.
16 Gay, *Freud*, 95.
17 Gay, *Freud*, 95.
18 Masson, 188.
19 Masson, xxi.
20 Crews, 666.
21 Ernst Freud, 134; translations by NL.
22 Mendes-Flohr, 278.
23 Gay, *Godless*, 125.
24 Gresser, 51–53, and Berke, 85–87.
25 Gay, *Freud*, 600.
26 Ernest Jones, quoted in Roazen, 89.
27 Richards, 70.
28 Gay, *Freud*, 54.
29 Letter of July 23, 1882.
30 Roazen, 79.
31 Roazen, 255.

32 Gay, *Freud*, 45.

33 Gay, *Freud*, 62.

34 Autobiographical Study, 1925.

35 Gay, *Freud*, 67.

36 Letters of May 25 and November 8, 1895.

37 Roazen, 96.

38 Letter of October 3, 1897.

39 Norman Lebrecht interview with Obholzer, February 1983.

40 Roazen, 172.

41 Prochnik, 96.

42 Roazen, 238–39.

43 Gay, *Godless*, 120.

44 Roazen, 266.

45 Mr. Purrington, "Carl Jung on 'Jews' 'Anti-Semitism,'" January 17, 2019, https:// carljungdepthpsychologysite.blog/2019/01/17/carl-jung-on-jews-anti-semi tism/#.XSSdcv57kuU.

46 Roazen, 267.

47 Schermer, 49.

48 Schermer, 50.

49 Falzeder, letter dated May 11, 1908, 2.

50 Rupprecht, 103–111.

51 Gay, *Godless*, 153.

52 https://josephjoachim.com/2014/09/26/villa-joachim-berlin/.

53 Dose, 34.

54 Sigusch, https://www.ncbi.nlm.nih.gov/pmc/articles/PMC3381530/#fnr107.

55 Dose, 66.

Chapter 8: 1905: The Known Unknowns

1 Donald Rumsfeld, press briefing, February 12, 2002.

2 Schwarz, Dorner: http://onlinelibrary.wiley.com/doi/10.1046/j.1365-2141.2003 .04295.x/pdf.

3 *Guardian* front page, February 12, 2016.

4 Pais, 150.

5 Gimbel, *Jewish*, 36.

6 Letter, February 12, 1950, trans. Calaprice, 206.

7 https://www.theguardian.com/science/2008/may/12/peopleinscience.religion.

8 Clark, 413–14.

9 Calaprice, 80.

10 Damasio, 280.

11 Walter Isaacson, in https://www.theatlantic.com/magazine/archive/2009/12/how -einstein-divided-americas-jews/307763/.

12 Isaacson, 308.

13 Gimbel, *Jewish*, 168.

14 Commentary to Mishnah—Sanhedrin 10.

15 James et al., 14.

16 Stern, *Einstein*, 77.

17 Isaacson, 187.

18 James et al., 24–25.

19 Friedrich and Hoffman, "Clara Haber."

20 Ibid.

21 Stern, *Einstein*, 124.

22 Stolzenberg, 191.

23 https://pdfs.semanticscholar.org/a596/a3016881e0525e2c81a66a9349b8bef5bad0
.pdf.

24 Trial report: http://www.worldcourts.com/imt/eng/decisions/1946.03.08_United
_Kingdom_v_Tesch.pdf.

25 Stern, *Einstein*, 138.

26 Chris Bowlby, BBC documentary, April 2011.

27 Stern, *Einstein*, 143.

28 Charles, np.

29 Eva Lewis, BBC documentary.

30 Stern, *Einstein*, 155.

31 Stern, *Einstein*, 157.

32 Stolzenberg, 202.

33 Stern, *Five Germanys*, 104.

34 Charles, 206.

35 Charles, 203.

36 Macintyre, *The Times*, April 14, 2018.

37 Charles, Ch. 12, np.

Chapter 9: 1911: Blues 'n' Jews

1 Bergreen, 56–57.

2 Goldberg, 56.

3 Banfield, 61.

4 Information from Peter Duchin.

5 Horowitz, 163.

6 Armitage, 120.

7 NL interview with Michael Tilson Thomas, Thomashefsky's grandson.

8 NL interview with Nuria Schoenberg-Nono.

9 Armitage, 164.

10 Edward Jablonski, letter to the *New York Times*, October 25, 1988.

11 http://www.richardgerstl.com/thesis-2/timeline-gmunden-1908-december-1908.

12 Auner, 58.

13 Lebrecht, 158.

14 Auner, 99.

15 Stuckenschmidt, 277.

16 Covach 155.

17 Schoenberg, *Style and Idea*, 214–15.

18 Stuckenschmidt, 341–42.

19 Ringer, 143.

20 Ringer, 135–37.

21 Ringer 141–42.

22 Ringer, 153–54.

23 Stuckenschmidt, 370.

24 Auner, 281.

25 Stuckenschmidt, 412–13.

26 Stengel, np.

27 Information supplied by Nuria Schoenberg-Nono.

28 Information from his descendant, Sir Charles Mackerras.

29 Idelsohn, 24.

30 There are thirty-eight letters in the Israel National Library, dated 1913 to 1929.

31 http://www.jewish-music.huji.ac.il/content/hava-nagila-0.

32 https://www.youtube.com/watch?v=8tnWx7BtDwE.

33 Werner, 17–18.

34 Idelsohn, np.

35 Robert Lachmann Oriental Music, programme 1.

36 Katz, 277.

Chapter 10: 1917: Dear Lord

1 Maria (Haralambakis) Cioată, Representations of Moses Gaster (1856–1939) in Anglophone and Romanian Scholarship, Bucharest (New Europe College), 2013, http://www.nec.ro/data/pdfs/publications/nec/2012-2013/MARIA%20HARA LAMBAKIS.pdf.

2 Schneer, 44.

3 Rose, 145.

4 Renton, *Zionist Masquerade*, 53.

5 Renton, *Zionist Masquerade*, 56.

6 Renton, *Zionist Masquerade*, 54.

7 Gaster papers, letter to Sykes, January 1917.

8 Rose, 75.

9 Gaster letter to Sykes, January 31, 1917, Gaster papers UCL.

10 All quotes, unless stated, are from a copy of the conference minutes consulted in the Gaster papers at UCL.

11 Rothschild, 237n.

12 Letter dated February 9, 1917, Gaster papers UCL.

13 Rosen, 150.

14 Fyvel, 168.

15 Sieff, 10.

16 Gaster papers, UCL.

17 JTA report, February 8, 1932.

18 Renton, "Reconsidering Chaim Weizmann and Moses Gaster," 130, 150.

19 Toller, 53.

20 Appelbaum, 139.

21 Appelbaum abstract: https://www.chester.ac.uk/sites/files/chester/conference-abstracts-09.04.14.pdf.

22 Simon, 18.

23 Cecil, 334.

24 Cecil, 339.

25 Peters, 85.

26 McGuinness, 158.

27 Ian Ground, "The Relentless Honesty of Ludwig Wittgenstein," *The Times Literary Supplement*, October 10, 2017.

28 Stern, 243–44.

29 Gitelman, 90.

30 Gitelman, 95.

31 Slezkine, 152.

32 Sebestyen: https://www.thejc.com/news/news-features/lenin-s-jewish-roots-1.447185.

33 Trotsky, *My Life*, 26. All Trostky quotes are from this vivid source.

34 Reed, 128.

35 Trotsky, *My Life*, Ch. 27.

36 Service, 223.

37 Translated in Slezkine, 175.

Chapter 11: 1924: Schoolboys

1 Zuckmayer, 281.

2 NL interviews, 1987–96.

3 Eleanor Rosé, NL interview.

4 Brod, epilogue to *The Trial*.

5 Brod, *Sternhimmel*.

6 Susskind, 106.

7 Brod, *Franz Kafka*, 66.

8 Gilman, 8.

9 Diamant, 48.

10 Diamant, 127.

11 All three statements from Brod's preface to *Das Prozess*.

12 Appelfeld, 150.

13 Hockaday, 77.

14 Hamann, 60.

15 Spotts, 141–42.

16 Carr, 147.

17 Jeffries, np.

18 Glatzer, 25–29.

19 Glatzer, 91.

20 Glatzer, 51.

21 Glatzer, 174.

22 Kestenberg, 97.

23 Interview with NL.

Chapter 12: 1933: Four Murders

1 Information mostly from Sima Arlozorov, in Teveth, 56–59.

2 Teveth, 308.

3 *The Arlosoroff Murder Trial*, 134–58.

4 *Tradition: A Journal of Orthodox Jewish Thought*.

5 https://www.haaretz.com/israel-news/.premium.MAGAZINE-israel-still-covering-up-murders-committed-by-jewish-militia-in-48-1.6245599.

6 Klabunde, 186–87.

7 Klabunde, 346n.

8 Baron, "Theodore Lessing," XXVI, 334.

9 Baron, "Theodore Lessing," XXVI, 335.

10 Grunfeld, 87.

11 Magida, 211.

12 Magida, 186.

13 http://www.taz.de/!1357838/.

Chapter 13: 1938: Cities of Refuge

1 Ehrentreu family memoir.

2 Blumenthal, 374.

3 See his daughter's memoir: https://www.youtube.com/watch?v=AW5k21o4ocM&fbclid=IwAR23fyOWHqIjWt42aSJhxedkE4ihEqbKdbmxcyy61d1zWQGG4x7EOcDOTxI.

4 Blumenthal, 380.

5 https://www.independent.co.uk/arts-entertainment/films/features/superman

-jewish-origins-film-adaptations-curse-jerry-siegel-christopher-reeve-henry-cav
ill-a8344461.html.

6　Isherwood, BBC interview, https://www.bbc.co.uk/news/world-europe-12737335.

7　Shepherd, 101.

8　Smith, 127.

9　Baker, 238.

10　Shepherd, 163.

11　NL interview with a family member.

12　Personal information, protected under privacy laws.

13　NL interviews with Ricci Horenstein, Menahem Pressler.

14　Ivinskaya, 66–69.

15　NL interview.

16　Lanouette, 24, 59.

17　http://www.dannen.com/lostlove/.

18　Lanouette, 137–38.

19　Rhodes, 292–93.

20　February 24, 1939.

21　Lanouette, 192.

22　Lanouette, 207.

23　Jungk, 109–11.

24　Lanouette, 244.

25　Szilard papers MSS 32: 40/1, University of California at San Diego.

26　Lanouette, 252.

27　Gleick, 160.

28　Rigden, 152.

29　Hardy and Sexl, 119.

30　Gorelik and Bouis, 220.

Chapter 14: 1942: Black Days

1　Peter Longerich, "Davon haben wir nichts gewusst!" *Die Deutschen und die Juden-verfolgung, 1933–1945* (München: Siedler, 2006).

2　See Stangneth, 172.

3　Emory University lecture, March 14, 2011. https://www.youtube.com/watch?v=oW
jI9WmuIk4.

4　Conversation with NL.

5　Cesarani, *Eichmann*, 368.

6　https://www.youtube.com/watch?v=pHgYRtefUqs.

7　The line serves as the title of a 1994 biography of Heidegger by Rüdiger Safranski.

8　Gilman and Zipes, 718.

9　Jenni Frazer, "Elie Wiesel: Yes We Really Did Put God on Trial," *Jewish Chronicle*,
September 19, 2008.

10 Oshry, 36–37.

11 Wiesel, *Dawn*, 12.

12 Wiesel, *Night*, 31.

13 Kulka, 98.

14 Imre Kertész, *Gályanaplo* (Galley Boat-Log, 1992), quoted in *Guardian* obituary, March 31, 2016, https://www.theguardian.com/world/2016/mar/31/imre-kertesz-obituary.

15 Schneersohn, 233–34.

16 Frankl, 98.

17 Translation by NL from a manuscript at the Hebrew University library.

18 Marton, 122.

19 Harmetz, 121.

20 Canham, 52.

21 Harmetz, 332.

22 Marton, 122.

23 Harmetz, 331.

24 Marton, 206.

25 https://archive.nytimes.com/www.nytimes.com/learning/general/onthisday/bday/0409.html.

26 https://www.telegraph.co.uk/news/health/news/11217750/Sex-will-soon-be-just-for-fun-not-babies-says-father-of-the-Pill.html.

27 https://www.theguardian.com/lifeandstyle/2010/oct/30/carl-djerassi-inventor-of-contraceptive-pill.

28 Cohn, 24.

29 Grunfeld, 140.

30 Grunfeld, 143.

31 Sonino, 122.

32 Pinsker, 282.

Chapter 15: 1947: New York, New York

1 Simeone, 225.

2 Simeone, 225.

3 NL interview, 1985.

4 Simeone, 481–82.

5 https://www.youtube.com/watch?v=kke4SyaP25c.

6 Exodus, 12:30.

7 Rigg, 74.

8 Höhne, 361.

9 Rigg, 123.

10 Telushkin, 471.

11 Telushkin, 74.

12 Yetev Lev epistle dated November 20, 2018.
13 Telushkin, book cover.
14 Symonette and Kowalke, 472.
15 Betz, 199.
16 Freedland, 215–18.
17 Schoenberg, 120.
18 NL, interview with Nuria Schoenberg-Nono.
19 NL interview, 1984.
20 Glynn, 132.
21 Maddox, 231.
22 Maddox, 313.
23 Maddox, 61.
24 https://www.youtube.com/watch?v=AU838zh5ysw.
25 https://www.youtube.com/watch?v=vOhqy9mB6TY.
26 Mandelstam, 361.
27 Slezkine, 291.
28 Sebag Montefiore, 508.
29 *Pravda*, January 13, 1953.
30 Morris, 51.
31 UN Oral History Project, June 20, 1990.
32 Meir, 172.
33 Morris, 75.
34 Conversation with NL, 2015.
35 Letters, 341.
36 Vermes, 72.
37 Bromberg-BenZvi, 151.

BIBLIOGRAPHY

Essays, Conference Papers, Theses, Websites,
Symposia, Unpublished Manuscripts

Sylvie Aprile and Delphine Diaz. "Europe and its Political Refugees in the 19th Century." *Books & Ideas*. April 18, 2016.

John Baron. "A Golden Age for Jewish Musicians in Paris, 1820–1865. *Musica Judaica* XII: 1991–92.

Murray Baumgarten. "The Other Woman." Johns Hopkins University Press, *Dickens Quarterly* 32, no. 1 (March 2015): 44–70.

Isaiah Berlin. "Benjamin Disraeli, Karl Marx, and the Search for Identity." *Transactions & Miscellanies* (Jewish Historical Society of England) 22 (1968–1969): 1–20.

Jeffrey Erik Berry. "Sigmund Freud, Arthur Schnitzler and the Birth of Psychological Man." Honors thesis, Bates College, 2012. http://scarab.bates.edu/honors theses/10.

J. Bogousslavsky and M. G. Hennerici, eds. "Neurological Disorders in Famous Artists—Part 2." *Frontiers of Neurology and Neuroscience* 22 (2007): 89–104.

Peter Brier. *Matthew Arnold and the Talmud Man*. http://www.academia.edu/10079411 /Matthew_Arnold_and_the_Talmud_Man.

Bryan Cheyette. *An Overwhelming Question: Jewish Stereotyping in English Fiction and Society, 1875–1914*. PhD thesis, University of Sheffield, May 1986.

John Covach. *Music and Theories of Josef Mathias Hauer*. PhD diss., University of Michigan, 1990.

Antonio Damasio. "Feelings of Emotion and the Self." *Annals of the New York Academy of Sciences* 1001, no. 1 (2003): 253–61. doi:10.1196/annals.1279.014.

Lydia Davis. "A Proust Alphabet." *The Cahiers Series*, 2007.

Mikhal Dekel. " 'Who Taught This Foreign Woman about the Ways and Lives of the Jews?': George Eliot and the Hebrew Renaissance." https://mikhaldekel.files .wordpress.com/2015/09/mikhal-dekel-who-taught-this-foreign-woman-about -the-ways-and-lives-of-the-jews-george-eliot-and-the-hebrew-renaissance.pdf.

Brandon Dupont, Drew Keeling, and Thomas Weiss. *Passenger Fares for Overseas Travel in the 19th and 20th Centuries*. Paper prepared for the Annual Meeting of the Economic History Association of Vancouver, BC, Canada, September 21–23, 2012. http://eh.net/eha/wp-content/uploads/2013/11/Weissetal.pdf.

BIBLIOGRAPHY

Jonathan M. Elukin. "A New Essenism: Heinrich Graetz and Mysticism." *Journal of the History of Ideas* 59, no. 1 (1998): 135–48.

Bretislav Friedrich and Dieter Hoffman. "Clara Haber, nee Immerwahr (1870–1915): Life, Work and Legacy." *Zeitschrift für Anorganische und Allgemeine Chemie* 642, no. 6 (March 2016): 437–48.

Andrew Gasson and William Baker. "Forgotten Terrain: Wilkie Collins's Jewish Explorations." Northern Illinois University (DeKalb, Illinois), 2016.

James W. Hamilton. "Freud and the Suicide of Pauline Silberstein." *The Psychoanalytic Review* 89, no. 6: 889–909. https://doi.org/10.1521/prev.89.6.889.22099.

Abraham Zvi Idelsohn. "My Life (A Sketch)." *Jewish Music Journal* 2, no. 2 (1935): 8–11.

Nimit Jain. "A Cross-Evaluation of Time in Proust and Einstein." Yale Seminar, Spring 2010. https://plastictime.wordpress.com/2010/03/14/a-cross-evaluation -of-time-in-proust-and-einstein/.

Viktoria Khiterer. "The Social and Economic History of the Jews in Kiev before February 1917." Doctoral thesis, Brandeis University, August 2008.

F. R. Leavis. "Gwendolen Harleth." *London Review of Books* 4, no. 1 (January 21, 1982): 10–12.

Peter Longerich. *The Wannsee Conference in the Development of the "Final Solution."* London: The Holocaust Educational Trust, 2000.

Ben Macintyre. "Twisted Mind That Gave Us Chemical Warfare." *The Times*, April 14, 2018, 27.

Michael L. Miller. "Samson Raphael Hirsch and the Revolution of 1848." http://web .ceu.hu/jewishstudies/pdf/02_miller.pdf.

Yukirou Murai. "The 'Esquisses' and Their Visual Programme: An Interpretation as a 'Book on Music Theory Dedicated to God.'" http://www.alkansociety.org/Publi cations/Society-Bulletins/Bulletin92.pdf.

Elizabeth L. Ray, Kristin E. Renault, and Meghan A. Roache. "Fritz Haber: The Protean Man." Submitted to the Faculty of Worcester Polytechnic Institute in partial fulfillment of the requirements for the Degree of Bachelor of Science, March 5, 2009.

Stefan Reif. "Giblews, Jews and *Genizah* views." *Journal of Jewish Studies* IV, no. 2 (Autumn 2004). http://www.jjs-online.net/archives/fulltext/2555.

———. "Jenkinson and Schechter at Cambridge: An Expanded and Updated Assessment." *Jewish Historical Studies* 32 (1990–92): 279–316.

Paul Ritterband. "Counting the Jews of New York, 1900–1991." Department of Sociology, University of Haifa, September 1998.

Julius H. Schoeps et al. *Juden in Berlin: 1671–1945, Ein Lesebuch.* Berlin: Nicolai, 1988.

Volkmar Sigusch. "The Sexologist Albert Moll—Between Sigmund Freud and Magnus Hirschfeld." *Medical History* 56, no. 2 (April 2012): 184–200. doi: 10.1017 /mdh.2011.32.

Willa Z. Silverman. "Sarah Bernhardt Exhibition Review." *Nineteenth Century Art Worldwide* 5, no. 2 (Autumn 2006).

BIBLIOGRAPHY

Jeffrey Sposato. "Creative Writing: The [Self-] Identification of Mendelssohn as Jew." *The Musical Quarterly* 82, no. 1 (Spring 1998): 190–209.

David A. Stern. "Was Wittgenstein a Jew?" *Inquiry*, December 2000.

Martin Sugarman. "Breaking the Codes: Jewish Personnel at Bletchley Park." *Jewish Historical Studies* 40, Jewish Historical Society of England (2005).

Arnold White. "The Jewish Question: How to Solve It." *North American Review* 178, no. 566 (1904): 10–24.

http://www.arthur-schnitzler.de

http://judaisme.sdv.fr/: *Le Judaisme d'Alsace et de Lorraine*

Series

Journal of Jewish Studies (ed. Géza Vermes), Oxford

Leo Baeck Yearbook

Transactions of the Jewish Historical Society of England

Published Books

Elkan Nathan Adler. *Jews in Many Lands*. London: Macmillan, 1905.

Peter C. Appelbaum. *Loyalty Betrayed: Jewish Chaplains in the German Army in the First World War*. London: Vallentine Mitchell, 2014.

Aharon Appelfeld. *The Story of a Life*. Translated by Aloma Halter. London: Penguin Books, 2006.

Merle Armitage. *George Gershwin*. New York: Longmans Green & Co., 1938.

Michael Aronson. *Troubled Waters: Origins of the 1881 Anti-Jewish Pogroms in Russia*. Pittsburgh: University of Pittsburgh Press, 1990.

Joseph Auner. *A Schoenberg Reader*. New Haven, CT: Yale University Press, 2003.

Klaus Bade. *Migration in European History*. Oxford: Blackwell Publishing, 2003.

David Bakan. *Sigmund Freud and the Jewish Mystical Tradition*. Boston: Beacon Press, 1957.

Leonard Baker. *Days of Sorrow and Pain: Leo Baeck and the Berlin Jews*. New York: Macmillan, 1978.

Mikhail Bakunin. *Oeuvres*. Vol. 1. 5th ed. Paris: P. V. Stock, 1907.

Robert Baldick, ed. *Pages from the Goncourt Journal*. Oxford: Oxford University Press, 1978.

Benjamin Balint. *Kafka's Last Trial: The Case of a Literary Legacy*. New York: W. W. Norton, 2018.

Stephen Banfield. *Jerome Kern*. New Haven, CT: Yale University Press, 2006.

Yoram Bar-David. *Kafka Udemuyotav*. Jerusalem: Tsur-Ot, 1998.

Eliezer Be'eri. *Reshit Hasihsuh Israel-Arav, 1882–1911*. Haifa, Israel: Sifriyat Po'alim/ Haifa University Press, 1985.

BIBLIOGRAPHY

Nikolaj Beier. *Vor allem bin ich ich: Judentum, Akkulturation und Antisemitismus in Arthur Schnitzlers Leben und Werk*. Göttingen, Germany: Wallstein, 2008.

Alex Bein. *Theodor Herzl*. New York: JPSA, 1956.

Steven Beller. *Herzl*. London: Peter Halban, 1991.

Norman Bentwich. *Solomon Schechter: A Biography*. Philadelphia: Jewish Publication Society of America, 1938.

Lawrence Bergreen. *As Thousands Cheer: The Life of Irving Berlin*. London: Hodder & Stoughton, 1990.

Joseph H. Berke. *The Hidden Freud: His Hassidic Roots*. London: Karnac Books, 2015.

Michael Berkowitz, ed. *Nationalism, Zionism and Ethnic Mobilization of the Jews in 1900 and Beyond*. Leiden, Netherlands: Brill, 2004.

Isaiah Berlin. *Karl Marx*. 4th ed. Oxford: Oxford University Press, 1978.

Chaim Bermant. *London's East End: Point of Arrival*. New York: Macmillan, 1975.

Sarah Bernhardt. *My Double Life*. London: Arrow Books, 1984.

Albrecht Betz. *Hanns Eisler: Political Musician*. Cambridge: Cambridge University Press, 1982.

David Biale. *Gershom Scholem, Master of the Kabbalah*. New Haven, CT: Yale University Press, 2018.

Stephen Birmingham. *Our Crowd: The Great Jewish Families of New York*. New York: Harper & Row, 1967.

Robert Blake. *Disraeli*. London: Eyre & Spottiswoode, 1967 (Rev. 1998).

Joshua Blau. *The Renaissance of Modern Hebrew and Modern Standard Arabic: Parallels and Differences in the Revival of Two Semitic Languages*. Oakland, CA: University of California Press, 1981.

Gerald J. Blidstein. *Judaism's Encounter with Other Cultures: Rejection or Integration?* Lanham, MD: Rowman & Littlefield, 2004.

Evelyne Bloch-Dano. *Madame Proust: A Biography*. Paris: Grasset, 2004.

Harold Bloom, ed. *Gershom Scholem*. New Haven, CT: Chelsea House, 1987.

W. Michael Blumenthal. *The Invisible Wall: Germans and Jews*. Washington, DC: Counterpoint, 1998.

Walter Boehlich, ed. *The Letters of Sigmund Freud to Eduard Silberstein, 1871–1881*. Cambridge, MA: Harvard University Press, 1992.

Alain de Botton. *How Proust Can Change Your Life*. London: Picador, 1997.

Malcolm Bowie. *Freud, Proust and Lacan: Theory as Fiction*. Cambridge: Cambridge University Press, 1987.

Chris Bowlby and Eva Lewis. "The Chemist of Life and Death." BBC Radio 4. April 12, 2011.

Jonathan Boyarin and Daniel Boyarin, eds. *Jews and Other Differences: The New Jewish Cultural Studies*. Minneapolis: University of Minnesota Press, 1997.

Peter Branscombe, ed. and trans. *Heinrich Heine: Selected Verse*. London: Penguin, 1968.

Mary Flowers Braswell. *The Forgotten Chaucer Scholarship of Mary Eliza Haweis, 1848–1898*. London: Routledge, 2016.

BIBLIOGRAPHY

Max Brod. *Chayei Meriva*. Tel Aviv: Hasifriyah Hatsionit, 1967.

———. *Franz Kafka: A Biography*. New York: Schocken, 1960.

———. *Heinrich Heine: The Artist in Revolt*. London: Vallentine Mitchell, 1956.

———. *Prager Sternenhimmel*. Vienna: Paul Zolnay Verlag, 1966.

Hava Bromberg Ben-Zvi. *We Who Lived: Two Teenagers in World War II Poland*. Jefferson, NC: McFarland, 2017.

Margarete Buber-Neumann. *Milena*. London: Collins Harvill, 1990.

———. *Under Two Dictators*. London: Victor Gollancz, 1949.

E. M. Butler. *Heinrich Heine*. London: Hogarth Press, 1956.

Alice Calaprice. *The New Quotable Einstein*. Princeton, NJ: Princeton University Press, 2005.

Jimena Canales. *The Physicist and the Philosopher: Einstein, Bergson and the Debate That Changed Our Understanding of Time*. Princeton, NJ: Princeton University Press, 2015.

T. Carmi, ed. *The Penguin Book of Hebrew Verse*. London: Penguin Books, 1981.

Jonathan Carr. *The Wagner Clan*. London: Faber & Faber, 2007.

William C. Carter. *Marcel Proust: A Life*. New Haven, CT: Yale University Press, 2000.

Lamar Cecil. *Albert Ballin, Business and Politics in Imperial Germany, 1888–1918*. Princeton, NJ: Princeton University Press, 1967.

David Cesarani. *Disraeli: The Novel Politician*. New Haven, CT: Yale University Press, 2016.

———. *Eichmann: His Life and Crimes*. London: William Heinemann, 2004.

Daniel Charles. *Between Genius and Genocide: The Tragedy of Fritz Haber, Father of Chemical Warfare*. London: Jonathan Cape, 2005.

Bryan Cheyette. *Constructions of "The Jew" in English Literature and Society: Racial Representations 1875–1945*. Cambridge: Cambridge University Press, 1993.

Stanley F. Chyet, ed. *Lives and Voices*. Philadelphia: Jewish Publication Society, 1972.

Cumberland Clark. *Charles Dickens and His Jewish Characters*. London: Chiswick Press, 1918.

Ronald W. Clark. *Einstein: The Life and Times*. New York: World Publishing Co., 1971.

Derek Cohen and Deborah Heller, eds. *Jewish Presences in English Literature*. Toronto: McGill-Queen's University Press, 1990.

Naomi W. Cohen. *Jacob H. Schiff: A Study in American Jewish Leadership*. Hanover, NH: Brandeis University Press, 1999.

Hans W. Cohn. *Else Lasker-Schüler: The Broken World*. Cambridge: Cambridge University Press, 1974.

Committee for Assisting the Defence. *The Arlosoroff Murder Trial: Speeches and Relevant Documents*. Jerusalem: Hassolel Partnership (S. White and Co.), 1934.

David Conway. *Jewry in Music*. Cambridge: Cambridge University Press, 2012.

Roger F. Cook, ed. *A Companion to the Works of Heinrich Heine*. London: Boydell & Brewer, 2002.

Frederick Crews. *Freud: The Making of an Illusion*. New York: Macmillan, 2017.

Minna Curtiss. *Bizet*. New York: Knopf, 1958.

BIBLIOGRAPHY

————. *Other People's Letters.* London: Macmillan, 1978.

Anthony David. *The Patron: A Life of Salman Schocken.* New York: Metropolitan Books, 2003.

Michael Davitt. *Within the Pale: The True Story of Anti-Semitic Persecutions in Russia.* London: Hurst & Blackett, 1903.

Emanuel Deutsch. *Literary Remains of Emanuel Deutsch.* London: John Murray, 1874.

Kathi Diamant. *Kafka's Last Love.* London: Secker & Warburg, 2003.

Carl Djerassi. *The Pill, the Pygmy Chimps, and Degas' Horse.* New York: Basic Books, 1992.

Ralf Dose. *Magnus Hirschfeld: The Origins of the Gay Liberation Movement.* New York: Monthly Review Press, 2014.

William Alexander Eddie. *Charles Valentin Alkan: His Life and His Music.* Farnham, UK: Ashgate Publishing, 2007.

John T. Edge. *Hamburgers and Fries: An American Story.* New York: Putnam, 2005.

Jonathan Eigg. *The Birth of the Pill.* London: Macmillan, 2014.

Amos Elon. *The Israelis: Founders and Sons.* New York: Holt, Rinehart & Winston, 1971.

————. *The Pity of It All: A Portrait of German Jews, 1743–1933.* London: Allen Lane, 2003.

————. *Theodor Herzl.* New York: Holt, Rinehart & Winston, 1975.

Todd M. Endelman and Tony Kushner, eds. *Disraeli's Jewishness.* London: Vallentine Mitchell, 2002.

Richard J. Evans. *Death in Hamburg: Society and Politics in the Cholera Years, 1830–1910.* London: Penguin Books, 1987.

Ernst Falzeder, ed. *The Complete Correspondence of Sigmund Freud and Karl Abraham 1907–1925.* London: Karnac Books, 2002.

Jack Fellman. *The Revival of the Classical Tongue: Eliezer Ben-Yehuda and the Modern Hebrew Language.* The Hague: Mouton & Co. N.V., 1973.

Niall Ferguson. *The House of Rothschild.* London: Penguin, 2000.

————. *Paper and Iron: Hamburg Business and German Politics in the Era of Inflation, 1897–1927.* Cambridge: Cambridge University Press, 2002.

Michael R. Finn. *Proust: The Body and Literary Form.* Cambridge: Cambridge University Press, 1999.

Lorenza Foschini. *Proust's Overcoat.* Translated by Eric Karpeles. London: Portobello Books, 2010.

Brigitte Francois-Sappey, ed. *Charles Valentin Alkan.* Paris: Fayard, 1991.

William Frankel, ed. *Friday Nights: A Jewish Chronicle Anthology, 1841–1971.* London: Jewish Chronicle Publications, 1973.

Viktor E. Frankl. *Man's Search for Meaning: An Introduction to Logotherapy.* London: Hodder & Stoughton, 1964.

Michael Freedland. *Witch-Hunt in Hollywood.* London: JR Books, 2009.

Sigmund Freud. *The Interpretation of Dreams.* London: George Allen, 1913.

BIBLIOGRAPHY

Sigmund Freud and Ernst L. Freud. *Letters of Sigmund Freud*. New York: Basic Books, 1960.

Judith Friedlander. *Vilna on the Seine: Jewish Intellectuals in France Since 1968*. New Haven, CT: Yale University Press, 1990.

Tosco Fyvel. "Weizmann and the Balfour Declaration." In *Weizmann: A Biography by Several Hands*. Meyer Weisgal and Joel Carmichael, eds. London: Weidenfeld & Nicolson, 1962.

Peter Gay. *Freud: A Life for Our Time*. London: J. M. Dent, 1988.

——. *Freud, Jews and Other Germans*. New York: Oxford University Press, 1978.

——. *A Godless Jew*. New Haven, CT: Yale University Press, 1987.

——. *Reading Freud*. New Haven, CT: Yale University Press, 1990.

——. *Schnitzler's Century*. New York: W. W. Norton, 2002.

Ruth Gay. *The Jews of Germany: A Historical Portrait*. New Haven, CT: Yale University Press, 1992.

Johannes Gerhardt. *Albert Ballin*. Hamburg: Hamburg University Press, 2010.

Sander L. Gilman. *Franz Kafka, the Jewish Patient*. New York and London: Routledge, 1995.

Sander L. Gilman and Jack Zipes, eds. *Yale Companion to Jewish Writing and Thought in German Culture, 1096–1996*. New Haven, CT: Yale University Press, 1997.

Steven Gimbel. *Einstein: His Space and Times*. New Haven, CT: Yale University Press, 2015.

——. *Einstein's Jewish Science*. Baltimore: Johns Hopkins University Press, 2012.

Zvi Gitelman. *A Century of Ambivalence: The Jews of Russia and the Soviet Union*. New York: Yivo Institute, 1988.

Nahum N. Glatzer. *Franz Rosenzweig: His Life and Thought*. New York: Schocken Books, 1961.

James Gleick. *Genius: The Life and Science of Richard Feynman*. New York: Pantheon, 1992.

Victoria Glendinning. *Anthony Trollope*. London: Hutchinson, 1992.

Jennifer Glynn. *My Sister Rosalind Franklin*. Oxford: Oxford University Press, 2012.

Harvey Goldberg, ed. *Sephardi and Middle Eastern Jewries*. Bloomington, IN: Indiana University Press, 1996.

Isaac Goldberg. *George Gershwin*. New York: Simon & Schuster, 1931.

Jonathan Goldstein. *Jewish Identities in East and Southeast Asia*. Berlin: Walter de Gruyter, 2015.

Edmond and Jules Goncourt. *Journals: Mémoires de la Vie Litteraire, 1851–1896*. Paris: Charpentier, 2014.

Benjamin L. Gordon. *Between Two Worlds: The Memoirs of a Physician*. New York: Bookman Press, 1952.

Gennady Gorelik and Antonina W. Bouis. *The World of Andrei Sakharov: A Russian Physicist's Path to Freedom*. New York: Oxford University Press, 2005.

Robert Gottlieb. *Sarah Bernhardt*. New Haven, CT: Yale University Press, 2010.

Moshe Gresser. *Dual Allegiance: Freud as a Modern Jew*. New York: State University of New York Press, 1994.

BIBLIOGRAPHY

Frederic R. Grunfeld. *Prophets Without Honour.* New York: Holt, Rinehart & Winston, 1980.

Jeffrey S. Gurock, ed. *American Jewish History.* New York: Routledge, 1988.

Frithjof Haas. *Hermann Levi: From Brahms to Wagner.* Translated by Cynthia Klohr. Lanham, MD: Scarecrow Press, 2012.

Jelena Hahl-Koch. *Arnold Schoenberg, Wassily Kandinsky.* London: Faber & Faber, 1984.

Reyndaldo Hahn. *Sarah Bernhardt: Impressions.* London: Elkin Mathews & Marrot, 1932.

Gordon S. Haight. *George Eliot: A Biography.* Oxford: Oxford University Press, 1968.

Brigitte Hamann. *Winifred Wagner: A Life at the Heart of Hitler's Bayreuth.* London: Granta Books, 2005.

Manfred Hammer and Julius Schoeps, eds. *Juden in Berlin, 1671–1945.* Berlin: Nicolai, 1988.

Anne Hardy and Lore Sexl. *Lise Meitner.* Reinbek, Germany: Rowohlt Verlag, 2002.

Aljean Harmetz. *The Making of Casablanca.* New York: Hyperion, 1992.

Daisy Hay. *Mr & Mrs Disraeli.* London: Chatto & Windus, 2015.

Robert Heilbroner. *The Worldly Philosophers.* New York: Simon & Schuster, 1953.

Andre Heller, ed. *Theodor Herzl, Ein echter Wiener.* Vienna: Edition Wien, 1986.

Deborah Hertz. *How Jews Became Germans.* New Haven, CT: Yale University Press, 2007.

Theodor Herzl. *The Diaries of Theodor Herzl.* New York: Dial Press, 1956.

Abraham Joshua Heschel. *The Earth Is the Lord's: The Inner World of the Jew in Eastern Europe.* New York: Farrar, Straus and Giroux, 1949.

Susannah Heschel. *Abraham Geiger and the Jewish Jesus.* Chicago: Chicago University Press, 1998.

Oliver Hilmes. *Cosima Wagner.* Translated by Stewart Spencer. New Haven, CT: Yale University Press, 2010.

Gertrude Himmelfarb. *The Jewish Odyssey of George Eliot.* London: Encounter Books, 2012.

Magnus Hirschfeld. *Sexual Pathology.* Newark, NJ: Julian, 1932.

Mary Hockaday. *Kafka, Love and Courage: The Life of Milena Jesenska.* London: Andre Deutsch, 1995.

Heinz Höhne. *The Order of the Death's Head: The Story of Hitler's SS.* New York: Penguin Press, 2001.

Joseph Horowitz. *On My Way: The Untold Story of Rouben Mamoulian, George Gershwin and* Porgy and Bess. New York: W. W. Norton, 2013.

Kathryn Hughes. *Victorians Undone.* London: Fourth Estate, 2017.

Bernhard Huldermann. *Albert Ballin.* London: William Cassell, 1922.

Jules Huret. *Sarah Bernhardt.* London: Chapman and Hall, 1899.

Paula E. Hyman. *The Emancipation of the Jews of Alsace.* New Haven, CT: Yale University Press, 1991.

Walter Isaacson. *Einstein.* London: Simon & Schuster, 2007.

BIBLIOGRAPHY

Olga Ivinskaya. *A Captive of Time: My Years with Pasternak*. Glasgow: Collins and Harvill Press, 1978.

Jarrel C. Jackman and Carla M. Borden, eds. *The Muses Flee Hitler*. Washington, DC: Smithsonian Institution Press, 1983.

Jeremiah James, Thomas Steinhauser, Dieter Hoffmann, and Bretislav Friedrich. *One Hundred Years at the Intersection of Chemistry and Physics: The Fritz Haber Institute of the Max Planck Society, 1911–2011*. Berlin: Walter de Gruyter, 2011.

Stuart Jeffries. *Grand Hotel Abyss*. London: Verso, 2016.

Ernest Jones. *The Life and Work of Sigmund Freud*. New York: Basic Books, 1953.

Leo Jung, ed. *Sages and Saints*. Hoboken, NJ: Ktav, 1987.

Robert Jungk. *Brighter than a Thousand Suns: The Story of the Men Who Made the Bomb*. Translated by James Cleugh. New York: Grove Press, 1958.

Ruth Kark and Michal Oren-Nordheim. *Jerusalem and Its Environs: Quarters, Neighborhoods, Villages, 1800–1948*. Detroit: Wayne State University Press, 2001.

Abraham J. Karp, *Golden Door to America: The Jewish Immigrant Experience*. New York: Viking Press, 1976.

Ruth Katz. *The Lachmann Problem: An Unsung Chapter in Comparative Musicology*. Jerusalem: Hebrew University Magnes Press, 2003.

Elie Kedourie, ed. *The Jewish World: Revelation, Prophecy and History*. London: Thames and Hudson, 1979.

Alex Keinan. *Kafka, Iyunim*. Haifa, Israel: Hadar, 1990.

Imre Kertez. "Gályanapló: Notes from a Galley 1992." In *Encyclopedia of Modern Jewish Culture*. Edited by Glenda Abramson. London: Routledge, 2005.

Leo Kestenberg. *Bewegte Zeiten*. Zurich, Switzerland: Möseler Verlag, 1961.

Harmut Kircher. *Heinrich Heine und das Judenthum*. Bonn, Germany: Bouvier Verlag, 1973.

Anja Klabunde. *Magda Goebbels*. Boston: Little, Brown, 2013.

John Klier. *Russians, Jews and the Pogroms of 1881–1882*. Cambridge: Cambridge University Press, 2011.

Eliyahu Meir Klugman. *Rabbi Samson Raphael Hirsch: Architect of Judaism for the Modern World*. Brooklyn, NY: Artscroll Mesorah, 1996.

Hadassa Kosak. *Cultures of Opposition: Jewish Immigrant Workers, New York City, 1881–1905*. New York: State University of New York Press, 2000.

Otto Dov Kulka. *Landscapes of the Metropolis of Death*. Cambridge, MA: Harvard University Press, 2013.

Rolf-Peter Lacher. *"Der Mensch ist eine Bestie." Anna Heeger, Maria Chlum, Maria Reinhard und Arthur Schnitzler*. Würzburg, Germany: Königshausen & Neumann, 2014.

Georg Mordechai Langer. *A Hunger Artist & Other Stories: Poems and Songs of Love*. Translated by Elana Wolff and Menachem Wolff. Toronto: Guernica Editions, 2014.

BIBLIOGRAPHY

William Lanouette and Bela Silard. *Genius in the Shadows*. New York: Skyhorse, 2013.

D. H. Lawrence. *The Letters of D. H. Lawrence*. Vol. 1. Cambridge, MA: Cambridge University Press, 1979.

Joyce Block Lazarus. *Geneviève Straus: A Parisian Life*. Brill | Rodopi, 2017. Ebook.

Norman Lebrecht. *The Book of Musical Anecdotes*. London: Andre Deutsch, 1985.

———. *Why Mahler?* London: Faber & Faber, 2010.

Jonah Lehrer. *Proust Was a Neuroscientist*. New York: Houghton Mifflin, 2007.

Theodor Lessing. *Der jüdische Selbsthaß*. Berlin: Jüdischer Verlag, 1930.

Primo Levi. *The Periodic Table*. Translated by Raymond Rosenthal. New York: Schocken Books, 1984.

Robert Liberles. *Religious Conflict in Social Context: The Resurgence of Orthodox Judaism in Frankfurt Am Main, 1838–1877*. Westport, CT: Greenwood Press, 1985.

Lyn Macdonald. *1915: The Death of Innocence*. London: Hodder Headline, 1993.

Angela Mace. *Mendelssohn Perspectives*. London: Routledge, 2012.

Brenda Maddox. *Rosalind Franklin: The Dark Lady of DNA*. London: HarperCollins, 2002.

Arthur J. Magida. *The Nazi Séance: The Strange Story of the Jewish Psychic in Hitler's Circle*. New York: Palgrave Macmillan, 2011.

Elena Mancini. *Magnus Hirschfeld and the Quest for Sexual Freedom*. New York: Palgrave Macmillan, 2010.

George Mandel. "Who Was Ben-Yehuda with in the Boulevard Montmartre?" Oxford Center for Postgraduate Jewish Studies. 1984. http://www.ochjs.ac.uk/wp-content/uploads/2011/09/MANDEL-George-Who-Was-Ben-Yehuda-with-in-Boulevard-Montmartre.pdf.

Nadezhda Mandelstam. *Hope against Hope*. London: Penguin, 1970.

Wilhelm Marr. *Der Sieg des Judenthums über das Germanethum: Vom nicht confessionellem Standpunkt*. Bern, Switzerland: Rudolph Costenoble, 1879.

Kati Marton. *The Great Escape*. New York: Simon & Schuster, 2000.

Jeffrey M. Masson. *The Complete Letters of Sigmund Freud to Wilhelm Fliess, 1887–1904*. New York: Belknap Press, 1985.

Brian McGuinness. *Wittgenstein: A Life: Young Ludwig, 1889–1921*. Oxford: Oxford University Press, 1988.

David McLellan. *Karl Marx: His Life and Thought*. London: Macmillan, 1973.

Rebecca Mead. *My Life in Middlemarch*. New York: Penguin Random House, 2014.

Golda Meir. *My Life*. New York: Putnam, 1975.

Paul Mendes-Flohr and Jehuda Reinharz. *The Jew in the Modern World: A Documentary History*. New York: Oxford University Press, 1980.

Michael L. Miller. *Rabbis and Revolution: The Jews of Moravia in the Age of Emancipation*. Stanford, CA: Stanford University Press, 2011.

———. "Samson Raphael Hirsch and the Revolution of 1848." http://web.ceu.hu/jewishstudies/pdf/02_miller.pdf.

Albert Moll. *Untersuchungen über die Libido sexualis*. Berlin: Fischer, 1897. English edition: *The Sexual Life of the Child*. New York: Macmillan, 1919.

Benny Morris. *Righteous Victims: A History of the Zionist-Arab Conflict, 1881–2001.* New York: Vintage Books, 2001.

Hanns Otto Münsterer. *The Young Brecht.* London: Libris, 1992.

Melanie A. Murphy. *Max Nordau's Fin-de-Siècle Romance of Race.* Bern, Switzerland: Peter Lang, 2007.

David F. Noble. *Beyond the Promised Land: The Movement and the Myth.* Toronto: Provocations, 2005.

Karin Obholzer. *Wolfman: Conversations with Freud's Patient Sixty Years Later.* London: Continuum, 1982.

Ephraim Oshry. *Responsa from the Holocaust.* New York: Judaica Press, 2001.

George D. Painter. *Marcel Proust: A Biography.* London: Chatto & Windus, 1965.

Abraham Pais. *Subtle Is the Lord: The Science and Life of Albert Einstein.* New York: Oxford University Press, 1982.

Susie J. Pak. *Gentlemen Bankers: The World of JP Morgan.* Cambridge, MA: Harvard University Press, 2014.

Michael F. Palmer. *Freud and Jung on Religion.* London: Routledge, 1997.

Esther L. Panitz. *The Alien in Their Midst: Images of Jews in English Literature.* Madison, NJ: Farleigh Dickinson University Press, 1981.

Michael A. Peters and Jeff Stickney, eds. *A Companion to Wittgenstein on Education: Pedagogical Investigations.* Singapore: Springer, 2017.

Shachar M. Pinsker. *A Rich Brew: How Cafés Created Modern Jewish Culture.* New York: New York University Press, 2018.

Evelyne Polt-Heinzl and Gisela Steinlechner, eds. *Arthur Schnitzler: Affairen und Affekte.* Vienna: Christian Brandstätter Verlag, 2006.

George Prochnik. *The Impossible Exile: Stefan Zweig at the End of the World.* London: Granta, 2014.

Marcel Proust. *Remembrance of Things Past.* London: Penguin, 2016.

John Reed. *Ten Days That Shook the World.* New York: Boni and Liveright, 1919.

Jehuda Reinharz. *Living with Antisemitism: Modern Jewish Responses.* Hanover, NH: Brandeis University Press and University Press of New England, 1987.

James Renton. "Reconsidering Chaim Weizmann and Moses Gaster in the Founding Mythology of Zionism." In *Nationalism, Zionism and Ethnic Mobilization of the Jews in 1900 and Beyond.* M. Berkowitz, ed. Leiden, Netherlands: Brill, 2004.

———. *The Zionist Masquerade: The Birth of the Anglo-Zionist Alliance, 1914–1918.* London: Palgrave Macmillan, 2007.

Richard Rhodes. *The Making of the Atomic Bomb.* New York: Simon & Schuster, 1986.

Arnold D. Richards, ed. *The Jewish World of Sigmund Freud: Essays on Cultural Roots and the Problem of Religious Identity.* Jefferson, NC: McFarland, 2010.

John S. Rigden. *Rabi: Scientist and Citizen.* New York: Basic Books, 1987.

Bryan Mark Rigg. *Rescued from the Reich: How One of Hitler's Soldiers Saved the Lubavitcher Rebbe.* New Haven, CT: Yale University Press, 2004.

Alexander L. Ringer. *Arnold Schoenberg: The Composer as Jew.* Oxford: Clarendon Press, 1990.

BIBLIOGRAPHY

Paul Roazen. *Freud and His Followers*. New York: Knopf, 1975.

Paul Lawrence Rose. *Wagner: Race and Revolution*. London: Faber & Faber, 1992.

Jeffrey Rosen. *Louis D. Brandeis: American Prophet*. New Haven, CT: Yale University Press, 2016.

Ludwig Rosenthal. *Heinrich Heine als Jude*. Berlin: Ullstein Verlag, 1973.

Franz Rosenzweig. *The Star of Redemption*. Frankfurt: Schocken, 1921.

Roy Rosenzweig and Elizabeth Blackmar. *The Park and the People: A History of Central Park*. Ithaca, NY: Cornell University Press, 1992.

Cecil Roth. *A History of the Jews in England*. Oxford: Clarendon Press, 1941.

Joseph Roth. *What I Saw*. Translated by Michael Hofmann. London: Granta, 2002.

Miriam Rothschild. *Walter Rothschild: The Man, the Museum and the Menagerie*. London: Natural History Museum, 2008.

Carol Schreier Rupprecht, ed. *The Dream and the Text: Essays on Literature and Language*. Albany, NY: State University of New York Press, 1993.

Reinhard Rürup. *Jüdische Geschichte in Berlin*. Berlin: Edition Hentrich, 1996.

Edward Said. *The Edward Said Reader*. Edited by Moustafa Bayoumi and Andrew Rubin. New York: Vintage, 2000.

Jeffrey L. Sammons. *Heine: A Modern Biography*. Princeton, NJ: Princeton University Press, 1979.

Ronald Sanders. *Shores of Refuge: A Hundred Years of Jewish Emigration*. New York: Schocken Books, 1989.

David Sassoon. *History of the Jews in Baghdad*. Letchworth, UK: S. D. Sassoon, 1949.

Jacob J. Schachter. *Judaism's Encounter with Other Cultures: Rejection or Integration?* Lanham, MD: Rowman & Littlefield, 1997.

Solomon Schechter. *Selected Writings*. Edited by Norman Bentwich. London: East and West Library, 1946.

Hartmut Scheible. *Schnitzler*. Reinbek bei Hamburg: Ro-Ro-Ro, 1976.

Victor L. Schermer. *Meaning, Mind and Self-Transformation: Psychoanalytic Interpretation and the Interpretation of Psychoanalysis*. London: Karnac Books, 2014.

Shimon and Naphtali Schischa. *Az Amar Shelomo*. Brooklyn, NY: private publication, 2009.

Isolde Schmidt-Reiter and Aviel Can, eds. *Judaism in Opera*. Regensburg, Germany: ConBrio, 2017.

Jonathan Schneer. *The Balfour Declaration*. New York: Random House, 2010.

R. M. M. Schneersohn. *Sefer HaSiḥot 5751*. Vol. 1. Brooklyn, NY: Kehot, 1992.

Arthur Schnitzler. *My Youth in Vienna*. Translated by Catherine Hutter. London: Weidenfeld and Nicolson, 1971.

———. *Tagebuch, 1879–1931*. Vienna: Verlag der Österreichischen Akademie der Wissenschaften, 2000.

———. *Die Weg ins Freie*. Berlin: S. Fischer, 1908.

Arnold Schoenberg. *Style and Idea*. New York: Philosophical Library, 1950.

E. Randol Schoenberg, ed. *The Doctor Faustus Dossier*. Oakland: University of California Press, 2018.

BIBLIOGRAPHY

Hans-Joachim Schoeps. *Theodor Herzl: A Pictorial Biography*. London: Thames and Hudson, 1997.

Gershom Scholem. *From Berlin to Jerusalem*. New York: Schocken, 1988.

———. *On Jews and Judaism in Crisis*. New York: Schocken, 1976.

———. *A Life in Letters, 1914–1982*. Translated and edited by Antony David Skinner. Cambridge, MA: Harvard University Press, 2002.

———. *Walter Benjamin: The Story of a Friendship*. London: Faber & Faber, 1982.

Esther Schor. *Emma Lazarus*. New York: Nextbook/Schocken, 2006.

Simon Sebag Montefiore. *Stalin: The Court of the Red Tsar*. London: Weidenfeld & Nicolson, 2003.

Robert Service. *Trotsky: A Biography*. London: Pan Macmillan, 2009.

Anita Shapira. *Land and Power: The Zionist Resort to Force 1881–1948*. Stanford, CA: Stanford University Press, 1999.

Naomi Shepherd. *A Refuge from Darkness*. New York: Pantheon Books, 1984.

Yvonne Sherratt. *Hitler's Philosophers*. New Haven, CT: Yale University Press, 2013.

Colin Shindler. *What Zionists Believe*. London: Granta, 2006.

Pierre Sichel. *Modigliani*. London: W. H. Allen, 1967.

Marcus Sieff. *Don't Ask the Price*. London: Weidenfeld & Nicolson, 1986.

Eisig Silberschag, ed. *Eliezer Ben-Yehuda: A Symposium in Oxford*. Oxford Center for Postgraduate Studies, 1981.

Nigel Simeone, ed. *The Leonard Bernstein Letters*. New Haven, CT: Yale University Press, 2013.

Ernst Simon. *"Unser Kriegserlebnis" in Brücken: Gesammelte Aufsatze*. Heidelberg, Germany: L. Schneider, 1965.

Geoffrey Skelton, ed. *Cosima Wagner's Diaries*. Vol. 2. New York: Harcourt Brace Jovanovich, 1980.

Eliza Slavet. *Racial Fever: Freud and the Jewish Question*. New York: Fordham University Press, 2009.

Yuri Slezkine. *The Jewish Century*. Princeton, NJ: Princeton University Press, 2004.

Michael Smith. *Foley: The Spy Who Saved 10,000 Jews*. London: Hodder & Stoughton, 1999.

Ronald Smith. *Alkan, the Enigma*. London: Kahn & Averill, 1976.

Claudia Sonino. *German Jews in Palestine, 1920–1948: Between Dream and Reality*. Translated by Juliet Haydock. Lanham, MD: Lexington Books, 2016.

Levi Soshuk and Azriel Eisenberg. *Momentous Century: Personal and Eyewitness Accounts of the Rise of the Jewish Homeland and State, 1875–1978*. New York: Herzl Press, 1984.

Paul Speiser. *Karl Landsteiner: Entdecker der Blutgruppen und Pionier der Immunologie*. 3rd ed. Berlin: Blackwell Ueberreuter-Wiss, 1990.

Pierre Spivakoff. *Sarah Bernhardt vue par les Nadar*. Paris: Hersch, 1982.

Jeffrey S. Sposato. *The Price of Assimilation: Felix Mendelssohn and the Nineteenth-Century Anti-Semitic Tradition*. Oxford: Oxford University Press, 2006.

Frederic Spotts. *Bayreuth: A History of the Wagner Festival*. New Haven, CT: Yale University Press, 1994.

BIBLIOGRAPHY

Bettina Stangneth. *Eichmann Before Jerusalem*. London: Bodley Head, 2014.

Larry Starr. *George Gershwin*. New Haven, CT: Yale University Press, 2011.

Gerick Stengel. *Lexikon der Juden in der Musik*. Berlin: Bernard Hahnfeld Verlag, 1941.

Fritz Stern. *Einstein's German World*. Princeton, NJ: Princeton University Press, 1999.

———. *Five Germanys I Have Known*. New York: Farrar, Straus and Giroux, 2006.

Desmond Stewart. *Theodor Herzl: Artist and Politician*. London: Hamish Hamilton, 1974.

Dietrich Stolzenberg. *Fritz Haber: Chemist, Nobel Laureate, German, Jew*. Philadelphia: Chemical Heritage Foundation, 2004.

Graham Storey and Kathleen Tillotson, eds. *The Letters of Charles Dickens*. Oxford: Oxford University Press, 1965.

Peter Franz Stubmann. *Mein Feld ist die Welt*. Hamburg, Germany: Christians, 1960.

H. H. Stuckenschmit. *Arnold Schoenberg: His Life, World and Work*. London: John Calder, 1977.

Charles Susskind. *Janáček and Brod*. New Haven, CT: Yale University Press, 1985.

Lys Symonette and Kim H. Kowalke, eds. *Speak Low, When You Speak Love: The Letters of Kurt Weill and Lotte Lenya*. Berkeley, CA: University of California Press, 1996.

Gerda Taranow. *Sarah Bernhardt: The Art within the Legend*. Princeton, NJ: Princeton University Press, 1972.

Kate Taylor. *Madame Proust and the Kosher Kitchen*. London: Chatto & Windus, 2003.

Joseph Telushkin. *Rebbe: The Life and Teachings of Menachem M. Schneerson, the Most Influential Rabbi in Modern History*. New York: HarperCollins, 2014.

Shabtai Teveth. *Retsach Arlosorov*. Jerusalem: Schocken, 1982.

Philippe Michel Thiriet. *The Book of Proust*. London: Chatto & Windus, 1989.

Hélène Tierchant. *Sarah Bernhardt, Madame "Quande même."* Paris: Editions SW Télémaque, 2009.

Ernst Toller. *I Was a German*. New York: William Morrow, 1934.

Leon Trotsky. *My Life*. New York: Charles Scribner's Sons, 1930.

Joseph H. Udelson. *Dreamer of the Ghetto: The Life and Works of Israel Zangwill*. Tuscaloosa, AL: University of Alabama Press, 1990.

Louis Untermeyer. *Heinrich Heine: Paradox and Poet*. New York: Harcourt Brace Jovanovich, 1937.

Antonina Vallentin. *Poet in Exile*. London: Victor Gollancz, 1934.

Shulamit Volkov. *Germans, Jews and Antisemites: Trials in Emancipation*. Cambridge: Cambridge University Press, 2006.

Renate Wagner. *Wie ein weiteres Land: Arthur Schnitzler und seine Zeit*. Vienna: Amaltheur, 2006.

J. B. Walker. *Fifty Years of Rapid Transit*. New York: Law Printing Company, 1918.

Richard Webster. *Why Freud Was Wrong: Sin, Science and Psychoanalysis*. London: William Collins, 1996.

Stanley Weintraub. *Charlotte and Lionel: A Rothschild Love Story*. London: Simon & Schuster, 2003.

BIBLIOGRAPHY

Eric Werner, ed. *Contributions to a Historical Study of Jewish Music*. Brooklyn, NY: Ktav, 1976.

Francis Wheen. *Karl Marx*. London: Fourth Estate, 1999.

Elie Wiesel. *The Night Trilogy*. New York: Hill & Wang, 1972.

Barbara Winton. *If It's Not Impossible: The Life of Nicholas Winton*. Kibworth, UK: Matador, 2014.

Charlotte Wolff. *Magnus Hirschfeld: A Portrait of a Pioneer in Sexology*. London: Quartet, 1986.

Charters Wynn. *Workers, Strikes and Pogroms: The Donbass-Dnepr Bend in Late Imperial Russia, 1870–1905*. Princeton, NJ: Princeton University Press, 2014.

W. E. Yates. *Schnitzler, Hofmannsthal and the Austrian Theatre*. New Haven, CT: Yale University Press, 1992.

Yosef Hayim Yerushalmi. *Freud's Moses: Judaism Terminable and Interminable*. New Haven, CT: Yale University Press, 1991.

Moshe Zimmermann. *Wilhelm Marr: The Patriarch of Antisemitism*. New York: Oxford University Press, 1986.

Otto Zoff. *Tagebücher aus der Emigration 1939–44*. Heidelberg, Germany: Lambert Schneider, 1968.

Carl Zuckmayer. *A Part of Myself: Portrait of an Epoch*. New York: Harcourt Brace Jovanovich, 1970.

Stefan Zweig. *The World of Yesterday*. London: Cassell & Co., 1943.

INDEX

INDEX

INDEX

INDEX

ABOUT THE AUTHOR

Norman Lebrecht has written several bestselling works of nonfiction, including *The Maestro Myth* and *Who Killed Classical Music?* He is also the award-winning author of the novels *The Song of Names* and *The Game of Opposites*, the first of which was adapted into a major feature film, starring Tim Roth and Clive Owen. He writes regularly for the *Wall Street Journal* and has presented major series for the BBC. He lives in London.